Whole Language Literature Activities for Young Children

WHOLE LANGUAGE LITERATURE ACTIVITIES FOR YOUNG CHILDREN

Over 1,100 ready-to-use,
content-based projects and activities
featuring 50 well-known children's books
and hundreds of alternative resources

MARY A. SOBUT
BONNIE NEUMAN BOGEN

THE CENTER FOR APPLIED
RESEARCH IN EDUCATION
West Nyack, New York 10995

10   9   8   7   6   5   4   3   2

Library of Congress Cataloging-in-Publication Data

Sobut, Mary A.,
     Whole language literature activities for young children
Mary A. Sobut / Bonnie N. Bogen.
        p.   cm.
     Includes bibliographical references (p.   ).
     ISBN 0-87628-973-1
     1. Early childhood education—Activity programs.   2. Language
experience approach in education.   I. Bogen, Bonnie Neuman.
II. Title.   III. Title: Whole language literature activities for
young children.
LB1139.35.A37B64   1993
372.6'044—dc20   93-2429
                                                                        CIP

Illustrated by Carrie Oesmann

ISBN 0-87628-973-1

**The Center for Applied Research
in Education,** Professional Publishing
West Nyack, New York 10995
Simon & Schuster

DEDICATION

We dedicate this book to teachers who help to instill the love of reading and literature in young children.

ACKNOWLEDGMENTS

Unless otherwise noted, the songs, fingerplays, and recipes presented here are original or have come from our collection of early childhood materials. We have made every effort to find the original sources of these materials and have been unsuccessful. If errors have occurred, they will be corrected in future editions.

We wish to thank the many authors and illustrators of the quality literature we reviewed for this resource.

Thank you to the staff at the Elmhurst Public Library for their assistance in suggesting literature and related resources included in the appendix and used while preparing this book. Thank you to the staff of the Junior Room at the Downers Grove Public Library for gathering books while this resource was being developed. Special thanks to friends on the "computer support team" from Conrad Fischer School and Elmhurst District 205 for their many hours of patient guidance and instruction.

Our families gave us support and encouragement while we were writing this resource. Their extra efforts at home provided us with the time to work. Thanks Michael, Andrew, Jeremy, and Elizabeth Bogen and Wally, Amy, and Frances Sobut.

ABOUT THE AUTHORS

Mary A. Sobut has more than 20 years of teaching experience in early childhood, special education, learning disabilities, and behavior disorders. She holds a B.A. in Special Education and an M.A. in Early Childhood Education and has completed many hours of postgraduate work. Ms. Sobut was instrumental in developing the early childhood special education program in Elmhurst, Illinois, which includes a comprehensive program of involvement, training, and support for parents. She has supervised student teachers and serves as a mentor to new teachers. She provides in-service training to college students, elementary teachers and staff, and consults with district ancillary personnel, as well as personnel from public and private agencies that work with young children and their families. Ms. Sobut is the teacher representative on the Early Childhood Advisory Committee for the North Central Regional Educational Laboratory. The committee reviews early childhood issues and advises the laboratory regarding its efforts in a seven-state region.

Bonnie Neuman Bogen has been a teacher in the field of special education for 12 years. She has taught early childhood special education and students with learning disabilities, and behavioral and emotional disorders. She tutors children with a wide range of special needs. Ms. Bogen earned her undergraduate degree in Child Development and Preschool Education from the University of Wisconsin. She earned her Master's Degree in Special Education from National Louis University. Ms. Bogen has expertise in student assessment, curriculum development, and facilitation of parental support and training groups. She is actively involved in community and school-based advisory groups.

Ms. Sobut and **Ms. Bogen** coauthored *The Complete Early Childhood Curriculum Resource* (1991) published by The Center for Applied Research in Education.

ABOUT THIS BOOK

Whole Language Literature Activities for Young Children seeks to make a young child's day meaningful by integrating the curriculum with developmental activities using children's literature. Children find it difficult to move from one activity to the next when the activities are unrelated. One goal of whole language is to integrate speaking and listening with reading and writing. Other goals that are perhaps even more important are to develop in children an interest in and love of literature, a desire to be read to, and eventually the ability to read independently.

This resource is a starting point for teachers of young children. It provides activities across the early childhood curriculum for expanding children's literature in a variety of categories. The literature chosen for this resource is only a small sampling of the quality children's literature which is available. The resource can be used to develop a curriculum while encouraging a variety of interests in young children using literature as the central focus. It can also be used to expand upon children's interests and themes that occur naturally in the classroom. Using this resource the teacher can extend ideas that stem from children's natural enthusiasm and curiosity across the preschool-first grade curriculum.

The activities were written to accommodate different classroom environments and teaching philosophies. The majority of activities can be used with individuals, small groups, or large groups. They can also be center or discovery based as well as teacher directed. Furthermore, the activities are not limited to the books selected for this resource—they can easily be adapted to other books. For your convenience, there is an annotated list of additional books in the appendix to assist you further in making selections for your students.

Mary A. Sobut
Bonnie Neuman Bogen

CURRICULUM AREAS

Preceding the actual activities for each book, there is a *Developmental Activities Chart* indicating which of the following areas will be emphasized in each particular activity.

Language/Cognitive Development.   Language development crosses all areas of the curriculum. It particularly relates to cognitive development pertaining to the child's ability to solve problems, evaluate and organize experiences, generalize concepts, and recall information. Examples of the cognitive curriculum include skills such as naming objects, colors, and shapes; using directional-positional concepts; and recognizing the function of everyday objects. The development of verbal reasoning skills, vocabulary, the ability to answer questions, and make predictions are also included in this area.

Fine Motor/Art.   These skills generally relate to the muscles of the hands, including dexterity, and the coordination and speed of the finger muscles, wrist flexibility, and eye-hand coordination. Fine motor activities can include block building, bead stringing, cutting, coloring, painting, printing, lacing, and finger-plays. Process-oriented art activities help to develop spontaneity, creativity, and imagination in children. Art experiences should provide opportunities for learning through many mediums. These experiences can be easily integrated with the whole language curriculum while still encouraging process rather than product. Since a child's self-concept may be diminished when he or she is expected to create a specific product, children are encouraged to work at their own developmental level. Examples of process-oriented art activities include the manipulation of paper, scissors, paints, crayons, markers, and various other mediums.

Gross Motor.   These abilities include balance, posture, muscle strength, and coordination. Some activities dependent upon gross motor skills include walking, running, skipping, climbing, and ball handling.

Perception.   These skills pertain to the senses of sight, hearing, taste, smell, and touch. Perception deals with how the brain processes the information acquired through the various senses. All information is received through one or more of the senses. Depending on the child's own learning style, one sense may predominate over the others. Activities in this area include puzzles, design copying, and patterning. Additional activities include experiences that enable the child to identify and compare sights, sounds, textures, tastes, and odors in the environment.

Social Skills.   This area involves the child's ability to interact with other people as well as the environment and objects found within. Examples of appropriate interaction with people include greeting others, turn taking, sharing, asking for and offering help, and attending to and following directions. A child's interaction with his or her environment includes handling objects and materials with care, cleaning up work and play materials, and developing the ability to work and play independently.

Math. This area provides children with learning opportunities to help them organize their world. Exploratory activities and interactions with manipulatives provide the foundation for the development of mathematical concepts. Examples of activities in this area are matching, sorting, patterning, comparing, classifying, ordering, measuring, and graphing. A child's ability to understand quantitative concepts, shapes, space, numbers, number symbols, one-to-one correspondence, and temporal concepts are also stressed in the math curriculum.

Dramatic Play. Individual and group experiences allow children to express themselves through play. Socialization and language development are further enhanced when children act out familiar or new experiences. Books, props, classroom visitors, field trips, stories, home or school experiences, and peer experiences provide children with a wealth of play themes that allow them to further understand, organize, and accept these events. A teacher who is aware of and in tune to children's interests and experiences of the past, present, and future can encourage dramatic play by providing materials and space relevant to these experiences.

Cooking/Snack. Cooking with children and daily snack time further helps to encourage integration of the curriculum. Fine motor skills, math, science, language and concept development, socialization, and sensory experiences are a natural part of cooking and eating. When the focus of preparing and enjoying food is learning through experience, manipulation, and exploration, opportunities for learning are abundant.

Science. Science in the preschool curriculum provides children with the opportunity to actively explore, investigate, and inquire about their environment while using the different senses. It builds on the child's natural curiosity about materials and objects and their relationship to the environment. The sensory-exploration table allows for individual or groups to experiment with various substances. A child is able to use all the senses when experimenting with water, sand, rice, shaving cream, corn meal, styrofoam, or pebbles. Other science experiences might include body awareness, water, air, weather, magnets, animals, and nature.

Music/Fingerplays/Poems. This area provides another natural way in which to integrate the curriculum. Children enjoy learning songs, poems, and fingerplays as well as singing and reciting old favorites. Rhythmic activities can help children to develop movement skills and spatial awareness. Children respond to music in an individual manner, allowing them to express their feelings and emotions. Fine and gross motor development can be encouraged through songs that involve physical activity. Music can be used to enrich the learning experience in areas such as concept and language development. Children can memorize the days of the week and learn about holidays, different cultures, weather, and many other subjects through songs, poems, and fingerplays. Many children with language and learning differences learn easily when music is the medium.

Suggested Home Activities. Research in the area of school success has repeatedly found that in the early years, the influence provided in the home by parents or other consistent caregivers outweighs the influence of the classroom experience. To achieve maximum effectiveness, the curriculum must seek to involve parents in a significant way. One way to achieve this goal is to provide parents/caregivers with information and activities for follow-up in the home environment. Most parents would agree that they would like to help ensure their child's future success in school. Unfortunately, many parents are not familiar with ways to effectively extend learning into the home environment. It is the responsibility of the teacher to frequently communicate with parents. School-home communication can take many forms, such as a daily or weekly newsletter, a daily or weekly note posted at the door, or frequent phone calls. Calendars, with suggestions for simple ideas to use each day, are another effective tool for extending the curriculum into the home. The intention of this type of communication is to keep parents informed on what is happening in the classroom and to provide ideas for follow-up. This resource provides ideas for extending activities for each book at home.

ENCOURAGING LANGUAGE DEVELOPMENT

Children learn during the early years that speaking and listening are useful tools. The first words spoken generally relate to what is most important to the child. But they also learn that language is a two-way process that involves a sender and a receiver. When adults are active listeners, children naturally speak more. There is much that adults can do to encourage a child's language development, but the most important is to be an active listener. This involves making and maintaining eye contact with the child during the conversation. It is important to make meaningful comments or ask for further information from the child. This sends the powerful message that, "What you say is important." It shows respect for the child. The following techniques that many teachers of young children use can be equally helpful for parents and should be shared with them.

HELPFUL TECHNIQUES
THAT ENCOURAGE LANGUAGE DEVELOPMENT

1. **Expansion.** This technique helps to increase the length of the child's statement. The listener repeats what the child says and adds to the statement. (Child: "See monkey." Listener: "I see a monkey eating a banana.")

2. **Correction.** The listener repeats the child's statement, but with correct grammar. (Child: "Me hungry." Listener: "I am hungry too.")

3. **Modeling.** This involves a conversation between an adult and child. The adult acts as an appropriate language model for the child using correct grammar and sentence structure. The two-way process of language is demonstrated through verbal turn taking.

---

4. **Open-Ended Questions.** The listener asks a question that will motivate the child to expand on his or her original thought. It is important to ask open-ended questions that encourage the child to think of and to verbalize a complete thought. Questions such as *"Why?" "When?" "Where?" "How?" "What might happen if . . . ?" "I wonder what . . ."* are all examples of open-ended questions that encourage problem-solving skills. The teacher can communicate to parents that although it isn't always possible for a parent or caretaker to drop what he or she is doing, an effort should be made periodically throughout the day to engage in really meaningful conversation with the child.

Provide parents with suggestions for talking about their activities as they are being performed. For instance, when the parent is preparing a meal, there are many language-enriching possibilities occurring. Objects can be labeled, and sequence and order can be discussed ("First we take the plates out, next we put them on the table, then we put the food on the plates, and so on."). Most important, the child is able to see the relationship between words and their corresponding actions.

ENCOURAGING PREREADING SKILLS

Children learn at an early age that just as language has an important function, so does reading. A child who sees his or her parents and teachers enjoying books, magazines, and newspapers, not only has an excellent model, but also learns that reading is fun and also functional. Reading aloud to children at an early age is unquestionably a prerequisite for eventual success in school as well as in motivating children to enjoy reading from childhood into adulthood. Reading aloud to children provides other valuable opportunities. When a child sits close to his or her parent, caregiver, or teacher, he or she feels a special closeness and a sense of being important as a result of the individualized focused attention. The association between the closeness and the enjoyment of the book fosters an early love for reading. When a child listens to the story, attending, memory, and vocabulary skills are strengthened. An early understanding of the relationship between written and spoken language is developed. This understanding is essential for the emergence of literacy. Much has been written regarding how to read to young children. The following suggestions pertain to teachers, parents, and other caregivers.

HOW TO ENCOURAGE PREREADING SKILLS

1. Provide a relaxed atmosphere in which to read. The setting should be comfortable, cozy, and well lit.

2. Set aside a special time to read each day. It should be a relaxed time, so there is time to talk about the book and the pictures. Don't limit yourself only to this time, however; take advantage of quiet moments, transition times, and other spontaneous opportunities throughout the day.

3. Visit the library regularly—parents and children should visit the library together as often as possible. Allow children to look for special books as well as to browse and find books that look interesting. Parents should also consider buying books that "belong" to their child. The teacher can arrange frequent field trips to the library and have the librarian visit for special story hours.

4. Stop to discuss the text and the pictures as you read. Ask open-ended questions that require the child to think and verbalize with more than a yes or no response.

5. Read the story many times if the child is interested. Children enjoy repetition. Stop before familiar lines and refrains or midsentence and let the child fill in the missing words.

6. Allow the child at home to hold the book and turn the pages if he or she is interested in doing so. At school, children can take turns being book holder and page turner.

7. Discuss the cover of the book, the title, and the author. Predict what the story might be about.

8. Talk about what might happen next while reading.

9. Talk about the beginning, middle, and end of the story when you have finished reading. Make up a new ending for the story or sequence the events of the story.

10. Discuss whether the story is real or make-believe.

11. Talk about the feelings of the characters. Ask the child how he or she would have felt. Relate the story to something in the child's past or present.

12. Tape record stories for children to "read" independently.

13. Be sensitive to the child's interest level. If the child is no longer enthusiastic, offer the opportunity to read the remainder at a later time. If the interest level is high, continue with discussion, a follow-up activity, or another book.

14. Be enthusiastic while you read. Children are naturally sensitive to adults' moods.

15. Expose children to literature from a wide range of categories.

ENCOURAGING WRITTEN LANGUAGE

In the early years' curriculum, written language can be broken into two primary components. The first component is the actual physical activity of writing. The development of fine motor–prewriting skills is a prerequisite to being able to print letters and words in the elementary grades. The second component is the developing awareness in children that written words correspond to spoken language. Children's fine motor–prewriting skills develop at different rates and ages. This variance occurs for different reasons, including physical and cognitive growth and development, motivation and interest, and exposure to materials. Physical skill development can be considered a prerequisite to writing (prewriting skills) and includes some of the following:

- The ability to pick up and hold a pencil, marker, or crayon
- The ability to make random marks on paper
- The ability to imitate simple shapes and designs
- The ability to copy simple shapes and designs
- The ability to copy letters and words

Activities that promote development of prewriting skills include a variety of fine motor manipulation activities, such as exposure to play dough, block building, bead stringing, completing form boards, assembling puzzles, and opportunities to handle and build with small manipulatives. Materials specific to the development of prewriting skills include writing utensils such as pencils, pens, markers, chalk, paints and brushes, fingerpaints, shaving cream (for fingerpainting), paper, Magic Slate™–type toys, and other writing surfaces. Children enjoy using envelopes, stationery, and other "office" materials. Opportunities for open-ended experimentation are critical in the development of fine motor–prewriting skills.

Just as children develop the physical skills necessary for writing at different rates, they also develop the awareness that there is a correspondence between spoken and written language at different rates and ages. This awareness comes through repeated exposure to written language. Reading books to children and supplying them with books they can handle independently provides many opportunities to view written language. Exposure to print in other mediums is also of importance. Children see printed language every day on road signs and billboards, on cans and boxes at the grocery store, and on the mail that comes into the house. As parents and teachers read signs and labels to children, their awareness slowly develops. Additional suggestions and activities for promoting awareness include acknowledging children's attempts at writing by making concrete observations (i.e., "What a lot of red lines you made.") and encouraging children to "write" at an early age. Children can "write" lists, letters, invitations, stories, or create new endings for old stories. They can make signs, write out directions, and make maps. Sometimes children want to pretend and write independently. Other times an adult, older student, or sibling can write while the child dictates; the child can then read the written language. Providing opportunities for children to use illustrations as another form of written language is also important.

The whole language curriculum seeks to integrate early language, reading, and writing experiences while respecting the developmental level of individual children. It should be understood that children will be working at different levels. All children must feel that what they are doing is important. The process-oriented approach helps to encourage this.

ADAPTING THE CURRICULUM FOR CHILDREN WITH SPECIAL NEEDS

This resource assumes that teachers of physically challenged students will have a variety of specialized materials for use with individual children. Examples of these materials might be specially designed writing implements and surfaces (including computers), special scissors, hand braces, pencil and crayon holders, book holders, large print or Braille for visually challenged students, and devices to augment sound for children with special hearing needs.

Teachers who have been specially trained to work with special needs students should try to consult and work closely with classroom teachers. Since all children learn at different rates and have different and unique learning styles, it is the responsibility of teachers of young children to be aware of these differences. In doing so, they can teach to each student's strengths while trying to develop weaker areas. Many students with special needs have been extensively evaluated, thus providing a detailed learning profile. Yet, many have not. Therefore, the teacher needs to observe each child to understand his or her particular learning style, strengths, and weaknesses. Much recent research in the field of education has been devoted to learning style. Some children learn best when information is presented in a sequential step-by-step manner. Others learn best simultaneously when all the information is presented at once in a holistic manner. These factors have been found to have immeasurable influence on how individuals learn. In addition, most individuals have a dominant sense through which they learn. Visual learners learn primarily by seeing and watching others perform tasks. Auditory learners learn primarily by listening to others or through self-verbalization. Kinesthetic learners need direct involvement with materials and need to be actively involved with the learning environment. Ideally, the early childhood curriculum provides activities that focus on all these learning styles each day. When children can be directly involved in activities that maximize the use of all the senses, optimal learning can occur. This resource provides teachers with a balance of activities that utilize all learning styles and senses.

Teachers should be familiar with the developmental stages children go through before mastering specific skills. It is important to break down and evaluate classroom activities to make it possible for children to approach them from their present developmental level. An example of this would be expecting a student to cut a circle before he or she can hold scissors appropriately. It should be noted that while some students learn easily in large groups with minimal teacher direction, other students may require small-group or individualized learning.

Some children may find it easier to be in a particular area of the room. A child who is a predominantly auditory learner may have difficulty blocking out extraneous sounds in a noisy area of the room, while a child who learns primarily through the visual channel may be unable to block out extraneous visual stimuli. Teachers of young children need to be sensitive to and aware of individual learning needs. Through this awareness all children can enjoy learning. The learning environment should be carefully and purposefully arranged, taking into account each child's learning style and unique needs.

CHOOSING CHILDREN'S LITERATURE

Quality children's literature is abundant. There are numerous categories of children's literature and hundreds of titles in most of the categories. When choosing literature to read with young children, there are a few things to keep in mind.

1. Consider the age and developmental level of the audience. Children have different interests and abilities at each age and level. For example, 3-year-olds might prefer simple pictures and text, while some 4-year-olds prefer repeated text and predictability. Older children enjoy not only the "fun" of the story, but may want to obtain information from books. Children's interest in various kinds of books can vary from day to day. Knowledge of the individual child and sensitivity to his or her ever-changing interests and ability is the key.

2. As a general rule, look for books with interesting pictures and bright colors. Pictures should be clear and not too busy.

3. Select books with characters who are similar to the children's age.

4. Look for books that contain repetition of words and themes.

5. Read more than one book by the same author. Children enjoy getting to "know" a particular author.

6. Use books that provide many opportunities for active participation and thus help maintain the child's attention span.

7. Look for themes and topics that are relevant to the child's world.

8. Choose books with happy endings to provide children with many positive experiences.

9. Consider books that are not only fun, but also reinforce new concepts, encourage new vocabulary, help children to deal with difficult situations (divorce, illness, moving, etc.), and reinforce current interests as well as encourage new ones.

10. Select a variety of books from different categories of literature. This resource contains ten categories of children's literature from which to choose. Try to use a variety of books from within each category.

CATEGORIES OF LITERATURE

Among the many categories of literature to choose, the following ten have been selected for use in this resource since they are representative of the types of literature that young children enjoy.

Readiness Books.   Readiness skills are generally thought of as prerequisites for future success in school. Readiness books reinforce concepts such as color and shape identification, understanding of opposites, rhyming, letters, numbers, and classification skills, to name a few.

Predictable Books.   Predictable books use word and/or picture repetition, language patterning, and plots that follow a predictable sequence. Children can predict what will come next once they understand the pattern in the book.

Multicultural Books.   Multicultural books represent cultural diversity. Individual differences are exemplified in both text and illustrations. These books allow children to see people, life-styles, and cultures that extend beyond their own world.

Science/Stories About the Earth.   These books deal with nature, animals, and natural phenomena such as water, air, and magnetism. Children's literature can be used to teach new concepts, explain natural occurrences, or reinforce science units which are presented in the classroom.

Personal Experience Books.   These books help children acknowledge and understand their own feelings. Children can relate to stories which deal with issues that are pertinent and timely. A few of these issues might include the birth of a sibling, death of a pet, moving to a new location, divorce, and hospitalization.

Winning Picture Books.   Some of these include the Caldecott, Parent's Choice, Best Books, Fanfare, and *School Library Journal* awards.

Folk and Fairy Tales.   This category of literature includes stories that probably originated orally and have since been interpreted and translated by more than one author. These stories are often about animals or imaginary characters such as princes and princesses, witches, or giants. They generally teach a lesson or reinforce a moral belief.

Books About Holidays and Special Occasions.   These books can be fact or fiction. The central theme is about a holiday or special day, and how it is celebrated or observed.

All-Time Favorite Books.   All-time favorites are generally thought of as books that have survived the "test of time." Some of the factors that contribute to their greatness include interesting characters, an exceptional story, or remarkable writing.

More Picture Books to Enjoy.   Books that are fun for children to listen to and read time and time again.

CONTENTS

Contents

Readiness Books

A Note to the Teacher About
Teaching Readiness Skills and Concepts

Children learn about and master concepts, including shapes, colors, numbers, letters, sizes, opposites, and rhyming in different ways and at different rates. Many children learn incidentally, that is, through simple exposure and discussion. These children probably do not need to spend weeks learning about one individual color, shape, or number. They can benefit from exposure to activities that emphasize all the colors and shapes or the numbers 1 through 10. Children with perceptual delays, language delays, weakness in short- and long-term memory, and other learning differences will benefit from exploring one concept (the color blue, the square shape, the number "3") at a time over the period of days and weeks. New concepts can be introduced at a gradual rate, once the previously taught concept is retained in the long-term memory.

The suggested activities for readiness or "concept" books can be presented in a variety of ways depending on the composition of the class and the individual learning styles of the children. Some teachers will choose to present a unit on color, presenting many colors at one time. It may benefit other classes to concentrate on activities which focus on only one color for a period of time. Different learning styles and learning rates occur within any classroom. The teacher might teach all the shapes to one child, while focusing on individual shapes with another. The activities in this unit should be presented in the way that best suits the individual children and/or the class as a whole.

ALPHABEARS: AN ABC BOOK
by
Kathleen Hague

Developmental Activities Chart	Language & Cognitive Development	Fine Motor Art	Gross Motor	Perception	Social Skills	Math	Dramatic Play	Cooking Snack	Science	Music, Fingerplays, Poems
1 Letters or Numbers	X					X				
2 Letter Hunt	X			X						
3 Alphabet Olympics	X		X							
4 Riddles	X									
5 Letter Bags	X	X								
6 Musical Alphabet	X		X							X
7 Oh Alphabet										X
8 Feeling Center				X						
9 Auditory Alphabet	X			X						
10 Hidden Letter		X		X						
11 Letter Sound Experiences	X									
12 Teddy Bear Match	X									
13 Touch and Name	X			X						
14 Name Verses	X				X					
15 Teddy Bear	X									
16 Letter Forms		X		X			X			
17 Cereal Spell and Math	X				X	X				
18 Alphabet Books	X	X								
19 Alphabet Game	X				X					
20 Alphabet Snacks								X		
21 Alphabet Fine Motor Activities		X								
22 Suggested Home Activities	X	X								
23										
24										
25										
26										
27										
28										
29										
30										

ALPHABEARS: AN ABC BOOK
by Kathleen Hague
Henry Holt, 1984

This rhythmic alphabet book introduces a teddy bear for each letter, from Amanda, who carries sweet apples, to Zak, who says zippers are better than buttons. The illustrations are warm and wonderful. Many other excellent alphabet books are also available. The following activities can be used with any alphabet book.

Letters or Numbers.   Children will be at many different levels in alphabet readiness. Make number cards from 0 to 10 and alphabet cards from A to Z; laminate the cards. Have children sort the numbers from the letters. This activity can also be done with commercially produced magnetic or rubber letters.

Letter Hunt.   Go on an alphabet hunt. Look for letters, words, names, and signs in school and around the neighborhood. Children can count the number of letters seen, print letters, or graph the letters.

Alphabet Olympics.   In an open area of the classroom or gym, children can use problem-solving skills to form each letter of the alphabet with their bodies.

Riddles.   The teacher gives clues related to an object and its beginning letter sound. Children listen to the clues and name the object. Picture cards can be placed on the table and used as visual cues. For example,

I am good to eat.
I can be round and have cheese and sausage.
I begin with the "p" sound.
What am I?

Letter Bags.   Children cut out a specific letter from magazines, catalogs, or newspapers and glue them on a brown bag. Each child brings his or her letter sound bag home. Together parent and child find an object that begins with the specific sound *and* fits inside the bag. Children return their bags to school, share the objects they brought, and display the objects on a letter sound table.

Musical Alphabet.   Laminate a large set of alphabet letters and tape them to the floor in an open area. Play lively music as children march around the alphabet. When the music stops, children name the letter on which they are standing. Children can also sit in a circle on the floor and pass letters around as the music plays. When the music stops, children name the letter they are holding.

Oh Alphabet   (to the tune of "Oh Christmas Tree")

> Oh alphabet, oh alphabet.
> The letters go from A to Z.
> Your letters spell the words we hear,
> And also tell us stories dear.
> Oh alphabet, oh alphabet.
> The letters go from A to Z.
> Oh alphabet, oh alphabet.
> The upper case match lower case.
> Your letters always stay the same,
> They never ever change their names.
> Oh alphabet, oh alphabet.
> The upper case match lower case.

Feeling Center.   Put fingerpaint or shaving cream on a tabletop or in the sensory table. Children can print the alphabet letters, spell their names, copy words, and so on. Children squeeze a heavy line of glue on a piece of tagboard or cardboard which has a teacher-prepared letter traced on it. They emboss the letter by putting sand, rice, elbow macaroni, and so on on the glue. Allow the letters to dry thoroughly. If each child creates a different letter, the class will have a complete set to use for touching and naming when they are blindfolded or have their eyes closed.

Auditory Alphabet.   Say three words, two of which have the same beginning sound and one which has a different beginning sound. Children can say the words that have the same sound or name the word that has a different sound, for example, boat-banana-deer.

Hidden Letter.   Select a simple picture from a favorite coloring book. Use a black pen or fine line marker to print and "hide" the letter you are working on in several places on the picture. Children find and circle the "hidden" letters and then color the picture. A picture showing an object with the specific letter sound would be an added reinforcement. See the black line master that is included.

Letter Sound Experiences.   While learning a specific letter sound, read stories which have themes or characters with that sound. Go on field trips and plan for class visitors that have a certain letter sound, for example, for "B" week, visit a bookstore or a bakery; for "P" week, have pets or police visit the class. Children dictate class stories about their experiences.

Teddy Bear Match.   Make a bear pattern from the black line master provided and cut 52 bears from construction paper. Print the upper-case and lower-case letters on the teddy bears' chests. Laminate the bears. Children match upper- and lower-case letter bears.

Touch and Name.   Use the objects on the letter sound table children have brought from home. Place one object at a time in a bag, pillowcase, or box that has an opening cut out so that children can reach inside. Children take turns reaching inside and trying to identify the object by touch.

Name Verses. When learning a specific letter sound, have children work together to dictate a nonsense verse for children whose name begins with that certain sound. The verses can rhyme, like the ones in the story, but that is not necessary and will depend upon the children's ability.

Teddy Bear. Cut out one brown bear using the pattern provided, laminate it, and staple it to a Popsicle™ stick or tongue depressor. Make a card for each letter of the alphabet, laminate them, and staple to Popsicle™ sticks or tongue depressors. Say a version of the familiar verse:

Teddy bear, teddy bear.	[Hold up the bear.]
What do you see?	[Hold up a letter card.]
I see letter ____ looking at me	
Letter ____, letter ____.	
What do you see?	[Continue with all the alphabet cards.]

End the verse with:
Teddy bear, teddy bear.
What did you see?
I saw the alphabet looking at me.

Letter Forms. Children can form the alphabet letters using play dough. Children can also form letters using thawed, Rhodes™ bread dough. Bake the letters. Eat and enjoy!

Cereal Spell and Math. Provide Alpha-Bits™ cereal for the children. They can identify letters, spell their names, and so on using the cereal. Provide a small container of cereal for cooperative groups of children. They can count their letters and sort and graph the letters that are the same.

Alphabet Books. Provide manila paper cut into the shape of the letter sound the children are learning. Each child finds and cuts three to five magazine/catalog pictures that begin with that sound (children can find pictures at home or school) and glue them on the paper. Each child writes/dictates a story about one of his or her pictures on the manila paper. Individual alphabet books can be made for each child or a class alphabet book for each letter can be made.

Alphabet Game. Make a set of 26 alphabet cards, print a letter of the alphabet on one side, and glue a picture of something beginning with that sound on the opposite side. Laminate the cards. Several games can be played with the cards. Place the cards, alphabet side up, on the table. Children name the letter and say a word that begins with that sound. If children are having difficulty, they can turn the card over to get a visual cue. Place the cards, picture side up, on the table. Children name the picture and tell its beginning sound.

Alphabet Snacks. Children will enjoy "eating their way through the alphabet." Have children assist in preparing/cooking foods that begin with the particular sound being learned. Consider snacks that are nutritious and healthy.

A,a   apples, applesauce, alfalfa sprouts, apricots, almonds, avocados
B,b   beans, biscuits, bananas, berries, bacon, bologna, bread
C,c   carrots, cucumbers, cabbage, cornbread, corn
D,d   donuts, dip, dates, date and nut bread
E,e   egg salad, enchiladas, egg rolls, eggnog
F,f   Fig Newtons™, fish sticks, fortune cookies, fudge, farina, fondue
G,g   gumbo soup, garlic bread, goulosh, graham crackers
H,h   honey, hash, hot dogs, ham, hamburgers, Hawaiian Punch™
I,i   Indian fry bread, Italian foods, ice cream
J,j   jam, jelly, juice, Jell-O™, jelly beans, Johnnycake
K,k   kiwi fruit, Kix™ cereal, Kool-aid™, chocolate kisses
L,l   lettuce, lemon bars, lemon or lime Jell-O™, Lucky Charms™ cereal
M,m   muffins, melons, meatballs, marshmallows, macaroni, marmalade
N,n   nuts, noodles, nachos, nut bread, nacho cheese
O,o   oriental foods, oranges, oatmeal, Oreo™ cookies
P,p   pancakes, potatoes, pudding, pizza, peaches, popcorn, peppers, peas
Q,q   quiche, quick bread
R,r   ravioli, rice, rye krisp, raisins, rolls, Ritz™ crackers
S,s   soup, sesame/sunflower seeds, sandwiches, sundaes, salads, salami
T,t   tacos, tuna, tostitos, tangerines, toast, tomatoes, tapioca, taffy
U,u   pineapple upside-down cake
V,v   vanilla pudding, vanilla ice cream, vanilla wafers, vegetables, Velveeta™
W,w   won tons, waffles, Waldorf salad, watermelon, wax beans, wafers
X,x   juice boxes, box lunch
Y,y   yogurt, yams, yellow foods
Z,z   zucchini, zucchini bread and muffins, zwieback toast

Alphabet Fine Motor Activities.   Children will enjoy the experience of creating a project for each letter sound or manipulating objects which have the sound. Try to incorporate some of these activities. The process is more important than the product.

A,a   print with apples, make a paper plate apple using tissue paper snips
B,b   play with blocks, string beads, button, make blotto prints with paint
C,c   clip clothespins on a line, make collages, clip coupons
D,d   make dot-to-dot pictures, trace diamonds or dinosaurs, print with dandelions
E,e   make colored eggshell mosaics, fold paper to put in envelopes
F,f   finger paint, make a folded paper fan using construction paper
G,g   sponge paint ghosts, print with classroom or kitchen gadgets
H,h   make handprints, lace around hearts, make a paper hat
I,i   stack and glue sugar cubes to make an igloo
J,j   make a junk collage, drop jelly beans in jars, screw lids on jars
K,k   make a paper bag kite, decorate, and add crepe paper streamers
L,l   make leaf rubbings, practice lacing, make a paper plate lion/lamb
M,m   make mosaics, mobiles, or masks, decorate a pair of mittens

N,n   crack nuts, screw nuts and bolts together, pound nails with hammers
O,o   sponge paint an ocean scene, trace and cut ovals
P,p   put pegs in pegboards, make potato prints, use a paper punch
Q,q   paint with Q-Tips™, make a class quilt, trace around quarters
R,r   make rubbings, make a robot using only rectangles, pour rice
S,s   cut with scissors, make a seed necklace, do a string painting
T,t   make letters with toothpicks, build block towers, trace objects
U,u   decorate a cut paper umbrella, practice unzipping and untying
V,v   print with vegetables, make a vase using wallpaper scraps
W,w   weave paper over and under, use watercolor paints
X,x   practice making X's, color an X-tra special picture
Y,y   try using a yo-yo, make a collage with thick and thin yarn
Z,z   practice zipping, use play dough to make a zoo animal

Suggested Home Activities.   Send home a synopsis of the book *Alphabears,* and inform parents that the children will be doing many alphabet-related activities throughout the school year. Remind them that the activities will provide exposure to the letters, but will not ensure mastery, since the children are at many different levels of readiness. Inform parents that reading to their child is the best readiness activity they can do with their child. Encourage parents to help their child find magazine pictures or objects with a specific letter sound. Let them be aware that children will be writing/dictating stories about the pictures and sharing objects at the letter sound table.

Related Literature

Aylesworth, Jim. *Old Black Fly.*
Ehlert, Lois. *Eating the Alphabet: Fruits and Vegetables from A to Z.*
MacDonald, Suse. *Alphabatics.*
Martin, Bill, Jr., and John Archambault. *Chicka Chicka Boom Boom.*

Look at the picture. Find all the *D*'s hidden in the picture and circle them. Color the picture.

Hidden Letter Activity

Teddy Bear Match and Teddy Bear Activities

TEN BLACK DOTS
by
Donald Crews

Developmental Activities Chart	Language & Cognitive Development	Fine Motor Art	Gross Motor	Perception	Social Skills	Math	Dramatic Play	Cooking Snack	Science	Music, Fingerplays, Poems
1 Number Hunt	X			X		X				
2 Number Collage		X				X				
3 Sorting	X			X	X	X				
4 Math Puzzles				X		X				
5 Shake and Roll	X				X	X				
6 Playing Cards	X			X	X	X				
7 Beanbag Toss	X		X			X				
8 Musical Numbers					X	X				X
9 Number Riddles	X				X	X				
10 Number Song						X				X
11 Dot Pictures	X	X				X				
12 Clothespin Math		X				X				
13 Making Numbers		X		X		X				
14 Touch and Name				X		X				
15 Telephone Time	X	X				X				
16 Estimating	X					X				
17 Calendar Math	X	X		X		X				
18 Obstacle Course Math			X			X				
19 Math-Science Predictions	X	X				X			X	
20 It's Your Business	X	X			X	X	X			
21 Play Dough Math	X	X				X				
22 Storytime	X					X				
23 Math Memory			X			X				
24 Find Your Partner	X				X	X				
25 Number Sounds				X		X				X
26 What Set Doesn't Belong?	X	X				X				
27 Caterpillar Puzzles		X			X	X				
28 Number Bingo					X	X				
29 Cook and Share	X				X	X		X		
30 Suggested Home Activities	X					X		X		

TEN BLACK DOTS
by Donald Crews
Greenwillow Books, 1986

Ten Black Dots is a delightful book that tells a simple rhyme for each number from 1 to 10 and shows what simple black dots can become. In each rhyme, a number is shown next to the printed word and the black dots in each picture are bold and easy to count. Children will enjoy listening to this rhythmic counting book over and over again.

Number Hunt.   After listening to the story, have children brainstorm a list of objects that have numerals, such as the door to their classroom, a clock, a measuring cup, and the calendar. After making the list, take a walk in the school building and around the school neighborhood to confirm their ideas and find other things with numerals (mailboxes, license plates, signs). Have children use problem-solving and thinking skills to tell why numerals are helpful and needed in our world.

Number Collage.   Provide magazines, newspapers, advertisements, and catalogs. Children look for numerals, cut them out, and glue them on a large piece of kraft paper to make a collage. Children can point to and try to name the individual numerals on the collage.

Sorting.   Prepare a set of 3" × 5" cards for children to sort. On each card write/draw a numeral, letter, "squiggle," or shape. Laminate the cards. Place the cards face down on a table, and have the children take turns picking a card, identifying it, and placing it in the correct pile.

Math Puzzles.   Cut white tagboard or cardboard into ten pieces, approximately 5" × 10" each. On the top of each piece write a numeral from 1 to 10; on the bottom, draw the corresponding number of black dots with a black marker. Cut each card into two pieces to make a puzzle. Vary each puzzle. Laminate the pieces. Children can assemble the puzzles by matching the numeral with the correct number of dots.

Shake and Roll.   Children will enjoy playing math games with dice.

- Each child takes a turn shaking a die in a cup or in his or her hand, then rolling it on a table. The child counts the dots and makes a set using the correct number of beans, keys, shells, buttons, and so on. Children with advanced skills can use two or three dice. Pairs of children can compare their sets: who has more, who has less?

- Two, three, or four children can be grouped together. Each child in the group rolls the die and makes a set. One member of the group can be a "recorder" and write the numeral each person rolled. The sets can be counted all together in this beginning addition activity.

Playing Cards.   Playing cards are a must in every classroom. Remove the face cards for each activity.

- Children sort the cards by number, 1 to 10.
- Sequence the cards in numerical order.
- Place cards face down on the table; have each child select a card and make a matching set with small manipulatives.
- Place a series of cards on the table: 4, 5, 7, 8; have children tell what number is missing.
- Place one card on the table; have children tell what numbers are more than or less than the number shown.
- Children are paired together to play "war." Each child gets up to ten cards. Both children show one card at the same time. The child with the larger number keeps both cards. If the two cards are the same, each child shows another card. The child with the larger numeral keeps all the cards. The winner is the child with the most cards. Another version of the game is for the child with the smaller numeral to keep the cards.

Beanbag Toss.   Prepare a set of cards with numerals from 1 to 10 on large pieces of construction paper. Laminate the cards. Secure the cards to the floor with masking tape in an open area. Children take turns tossing a beanbag on a card and saying the numeral. Another version is to have each child toss the beanbag to a specific numeral.

Musical Numbers.   Tape a laminated set of numerals, 1 to 10, in a large circle on the floor. Play lively music as children walk around the circle. When the music stops, each child must name the numeral he or she is standing on.

Number Riddles.   Children demonstrate numeral comprehension when answering number riddles; for example,

> I am a number.
> I am more than 4.
> I am less than 8.
> What number(s) can I be?

Groups of children can work together to solve the riddles; manipulatives should be provided for each group.

Number Song   (to the tune of "Ten Little Indians")

> One little, two little, three little black dots,
> Four little, five little, six little black dots,

Seven little, eight little, nine little black dots,
Ten little black dot pictures.

Dot Pictures.   Provide each child with a large piece of construction paper or heavy manila paper and a supply of large, precut black dots. Each child creates a picture using the dots, as in the story, and writes or dictates a rhyme or story about their picture, including the number of dots used. The pictures can be put together to make a class book. Consider laminating each page of the class book; it is likely to be a popular book students will "read" often.

Clothespin Math.   Children will strengthen fine motor skills as well as numeral comprehension with the following activities.

- Cover ten soup-size cans with construction paper or Con-Tact® paper. Write a numeral on each can. Children "clip" the correct number of clothespins around the rim of each can.

- Divide a pizza board or piece of heavy cardboard into sections. Glue pictures, 1 to 10, into each section. Cover the board with clear Con-Tact® paper. Write a numeral from 1 to 10 on spring-style clothespins using a permanent marker. Children "clip" a clothespin with the correct numeral on each set of pictures.

Making Numbers.   Children can form numerals using toothpicks, blocks, play dough, or bread dough. Bread dough numbers can be baked and eaten. Children will enjoy the sensory experience of forming numbers in fingerpaint, pudding, or a shaving cream–lined sensory table.

Touch and Name.   Make a set of numbers cut from course sandpaper and glue onto heavy tagboard of cardboard. Children close their eyes and try to identify the numeral by touch.

Telephone Time.   Write each child's telephone number on a notecard. Children can practice calling their home number using a rotary dial or touch-tone play phone. If possible, get donations of broken phones, or request the use of practice phones from the telephone company.

Estimating.   Place buttons, pieces of candy, pennies, keys, beads, plastic caps from milk and water containers, poker chips, and so on in a clear jar or zip-style bag. Children estimate how many objects are in the container. The teacher can record estimates on the chalkboard. Children check their predictions by counting the items. Using the chalkboard estimates, talk about which estimates were close and which were "way off." It is important not to label predictions as right or wrong.

Calendar Math.   Calendar activities teach young children many concepts in a fun and rhythmic way.

- Display a class calendar. Each day a new number symbol can be added on the calendar. Special events like birthdays, field trips, and class visitors can be shown on the calendar with a symbol, for example, a bus, a birthday cake, a star. Children can count how many more days/sleeps until a certain event occurs. Symbols can be patterned by color and/or object. Some children will be able to understand and follow a three-color/object pattern and anticipate what should come next on the calendar. Children can chant the days of the week, counting how many days have occurred and how many more days there will be in the week. They can be exposed to simple addition concepts when filling in the blanks and reviewing what has already been discussed. We've had *3* days, we still have *4* more days, 3 and 4 make *7, 7* days make a *week!* Temporal concepts, today, yesterday, tomorrow, can be reviewed at calendar time, as well as the ordinal positions of first, second, third, and last, depending on the children's level of understanding.

- Each child can make an individual calendar, completing it in a way that is meaningful to them. (An empty calendar is included that can be duplicated and decorated by the children.) Some children may fill the calendar with numerals, others may want to draw small pictures to show the weather for the day, while others may want to use stickers to represent events. Their ideas should be encouraged and shared with the class.

- Provide multicolored strips of paper so that children can make a paper chain calendar (seasonal colors can be provided, for example, fall—orange, yellow, brown; winter—white, black, dark blue; spring—pink, yellow, green). Each day children can add a new link to their calendar. Some can draw a picture of what the weather is like, write the date, or add a special sticker to represent a special event occurring at home or school. Calendars can be tacked around the classroom.

Obstacle Course Math.   Set up an obstacle course in the gym and number each station. Children complete the activities in the correct order. Include a wide range of materials including tires, a tunnel, mats, a balance beam, balls, and beanbags.

Math-Science Predictions.   Provide several types of seeds; marigold and bean seeds grow well. Children select what seeds they want to plant in peat pots or Styrofoam™ cups. Make a class chart recording how many seeds each child planted, their prediction about how many will grow, and the actual amount that did. Children can also record how well their plants are growing, for example, the marigold is one block tall and has three leaves, the bean plant is two blocks tall and has five leaves.

It's Your Business.   Allow children to decide what kind of store/restaurant they would like to open in the dramatic play area. Assist them in finding props they will need. Supply a telephone to take orders, play money, an adding machine, calculators, a cash register, bags, boxes, coupons, pencils, paper, price stickers, construction paper, and old magazines to cut apart to make advertisements or menus.

Play Dough Math.   Children can easily experiment with numbers and parts of a whole when using play dough.

- Children make flat pancakes or snakes with play dough. Provide dull knives children can use to divide their creations into three parts, five parts, and so on.
- Challenge children to make caterpillars, snakes, or worms following a variety of directions:

    Make it three unifix™ cubes long,

    Make it shorter than one Popsicle™ stick,

    Make it between four and five keys long.

Storytime.   Make up a story to tell children (On my way to school I saw three blue cars that were the same. I had to stop for two red lights and one schoolbus picking up children, and so on.) When children hear the number word they can raise their hands or clap. Encourage children to tell simple number stories for the class.

Math Memory.   Give children one- to four-step directions depending on their readiness/memory levels: "Clap 6 times, stamp your feet 1 time, and hop 3 times." The directions can be tailor made to meet the individual needs of the class.

Find Your Partner.   Give one-half of the children a card with a numeral from 1 to 10. Give the other children a card with black dots from 1 to 10. Children work together to find their number partner.

Number Sounds.   The teacher or a student sits behind a screen and makes a certain number of sounds with classroom objects, rhythm instruments, and so on. Children need to listen and tell the number of sounds heard, identify what made the sound, and then duplicate the correct number of sounds.

What Set Doesn't Belong?   Each day display a number and a variety of sets in small containers, boxes, trays, and so on on a "math discovery table." Children must decide which set(s) don't belong because they don't have the correct amount. Provide paper and crayons so that children can record their responses by drawing pictures of the set(s) that don't belong. Some children can indicate if the set contains too many or too few.

Caterpillar Puzzles.   Have children cut out a long construction paper shape to represent a caterpillar. Children write the numerals in order from 1 to 10 on the caterpillar, leaving some space between each numeral. Children cut the caterpillar apart by making wavy, zigzag lines, and so on. Puzzles pieces can be stored in zip-style bags. Children can trade bags so they have the opportunity to put different puzzles together. The teacher can prepare the caterpillar puzzles and laminate the pieces if the activity is too difficult for the children. A numbered caterpillar puzzle can be made out of flannel to be used as a group activity on the flannel board. Reinforce turn taking, number recognition, and ordinal positions.

Number Bingo.   Prepare enough bingo cards so that each child has one. Duplicate the bingo grid provided or make cards on tagboard. Fill in each space with a number, varying each card. Cards can be laminated. The teacher or student "caller" picks a numeral from a box, says the numeral, and/or shows it to the children. Players find and cover the number on their card with a poker chip or bingo disk. Play continues until a child fills a row or column to make "bingo"!

Cook and Share. Cooking is an excellent way for children to learn about numbers, parts of a whole, and units of measure. After making these cookies, have children figure out ways to evenly divide the cookies among themselves and decide what to do with the extras.

Applesauce-Oatmeal Cookies

¾	cup packed brown sugar	1	cup flour
½	cup softened margarine	½	cup raisins
1	egg	1¼	teaspoon salt
1	cup unsweetened applesauce	½	teaspoon baking powder
3	cups rolled oats	½	teaspoon baking soda
½	teaspoon cinnamon		

Preheat oven to 375 degrees. Cream sugar and margarine until light and fluffy. Beat in egg, then add applesauce. Stir in oats, flour, raisins, salt, baking powder, baking soda, and cinnamon. Drop by tablespoon on a greased cookie sheet. Bake for 12 to 15 minutes, or until lightly browned. Makes about 36 cookies.

Suggested Home Activities. Send home a synopsis of the story *Ten Black Dots,* and inform parents of some of the activities children will be doing at school. Continue to update parents about the math experiences that will be ongoing in the classroom. Encourage parents to help their child become more aware of numbers and math concepts in their environment. Children can set the table, practicing one-to-one correspondence, cook with parents, and count everything in their environment. Many children will demonstrate understanding of mathematical concepts if they are frequently heard. Encourage parents to use vocabulary in meaningful situations: more than–less than, empty–full, tall–short, long–short, big–little, whole–part, first–second–third, few–many, and so on. Remind parents to visit the library and select counting and math-related books. Some parents might appreciate receiving a short list of some of the books annotated in the bibliography.

Related Literature

Anno, Mitsumasa. *Anno's Counting Book.*
Carle, Eric. *1, 2, 3, to the Zoo.*
Ehlert, Lois. *Fish Eyes: A Book You Can Count On.*
Hague, Kathleen. *Numbears.*

Number Bingo

Number Bingo Activity

SUN	MON	TUE	WED	THU	FRI	SAT

Calendar Math Activity

OF COLORS AND THINGS
by
Tana Hoban

Developmental Activities Chart	Language & Cognitive Development	Fine Motor Art	Gross Motor	Perception	Social Skills	Math	Dramatic Play	Cooking Snack	Science	Music, Fingerplays, Poems
1 Exploring the Book	X			X	X	X				
2 Color Boxes	X									
3 Scavenger Hunt	X			X	X	X				
4 Color Cans		X		X						
5 Color Pizzas		X		X						
6 Color Riddles	X									
7 Icicle Painting		X								
8 Color Days	X	X		X						
9 Color Collage	X	X								
10 Beanbag Toss			X	X						
11 Color Tag			X	X						
12 Painter, May I?	X		X							
13 Balloon Chant			X							
14 Odd One Out				X						
15 Colored Lollipops	X		X							X
16 Class Big Book	X	X		X	X					
17 Candy Math				X		X		X		
18 Color Matching				X		X		X		
19 Patterns		X		X		X				
20 Color My World		X		X			X			
21 Bubble Pictures		X							X	
22 Color Mixing		X		X					X	
23 Syringe Painting		X		X						
24 Colored Shaving Cream		X							X	
25 Colored Snacks								X		
26 Color Game										X
27 Suggested Home Activities	X			X				X	X	
28										
29										
30										

OF COLORS AND THINGS
by Tana Hoban
Greenwillow Books, 1989

Colors of easily recognizable objects are represented in simple bold photographs in this wordless book. Each page contains four photographs—three with objects of one solid color and one with a multicolored object that incorporates the color of the page. The book lends itself to endless discussion and activities. The book can be used with *Shapes, Shapes, Shapes* or other books by Tana Hoban, in a unit based on the author, or with books that use real photographs to tell a story.

Exploring the Book. Take time to look at the book with individual children and small groups, as well as with the whole class. The children will want to share information about their experiences with the toys, food, and other common objects. Incorporate counting skills, classifying, shape recognition, discussion of texture, taste, size, and function, along with the children's personal experiences and object recognition.

Color Boxes. Cover boxes with different colors of Con-Tact® paper or construction paper and label them by color. The children can collect items at home and school to add to the color boxes. Provide time for the children to talk about the different items. They can name and describe the objects in terms of who might use it and where, when, and how it might be used.

Scavenger Hunt. Make a picture list of colored objects that children can collect from different classrooms or at home. Divide the class into teams of two or more children. The teams can use identical lists or different lists. When the children find the items, have them classify the items by color, function, size, and shape. They can count the items all together and the number of items in each category.

Color Cans. Cover empty aluminum cans such as soup or juice cans with colored Con-Tact® paper. Make a set of color-coded clothespins. The children will develop the small muscles of the hand when they pinch open the clothespin while matching/attaching it to the same-colored can.

Colored Pizzas. Divide a round pizza cardboard into six sections. Color or cover each section with a different color. Provide sets of colored toppings that match each section of the pizza. Examples are red tomatoes, green and yellow peppers, white mushrooms, brown sausage, and pink pepperoni. Cover the pizza with clear Con-Tact® paper and laminate the toppings to preserve them. The children can match the toppings to the corresponding piece of pizza.

Color Riddles. Use the pictures in the book or classroom objects to play a riddle game. Start out by giving one clue, "I'm thinking of something green." Give more clues as needed, using size, shape, function, and so on as additional attributes. Some children might be familiar with the game "I spy." Children take turns thinking of an object or picture and saying "I spy with my eye something that is . . . . (name a color)."

Icicle Painting. Add water mixed with tempera paint or food coloring to an empty ice cube tray or Popsicle™ mold. Place it in the freezer. When the mixture begins to solidify, place a tongue depressor into each section. Once frozen, the children can paint with their icicle on fingerpaint paper or on cardboard.

Color Days. Proclaim special color days in the classroom. Children can dress, eat a special snack, color and paint, and bring an item to share, all in the special color of the day.

Color Collage. Provide an assortment of collage materials such as paper, fabric, buttons, sequins, pipe cleaners, yarn, and so on. The children can make a color collage by using materials of only one color. Label the collage with the appropriate color word.

Beanbag Toss. Arrange and tape pieces of colored construction paper on the floor behind a chalk or masking tape line. Prepare a set of colored cards (five of each color) that match the construction paper. The children can take turns choosing a card and throwing a beanbag to the piece of construction paper that matches the color they chose.

Color Tag. This game is played like the regular tag game, except that, when "It" tags another child, he or she must say the name of a color that child is wearing.

Painter, May I? Choose one child at a time to wear a painter's cap or to hold a painter's brush. He or she is the painter and gives directions for the other children to follow. Examples might be, "Hop on one foot; jump on two feet; take two giant steps," and so on. The children respond by asking, "Painter, May I?" Painter responds by saying, "Only if you are wearing the color . . . ."

Balloon Chant. Use colored balloons to go with this chant:

> Green in the air. Green in the air.
> We only care to keep green in the air.

Substitute other colors for green or chant two colors at the same time. Children bat balloons with their hands, head, or feet to keep them in the air.

Odd One Out. Display a group of objects of the same color. Include one different-colored object. The children try and guess which object doesn't belong. Young children and children with delays in perceptual skills will be challenged by displays of solid-colored objects. Children who can easily recognize color differences can be challenged with more subtle differences in color. An example might be to display three sets, each containing three objects, for example, red, blue, and yellow. A fourth set can be displayed that contains red, blue, and green. The children can determine which set is different.

Colored Lollipops.   Make a set of different-colored lollipops by stapling colored circles onto tongue depressors. Prepare enough for everyone in the class; colors can be duplicated. Teach the children this lollipop song and have them follow the directions (to the tune of "Ten Little Indians").

> Blue and red and yellow lollipops.
> Green and orange and purple lollipops.
> Black and brown and white lollipops.
> If you're holding green jump up.

Vary the color and the direction to follow. For example, if you're holding purple touch your head.

Class Big Book.   The children can work cooperatively to make a class Big Book. Divide the class into groups of two, three, or four children. Each group can pick a colored slip of paper out of a hat. Provide them with magazines and catalogs, and have the group find and cut pictures that match the color they chose. Have the children glue their pictures onto sheets of tagboard. The class can vote to decide if the book should be wordless or have words. If they choose to have a book with words, they can dictate captions and text for their pictures. Assemble the book by punching holes and tying the pages together with yarn.

Candy Math.   Use colored M&Ms™ or jelly beans as a math manipulative. The children can make up patterns (red/green/red; red/green/red, . . .), sort and classify by color, count and make sets, design shapes, and measure classroom objects with the candy. Finally, the candy can be eaten.

Color Matching.   Label the sections of an empty egg carton with different colors by drawing a colored dot at the bottom of each section. Provide the children with colored candies or beads. The children can fill the sections with the matching color. If candy is used the children will enjoy the snack after the activity.

Patterns.   Use colored beads, cubes, blocks, unifix™ cubes, attribute blocks, buttons, or beans to set up patterns for the children to follow. Patterns can be single colored or multicolored, simple or complex, depending on the ability levels of the children.

Color My World.   The children will be able to view their world in their favorite color. Have them cut out the center circle of a paper plate. Provide them with different colors of cellophane paper. They can staple, tape, or glue the cellophane to the outer ring of the plate. Staple on a tongue depressor for a handle.

Bubble Pictures.   Add food coloring to bubbles. As children blow bubbles on paper they can watch them pop in color. Vary the activity by taping the paper to a wall or mounting it on an easel.

Color Mixing.   Use baby food jars or small clear glasses and an eyedropper. Half-fill the jars with clear water. Fill additional jars with water containing a high concentration of food coloring. The children can color their water by squeezing colored water into their eyedropper and then into their jar of water. Encourage them to experiment by mixing colors.

Syringe Painting.   Mix different colors of tempera paint with water so that they are quite runny. Provide the children with syringes to fill with the paint and then squirt the paint onto the paper.

Colored Shaving Cream.   Shaving cream can be colored with tempera paint and children can finger paint on the tabletop. Use the particular color that the children are learning about or a variety of colors for color mixing.

Colored Snacks.   Reinforce the concept of color by preparing snacks that emphasize a particular color.

> **Orange**—Oranges, tangerines, orange juice, cantaloupe melon, carrots, orange Jell-O™
>
> **Green**—Celery, green pepper, kiwi fruit, honeydew melon, Granny Smith apples, lime Jell-O™, green grapes, pickles, pistachio pudding
>
> **White**—Popcorn, vanilla ice cream, marshmallows, cream cheese, cottage cheese, white bread, vanilla yogurt, mozzarella cheese sticks
>
> **Red**—Apples, strawberry or raspberry jam on toast, strawberries, red peppers, red Jell-O™, raspberries, red licorice, tomato soup
>
> **Pink**—Strawberry ice cream, strawberry shakes, strawberry yogurt, pink grapefruit, pink fluff (Jell-O™ mixed with whipped topping)
>
> **Yellow**—Bananas, egg salad, yellow apples, yellow peppers, corn, toast with butter, yellow popcorn, yellow cupcakes, vanilla pudding
>
> **Purple**—Grapes, grape jam, grape juice, purple Popsicles™, purple cow (frozen grape juice mixed with milk)
>
> **Blue**—Blueberries, blueberry yogurt, blueberry muffins
>
> **Brown**—Wheat bread, chocolate ice cream, peanut butter, graham crackers, chocolate pudding, cinnamon and toast, pretzels, raisins
>
> **Black**—Black licorice, black jelly beans

Color Game.   Children sit in a circle and say this chant:

> Green, green, green, green, who is wearing green today?
> Green, green, green, green, who is wearing green?
> Anna's wearing green today, she'll come in the circle and play.
> Green, green, green, green, Anna's wearing green.

The child wearing that color comes to the middle of the circle. Repeat the chant with other colors.

Suggested Home Activities.   Send home a synopsis of the story *Of Colors and Things,* and inform parents of some of the activities the children are involved in at school. Suggest to parents that they reinforce color concepts during daily activities. Serve colorful meals and talk about the colors of food served. Talk about clothing colors while dressing. Children can help sort laundry by color, and match socks by color. A trip to the grocery store exposes children to almost any color imaginable. Parents can help children notice foods of different colors while shopping and then write them down from memory at home. The family can go for color walks around the neighborhood noticing the many colors of nature and the neighborhood.

Related Literature

Hoban, Tana. *Is It Red? Is It Yellow? Is It Blue?*
Martin, Bill, Jr. *Brown Bear, Brown Bear, What Do You See?*
Young, Ed. *Seven Blind Mice.*

SHAPES, SHAPES, SHAPES
by
Tana Hoban

Developmental Activities Chart	Language & Cognitive Development	Fine Motor Art	Gross Motor	Perception	Social Skills	Math	Dramatic Play	Cooking Snack	Science	Music, Fingerplays, Poems
1 Shape Walk	X			X						
2 See Them, Count Them	X			X		X				
3 Shape Collections	X			X	X					
4 Every Picture Tells a Story	X									
5 Body Shapes		X	X							
6 Class Shapes			X		X					
7 Beanbag Toss			X	X						
8 Hopscotch			X		X	X				
9 Shape Days	X	X		X	X					
10 Shape Snacks								X		
11 Cookie Shapes								X		
12 Shape Construction	X	X								
13 Instruments										X
14 Feely Bag				X						
15 Card Sort				X		X				
16 Completer Pictures	X	X								
17 String Pictures		X								
18 My Own Book	X	X								
19 Shape Prints		X								
20 Play Dough Shapes		X		X						
21 Calendar Shapes	X			X		X				
22 Top It				X						
23 Textured Shapes				X						
24 Share a Shape	X			X	X					
25 Shape Structures		X								
26 Scavenger Hunt	X				X	X				
27 Sizable Shapes	X			X		X				
28 Suggested Home Activities	X	X		X						
29										
30										

SHAPES, SHAPES, SHAPES
by Tana Hoban
Greenwillow Books, 1986

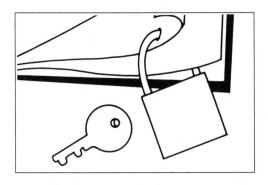

This wordless book presents a study of shapes that are common to our everyday environment. Tana Hoban selects photographs of familiar objects such as houses, windows, bicycles, bridges, and musical instruments, all rich with shapes. The book inspires readers, young and old, to see shapes all around. The book can be presented with *Of Colors and Things* or other books by Tana Hoban as a unit on the author and/or photography.

Shape Walk.   After looking at the book *Shapes, Shapes, Shapes,* go for a shape walk indoors or outdoors. Each child or group of children can be assigned a shape to look for, look for only one shape as a class, or look for many shapes. Upon returning, brainstorm about all the shapes that were seen.

See Them, Count Them.   Explore the book one page at a time finding all the repetitions of the shape. Have the children count how many times each shape is captured in one photograph.

Shape Collections.   This book will help to develop an awareness that there are shapes all around us. Label large boxes or baskets with pictures of a shape. The children can look for objects, photographs, and pictures representing each shape. Before putting their item in the collection box, the children can tell about it.

Every Picture Tells a Story.   While looking at the photographs in the book, ask the children to tell a story to go with each picture.

Body Shapes.   Challenge the children to make shapes with their bodies. Make a circle with arms, hands, and fingers. Make a triangle with fingers, feet, and legs. Make a square, rectangle, and diamond with fingers.

Class Shapes.   The children can lie on the floor and together make shapes. They can problem solve to figure out how to form themselves into various shapes. This activity can be done with the whole class or by dividing the children into groups.

Beanbag Toss.   Label index cards with different shapes. Make corresponding targets from construction paper or tagboard to place on the floor. The children can take turns choosing a shape card and tossing a beanbag onto the corresponding shape on the floor.

Hopscotch.   Children playing hopscotch are photographed in the book. Draw or tape a hopscotch game on the floor. Children take turns tossing a small stone or other marker onto a number and then hopping on one foot or jumping on two feet through the squares. The game continues until each child has thrown a marker on every numeral, in sequence.

Shape Days.   Designate a day for each shape. The children can wear clothing with the shape on it. Specially shaped snacks can be provided. The children can bring a show-and-tell item representing the particular shape. Children can paint, draw, and cut the shape.

Shape Snacks.   Prepare snacks that go with each shape.

> **Bread and Spreads**—Cut bread into any shape and top with cream cheese, peanut butter, jam, cheese, and so on.
>
> **Shaped Cereal**—Serve breakfast cereals in almost any shape.
>
> **Lunch Meat**—Cut or roll lunch meat into any shape.
>
> **Cheesy Shapes**—Cut pieces of cheese into any shape and serve with crackers.
>
> **Circle Snacks**—Cut circles of orange, apple, banana and carrots; serve Cheerios™, doughnuts, doughnut holes, Lifesavers™, circle crackers.
>
> **Triangle Snacks**—Break graham crackers into triangles; serve pizza slices, and sandwiches cut diagonally.
>
> **Square Snacks**—Serve square crackers and cookies.
>
> **Oval Snacks**—Cut eggs lengthwise or serve whole; cut deviled eggs lengthwise; serve jelly beans.
>
> **Rectangle Snacks**—Serve rectangle-shaped crackers, Granola Bars™, Jell-O™ cut into rectangles.
>
> **Arc Snacks**—Serve bananas; broken pretzels.

Cookie Shapes.   Purchase premade cookie dough or use the following recipe for cutting cookies. Use a variety of cookie cutter shapes when cutting the cookies.

1 cup butter	3½ cups flour
1 cup sugar	1 teaspoon cream of tarter
3 eggs	1 teaspoon nutmeg
1 teaspoon salt	pinch salt
1 teaspoon vanilla	

Preheat oven to 425 degrees. Cream butter and sugar, add eggs, then dry ingredients. Refrigerate dough until well chilled. Roll dough and cut into shapes. Bake for 6 to 8 minutes. Makes approximately 48 cookies.

Shape Construction.   Have the children cut paper shapes. Use a variety of shapes or use just one particular shape. Younger children and children with delays in the area of fine motor development can use precut shapes. The shapes can be glued on paper to make a variety of pictures. The children can use the shapes creatively or suggestions can be made. For example, use squares or rectangles and circles to make a train or car; rectangles, squares, and triangles to build a house; circles to make caterpillars and candy canes; triangles to make tall trees; squares to make a skyscraper.

Instruments. The book includes photographs of instruments representing a variety of shapes. Provide an assortment of instruments for the children to play. Include a triangle, sand blocks, a tambourine, cymbals, and so on. The children can experiment with playing loud and soft, fast and slow.

Feely Bag. Place a variety of different-shaped objects in a pillowcase or cardboard box with a cover. The children can take turns reaching in and trying to identify a shape by the way it feels. Vary the activity by asking the child to find a particular shape or find two shapes that are the same.

Card Sort. Use all the hearts and diamonds from a deck of cards. The children can sort through and separate the cards by shape. Have them count the number of hearts and diamonds.

Completer Pictures. Provide paper with a shape drawn or glued anywhere on the page. Challenge the children to finish the picture with crayons, markers, or paint or by gluing on additional shapes. Children can dictate a sentence story about their picture.

String Pictures. Provide the children with construction paper containing penciled-on shapes. The children can squeeze a glue bottle, putting glue on the shapes. They can cover the glue with brightly colored yarn, string, or ribbon.

My Own Book. Staple paper together to make a book for each child. Provide stencils of shapes for the children to trace on the pages of their books. They can label the shapes or leave the book wordless.

Shape Prints. The children can make shape prints by dipping different-shaped items into tempera paint and then on paper. Examples could include coins, erasers, cookie cutter shapes, buttons, barrettes, jar lids, blocks, noodles, and dice.

Play Dough Shapes. Use commercially prepared or homemade play dough. (See recipe on p. 42.) The children can roll the dough with a rolling pin and cut it into different shapes or roll it into snakes and form the snakes into shapes.

Classroom Stencils. The school environment is ripe with shapes. The children can find interesting classroom items and use them as shape stencils.

Calendar Shapes. Use shapes with numbers on the calendar. Pattern the shapes. The children can talk about today's shape, yesterday's shape, and tomorrow's shape. They can predict what shape will come next. They can count how many of each shape is on the calendar, and how that number will change tomorrow. Make up random patterns such as circle/diamond/triangle/circle/diamond/triangle, or pattern the days so Mondays are circles, Tuesdays are triangles, and so on.

Top It. Provide containers of different shapes and matching lids. The children can look at the shape of the container and the lid to find the correct match.

Textured Shapes.   Cut shapes out of different textures of paper and fabric. Use sandpaper, shiny paper, crepe paper, corduroy, felt, furry fabric, and so on. The children can find all the squares, triangles, circles, stars, hearts, and so on.

Share a Shape.   Cut paper shapes in half with zigzag or wavy lines to make puzzles. Laminate the shapes or cover them with clear Con-Tact® paper. Distribute the shapes, one-half to each child. The children can work together to find which classmate has the other half of the shape.

Shape Structures.   The children can use pipe cleaners, toothpicks, Popsicle™ sticks, or cotton swabs to make shape structures. The structures can be glued onto paper.

Scavenger Hunt.   The children can go on a scavenger hunt to other classrooms or at home. They can ask for objects that are circles, squares, rectangles, diamonds, hearts, and ovals. Divide the children into groups; each group can be responsible for finding objects of a specific shape. List and graph the objects. Determine how many of each shape was found. Determine most, least, and the same.

Sizable Shapes.   Cut a variety of shapes in small, medium, and large sizes. The children can classify the different shapes by putting all the like shapes together or by putting all the same size shapes together.

Suggested Home Activities.   Send home a synopsis of *Shapes, Shapes, Shapes,* and inform the parents of the kinds of activities in which the children are involved. Suggest that they reinforce the concept of shapes at home by helping their children be aware of shapes all around them. The parents and their children can look at the outside of their car and list all the shapes they see. They can do the same on the inside of the car. Ask them to stand in front of their house and look for shapes as they notice windows, doors, door knobs, bricks, and so on. Ask them to make a list of the shapes they find and send it to school. Children can practice making shapes at home in the bathtub with shaving cream and on foggy windows and mirrors.

Related Literature

Hoban, Tana. *Circles, Triangles, and Squares.*
————. *Round, Round, and Round.*

Traffic
by
Betsy and Giulio Maestro

Developmental Activities Chart	Language & Cognitive Development	Fine Motor Art	Gross Motor	Perception	Social Skills	Math	Dramatic Play	Cooking Snack	Science	Music, Fingerplays, Poems
1 The Bridge	X	X								
2 Country to City	X	X			X		X			
3 Maps	X	X		X		X				
4 Traffic Lights	X	X		X						
5 Traffic Patrol	X		X		X		X			
6 Listen to the Beat			X	X						X
7 Silly Song	X		X							X
8 Right and Left	X		X	X						
9 Walk Right, Walk Left	X		X							
10 Dark and Light	X					X				
11 Wide and Narrow	X		X			X	X			
12 Tollbooth	X		X		X					
13 Hand Tracing	X	X								
14 Opposite Book	X	X		X						
15 Opposite Snacks				X				X		
16 Opposite Changes	X			X					X	
17 Open Close Them	X	X								X
18 Path Trace		X		X						
19 Far and Near	X			X					X	
20 Empty and Full	X	X		X		X			X	
21 Front and Back	X		X							X
22 Tall/Short and Long/Short	X	X		X		X				
23 Big/Little	X					X				
24 Up, Up	X		X							X
25 Suggested Home Activities	X									
26										
27										
28										
29										
30										

TRAFFIC
by Betsy and Giulio Maestro
Crown, 1981

Traffic follows a little car's journey from the city to the country. The fast and slow journey takes the little car over and under bridges and through light and darkness on its way from the city to the country. This concept book introduces the meaning of opposites. The illustrations are bold and simple. Even the youngest children can understand the concepts introduced throughout this story.

The Bridge.   On its way home the car had to go over and under a bridge. The children can make bridges out of large or small building blocks or out of unifix™ cubes. Provide toy cars for the children to play with, driving them over and under the bridge.

City to Country.   The car had a long ride from the city to the country. After reading the book a few times, ask the children how they could set up a similar route in the classroom. Together, brainstorm ideas. The children will need to remember what the car passed on its route. They will need to decide how to create a dark tunnel, a wide and narrow road, a high hill and a low valley, among other things. Write down ideas and suggestions. Use picture words when possible. Once complete, provide enough toy cars for all the children to enjoy the drive.

Maps.   Introduce children to the concept of a map. Draw a map of the journey from the city to the country. Draw a map of the route the children set up in the classroom. Encourage the children to make simple maps of the classroom to the playground, or of their bedroom to the kitchen. The objective is for them to understand that a map gives a visual representation of a location and it helps people get from point A to point B.

Traffic Lights.   Traffic lights helped the little car know when to go and when to stop. Simple traffic lights can be made from a blue rectangle and green, red, and yellow circles. Make cardboard stencils for the children to trace and cut. The teacher can modify the activity for children with delays in fine motor or perceptual skills. The teacher may provide predrawn or precut shapes. The lights can be assembled by the children by following auditory directions or by following a visual model. Use the terms top, middle, and bottom, as well as stop/go/slow.

Traffic Patrol.   The children can pretend to be cars, or they can use big wheels or scooter boards if there are enough for everyone. In a wide open area such as the gym or playground, cars can move by following directions which are given by a traffic control person. Use the terms fast/slow, stop/go, right/left. The traffic control person can use props such as a whistle, stop/go sign or light, and, of course, a hat. Children will enjoy taking turns being the traffic control person.

Listen to the Beat.   Provide music with fast and slow tempos. Children will move fast or slow depending on the tempo of the music. When the music stops, the children stop. When the music goes, the children move to the beat of the music. Children can move freely, performing any motion they wish, or the teacher or a leader can tell the children how to move. Suggestions are hopping, skipping, walking, running, crawling, rolling, twirling, or wiggling.

Silly Song.   This jump rope activity will reinforce the concepts of high/low and over/under. Two people hold opposite ends of the rope. When they hold the rope high, children move under it. When they hold the rope low, children move over it. Teach this silly song to the tune of "It's Raining, It's Pouring." Ask them to demonstrate, using the jump rope, why the song is silly.

> High, low, how should we go?
> Under on high and over on low.
> Don't get confused or you will go
> Over on high and under on low.

Right and Left.   Discuss the fact that everybody has a right and left side, such as a right and left eye, ear, arm, shoulder, elbow, hand, hip, leg, and foot.

- Play a direction-following game that incorporates the sides of the body. Examples: hold out your right arm, close your left eye, hop on your right foot, pound your left fist, touch your right elbow, and so on. Children might enjoy playing "Simon Says" or "Captain, May I."
- Divide the classroom into a right and left side using a chalk line or by putting masking tape on the floor. Label the sides right and left with a sign. Children can follow simple directions which incorporate the concept of right and left. Examples are everyone move to the right side, eat snack on the left side, find a hidden object on the left side, or read a book on the right side.

Walk Right, Walk Left.   After talking about the concept of right and left, go for two walks around the block. On the first walk only turn right. On the second walk only turn left. Ask the children how the two walks were different.

Dark and Light.   Children can experiment with the concept of dark and light, even during the day. Make a fort by covering a table with a blanket. The children can huddle together under the table in the dark or come out where it is light. Children will enjoy sharing tales, fears, and experiences about being in the dark.

Wide and Narrow.   Make wide and narrow roads by drawing chalk lines on the sidewalk or by placing masking tape on the floor. Provide children with toy cars, big wheels, tricycles, doll buggies, shopping carts, and so on. The children can drive or push their wheeled objects along the roads. Discuss the difference in the two roads. How many cars can go side by side on the narrow road and on the wide road?

Tollbooth.   Human tollbooths can be created by having children hold hands. When the gate of the tollbooth is closed, children hold hands with arms held out to the sides; when the gates open, hands are dropped. Children can combine the game of tollbooth with wide and narrow roads. The game teaches the concept of open and close. Another way to play tollbooth is by dividing the class into two groups. One group is the tollbooth, the other group are cars. When the teacher calls "Close," the gate is closed. When the teacher calls "Open," the cars try to run through the gate before it closes.

Hand Tracing.   Children will learn and see the concept of wide when their hands are traced with fingers spread apart. They will learn and see narrow when their hands are traced with fingers close together.

Opposite Book.   Children can make pictures or find magazine pictures depicting opposite concepts. The pictures can be compiled into book form by the teacher. Make one large book or an individual book for each child. Concepts to include are dark/light, open/close, stop/go, fast/slow, narrow/wide, long/short, tall/short, front/back, far/near, empty/full, and large/small.

Opposite Snacks.   Serve snacks that can be found in opposite pairs. Examples include:

> **Wet/dry snacks**—Crackers, popcorn, cookies, bread sticks, or pretzels, with juice, water, or milk.
>
> **Long/short snacks**—Carrot and celery sticks cut in different lengths. The same can be done with bread sticks, licorice, strands of cooked spaghetti, string cheese, hot dogs, and buttered toast cut into long and short strips.
>
> **Hard/soft snacks**—Hard cheese and cottage cheese, pudding and crackers, milk shakes and popcorn, Jell-O™ and toast, ice cream and cones, and bagels and cream cheese.
>
> **Sweet/sour snacks**—Sweet and sour varieties of apples, bananas and grapefruit, oranges and lemons, and Kool-aid™ and lemonade.

Opposite Changes.   Children can observe matter changing from hard to soft when they watch an ice cube or a Popsicle™ melt. They can watch water change from soft to hard when they observe an ice cube freezing. They can observe the change in cookie dough—soft when it's raw and hard when it's baked. Watching Jell-O™ change from a liquid to a solid is another way to help children observe opposite concepts within their environment.

Open Close Them.   Teach the familiar fingerplay to the children to reinforce the opposite concepts of open and closed. Hands simply do what the words say.

Open close them. Open close them.
Give a little clap.

Open close them. Open close them.
Put them in your lap.

Path Trace.   Reproduce the black line master of the little car's journey from the city to the country. The children can follow the path first with their finger, then with a little car, and finally with a pencil, crayon, or marker.

Far and Near.   Take the children outside if the weather permits; otherwise, look out the window. Tell the children to name as many things as they can that are far and near. Brainstorm a list. Are more things near or far? Bring a pair of binoculars to school. Allow the children to observe the items that were far away. Do they still look far away when using the binoculars?

Empty and Full.   Children will experience the concept of empty and full using the exploration table or buckets filled with water, sand, rice, gravel, and other materials. Provide a variety of containers in different sizes and shapes for children to empty and fill with the different substances.

Front and Back.   Teach the concept of front and back with this simple chant. One or two children at a time repeat the chant. After they have said it they jump facing front or back and the classmates must say which way they are facing.

Jump to the front.
Turn to the back.
Guess which way I am now.

Tall/Short and Long/Short.   Use blocks to reinforce the concept of tall/short and long/short. Children can build tall and short buildings and long and short trains. Long and short can also be reinforced by stringing beads into long and short lengths or by cutting string into long and short lengths. The string can be glued onto paper to create long and short designs. Provide children with colored chalk. The children can use the chalk to draw long and short and tall and short lines on the sidewalk.

Big and Little.   Provide two baskets, one for big items and one for little items. Play this listening game with the children. Describe a classroom item by giving clues (it is big, it is blue, you can throw and catch it). The child who guesses the item correctly takes it from its place in the classroom and deposits it in the correct basket. Repeat the game with other classroom objects until each child has had a turn to find and classify an item.

Up, Up.   Teach the children this action song, which is sung to the tune of "Here We Go Looby Loo." As they say the words, they can act out the movements.

Here we go up, up, up.
Here we go down, down, down.
Here we go backwards and forwards.
And here we go round and around.

Suggested Home Activities.   Send home a synopsis of *Traffic,* and inform parents of some of the activities the children are doing in school. Encourage parents to be aware of opposites which occur in the environment. In the car, they can talk about things that are near and far. If a bridge is on a familiar route, they can go over it and talk about what is under it. They can compare the height of family members: who is tall? who is short? They can talk about foods the family eats: what is hard and what is soft? Is the bath water too cold, too hot, or just right? Children will soon recognize opposites as well as understand the meaning of the concepts.

Related Literature

Dorling Kindersley Book. *My First Look at Opposites.*
Hoban, Tana. *Exactly the Opposite.*
———. *Push, Pull, Empty, Full.*

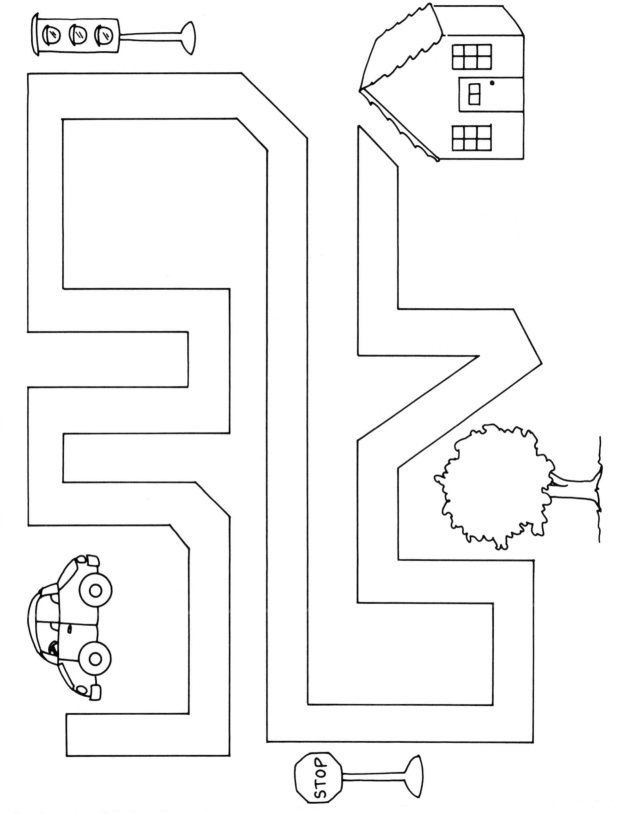

Path Trace Activity

STOP

Predictable Books

POLAR BEAR, POLAR BEAR, WHAT DO YOU HEAR?
by
Bill Martin, Jr.

Developmental Activities Chart	Language & Cognitive Development	Fine Motor Art	Gross Motor	Perception	Social Skills	Math	Dramatic Play	Cooking Snack	Science	Music, Fingerplays, Poems
1 Story Dramatization	X				X		X			X
2 Animal Riddles	X									
3 Window Game				X						
4 Crazy Creatures	X	X		X						
5 Animal Estimations						X				
6 Easel Animals		X								
7 Masks		X					X			
8 Class Zoo							X			
9 Scissor Snakes		X				X				
10 Animal Shapes		X		X				X		
11 Unique Animals		X							X	
12 Color Mixing		X							X	
13 Animal Habitats	X									
14 Animals on the Go			X				X			
15 Animal Crackers								X		
16 Polar Bear, Polar Bear	X									
17 Animal Sounds	X								X	
18 Suggested Home Activities	X	X			X				X	
19										
20										
21										
22										
23										
24										
25										
26										
27										
28										
29										
30										

POLAR BEAR, POLAR BEAR, WHAT DO YOU HEAR?
by Bill Martin, Jr.
Henry Holt, 1991

Simple text and bold colorful pictures help to keep young listeners' attention. This word patterning book sparks the imagination and encourages even the youngest children to follow along and predict what comes next. Children are anxious to name the animals, make animal sounds, and say the words of this book.

Story Dramatization. Read and reread the story, having the children chant along. Reproduce the black line master animal pictures. Allow each child to choose his or her favorite animal. Depending on the children's age and interest level, they may want to cut and color the animal pictures. Sitting in a circle, seat the same "animals" together, and let them retell the story. The children can hold up their picture and chant the words to their part of the story.

Animal Riddles. Using the animals from the story, make up riddles. The children can guess the animal by the clues you give. The difficulty of the clues depends on the age and ability level of the children. For example,

I am brown.
I have a long tail.
I have a fluffy mane. What am I?

Window Game. Make copies of the "Windows Game" black line master and the animal pictures. Color and cut out the animal pictures from the "Story Dramatization" activity (or use other favorite pictures of animals). Cut out the window flaps. Paper clip a copy of window flaps over each of the animal pictures, keeping the flaps closed. The children try to identify the animals by opening as few windows as possible. Before presenting a picture to the children, have them guess how many windows they will have to open to identify the animal. Once the children have identified the animal, ask which characteristics helped them with the identification.

Crazy Creatures. Have the children invent new animals. Depending on their age and ability levels, the teacher or children can color and cut animal pictures or use pictures cut from magazines. Cut the pictures in two to four parts and combine the parts to make new animals. Have the children make up new names, sounds, and movements for the crazy creatures.

Animal Estimations. Using the illustrations in the book, ask the children to estimate how many spots there are on the peacock, leopard, or snake. Have the group of children touch and count the spots. The children can also estimate how many stripes are on the zebra, teeth on the lion, and so on. The activity can be extended by placing representations of spots, stripes, teeth, and other characteristics on the flannel board or table in a row so that the children can visualize the amount in a different way. Help the children to understand the number by jumping or clapping the same number of times.

Easel Animals.   Cut easel paper into animal shapes. When painting or coloring at the easel, the children can paint stripes or spots on the animals. Children will also have fun designing their own silly animals.

Masks.   The children in the story dress like animals. Have the children make animal masks from paper plates or paper bags. Provide markers, colored paper, glue, feathers, string for whiskers, and varied colors and shapes for eyes, ears, spots, and stripes. Encourage the children to wear the masks for dramatic play.

Class Zoo.   A zoo can be created in the classroom. Children can dress like the animals using masks. Be sure to include a hat and food pails for the zookeeper. The children can be reminded that zoo animals follow a daily routine just as they do. The routine, including feeding, napping, cleaning, exercising, and playing, can be simulated by the children.

Scissor Snakes.   Children can make boa constrictors like the one in the story by cutting around a piece of paper. Encourage them to start cutting around the paper from the outside in. They can decorate their boas with crayons or markers or by gluing paper dots onto the boa. Provide the children with different sizes of paper to cut. They can estimate and then measure the length. Encourage the children to be creative with measuring tools. They might measure with erasers, crayons, or Match Box™ type cars. Older children might be interested in measuring in inches and centimeters. The snakes can be sequenced from longest to shortest or shortest to longest.

Animal Shapes.   Make play dough using the following recipe. Provide the children with animal-shaped cookie cutters. The children can also make animals by rolling and forming the dough into different shapes. The children will enjoy using their imaginations when playing with their animal shapes.

Play Dough Recipe

Mix:		*Combine and add:*	
1	cup flour	1	cup water
¼	cup salt	2	teaspoons food coloring
2	tablespoons cream of tarter	1	tablespoon oil

Cook over medium heat and stir (3 to 5 minutes). When it forms a ball in the center of the pot, remove and knead. Store in an airtight container.

Unique Animals.   Provide the children with cutout shapes of animals that are spotted. Examples from this book include a leopard, a peacock, and a boa constrictor. Have the children dip their thumbs or fingers into paint or use a stamp pad. The children decorate the animal shapes with their own fingerprints. Compare fingerprints and note the differences in size, shape, and design. Discuss with the children that everybody has unique fingerprints. Discuss the differences in the animal spots and how an animal's coat makes it unique. The children will also find it interesting to learn that an animal's appearance helps to protect it in its natural environment.

Color Mixing.   This book uses bold colors in the illustrations. The children can experiment with color when the teacher provides them with clear jars (baby food jars work well) and small pieces of colored tissue paper. Cut small squares of tissue paper in the primary colors (red, blue, and yellow). Using tweezers, the child picks up a small square and places it in a jar filled with water. The dye from the paper will color the water. Have the children start by using one primary color per jar, and later experiment with mixing colors, by adding two primary colors to produce a secondary color.

Animal Habitats.   While looking at the illustrations, discuss the animal's natural habitat. Talk about how an animal's appearance often reflects its natural habitat. Make simple sketches representing snow, water, grass, and dry land. Ask the children to guess where each animal might live.

Animals on the Go.   Have the children move around the room or play area like the animals do. Practice slithering like snakes, swaying like elephants, swimming like a walrus, galloping like a zebra, running like a lion, and standing on one foot like a flamingo. An obstacle course can be set up providing the "animals" the opportunity to move around chairs, under tables, through a tunnel, and over a mountain (could be made of large blocks).

Animal Crackers.   The children will enjoy making their own animal crackers. Using the following recipe, the dough can be mixed and refrigerated one day and cut and baked the next, or you may choose to mix it in the morning and cut and bake later in the day.

½	cup butter-flavored shortening	½	teaspoon vanilla
⅔	cup sugar	¼	teaspoon baking powder
1	egg	1¼	cups flour
1	tablespoon milk	¼	teaspoon salt

Preheat oven to 425 degrees. Thoroughly blend the first five ingredients. Mix together dry ingredients and add to above mixture. Chill for 2 to 3 hours or overnight. Roll dough on a floured surface and cut with animal-shaped cookie cutters. Bake on a greased cookie sheet about 5 minutes or until golden brown. Makes 24 to 36 cookies, depending on the size.

Polar Bear, Polar Bear.   While reading the story to the children, allow them to take turns anticipating and reciting the lines. First, try it with the pictures; then, see if you can "trick" the children by asking them the question, "Polar bear, polar bear, what do you hear?" Without showing them the pictures, see if they can guess the answer. Give the children the opportunity to reverse roles: let them ask the question, while the teacher gives the answer.

Animal Sounds.   Have the children make the animal sounds that are described in the book. Encourage them to experiment with different sounds. Discuss the adjectives used to describe the sounds. Is fluting loud or soft? musical or thundering? Is hissing a short or long sound? How does yelping compare with roaring? Help the children understand that animals make different sounds, and that they use sound as one way to communicate with each other, and with different species.

Suggested Home Activities.   Send home a synopsis of *Polar Bear, Polar Bear, What Do You Hear?* Tell parents about the activities their children are doing at school.

- Plan a class field trip to the zoo. Invite parents to accompany their child on the field trip. If your school does not take class field trips, encourage parents to take their own child.
- Have the parents and child write a short paragraph about their last trip to the zoo.
- Parents and children might enjoy making a simple animal costume by decorating a plain white T-shirt with stripes or spots. The shirt could represent a real or invented animal.

Related Literature

Martin, Bill, Jr. *Brown Bear, Brown Bear, What Do You See?*

Story Dramatization Activity
Lion

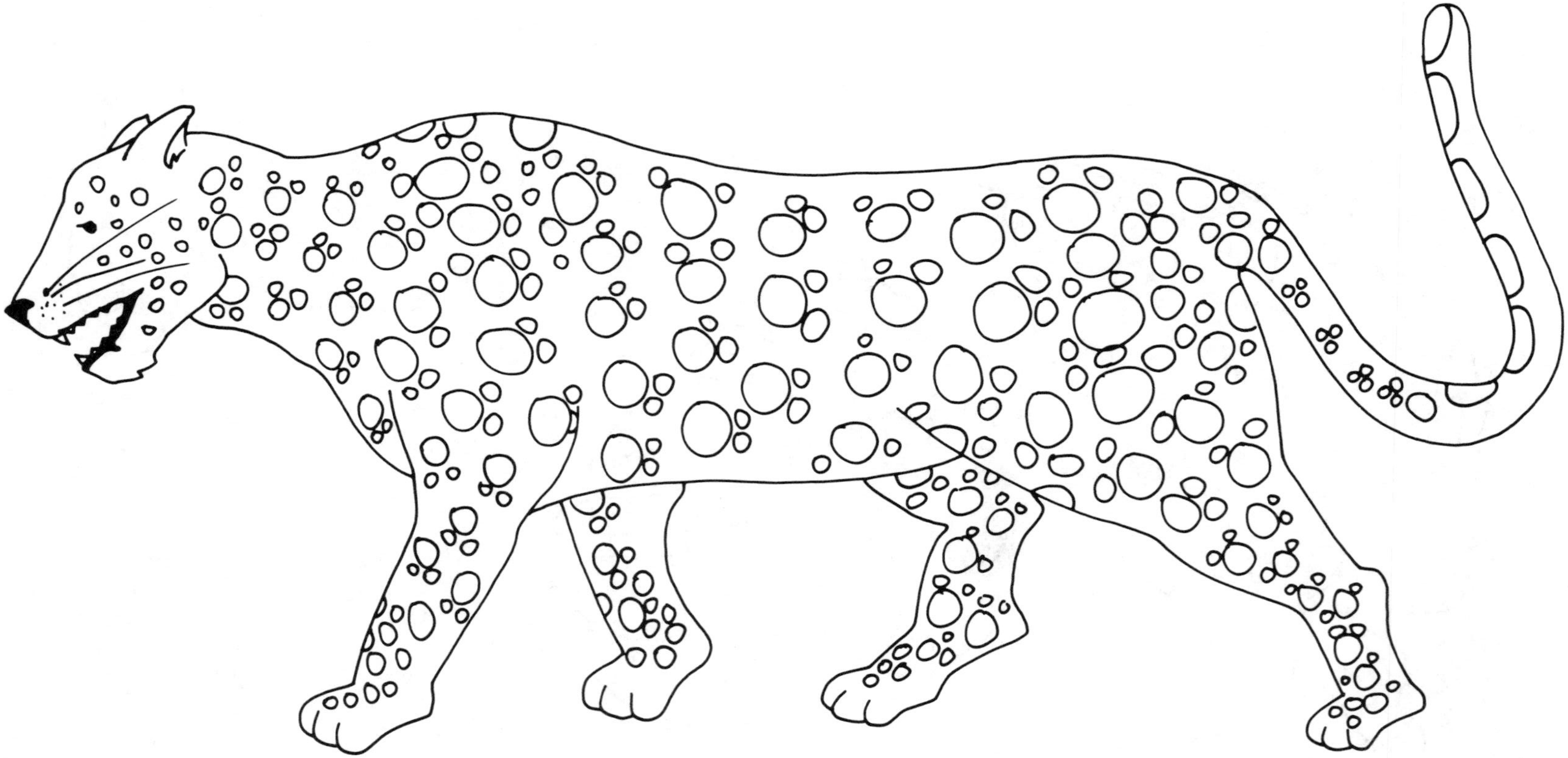

Story Dramatization Activity
Leopard

Story Dramatization Activity
Elephant

Story Dramatization Activity
Polar Bear

© 1993 by The Center for Applied Research in Education

Story Dramatization Activity
Hippopotamus

Story Dramatization Activity
Zebra

Story Dramatization Activity
Boa Constrictor

Story Dramatization Activity
Peacock

Story Dramatization Activity
Flamingo

Story Dramatization Activity
Walrus

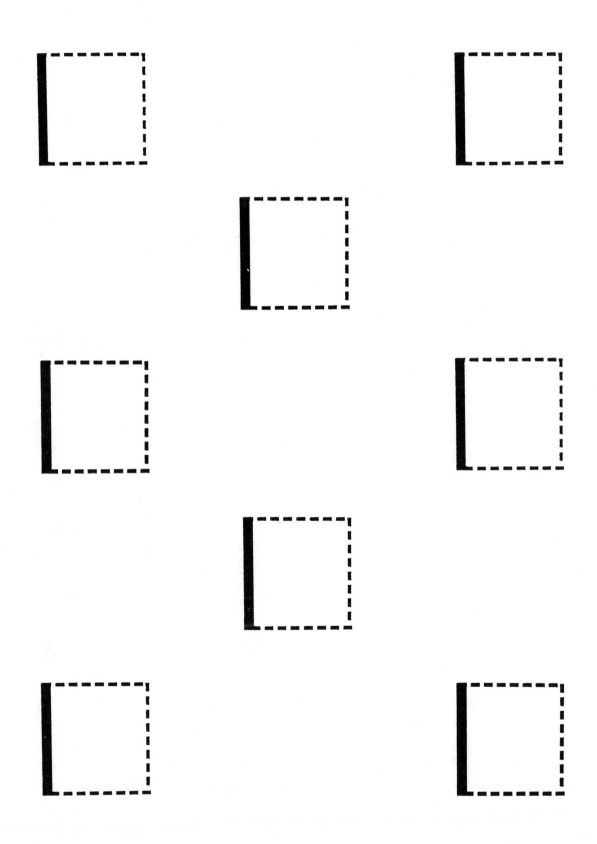

© 1993 by The Center for Applied Research in Education

Window Game Activity
(cut on broken lines)

THE VERY HUNGRY CATERPILLAR
by
Eric Carle

Developmental Activities Chart	Language & Cognitive Development	Fine Motor Art	Gross Motor	Perception	Social Skills	Math	Dramatic Play	Cooking Snack	Science	Music, Fingerplays, Poems
1 Life-Cycle Sequencing	X	X							X	
2 Days of the Week Chant	X	X		X		X				X
3 Estimating	X					X				
4 Estimate the Seeds	X			X		X				
5 A Week to Eat	X	X								
6 Butterfly Movements			X							
7 Butterfly Dance			X							X
8 Caterpillar Construction	X	X				X				
9 Comparing Fruit	X			X						
10 Planting Seeds		X							X	
11 Search and Sort	X			X		X				
12 Leaf Rubbings		X								
13 Getting Bigger!	X								X	
14 Graphing	X					X				
15 Paper Chain Caterpillar	X			X						
16 Ordering Caterpillars	X				X	X				
17 Apple Cupcakes Recipe	X	X				X		X		
18 Blotto Butterflies		X								
19 Sandwich Making						X		X		
20 Tell Me More	X								X	
21 Caterpillar Poems										X
22 Suggested Home Activities	X							X	X	
23										
24										
25										
26										
27										
28										
29										
30										

THE VERY HUNGRY CATERPILLAR
by Eric Carle
Putnam Publishing Group, 1981

This book presents a delightful story that traces the life-cycle of a butterfly. For one week a caterpillar munches his way through a huge variety of foods before building himself a cocoon. After two weeks inside, a beautiful butterfly emerges from the cocoon.

Life-Cycle Sequencing.   Give each child a set of picture cards that shows the life-cycle of a butterfly; include a picture of an egg on a leaf, a caterpillar, a cocoon, and a butterfly. (See black line master.) Children can arrange the pictures in the correct order after hearing the story, or they can arrange the pictures in order as the teacher rereads the story. Children might enjoy coloring the pictures before bringing them home.

Days of the Week Chant.   Have children chant and clap the names of the days of the week. They can clap one time for each day. As children become proficient in doing the activity, increase the difficulty by patterning the hand movements performed for each syllable: Sun-day, Mon-day, Tues-day, Wednes-day, Thurs-day, Fri-day, Sat-ur-day. Examples might include tap-clap tap-clap, snap-nod snap-nod, and so on. Encourage children to make up the movement pattern for the days of the week chant. Be sure to think of simple movements that children with special needs can perform.

Estimating.   Have children estimate how many pieces of food the caterpillar ate through. Children's estimates can be recorded on the board. The correctness of a response is not the goal, since young children are just beginning to develop number sense. The teacher may prepare construction paper or felt pieces of the food eaten by the caterpillar in advance of the estimating activity, then display them as the story is retold. Teacher and students can touch and count the number of food items eaten by the hungry caterpillar.

Estimate the Seeds.   The hungry caterpillar ate through many fruits. Have children estimate how many seeds there would be in a real apple. Write their estimates on a paper plate. With teacher assistance, children cut the apple into parts very carefully, pick out the seeds, and place them on the plate for counting. The same can be done for a pear. Talk about how the seeds are the same and how they are different.

A Week to Eat.   Encourage the children to retell the story of the hungry caterpillar. Given a supply of paper, crayons, and markers children might enjoy making food items that their caterpillar would eat throughout the week, while others could cut out food pictures from magazines or grocery ads. Individual or small groups of children might enjoy telling and showing their version of the story with the handmade props.

Butterfly Movements.   Encourage children to position or move their bodies: lie still like the egg, move through an apple like a hungry caterpillar, move like a stuffed caterpillar, pretend your body is inside a small cocoon, move like a butterfly just coming out of the cocoon, move like a butterfly, and so on.

Butterfly Dance.   Play instrumental music. Give children streamers or colorful scarves as they move like butterflies to the sound of the music.

Caterpillar Construction.   Provide children with a variety of green blocks, green unifix™ cubes, or precut green ovals to use to assemble a caterpillar of their own. Encourage small groups of children to compare the lengths of their caterpillars: which is the longest? which is the shortest? which are the same? Some children will be ready to count the number of green segments that make up their caterpillar.

Comparing Fruit.   Have children examine an apple, pear, and plum. Have them brainstorm ways the fruits are the same and how they are different. Cut the fruit open and have them compare how the seeds of the fruit are the same or different.

Planting Seeds.   Give children an opportunity to plant apple seeds in soil-filled Styrofoam™ cups or commercial peat pots.

Search and Sort.   Children go for a walk and collect leaves. They can then sort the leaves by color, shape, size, or other characteristics they choose.

Leaf Rubbings.   Tape a variety of different-sized and shaped leaves on a tabletop, vein side up. Show children how to gently make leaf rubbings using thin newsprint-type paper and a crayon.

Getting Bigger!   Provide children with hand-held magnifying glasses, a large magnifier, leaves, and possibly insects at the science center. Encourage children to verbalize what they see and record their observations. Observing a real caterpillar would be ideal!

Graphing.   Children can graph their favorite fruit in a variety of ways.

> **Real graph**—Each child brings his or her favorite fruit from home to place on a large graph made on a shower curtain liner or butcher paper.
>
> **Pictorial graph**—Each child puts a picture of his or her favorite fruit under a picture of the fruit on the top of the graph.
>
> **Symbolic graph**—Each child puts a picture or representation of himself or herself under his or her favorite fruit on the graph.

Compare results of the graphing experience, stressing concepts of more than, less than, and the same. Other favorites to graph are ice cream, lollipop, or cupcake flavor.

Paper Chain Caterpillar.   Provide children with two or three shades of green paper strips about 1½ inches wide by 8 inches long. Children glue ends together and connect to the previous loop to make a caterpillar. Some children might want to pattern the green shades for their caterpillar: light green, medium green, dark green, and repeat.

Ordering Caterpillars. Arrange children in small groups on the rug area. Using their paper chain caterpillars from the preceding activity, have children put the caterpillars in order from shortest to longest or from longest to shortest.

Apple Cupcake Recipe. Help children pour, measure, and stir to make the hungry caterpillar's favorite cupcakes.

1	egg	2	cups Bisquick™
⅓	cup sugar	⅔	cup milk
2	tablespoons vegetable oil	¾	cup apple pieces

Preheat oven to 400 degrees. Beat egg slightly in a medium bowl, stir in remaining ingredients, except apples, just until moistened. Fold apple pieces into batter. Divide batter evenly among cups. Bake 15 to 18 minutes or until golden brown. Makes 1 dozen regular-sized muffins or 2 dozen mini-sized muffins. Before pouring the batter into muffin cups, have children estimate how many cupcakes the batter will make.

Blotto Butterflies. Have children fold a large piece of paper in half. Let them drop or dab bright colors of tempera paint on one side of the paper. Refold the paper on the fold line, and rub the paper in a circular motion to spread the colors. Open the paper to find a butterfly.

Sandwich Making. Provide bread, Swiss cheese, and salami for sandwich making at snacktime. Children can decide what kind of sandwich they will make: Swiss cheese sandwich, salami sandwich, or salami and cheese sandwich. Tally the sandwich choices to determine which was the class favorite.

Tell Me More. Have children dictate a class story or individual stories about what happened to the hungry caterpillar after he turned into a beautiful butterfly.

Caterpillar Poems

THE CATERPILLAR

Brown and furry
   Caterpillar in a hurry;
Take your walk
   To the shady leaf or stalk.

May no toad spy you
   May the little birds pass by you;
Spin and die,
   To live again a butterfly.

Christina G. Rossetti
Sing a Song of Popcorn
Every Child's Book of Poems
Selected by Beatrice Schenk de Regniers
Scholastic, 1988

FUZZY WUZZY CATERPILLAR

Fuzzy wuzzy caterpillar
Into a corner will creep.   [Make fingers creep.]
He'll spin himself a blanket,
And then go fast asleep.   [Rest head on hands, close eyes.]
Fuzzy wuzzy caterpillar
Wakes up by and by   [Children awaken.]
To find he has wings of beauty
Changed to a butterfly.

Suggested Home Activity.   Send home a synopsis of *The Very Hungry Caterpillar,* and inform parents about some of the activities their children will be doing at school. Invite parents to cook with their child to demonstrate how substances can change in appearance while cooking or during preparation. Simple examples include making Jell-O™ or popcorn.

Related Literature

Carle, Eric. *The Very Quiet Cricket.*
Ryder, Joanne. *Where Butterflies Grow.*

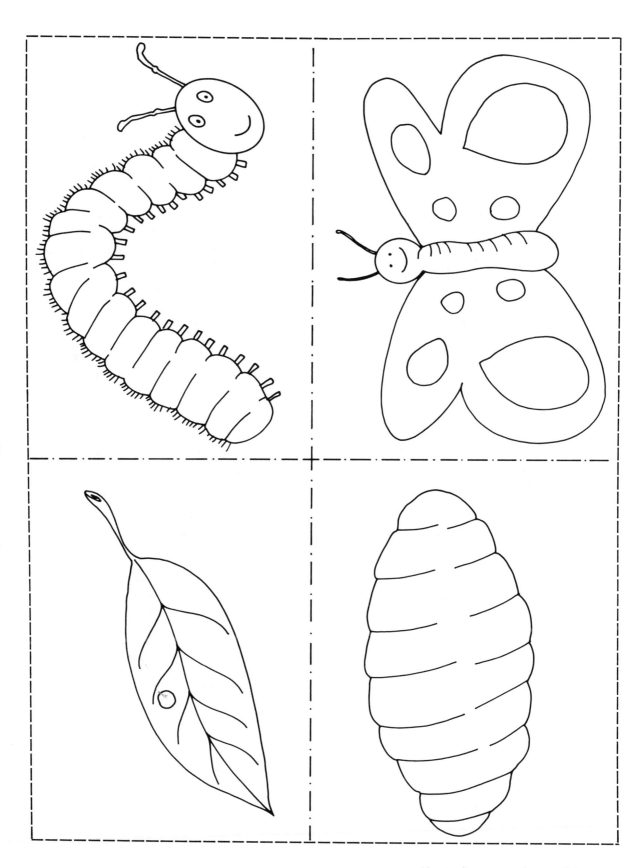

Life-Cycle Sequencing Activity

THE DOORBELL RANG
by
Pat Hutchins

Developmental Activities Chart	Language & Cognitive Development	Fine Motor Art	Gross Motor	Perception	Social Skills	Math	Dramatic Play	Cooking Snack	Science	Music, Fingerplays, Poems
1 Cookie Math	X					X				
2 The Real Thing!	X					X				
3 Cooking Baking Song										X
4 Raisin Cookies	X	X				X		X		
5 Chocolate Chippers	X	X				X		X		
6 Remember and Sequence	X									
7 Cookie Concoctions	X									
8 Sensory Experiences		X		X						
9 Estimating	X					X				
10 Graphing	X					X				
11 Cookie Fingerplay										X
12 Problem Solving	X				X	X				
13 Sharing	X				X					
14 Patterning	X			X						
15 Dramatize	X				X		X			
16 Grandma's Bakery	X	X			X	X	X			
17 Cookie Relay			X		X					
18 Find the Cookie	X					X				
19 Suggested Home Activities	X				X	X		X		
20										
21										
22										
23										
24										
25										
26										
27										
28										
29										
30										

THE DOORBELL RANG
by Pat Hutchins
Greenwillow Books, 1986

Ma has made a plate of cookies for her two children to share. Their portion gets smaller and smaller as they must share them with company each time the doorbell rings. Grandma arrives to save the day for the disappointed children by bringing them an enormous tray of cookies.

Cookie Math. In the story, it appears that Ma has made chocolate chip or raisin cookies. Prepare 33 large, light-brown circle shapes out of construction paper to represent the cookies. On one set of 11 cookies, write a numeral from 0 to 10 on each. On the remaining two sets of cookies, use a brown crayon or marker to draw from 0 to 10 "chocolate chips" or "raisins." Laminate the cookies. Children can then match the correct "numeral cookie" to its corresponding "chocolate chip/ raisin" cookie. Individual children can take turns matching the set of cookies that have two chips, five raisins, and so on.

The Real Thing! Prepare enough laminated cookie shapes so that each child has one. Have a container of chocolate chips and/or raisins in front of each child. The teacher says a numeral and children practice their counting skills by putting the correct number of chips or raisins on their cookie. The teacher can individualize the lesson for students by having children put a smaller or larger amount of chips or raisins on their cookie depending on their number readiness skills. Naturally, the children can eat the cookie ingredients when the activity is over.

Cookie Baking Song (to the tune of "Are You Sleeping?")

Baking cookies, baking cookies
Fun, fun, fun. Fun, fun, fun.
Eggs, vanilla, butter, nuts.
Flour, sugar, chocolate chips.
Stir, stir, stir. Stir, stir, stir.

Baking cookies, baking cookies
Done, done, done. Done, done, done.
Pour the milk, then count them out.
Pour the milk and pass them out.
Gone, gone, gone! They're all gone!

Raisin Cookies. Children can help make their own version of the cookies Ma made in the story. Review health and safety rules before beginning.

1	cup raisins	1	cup sugar
½	cup water	1	cup solid vegetable shortening
1¾	cups unsifted all-purpose flour	1	extra large or 2 small eggs
½	teaspoon each: baking powder, baking soda	½	teaspoon vanilla
¼	teaspoon salt	¼	teaspoon cinnamon

Preheat the oven to 375 degrees. Have ungreased baking sheets ready. Stir together the flour, baking powder, baking soda, and salt; set aside. Beat ¾ cup of the sugar with the shortening in the bowl of an electric mixer on high speed, until light and fluffy, about 2 minutes. Add the egg(s), mixing well. Add the vanilla. Stop the mixer and add the dry ingredients and mix until smooth. With a large spoon, mix in the raisins.

Children roll the dough into balls about the size of small walnuts. Combine the remaining sugar with the cinnamon and roll the cookies in the cinnamon-sugar. Arrange on the baking sheets, spacing 1½ inches apart.

Bake until set, 9 to 11 minutes. Transfer to a wire rack to cool. Yields 2½ to 3 dozen cookies.

Chocolate Chippers. This is one version of the all-time favorite chocolate chip cookies. Review health and safety rules before beginning.

½	cup shortening	1	teaspoon vanilla
½	cup sugar	1	cup sifted all-purpose flour
¼	cup brown sugar	¾	teaspoon salt
1	egg	½	teaspoon baking soda
1	6-ounce package semi-sweet chocolate chips	½	cup broken nuts

Preheat oven to 375 degrees. Cream shortening, sugars, egg, and vanilla until light and fluffy. Sift together dry ingredients; stir into creamed mixture. Blend well. Add chocolate chips and nuts. Drop from a teaspoon 2 inches apart onto a greased cookie sheet. Bake 10 to 12 minutes. Remove from the baking sheet immediately to cool. Makes about 3 dozen cookies.

Remember and Sequence. After making a batch of cookies, ask children to remember and name as many of the ingredients used as they can. Have them sequence the main events of baking cookies. Their responses can be written on an experience chart.

Cookie Concoctions. Have children brainstorm as many different kinds of cookies that they can think of. Allow children to write or dictate a cookie recipe of their own. These recipe concoctions can be put together to make a delightful book that can be duplicated and sent home for parents to enjoy!

Sensory Experiences. Put flour into the sensory table. Supply the children with sifters, measuring spoons, and cups with which to experiment and explore. Later, the teacher may consider providing children with spoons, baking sheets, spatulas, and water or colored water to add to the flour so children can make their own cookie dough.

Estimating.   Place a small amount of chocolate chips or raisins in a glass jar. Have children estimate how many chips or raisins are inside. Record responses. Children can then touch and count to see how close they came to the correct number. If a large number of chips or raisins was displayed, children can count the pieces by placing them in portion cups of ten, then counting the ten-cups and the extras (2 ten-cups plus 5 equal 25). This activity would be appropriate for children who display a good understanding of number concepts.

Another estimation activity would be for children to estimate how many spoonfuls of flour are in a container. Children can check their responses by actually tallying how many spoonfuls there are.

Graphing.   Have the class make a real and/or a picture floor graph of their favorite kind of cookie: chocolate chip, chocolate chip with nuts, or raisin. This activity can be done after children have baked cookies in school. Children can interpret results by comparing:

Which cookie has the most votes?

Which cookie has the least?

Are any of the columns the same?

How many more or less are there?

How many children voted? How can we tell?

Cookie Fingerplay

Five warm cookies lying on the tray.   [Show 5 fingers.]

(Child's name) came in from play,   [Rub stomach.]

And then there were four.   [Show 4 fingers.]

Four yummy cookies cooling all alone.   [Show 4 fingers.]

(Child's name) snatched one,   [Rub stomach.]

And then there were three.   [Show 3 fingers.]

Three tasty cookies lying on a plate.   [Show 3 fingers.]

(Child's name) couldn't wait,   [Rub stomach.]

And then there were two.   [Show 2 fingers.]

Two chocolate chippers cooled just right.   [Show 2 fingers.]

(Child's name) reached for one,   [Rub stomach.]

And then there was one.   [Show 1 finger.]

One big cookie by the glass of milk.   [Show 1 finger.]

(Teacher's name) enjoyed the last one,   [Rub stomach.]

And now there are none!

This activity can be done on a flannel board by making laminated cookies that have a small piece of Velcro™ placed on the back of each piece.

Problem Solving.   Have children work in small groups of three or four. Give each group 10 to 12 real cookies or laminated construction paper cookies and challenge them to divide the cookies among themselves as Victoria and Sam did in the story. Check with each group to see how they divided the cookies and what they did with the extras.

Sharing.   Brainstorm two lists with the children—things that are easy to share and things that are difficult to share. Record responses on butcher paper. Children may want to illustrate their response with a drawing or magazine picture. This activity can be followed up with a book about sharing, such as *It's Mine—A Fable* by Leo Lionni, Alfred A. Knopf, 1986.

Patterning.   Children can practice patterning with brown and golden raisins, mini- and regular-sized chocolate chips, or any combination of these cookie ingredients.

Dramatize.   Have children reenact the story in the housekeeping area while the teacher rereads the story. Have children make a list of props that are shown in the story. They can assist in collecting the props or the teacher can supply them: bucket, mop, tray, tablecloth, bell, oven mitts, and so on. Leave the props in the housekeeping area and children will enjoy making different versions of the story on their own.

Grandma's Bakery.   Have children make cookies that look and smell as good as those baked by Sam and Victoria's grandma. Provide a variety of cookie cutters, and try this no-cook play dough recipe.

> 2½   cups peanut butter
> 2   tablespoons honey
> 2   cups powdered milk
>   mini chocolate chip and/or raisins to decorate

Measure and place the first two ingredients into a large bowl. Children can mix the ingredients well with cleaned hands. Continue adding the powdered milk until the dough feels soft and not sticky. Children can decorate their cookies with the mini chocolate chips or raisins. This play dough is safe to eat.

Cookie Relay.   Divide children into teams for this relay game. Each team will need a brown bag or tray to put their cookies in or on. Tape a line on the floor in front of the children and place an equal number of laminated construction paper cookies behind the masking tape line. When the teacher rings the "doorbell," the first child in each team runs to the line, picks up a cookie, puts it in the bag or on the tray, and runs back to his or her team. The next child repeats the process and the relay continues until all the cookies have been picked up. The children can count the cookies on each tray/bag. Ask them how many cookies there are altogether.

Find the Cookie.   Give each child a copy of the black line master. Children count and find the cookie with the same number of chocolate chips as the sample.

Suggested Home Activities.   Send home a synopsis of the story *The Doorbell Rang,* and inform parents about some of the activities their children will be doing at school. A natural follow-up activity for parents to do with their child is to choose a favorite family cookie recipe and prepare it together, maybe even inviting grandma or some friends over to share the cookies! You may also wish to make copies of the black line master to send home with children.

Related Literature

McMillan, Bruce. *Eating Fractions.*
O'Keefe, Susan Heyboer. *One Hungry Monster: A Counting Book in Rhyme.*

Count the chocolate chips in the first cookie. Mark the cookie with the *same* number of chips.

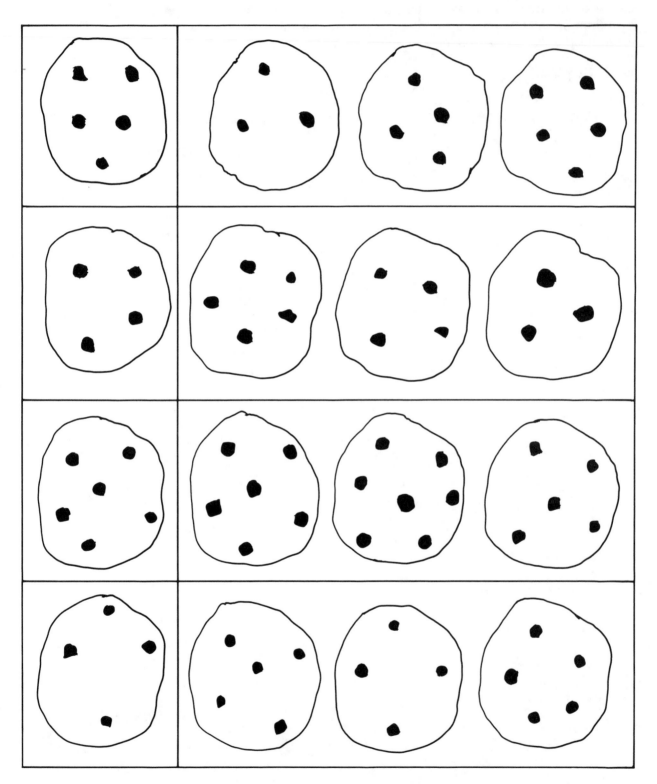

Suggested Home Activity

IF YOU GIVE A MOOSE A MUFFIN

by
Laura Joffe Numeroff

Developmental Activities Chart	Language & Cognitive Development	Fine Motor Art	Gross Motor	Perception	Social Skills	Math	Dramatic Play	Cooking Snack	Science	Music, Fingerplays, Poems
1 Go Togethers	X									
2 Go-Together Pictures	X			X						
3 Go-Together Puzzles	X	X		X						
4 Fit the Lid		X		X						
5 Pick It, Name It	X									
6 How Big Is a Moose?	X	X		X		X				
7 A Moosey Menu	X					X		X		
8 A Shapely Moose	X	X								
9 Moose Puppets	X				X		X			
10 Moose Prints	X	X				X				
11 The Moose and Muffin Song										X
12 Silly Stories	X									
13 Muffin Tin Sets						X				
14 Counting Blackberries						X				
15 Sewing Sets		X				X				
16 Sheet Shenanigans			X		X		X			
17 Sock Puppets	X	X			X		X			
18 Sew Fun		X								
19 Pick It Up		X		X		X				
20 Blueberry Muffins	X	X			X	X		X		
21 Suggested Home Activity				X		X				
22										
23										
24										
25										
26										
27										
28										
29										
30										

IF YOU GIVE A MOOSE A MUFFIN
by Laura Joffe Numeroff
HarperCollins, 1991

A young boy finds out what can happen when you give a muffin to a moose. Children enjoy the repetitiveness and predictability of the text. The descriptive pictures bring the story to life, as the moose demands jam and more muffins, which of course requires a trip to the store, which inspires more and more hilarious demands.

Go Togethers. Throughout the story the moose is reminded of things that go together, which prompt his demands on the boy. Look at the pictures in the book and talk about the go-togethers. Use real objects or pictures of things that go together. Have the children tell how the items are used and how/why they go together. Examples are: pencil and paper, juice and glass, socks and shoes, bread and butter, knife and fork.

Go-Together Pictures. Prepare pairs of picture cards of things that go together. Glue one item on each card or buy premade cards. Shuffle the cards and have children find the two cards that go together. Play "concentration" with the cards; the children can make pairs of go-togethers.

Go-Together Puzzles. Provide the children with magazine and catalog pictures. Ask them to find and cut pictures of things that go together. They can mount the pictures on tagboard and cut the tagboard in half with a zigzag line to make puzzle pictures. Laminate the pieces or cover them with clear Con-Tact® paper. The children put the puzzles together by finding the go-together pictures, making sure the puzzle pieces fit together.

Fit the Lid. Provide a variety of different-sized containers and lids. The children can find the lid that goes with the container.

Pick It, Name It. Fill a bag or box with items that have an obvious go-together. The children take turns picking an item from the bag, naming it, and thinking of an item that goes with it.

How Big Is a Moose? The children will develop an understanding about the size of a moose when they can visualize it with this activity. Cut a simple moose shape from brown kraft paper. Use one of the illustrations as a model. The average moose stands 6½ feet at the shoulder and weighs 800 to 1,400 pounds. The width of the antlers is 5 to 6 feet. Measure out the outline of a moose using masking tape, chalk, or kraft paper. Trace, cut, and stack the children's hands to form antlers. The children can measure the antlers and the moose using their hands as a unit of measure.

A Moosey Menu.   Discuss with the children that real moose eat woody plants and shrubs. Compare their diet with the human diet. Ask the children to name their favorite foods and drinks and the foods and drinks their parents prepare. List the children's responses according to food groups. Point out to the children that the foods they eat fit into the four food groups. Favorite foods can be graphed. Count the responses to determine which foods are the most favored.

A Shapely Moose.   The children can make a moose by cutting a triangle for the head. Hold the triangle point side down. Glue on two circle eyes, a circle nose, and a triangle mouth. Trace both of the children's hands. The children can cut them out and glue them to the top of the head for antlers.

Moose Puppets.   Make a moose puppet from a lunch-size brown paper bag. Have the children draw or glue a face on the bottom of the bag. The fold can be the mouth. Trace, cut, and glue on each child's hand for antlers. The children can use their puppets for dramatizing the story.

Moose Prints.   The children can make moose prints on paper by dipping the under side of their index and middle fingers in tempera paint and then placing them in a narrow "V" on construction paper. Larger moose prints can be made by the teacher's fingers. The children can compare the size of the prints by finding the smallest, largest, and medium-sized prints.

The Moose and Muffin Song   (to the tune of "My Bonnie Lies Over the Ocean")

> I once gave a moose jam and muffins.
> He decided he wanted to stay.
> The moose was so busy at my house.
> I couldn't make the moose go away.
> Help me. Help me.
> I can't make the moose go away, away.
> Help me. Help me.
> I can't make the moose go away.

Silly Stories.   The children can write a class story similar to *If You Give a Moose a Muffin*. Make up a silly story starter such as "If you give a pig some popcorn" or "If you give a dog a doughnut." Use pictures of go-togethers to give the children ideas for the story.

Muffin Tin Sets.   Label each section of a muffin tin with a numeral, or a pictorial set. Provide counters such as raisins, Cheerios™, nuts, or inedible manipulatives. The children can put the appropriate number of counters in each section.

Counting Blackberries.   When the moose saw the mother picking blackberries, he was reminded of blackberry jam. Draw a bush with leaves on a sheet of tagboard. Laminate it or cover it with clear Con-Tact® paper to preserve it. Cut 50 blackberries from construction paper and laminate them. Place the berries on the bush. The children can take turns shaking a die or pair of dice and picking the corresponding number of blackberries from the bush.

Sewing Sets.   When the moose borrowed a sweater, he noticed it was missing a button so he asked for a needle and thread. The boy took out the sewing basket. Make pincushions by cutting sponges into assorted shapes; mount them on cardboard. Label each pincushion with a numeral or pictorial set. Purchase pins with ball heads or oversized heads. The children can stick the corresponding number of pins into the pincushion.

Sheet Shenanigans.   When the moose hid behind the couch for his puppet show, his antlers stuck out. He asked for a sheet to cover them up. Bring an old sheet to the classroom and let the children find creative ways to use it. Try using it as a parachute in an open area. Children stand all around the outside edges of the sheet. Make waves with the sheet. Catch air under it by throwing it into the air while holding onto it. Children can run under it while it is in the air. Move around the sheet in different ways (run, skip, gallop) while holding the edges.

Sock Puppets.   When the moose sewed the button on the sweater, he was reminded of the sock puppets his grandmother used to make. Purchase one or two six packs of tube socks, or ask parents to send a pair of tube socks. Provide the children with an assortment of old buttons, yarn, ribbon, sequins, plastic eyeballs, felt or fabric scraps, and fabric glue. Children can make sock puppets which represent characters from this story or other favorite stories or nursery rhymes. They can use the finished puppets to dramatize their stories or rhymes.

Sew Fun.   Purchase large buttons with oversized holes, large embroidery needles, heavy fabric such as felt, and heavy thread or yarn. Show the children how to sew the button onto the fabric just as the moose did when he sewed the button on the sweater.

Pick It Up.   Provide a muffin tin, enough small beads or other manipulatives for each section, and tweezers. The children will practice skills in fine motor, perception, and one-to-one correspondence when they pick up one bead at a time and place it in a section of the muffin tin.

Blueberry Muffins.   Have the children place one liner in each section of a muffin tin.

$\frac{1}{2}$	cup butter	$\frac{1}{2}$	cup milk
1	cup sugar	2	cups flour
2	eggs	2	teaspoons baking powder
1	cup blueberries	$\frac{1}{4}$	teaspoon salt

Preheat oven to 375 degrees. Cream butter and sugar. Add eggs. Beat thoroughly. Sift dry ingredients. Add alternately with milk. Fold in berries. Pour into lined muffin tins. Bake for 25 minutes. Before pouring the batter, have children estimate how many muffin tins will be filled. Makes 12 regular-size muffins or 24 mini muffins.

Suggested Home Activities.   Send home a synopsis of *If You Give a Moose a Muffin*. Inform the parents of some of the activities the children are involved in at school. Suggest to parents that they can make up a simple sorting game for their children using a muffin tin and household objects. Parents prepare a bag containing different categories of like objects, such as paper clips, pennies, nickels, dimes, rubber bands, buttons, bottle tops, and colored chips. The children can remove the items from a bag and sort them into different sections of the muffin tin.

Related Literature

Numeroff, Laura Joffe. *If You Give a Mouse a Cookie.*

THE VERY BUSY SPIDER
by
Eric Carle

Developmental Activities Chart

	Language & Cognitive Development	Fine Motor Art	Gross Motor	Perception	Social Skills	Math	Dramatic Play	Cooking Snack	Science	Music, Fingerplays, Poems
1 Dramatize	X				X		X			
2 Persistence	X				X	X				
3 Paper Plate Masks	X	X					X		X	
4 Busy Spider										X
5 Insects and Spiders	X			X					X	
6 Walk and Stalk	X				X				X	
7 Spider Graphing	X				X				X	
8 Mom and Babies	X								X	
9 Eensy Weensy Spider		X								X
10 Spider Fun		X							X	
11 Little Miss Muffet				X			X			X
12 Spider Webs		X						X	X	
13 Sticky Webs		X							X	
14 Spider, Spider, Insect!			X	X						
15 Catch a Bug!			X	X						
16 Spin a Web	X				X				X	
17 Finish the Web		X								
18 Observing the Wind	X			X					X	
19 Spider Game	X				X	X			X	
20 Suggested Home Activities	X	X	X						X	
21										
22										
23										
24										
25										
26										
27										
28										
29										
30										

THE VERY BUSY SPIDER
by Eric Carle
Philomel Books, 1984

Early one sunny morning, the wind carries a spider across the field to a fence post. There she begins to spin a web. Many barnyard animals try to distract her by suggesting she stop and engage in activities with them, like running in the meadow, taking a nap, and rolling in the mud. The spider ignores their requests and busily spins herself a beautiful and useful web. Children can *feel* the spider's web and see how it changes as it is being built.

Dramatize.   Children will enjoy dramatizing this simple, predictable story. The child who is the spider can hold a string or a piece of yarn and "balloon" across the room as her silky threads catch the wind and carry her to the fence post. Children act out the parts of the barnyard animals who tried to distract the spider: horse, cow, lamb, goat, pig, dog, cat, duck, rooster, and owl. Children may think of and act out other animals to distract the spider and suggest different activities to entice her to stop working. While each animal speaks to the spider, she can be spinning a web using chalk on a chalkboard or sticking masking tape on a flannel board. A pesky fly should be flying around the animals, just as in the story.

Persistence.   Have a discussion about the spider's behavior. Encourage children to share their ideas about why the spider didn't stop spinning. Make a yes/no graph to record if children think the spider was being rude or unkind when she refused to stop spinning her web instead of engaging in other activities with the animals. Introduce the word "persistent" and its meaning. Would the definition fit the qualities demonstrated by the busy spider? Have children share stories about times they have cleaned their rooms or finished a project even though there may have been something better to do.

Paper Plate Masks.   Give each child a large paper plate that has two cutout eyes. Allow children time to look at the illustrations of the barnyard animals and select one they would like to make. Talk about the facial characteristics of the animals, for example, the pig's round, flat nose, the goat's beard, and the cow's spots. Provide crayons, markers, yarn, fabric, felt, feathers, construction paper, cotton balls, and pipe cleaners for children. When the masks are completed, assist the children in stapling a tongue depressor to the bottom of the mask. Hand-held masks are easy and comfortable for children to use. These masks can be used when children dramatize the story.

Busy Spider   (to the tune of "The Farmer in the Dell")

The spider spins her web.
The spider spins her web.
She works all day,
Won't stop to play.
The spider spins her web.
Night fell on the farm.
Night fell on the farm.
The spider rests,
She's done her best.
Night fell on the farm.

The spider traps a fly.
The spider traps a fly.
She caught her lunch,
It's time to munch.
The spider traps a fly.

Insects and Spiders.   Tell children that spiders do not belong to the insect family. Insects have six legs, and spiders have eight. Insects usually have wings. Spiders never do. Insects have three parts to their bodies, spiders have two. Insects go through different stages in their life. Spiders emerge from eggs looking just like their parents, only smaller. Insects have two eyes, most spiders have two rows of four eyes each, or eight eyes altogether. Select some books from the library, and show children pictures of different kinds of spiders and insects. The class can make a chart pinpointing the many ways spiders are different from insects.

Walk and Stalk.   Take a walk and spend 5 to 10 minutes each day for one week looking for insects and spiders. Children can keep a tally of how many insects/spiders have been seen. When outside, suggest that children look in shrubs, on trees, in the grass, on leaves, under rocks, in holes in the ground, and under windowsills. If children locate a spider web, spraying it with water will make the web more visible and easier for the children to examine. Inside the school building, children can look for insects and spiders in corners; in the basement, storage room, or boiler room; or in all sorts of cracks and crevices. Children can count how many spiders and insects have been seen altogether during the one-week period. Children can compare if more/fewer insects were seen than spiders.

Spider Graphing.   Many adults and children are afraid of spiders. Share some nonthreatening facts with children to help ease their fears: most spiders are harmless and are very helpful, especially in gardens, where they eat insects that could harm flowers and plants. Make a yes/no graph. Children vote if they like or don't like spiders. Compare results and discuss children's reasons for voting as they did. If children's votes are based on incorrect information, be prepared to supply accurate information.

Mom and Babies.   Name all the farm animals shown in the story. Have children tell what their babies are called—cow-calf, pig-piglet, cat-kitten, and so on. Tell children that baby spiders are called spiderlings.

Eensy Weensy Spider   (traditional song)

> The eensy weensy spider went up the water spout.
>> [Left thumb to right pinkie, then right thumb to left pinky, make a climbing motion.]
>
> Down came the rain and washed the spider out!
>> [Hands sweep down and out to the sides.]
>
> Out came the sun and dried up all the rain.
>> [Touch fingertips overhead.]
>
> And the eensy weensy spider went up the spout again.
>> [Repeat the climbing motion with thumbs and pinkies.]

Spider Fun.   Spiders can be green, yellow, or red, but most are brown, gray, or black. Provide children with colored construction paper. Review what children have learned about a spider's body: it has two body parts, eight legs, and eight eyes. Allow children to create their own version of the very busy spider.

Little Miss Muffet.   Have children learn, recite, and dramatize the traditional nursery rhyme. Talk about the meaning of a tuffet and the definition of curds and whey. Provide some simple props: a stool, a bonnet for Miss Muffet, a bowl and spoon for her curds and whey, and a spider (use one the children have made). Repeat the dramatization, so that everyone has a turn over a several-day period.

> Little Miss Muffet
> Sat on a tuffet.
> Eating her curds and whey.
> Along came a spider
> And sat down beside her
> And frightened Miss Muffet away!

Spider Webs.   Spiders build webs in many shapes and sizes. A spider's web is made of fine silk that the spider makes inside its body in a tiny body part called a spinneret. The silk starts as a sticky liquid and then hardens to form a thread that is light but very strong. Children can make their own webs on black construction paper. They gently squeeze white glue onto the paper or dip a cotton swab into glue to form a web design. The webs may take several days to dry, depending on their thickness. Children can also make edible webs on waxed paper. The teacher melts vanilla-flavored almond bark and puts it inside a squeeze container like that used for ketchup. Children squeeze the container to form their web. Carefully remove the web from the paper after it has dried. Children can also brainstorm food items to put on their webs to represent insects that get stuck in the web.

Sticky Webs.   Children can make a sticky web to use outside for catching insects. Reshape pliable coat hangers into different shapes. Children wrap double-sided sticky tape all around the hanger to form a weblike design. The curved hook of the hanger can be squeezed together and wound with masking tape to form a safe handle. The children will enjoy hunting for insects!

Spider, Spider, Insect!   Play a version of the familiar game "Duck, Duck, Goose." Children brainstorm a list of insects that would be tasty treats for a hungry spider, for example, a fly, moth, beetle, locust, mosquito, ladybug, or grasshopper. One child is chosen to be "It" and he or she walks around the circle of children touching each child. If "It" goes around the circle and says "spider, spider, ladybug," for example, the "ladybug child" would run around the circle chasing the spider in hopes of tagging him or her before returning to the empty space. If "It" walks around the circle and names something a spider would *not* like to eat, the child touched in the circle should not get up to chase the spider. "It" must name something the spider likes to eat.

Catch a Bug!   Children join hands to form a large circle. Two children are chosen to be bugs. They walk carefully in and out of the circle under the children's outstretched arms, trying not to get trapped inside. When *both* bugs are inside, the children quickly lower their arms to trap the bugs. Once caught, they join the other children in the circle and new bugs are selected.

Spin a Web.   Small groups of three or four children sit in a circle and make a spider's web as they tell a fact they know about spiders or make up a story about an imaginary spider. The first child holds on to the end of a ball of yarn. When he or she contributes a spider fact or story event, the ball of yarn is passed to someone else in the circle. That child holds on to the yarn, makes a statement, and passes the ball around to someone else. The yarn will form a weblike design.

Finish the Web.   Children connect the lines to complete the spider web black line master provided. Children can paint thumbprint spiders on the web.

Observing the Wind.   In the story, the wind carried the busy spider across the field to a fence post near the farmyard. Have children brainstorm a list of things they think can be blown or moved by the wind. They can bring these items outside on a windy day to test their predictions. Give children the opportunity to observe things the wind is blowing, such as clouds, leaves, litter, feathers, and the school flag.

Spider Game.   The teacher prepares at least five sets of body parts out of construction paper, including the head, abdomen, eight legs, and eight eyes for each spider, using the black line master pattern. Laminate all the pieces. A group of children play the game by sorting the parts that are the same. Each child then takes a turn to roll a die. The number on the die will determine what part(s) the child takes to complete his or her spider. The first child to complete a spider wins.

    A roll of 1—head
    A roll of 2—abdomen
    A roll of 3—four eyes
    A roll of 4—four legs
    A roll of 5—four eyes
    A roll of 6—four legs

Suggested Home Activities.   Send home a synopsis of the story *The Very Busy Spider,* and inform parents about some of the activities the children will be doing at school. Encourage parents to reinforce and extend their child's interest by helping them collect and observe spiders and insects and by selecting books at the library to extend concepts. Parents can provide markers, a large paper bag, or an old pillowcase for children to make a spider. A piece of yarn can be attached to the bag or pillowcase. Children can take their spider outside, run with it to catch the wind, and watch their spider ballooning in the air.

Related Literature

Carle, Eric. *The Very Hungry Caterpillar.*
————. *The Very Quiet Cricket.*
Parker, Nancy Wilson and Joan Richards Wright. *Bugs.*

Connect the lines to complete the spider's web. Add a thumbprint spider.

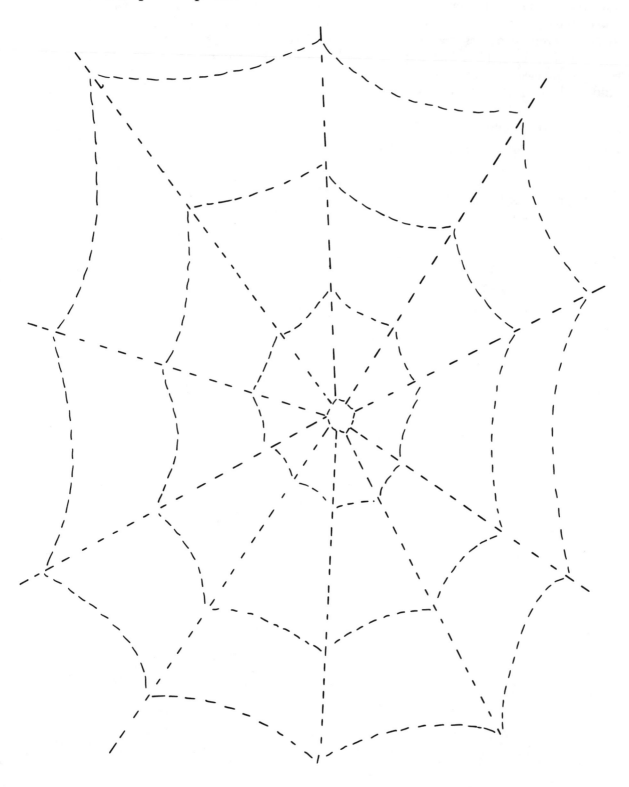

Finish the Web

Make 1 head, 1 abdomen, 8 legs, and 8 eyes for each spider.

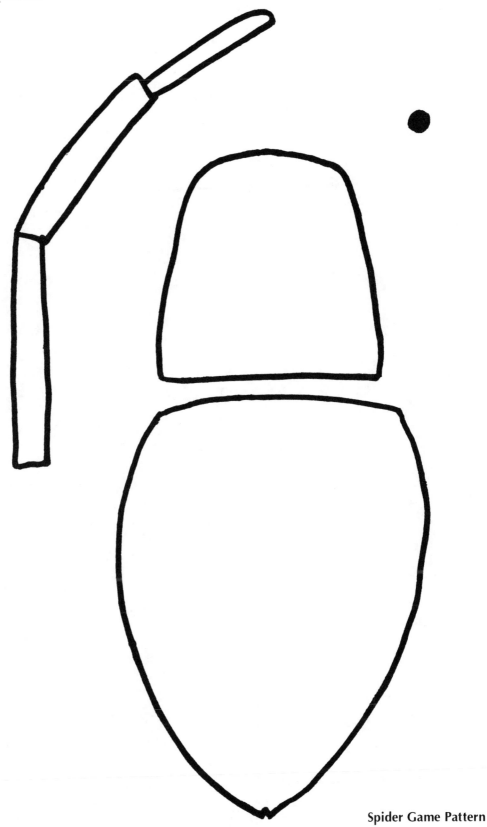

Spider Game Pattern

Multicultural Books

WHEN AFRICA WAS HOME
by
Karen Williams

Developmental Activities Chart	Language & Cognitive Development	Fine Motor Art	Gross Motor	Perception	Social Skills	Math	Dramatic Play	Cooking Snack	Science	Music, Fingerplays, Poems
1 Different Homes	X				X					
2 Dramatic Play							X			
3 Toys	X			X	X					
4 Clay Dolls		X								
5 Moving Memory Game	X			X						
6 Suitcase Memory Game	X			X						
7 Sweet Snacks	X			X		X		X		
8 Exploration Table									X	
9 Snack Ideas								X		
10 Barefoot Fun				X						
11 Bead Stringing		X		X		X				
12 Noodle Necklaces		X				X				
13 Drums	X	X		X						X
14 Sand Pictures		X								
15 Sand Exploration		X				X			X	
16 Sand Paintings		X								
17 Games			X							
18 Suggested Home Activities	X				X			X		
19										
20										
21										
22										
23										
24										
25										
26										
27										
28										
29										
30										

WHEN AFRICA WAS HOME
by Karen Williams
Orchard Books, 1991

Peter is a young boy who spent his first few years living in a small African village. When his father's job ends, the family moves back to America where life is very different. Peter misses many things about his simple life in Africa and wishes to go back. The descriptive pictures and touching story exemplify to young children everywhere how life in a small African village differs from their own.

Different Homes.   This book offers an excellent opportunity to introduce children to the concept of individual and cultural differences. The difference in homes is easy to recognize. Discuss with children how Peter's home in Africa differed from his home in America. Extend the activity by discussing the many different types of homes people live in. Make a picture list of the different home types of children in the class. Examples might include apartments, duplexes, town homes, condominiums, single-family homes, one-story or two-story homes, mobile homes, homes made of wood, brick, adobe, and so forth. The list will differ depending on geographical location. Graph how many children live in each type of home. Compare the results of the graph in terms of most, least, more than, less than. Count how many different home types there can be in just one class. Encourage the children to share pictures of their homes.

Dramatic Play.   Create a village, similar to the one in which Peter lived. Peter sat on the floor, ate with his fingers, slept with mosquito netting, and didn't wear shoes. Provide blankets on which children can sit. If mosquito netting is available, surround areas of the "village" with it; allow the children to eat finger-food snacks on the floor and remove shoes while in the "village." Encourage the children to brainstorm other ways to simulate village life.

Toys.   In Africa toys are different from those with which we play. Dolls are made with wet earth from the riverbed; other toys are made from corn stalks. Ask children to bring their favorite toy to school. Children can take turns showing off their toy, describing what they like to do with it, and sharing toys with each other. Expand the activity by classifying the toys. Possible categories might include large, medium, and small toys; toys with wheels; toys with moving parts; dolls; and animals. The children can graph the number of toys in the various categories. First, list the categories at the top; then, put the toy under the category.

Look at which category has the most toys, least toys, biggest toys, smallest toys, and so forth.

Clay Dolls.   Provide the children with clay. Point out that it is like the wet earth from the riverbed. Let them fashion their own toys from the clay.

Moving Memory Game.   Ask the children to pretend that they are Peter and it is time to move back to America. Sit in a circle and chant, "I'm moving to America and bringing back a . . ." Each child thinks of one thing he or she would bring with him or her. Each turn, the child repeats what the other children would bring and adds his or her own item to the list. Change the game by saying "I'm moving back to Africa and bringing back a . . ."

Suitcase Memory Game.   Place a few items in a suitcase (the amount will depend on the age and developmental level of the children). Have the children name the items. Remove one or two items from the suitcase and ask the children to guess what is missing. Vary the categories of items; choose from clothing, toys, toy animals, and so on.

Sweet Snacks.   In Africa, Peter and his friends snacked on sweet stringy pieces of sugarcane. His mother promised he'd have Popsicles™ in America. Peter didn't even know what Popsicles™ or ice were. Provide the children with sugarcane for snack. Most large supermarkets or specialty food stores carry it. Have the children compare the sugarcane to Popsicles™ and list adjectives describing each. Determine what might be the same or different with the two snacks. Both are sweet, one is cold, one is rough. Count the characteristics they have in common and those they don't. Take a class vote regarding which tastes better, sugarcane or Popsicles™. Tally the results; use the terms more, less, the same.

Exploration Table.   Fill the exploration table with ice cubes. Watch what happens over the course of the day. The children will enjoy playing in the water and watching it change from ice to cold water to warmer water. Provide containers with which to measure, fill, and empty. Have the children time how long it takes for the ice to melt partially and to melt completely. Experiment by taking a container of ice outside. Does the ice melt faster or slower? What happens to the water if the ice melts on a warm sidewalk? Adding food coloring to the ice cubes will add another dimension to this activity. Ice cubes of different colors can be combined in a clear container. What happens to the color when the ice cubes melt together? Be sure to ask the children which home Peter would have to live in if he wanted to do a similar activity.

Snack Ideas.   The foods Peter ate in Africa were different from what he ate in America. Corn or maize is grown in Africa, and is a primary source of nutrition. Flat breads are commonly eaten instead of the yeast bread we eat. Serve pita bread for snacks. Try it with butter and jam, or make sandwiches with cheese, meat, or peanut butter. The children will enjoy sitting on the floor to eat as Peter did.

Try the following recipe for corn bread, or use a mix.

Corn Bread Recipe

1	cup flour	1	cup cornmeal
⅓	cup sugar	2	eggs
½	teaspoon salt	1	cup milk
4	teaspoons baking powder	¼	cup margarine

Preheat oven to 450 degrees. Sift together dry ingredients, add eggs, milk, and margarine. Beat until smooth. Bake in a 9-inch pan for 20 minutes.

Barefoot Fun. In Africa, Peter enjoyed going barefoot and feeling the warm earth on his feet. Play a sensory game with bare feet. Set up containers large enough for a child's foot. Fill one container with sand, one with water, one with corn meal, and one with gravel. Allow the children to experiment with the various substances so they are familiar with them. Next, without allowing the children to see what is in each container, have them place a bare foot in one container at a time. Using only the sense of touch with bare feet, ask the children to identify the substance. The substances in the containers can be substituted or varied depending on what substances are easily accessible. Examples are feathers, grass clippings, leaves, and crushed ice.

Bead Stringing. People in Africa wear brightly colored beads. Provide the children with beads of different colors and sizes and stiff string with which to string the beads. Children can make up bead patterns, alternating colors and sizes of the beads. The children might enjoy making up a pattern for classmates to follow or following a pattern made up by the teacher.

Noodle Necklaces. The children can make beaded jewelry with colored macaroni. Color macaroni by mixing ¼ cup alcohol with a few drops of food coloring in a plastic zipper bag. Add uncooked macaroni noodles and shake the bag until the noodles are coated with color. Dry the noodles on a paper towel. Prepare yarn for stringing by making a large knot at one end and wrapping masking tape at the other end to stiffen it for ease in stringing. The children may want to create patterns in their jewelry by alternating colors.

Drums. One of the familiar African sounds Peter missed when he was in America was the sound of the distant drums. Drumming is a common musical form in African villages. Have the children make simple drums by decorating oatmeal canisters. The canisters can be painted with tempera, decorated with markers or crayons, or covered with Con-Tact® or other colored paper. The children can make up special beats on their drums alternating fast and slow or loud and soft taps. An excellent auditory activity involves asking the children to repeat sound patterns made up by the teacher. Begin with two or three tap patterns, for example, long-short-long. Increase the difficulty depending on the age and developmental level of the children. Try tapping names and ask the children to guess whose name was tapped.

Sand Pictures. Children in small African villages spend time experimenting with substances easily found in their environment. Playing in the dirt and sand is a common pastime. Sand collages can be made by having the children make a design with glue on a piece of cardboard. Have them sprinkle sand over the glue and let it dry. Children might try writing their names in the sand or using glue and sand.

Sand Exploration.   Put sand in the exploration table. Provide containers for pouring, measuring, and sifting, in addition to other common sand toys. In Africa, Peter ran up and down the anthills. Challenge the children to make anthills of varying sizes in the exploration table. Take a walk outside and look for anthills; compare the size of those you find with the anthills pictured in the book.

Sand Paintings.   Try mixing sand in tempera paint at the easel. The children's pictures will be textured by the sand. Use bright colors, which are popular in Africa. The children might enjoy creating designs with the paint similar to those on the hat Peter's mother made him, which reminded him of Africa. Ski hat shapes could be cut out of easel paper and hung at the easel for the children to decorate with the sand-textured paint.

Games.   Peter and his friends in the African village enjoyed playing simple games from morning until night. They climbed trees, chased animals, raced up anthills, and danced in the moonlight. The children will enjoy playing different versions of tag, depending on age and developmental level. Very young children enjoy playing shadow tag. When outside, the children can try to tag each other's shadows. Older children can play African animal tag. Animals mentioned in the book were monkeys, antelopes, hippos, hyenas, and giraffes. When tagging another child they need to say the name of an animal. If there is a nearby hill, have children race to the top, pretending it is a giant anthill. Try setting up a race course around the village. Set up markers representing huts, anthills, nearby water, and so on. Let the children run races around the course.

Suggested Home Activities.   Send home a synopsis of the story *When Africa Was Home.* Tell parents about the activities the children are doing at school. Because this story is an excellent introduction to other cultures, encourage parents to share a special recipe or custom from their family or cultural background. If any parents have visited or lived in Africa or another country, ask them to come into the classroom and share photographs, artifacts, and experiences.

Related Literature

Ekoomiak, Normee. *Arctic Memories.*

Lewin, Hugh. *Jafta.*

———. *Jafta and the Wedding.*

———. *Jafta's Father.*

———. *Jafta's Mother.*

———. *Jafta—The Journey.*

———. *Jafta—The Town.*

Porter, A. P. *Kwanzaa.*

Williams, Karen Lynn. *Galimoto.*

NOT SO FAST, SONGOLOLO
by
Niki Daly

Developmental Activities Chart	Language & Cognitive Development	Fine Motor Art	Gross Motor	Perception	Social Skills	Math	Dramatic Play	Cooking Snack	Science	Music, Fingerplays, Poems
1 Shoe Collage	X	X								
2 Shoe Categories	X			X						
3 Shoes On!		X			X					
4 City Trip	X			X						
5 Kick the Can			X							
6 Bus Ride		X								X
7 Store Games	X			X						
8 Category Collages	X			X						
9 Traffic Light	X	X								
10 Safety Verse										X
11 Red Light, Green Light			X		X					
12 Shoe Store	X			X	X	X	X			
13 Measure Up	X			X		X				
14 What a Pair!	X									
15 Shoe Stepping	X		X							
16 Foot Moves	X		X			X				
17 Footprints		X								
18 Sensory Walk				X		X				
19 South African Cooking	X	X				X		X		
20 Shoe Matching	X	X		X						
21 Footwear Patterning	X			X		X				
22 Suggested Home Activities	X									X
23										
24										
25										
26										
27										
28										
29										
30										

NOT SO FAST, SONGOLOLO
by Niki Daly
Atheneum, 1986

Young Malusi accompanies his large, old, slow-moving granny on a shopping trip to the busy city. Their special day is filled with many sights and sounds, and old GoGo surprises Malusi by buying him a beautiful pair of new red and white sneakers, or tackies, as they are called in South Africa.

Shoe Collage. Talk about some of the reasons why people need to cover their feet, and then brainstorm with children all the things that people wear on their feet. Provide children with magazines, catalogs, and newspaper ads, and have them cut out and glue all the different kinds of shoes that they see to make a large shoe collage.

Shoe Categories. Cut out, mount, and laminate pictures of a wide variety of shoes found in magazines, catalogs, newspapers, and so on. Children can sort the shoes into categories, such as those with straps, those with no straps, those with Velcro™ closures, high heels, low heels, shoes with ties like Malusi's tackies, and shoes with buckles like GoGo wore.

Shoes On! Provide a variety of clean, old shoes in the housekeeping corner. Children can practice putting them on, lacing, tying, and buckling the shoes on themselves or their friends.

City Trip. Malusi and GoGo shopped in a busy city of South Africa. Take a field trip to a busy city where children can enjoy the variety of things to see and do. Upon returning, children can compare what they saw and did with what Malusi saw and did. Brainstorm things seen and heard that make the description "busy" fit: lots of cars and traffic, many traffic lights and stop signs, police directing traffic, many stores, many shoppers, parking meters, loud sounds, crowded restaurants, to name just a few.

Kick the Can. Malusi entertained himself while walking to the bus stop by kicking a can. In a large open area, children can have fun and practice eye-foot coordination by kicking a can as they walk. They can also see who can kick a can the farthest. Provide cans with no sharp edges.

Bus Ride. Malusi and GoGo traveled by bus to the city. Sing the old, familiar song, "Wheels on the Bus."

The wheels on the bus go around and around,
Around and around, around and around.
The wheels on the bus go around and around,
All through the town.

Include other verses:
people go jabber, jabber, jabber
horn goes beep, beep, beep
brakes go squeak, squeak, squeak
windows go up and down, up and down
money goes clink, clink, clink

Have children think up other verses to add to the song.

Store Games. Sort teacher-prepared or commercial pictures into the "store" where each item could be found. Categories to include might be a toy store, clothing store, shoe store, pet store, grocery store, flower store, and fabric store. Another activity would be having children brainstorm as many things as they can that could be found in a particular store. Last, the teacher can collect a variety of objects and put them into a bag. Items to include are a leash, belt, scissors, socks, a puzzle, and shoe laces. The teacher explains that all the items were wrong, didn't fit, and need to be returned. The children can name each item and help the teacher decide which store will accept the merchandise.

Category Collages. Children cut out shoe pictures from magazines, ads, and catalogs. Pictures are glued on paper into separate categories: work shoes, shoes for play, and dress-up shoes.

Traffic Light. On the way to the city, Malusi and GoGo saw many traffic lights. Children can make a light by cutting one large black rectangle and three circles, one red, one yellow, and one green, that will fit vertically on the rectangle. Talk about the meaning of the colored lights as children glue on the circles.

Safety Verse. Teach the safety verse and practice it as the class takes a walk around the school neighborhood.

Stop, look, and listen.
Before you cross the street.
Use your eyes, your ears, and
Then you use your feet.

Red Light, Green Light. In an open area outside or in the gym, teach the children the running game "Red Light, Green Light." Children stand behind a line or at a designated starting point. When the teacher shouts "green light," children run forward. When they hear the words "red light," they immediately stop. Anyone who fails to stop must go back to the starting point. The winner is the first child to reach the finish line.

Shoe Store. Set up a shoe store in the dramatic play area, where children can enact what happens when someone buys a pair of shoes. Provide a variety of shoes, boots, slippers, play money, old receipts, a cash register, and some rulers children can use to measure each other's feet. If boxes are available, children can also practice getting shoes into appropriately sized boxes.

Measure Up. Have children arrange the footwear in the shoe store from longest to shortest or shortest to longest.

What a Pair!   Show children a pair of shoes and a pair of mittens. Ask them to think of how the sets are the same. If necessary, explain that a pair is a set of two items that look the same and are used the same way. Encourage children to think of other things that come in pairs—socks, pants, eyeglasses, earmuffs, shoelaces, and so on.

Shoe Stepping.   Set up an object course in the classroom or gym. Children can take turns walking heel-toe from one object to the next, counting how many steps it takes to get from one object to the next. Ask children if they know why it might take a different number of steps for everyone.

Foot Moves.   Children stand in a row at a designated place and move when given directions by the teacher or leader. Children can take a certain number of steps, they can walk fast or slow, backward or forward, on tip toes, using baby steps or giant steps.

Footprints.   Gym shoes and sneakers typically have some pattern on the bottom. If an old pair is available, children will enjoy making shoe prints by putting the shoe in a shallow pan that contains paint and pressing onto paper.

Sensory Walk.   Children will enjoy the feeling of walking barefoot in sand, water, grass, in high heels, boots, and other types of shoes. Take a class vote and tally what felt best on the children's feet!

South African Cooking.   In South Africa, Malusi and his family ate foods like rice, beans, dried peas, lentils, and corn. Children can prepare a rice dish that Malusi may have eaten.

Geelrys (Yellow Rice)

6	tablespoons margarine	1	teaspoon tumeric (adds an orange-yellow tint to food)
2	cups uncooked long grain white rice		
2	cinnamon sticks	2	cups raisins
1	teaspoon salt	½	teaspoon sugar

Melt margarine over moderate heat in a large pot. Add rice and stir until the grains are coated. Add cinnamon, salt, tumeric, and four cups of water. Cook on high and stir occasionally until the mixture comes to a boil. Cover and simmer for about 20 minutes until the rice is tender and all the water is absorbed. Remove from heat and add the raisins and sugar. Stir and fluff with a fork. Makes 12 to 15 servings.

Shoe Matching.   Give each child a copy of the black line master that accompanies this activity set. The children can talk about where they might wear the shoes, and what they might do while wearing them. Have the children color the shoes and draw lines to match shoes that are the same.

Footwear Patterning.   Use the footwear patterns to make at least 12 pairs of the boots, shoes, and slippers that are included. The footwear can be colored or cut from construction paper. Laminate the pieces. Children can sort the footwear and then make patterns or copy patterns created by the teacher, for example: slipper, gym shoe; high heel, boot, running shoe.

Suggested Home Activities. Send home a synopsis of the story *Not So Fast, Songogolo,* and inform parents about some of the activities their children will be doing at school. Ask parents to assist their child in making a shaker instrument that they can use at home or bring to school. Children can put dried peas, beans, rice, or lentils in a 6-ounce orange juice container, preferably one that has a plastic lid. They can decorate the can with pieces of Con-Tact® paper or colored masking tape, overlapping the pieces. If children bring their shaker instruments to school, they can compare the sounds that their instruments make. Children can shake and dance as they listen to music.

Related Literature

Cleary, Beverly. *The Growing-Up Feet.*
Hughes, Shirley. *Alfie's Feet.*
Ungerer, Tomi. *One, Two, Where's My Shoe?*
Winthrop, Elizabeth. *Shoes.*

Match the shoes that are the same.

Shoe Matching Activity

Footwear Patterning Activity

BIGMAMA'S
by
Donald Crews

Developmental Activities Chart	Language & Cognitive Development	Fine Motor Art	Gross Motor	Perception	Social Skills	Math	Dramatic Play	Cooking Snack	Science	Music, Fingerplays, Poems
1 Train Ride	X									
2 Railroad Workers	X									
3 Dramatic Play	X				X	X	X			
4 Vacation Dreams	X									
5 Families	X				X					
6 I Love My Family		X								X
7 Going on a Trip	X									
8 Suitcase Math	X				X	X				
9 The Conductor Says			X		X					
10 Feeling Feet	X			X		X				
11 Fishing		X			X					
12 Summer at Bigmama's	X					X				
13 Country or City	X									
14 City-Country Comparisons	X									
15 Summer Song										X
16 Look and Listen	X			X						
17 Barbecued Chicken Wings	X	X				X		X		
18 Egg Math	X					X		X		
19 Eggs-actly				X	X					
20 Egg Puzzles	X			X						
21 Farm Science	X							X		
22 Suggested Home Activities	X	X			X					
23										
24										
25										
26										
27										
28										
29										
30										

BIGMAMA'S
by Donald Crews
Greenwillow Books, 1991

Donald Crews grew up in New Jersey, but spent his summers in Cottondale, Florida. In the story, young Donald once again visits Bigmama's house in the country and finds everything just the same inside and outside. He loves playing and exploring with his cousins and the dinnertime talks with friends and family during the hot summer days at Bigmama's.

Train Ride. The family traveled by train to get to Bigmama's. Give children an opportunity to tell about their experiences riding on a train. Where did they go? What did they do? How long did it take? Talk about the different cars on a passenger train: coach, sleeping car, dining car, baggage car, and observation car. Ask children to speculate about how the cars are different and why they are all needed.

Railroad Workers. Many people work for the railroad to ensure that passengers safely get from one place to another. Talk about the job of the ticket agent, engineers, brakemen, conductors, porters, cooks, and waiters. Children can dictate stories about the jobs of the workers and tell why each is important.

Dramatic Play. Children can line up chairs or use large grocery or storage boxes to set up a train station and train cars in the dramatic play area. Children can take turns being passengers or railroad workers. Provide a hole punch and blank paper to make tickets, play money, a conductor's hat, an engineer's hat, old newspapers and magazines for the passengers to read, dining utensils, a bell, a "train whistle," old suitcases, and clothing.

Vacation Dreams. Donald and his family spent part of every summer at Bigmama's. It was a vacation everyone looked forward to with great anticipation. Children can write or dictate a story about a place they would like to visit—a new place or somewhere they have already visited. They can imagine what they might do on their vacation, what they might see, and what their vacation spot would be like.

Families. Bigmama, Bigpapa, Uncle Slank, and all the cousins were part of a large, close-knit family. Send home a self-adhesive page from a photo album with each child. Together, parents and their child can fill the album page with pictures of important family members. Children can share pictures with classmates and talk about special events shown in them. Photos can be kept in the school photo "family album" and be sent home at the end of the school year.

I Love My Family   (fingerplay)

    Some families are large.   [Spread arms out wide.]
    Some families are small.   [Bring arms close together.]
    But I love my family,   [Cross arms over chest.]
    Best of all!

Going on a Trip.   Play a memory game. Provide a small suitcase and pictures/objects children might use on a trip. Place three to six objects/pictures in the suitcase, and have children repeat the sequence of items in the order they were placed in the suitcase.

Suitcase Math.   Provide a suitcase (use black line master) for each child cut from construction paper. Cut pictures of toys, toiletries, clothing, books, and other items that might be needed for a vacation trip. Mount the pictures on small cards and laminate all the pieces. Place a set of numeral cards, 0 to 10, on the table. Children take turns picking a card, reading the numeral for all, and placing the correct number of items in their suitcase.

The Conductor Says.   Play a version of the familiar game "Simon Says." One child is chosen to be the conductor. The conductor tells the children to perform an action, move a number of steps, and so forth. If the conductor doesn't say "Conductor says" before giving the directions, children should not perform the action, and go back to a starting point.

Feeling Feet.   When the children arrived at Bigmama's, one of the first things they did was to take off their shoes and socks. Have children remove shoes and socks and get an opportunity to walk on/in different surfaces, for example, grass, concrete, dirt, asphalt, leaves, gravel, and sand. Children can describe how each surface felt, make a graph showing their favorite and most unfavored surface, and compare results. Last, with adult supervision, children can walk through a small wading pool filled with soapy water to clean their feet.

Fishing.   Down on the path, past the cow pen and the pig pen was a pond where the children went fishing. Cut about five fish shapes from at least eight or more colors of construction paper. Laminate these pieces and place a paper clip on the end of each fish. Attach a magnet to a string that is tied to a dowel rod. This becomes the fishing pole. Make a pond out of blue kraft paper, or use yarn to make an outline of the fishing area. Place fish in the water, and children can take turns "catching" fish in the pond.

Summer at Bigmama's.   Children pretend they are returning from a summer vacation at Bigmama's and retell the story on their long train ride home. Cut rectangular shapes from felt to represent the train cars. Children put up a different train car for each event they remember from their summer experiences at Bigmama's, for example, "We drank water from the well." "We looked for nests by the tool shed." "We saw Nancy and Maude in the stable." When finished, children can count the train cars.

Country or City.   The teacher makes a statement and children decide if it better describes life in the country or life in the city.

I wash my face in the bathroom.
I wash my face outside in the washstand.

I swim at the pool.
I swim in the pond.

I ride my horse.
I ride my bike.

I get a drink from a well.
I get a drink from the faucet.

I get eggs from the grocery store.
I get eggs from the chicken coop.

City-Country Comparisons.   Children use creative thinking, problem-solving skills, and the illustrations from the story to complete the comparisons.

In the city an alarm clock wakes me up. In the country _____ wakes me up.

In the city cars drive on paved streets. In the country cars drive on _____.

In the city my job is to walk the dog. In the country my job is to _____.

In the city I get vegetables from the grocery store. In the country I get vegetables from _____.

In the city I wear sandals and sneakers. In the country I _____.

In the city my backyard has a swing set. In the country my backyard has _____.

In the city we use toilets and bathrooms. In the country we use _____ and _____.

Summer Song (to the tune of "You Are My Sunshine")

It is the summer.
It is the summer.
We'll take vacations and take the train.
We'll all go barefoot out in the country.
In the summer.
When school is out.

We're in the country.
We're in the country.
We feed the chicks and gather eggs.
We ride the tractor and climb the pear trees.
In the summer.
When skies are blue.

Look and Listen.   Children listen carefully to the story and look at the illustrations. They brainstorm a list of sounds they might hear at Bigmama's, such as the train whistle, chicks cheeping, dogs barking, roosters crowing, horses neighing, the wind-up record player, the clock over the fireplace, turkeys gobbling, the tractor motor, children splashing in the pond, and the family talking and laughing.

Barbecued Chicken Wings.   The chicken coop was the place "where Sunday dinner's chicken spent its last days." Children will enjoy preparing this recipe.

16	chicken wings (about 2½ pounds)	¼	teaspoon ginger
1	cup mild barbecue sauce	⅛	cup honey
¼	cup teriyaki sauce	¼	cup toasted sesame seeds

Preheat oven to 425 degrees. Remove tips from chicken wings, and cut each wing apart at joint to make two pieces. Mix ingredients except sesame seeds in a large bowl. Place chicken wings in a single layer in a shallow baking pan; brush with half the sauce. Bake for about 30 minutes until glazed and crispy, basting with extra sauce after 15 minutes. Sprinkle with sesame seeds. Reserved sauce can be used for dipping.

Egg Math.   Children will enjoy a variety of egg activities:

- Make a graph of children's favorite kind of eggs—fried, scrambled, or boiled. Compare results. Children prepare their favorite type of egg for a snack.
- Give each child a length of yarn. They estimate the circumference of an egg and cut their yarn piece to match their guess. Graph results—which estimates were too short, too long, and how many were just right.
- Use a balance scale and have children estimate, then determine exactly how many buttons, paper clips, blocks, and so on, weigh the same as the egg.

Eggs-actly.   The children at Bigmama's looked in the barn and under the tractor for eggs. Students can match eggs that are exactly the same. Cut out about 24 egg shapes from construction paper. Decorate the eggs so that there are 12 exact pairs. Laminate the pieces. Hide the eggs under chairs and tables, and have children hunt and work together cooperatively to find and match egg pairs.

Egg Puzzles.   Cut out at least 12 large egg shapes from construction paper. Cut apart/crack each egg in half by making wavy lines, zigzag lines, and so on. Laminate the pieces. Children put the egg puzzles together.

Farm Science

- Have children predict if a boiled egg will weigh the same as a raw egg. Check predictions.
- The children dug for worms at Bigmama's to use for fishing. Students can pick worms up off the sidewalks in the school neighborhood after a heavy rain, buy them at bait stores, or dig in a spot where they have been watering to find worms. Small groups of children can observe their worms. Tell children that

worms have sensitive skin that must remain moist for them to breathe. Remind children to handle the worms gently. Encourage children to look for eyes and ears on their worm. Use a magnifying glass if one is available. Explain that the head is the thicker of the two end segments. When eyes and ears can't be located, inform children that the worm *does* have a mouth and a nose with a good sense of smell. They can compare the color of worms, graph and compare the length of the worms, watch them move, and so on. Have a supply of wet wipes and paper towels on hand for the children to use after handling the worms. Be sure to release the worms safely outdoors.

Suggested Home Activities.   Send home a synopsis of the story *Bigmama's,* and inform parents of some of the activities the children will be doing at school. Encourage parents to visit a train station with their child. If possible, take a short trip and observe the sights and sounds along the way. Another fun family activity would be to plan a day of fishing at a nearby lake or pond. Remember to bring the worms!

Red Wigglers can be purchased at a bait shop or through:

> Flowerfield Enterprises
> 10332 Shaver Road
> Kalamazoo, Michigan 49002
> (616) 327-0108

Parents can send for a free brochure and get more information about worm composting.

Related Literature

Crews, Donald. *Shortcut.*
Howard, Elizabeth Fitzgerald. *The Train to Lulu's.*
Hurd, Edith Thacher. *I Danced in My Red Pajamas.*
Rylant, Cynthia. *The Relatives Came.*
Stanovich, Betty Jo. *Big Boy, Little Boy.*

Children need a suitcase to play the game and get ready for their vacation. Talk about all the things they'll need.

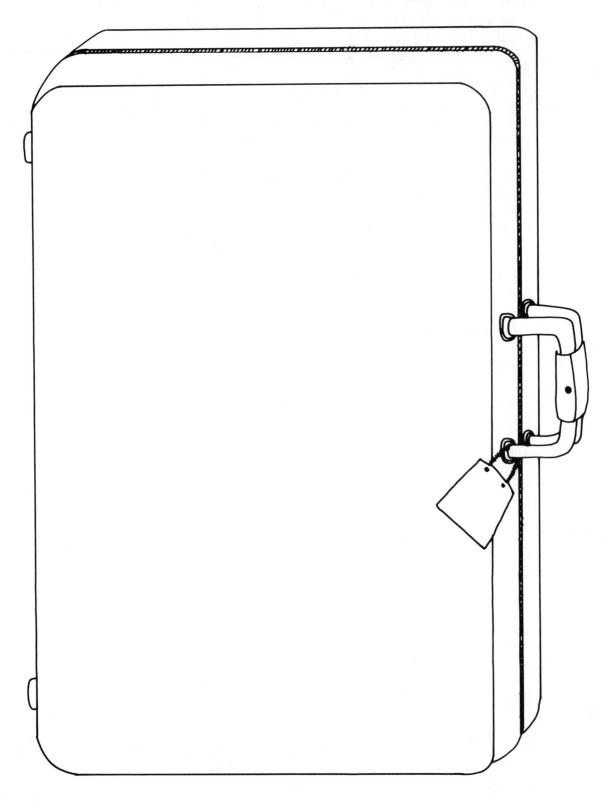

Suitcase Math Activity

EVERYBODY COOKS RICE
by
Norah Dooley

Developmental Activities Chart	Language & Cognitive Development	Fine Motor Art	Gross Motor	Perception	Social Skills	Math	Dramatic Play	Cooking Snack	Science	Music, Fingerplays, Poems
1 Phone Numbers	X									X
2 Rice Rations	X	X				X				
3 Rice Relays		X	X			X				
4 Rice Table		X		X		X			X	
5 Rice Collages		X							X	
6 Write on Rice		X		X						
7 Measuring/Sorting	X	X		X		X				
8 Rice Cakes								X		
9 Rice Pudding								X		
10 Rice Song										X
11 Dramatic Play					X		X			
12 Around the World	X	X			X	X	X			
13 Map Your Trip	X									
14 Country Punchouts		X								
15 Puerto Rico		X				X				
16 India	X	X						X		
17 Chutney								X		
18 Italy	X	X		X						
19 Barbados		X		X			X			
20 China		X						X		
21 Vietnam			X		X		X	X		
22 Haiti	X	X		X						
23 Suggested Home Activities	X	X						X		
24										
25										
26										
27										
28										
29										
30										

EVERYBODY COOKS RICE
by Norah Dooley
Carolrhoda, 1991

Hungry Carrie was sent out to find her younger brother, Anthony, and bring him home for dinner. As she went from neighbor to neighbor, looking for Anthony, she discovered that every family in her culturally diverse neighborhood was cooking a rice dish.

Phone Numbers. Even though Carrie enjoyed looking for Anthony, it would have been better if Anthony had called home to inform his family where he was. It is very important that children know their own phone numbers so they can call home when necessary. Have children draw pictures of themselves. Each picture should be labeled with the child's phone number. Children can recite their numbers until they have been memorized. Use this song to help children memorize their phone numbers. Sing the song to the tune of "Here We Go Looby Loo."

I know a phone number song.
It tells me what to do.
When I need to call.
It helps me remember it all.

(Each child sings his or her own phone number four times.)

222-2222, 222-2222, 222-2222, 222-2222.

Rice Rations. Label baby food jars or margarine containers with a numeral from 1 to 10. Provide a bowl of uncooked rice and a spoon. Children can read the numeral and put the corresponding number of spoonfuls of rice into the container.

Rice Relays. Divide the children into teams of three or four. Mark off a starting and finish line. The distance between them will depend on the age and physical abilities of the children. Place one container of rice and a tablespoon for each team at the starting line. Place an empty bowl for each team at the finish line. The first child on each team puts rice on the spoon and carefully walks (or runs) with the spoonful of rice to the empty bowl. He or she places the rice into the bowl, runs back to the starting line, and hands the spoon to the next child in line. Play continues until all the rice is deposited into the bowl at the finish line. The game can be modified for children in wheelchairs by placing the bowls on tables that are level to the chair. Leave enough space for children to maneuver their chairs easily.

Rice Table. Put rice in the exploration table or in plastic bins. The children can empty and fill containers, pour rice, measure rice with measuring cups and spoons, compare amounts, and experiment with the texture of the substance.

Rice Collage. Place a cup of rubbing alcohol mixed with a few drops of food coloring into a large plastic zipper bag or into a bowl. Add rice. The longer the rice sits in the alcohol and food coloring, the bolder the colors will become. Primary colors can be mixed to create secondary colors. Place the rice on a paper towel to dry. Make designs by squeezing glue on paper and sprinkling rice over the glue.

Write on Rice. Line a tray or box with a layer of rice. Children can practice making letters, shapes, or numerals or writing their names with their fingers in the rice. Younger children can practice making roads. Small cars can be driven through the rice on the road.

Measuring/Sorting. The recipes in the book call for additional ingredients. Some of those ingredients are red beans, green peas, and black-eyed peas. These items can be purchased in the grocery store. Purchase a bag of each item. Pour the peas and beans into a single bowl. Children can separate and sort the legumes. The children can also use the legumes for measuring small items and graphing their lengths. Each item can be measured separately with each legume. Prepare a graph by drawing a picture of the items being measured across the top of the paper. The children can glue the number of legumes it took to measure each item. Compare the length of each item using the terms "longer than" and "shorter than."

Rice Cakes. Rice cakes can be purchased in different flavors. They can be topped with peanut butter, butter, jam, cream cheese, or cheese spread. Add toppings such as raisins, nuts, or pieces of fruit or vegetable to the spreads to make faces and designs.

Rice Pudding. The children will enjoy cooking and eating this simple but tasty dish.

¼	cup uncooked rice	2	teaspoons vanilla
4	eggs	3	tablespoons melted butter
½	cup sugar or to taste	3½	cups milk

Preheat oven to 350 degrees. Cook rice. Beat eggs with sugar and vanilla; add butter and milk and combine thoroughly. Add rice. Place in buttered 5" × 7" loaf pan. Bake for 1 hour. Makes 6 to 8 servings.

Rice Song (to the tune of "Ten Little Indians")

Rice with beans.
Rice with peas.
Rice with vegetables.
Give me more please.
Put it in a pot.
Add the water.
Put on the lid.

And wait for it to boil.
Rice tastes great.
Rice tastes good.
Rice is everybody's favorite food.
Rice with beans.
Rice with peas.
Rice with vegetables.
Give me more please.

Dramatic Play. The dramatic play area can be set up as a kitchen. Provide pots and pans with lids, measuring cups and spoons, dishes, silverware, dishcloths and towels, glasses or cups, and other kitchen items. Ask parents to donate empty food boxes and containers. A high chair can be provided for young "parents" to use when feeding their "babies." Be sure to provide a phone for children to use when they are going to be late for dinner. The children may want to role play the story *Everybody Cooks Rice*. The teacher can help them sequence whose house Carrie visited first, second, third, and so on.

Around the World. Many countries were represented in one culturally diverse neighborhood. The children can get a better look at some of these countries by taking a trip around the world. As the children visit the countries mentioned in the book, they can participate in an activity representative of that country. They might also enjoy cooking the rice dishes from each country. The recipes are given in *Everybody Cooks Rice*. Begin the around-the-world trip by making passports and airplane tickets. Passports can be made by stapling a few sheets of paper together in book form. The children can draw a picture of themselves on the front page. As each country is visited, it should be recorded on the passport. The children can make their own airline ticket to use each time they board the airplane. A seat number should be written on each ticket. As the children board, they will need to find the correct seat. An airplane interior can be made by lining up rows of chairs, two and three across. Each seat should be labeled with a seat number corresponding to those written on the tickets. Remind the passengers to buckle their seat belts. Children can take turns acting as the pilot, copilot, flight attendant, and passengers.

Map Your Trip. Begin the journey by mapping out the route. Look at a world map and locate the countries you will be visiting. Stretch a colored string between the countries marking where you will be visiting first, second, third, and so on. Discuss which countries are close together and which are far apart. Talk about how long it might take to get from place to place. Look at the oceans that you will be flying over along the way.

Country Punchouts. Make country outlines by tracing each country with tracing paper and then transfer the outline to construction paper. Place the paper on a carpet square or similar soft flat surface. The children can use pushpins to punch out the outline of the country.

Puerto Rico. While "visiting Puerto Rico," the children can make a Puerto Rican flag. The children can cut out three predrawn red stripes, one blue triangle, and one white star and assemble them on white construction paper. (See black line master.) Older children and those with more developed fine motor skills can trace stencils instead of using predrawn shapes. Flag assembly can be done by providing auditory directions, a visual model, or a combination of both.

India. Wall paintings are paintings that extend around the walls of a room and tell a story. Tape kraft paper to a wall, extending around a corner. While Anthony was visiting neighbors, he and Mei-Li were seen blowing bubbles out of a window. The children can decorate the wall painting by blowing bubbles mixed with food coloring onto the paper. When the bubble pops it will make a design on the paper. The children can dictate sentence stories about their pictures for the teacher to record on the paper.

Chutney. Chutney is a condiment that is popular in India. It is made from a mixture of mangoes or peaches, peppers, and spices. Chutney can be purchased at most grocery stores. Children will enjoy eating it over vanilla ice cream, while "visiting India."

Italy. Michelangelo was a very famous Italian artist who spent his life painting and sculpting. He is probably most famous for his painting that covers the ceiling of the Sistine Chapel at the Vatican in Rome. Show children pictures of some of Michelangelo's works, which can be found in encyclopedias or art books in the library. Tell the children that Michaelangelo laid on his back while painting the Sistine Chapel, so that he could paint the ceiling above him. The children can experience this by lying on the floor and painting or drawing on paper that has been taped to the bottom of classroom chairs and tables. If tempera paint is used, thicken it by adding flour or cornstarch, or mix it using less water. When the children are finished with their artwork, ask them how Michaelangelo might have felt painting in that position for approximately four years (the lifetime of most preschoolers). Display the artwork on the ceiling of the classroom.

Barbados. Barbados is best known for its tourist industry. Mr. D. explained to Carrie that people swim and fish there, even in December. While visiting Barbados, the children can play in the sand and pretend they are at the beach. Fill the exploration table or bins with sand. Provide shovels, pails, and other sand toys for the children to enjoy on their day at the beach. Props to pack in the suitcase might include sun hats, sun glasses, flip flops to wear on feet, a sun umbrella, and sand chairs. Fishing poles can be made by tying string on a long stick. Place a magnet on the end of the string. Cut colorful tropical fish out of paper. Attach a paper clip to each fish. Place the fish in an inflatable swimming pool or in a bucket. The children can fish while on vacation in Barbados.

China. It is traditional to eat with chopsticks while "visiting China." Children can learn to control chopsticks quite simply. Tightly stretch a rubber band around the top of a pair of chopsticks. Fold a napkin or small piece of paper into a small wad and wedge it between the chopsticks directly under the rubber band. Children control the chopsticks by squeezing their thumb (which is placed on the bottom chopstick) and their middle and index fingers (which are placed on the top chopstick) together. The children can use the chopsticks to eat snacks (little pieces of rice cakes or chunks of vegetable or fruit). Chopsticks can also be used to pick up small items and deposit them in containers (e.g., small beads, marbles, chunks of play dough). Chopsticks can be purchased at large supermarkets or specialty food stores.

Vietnam. In Vietnam, people buy and sell food, crafts, and clothing in a central outdoor market. Some farmers still carry their produce with a carrying pole called a *don ganh*. A don ganh is made from a bamboo stem; it is very sturdy and can carry quite a bit of weight. The children can make don ganhs from long poles or dowel rods. A plastic grocery bag of fruit and vegetables can be tied to both ends of the pole. The children can practice balancing the poles on their shoulders. The children might choose to cooperate and help each other balance their don ganhs. Set up a course for children to travel with their don ganhs, pretending to go to the market. Once there, they can trade fruits and vegetables with each other. The produce can be washed and eaten for snacks.

Haiti. Coffee is grown in Haiti and exported to other countries. Most children are familiar with a cup of coffee, but not with coffee beans and ground coffee. Purchase a bag of coffee beans and a bag of ground coffee. The children can use the two forms of coffee to make coffee collages. The children can squeeze glue on paper and cover it with coffee beans and ground coffee. Talk with children about the smell and texture of coffee. Explain how the beans are ground. If possible, bring in a coffee grinder for a demonstration.

Suggested Home Activities. Send home a synopsis of *Everybody Cooks Rice.* Inform parents of the kinds of activities in which their children are involved. Parents can reinforce the ideas from the book by preparing a favorite rice dish at home. They can talk with their children about the ingredients and where the recipe originated. Ask them to send their favorite rice recipe to school. The recipes can be compiled into a class rice recipe book. The children can illustrate the book with pictures of their families eating rice. The book can be duplicated and sent home.

Related Literature

Ashley, Bernard. *Clever Sticks.*
Morris, Ann. *Bread, Bread, Bread.*
———. *Hats, Hats, Hats.*
———. *Houses and Homes.*
———. *Loving.*
———. *Tools.*

red
white
blue
white
red
white
red

Puerto Rican Flag Pattern

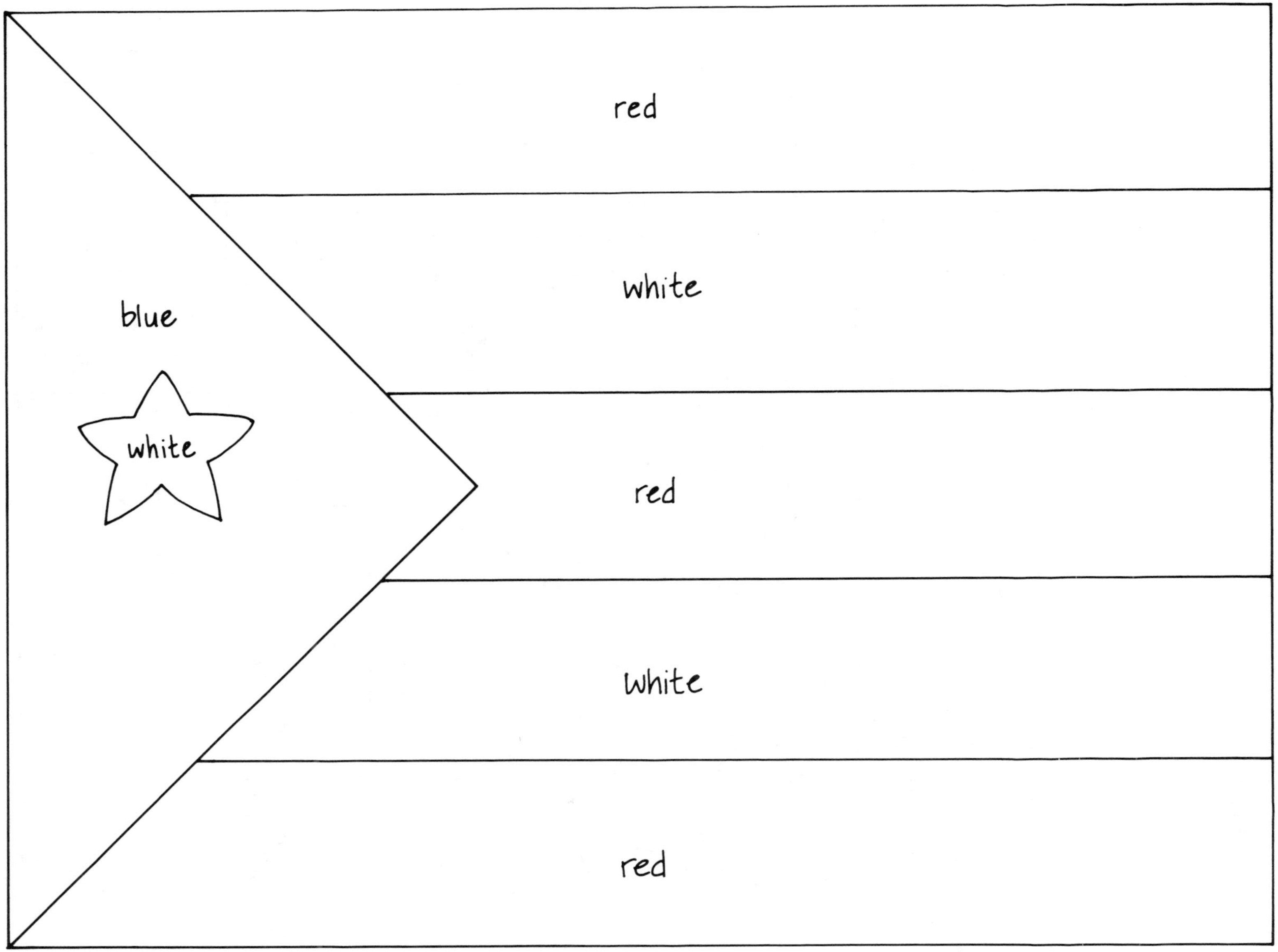

ABUELA
by
Arthur Dorros

Developmental Activities Chart	Language & Cognitive Development	Fine Motor Art	Gross Motor	Perception	Social Skills	Math	Dramatic Play	Cooking Snack	Science	Music, Fingerplays, Poems
1 Where Do We Come From?	X				X					
2 Grandma	X	X			X					
3 Grandmother Books	X	X								
4 Spanish-English Song										X
5 Fact/Fantasy	X									
6 Fancy Fabrics				X						
7 Fly Away	X	X			X		X			
8 Banana Plants	X					X				
9 Far-Away Fruits	X			X				X		
10 Tempting Tostadas								X		
11 Banana Buena								X		
12 Statue of Liberty	X									
13 Statue Games			X							
14 Statue Building		X		X			X	X		
15 Cloud Sculptures		X		X						
16 Cityscapes		X								
17 Statue of Liberty Hats		X					X			
18 City Tour					X					
19 Bus Play	X	X				X	X			
20 Los Pollitos										X
21 Head, Shoulders Song	X		X							X
22 Suggested Home Activities	X				X					
23										
24										
25										
26										
27										
28										
29										
30										

ABUELA
by Arthur Dorros
Dutton Children's Books, 1991

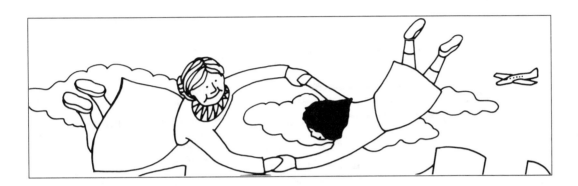

Rosalba, a young Hispanic girl, narrates an imaginary adventure tale. She and Abuela, the Spanish word for "grandma," take a bus ride to the park. While there, Rosalba imagines herself and Abuela flying high above New York City. They observe the sights and sounds of the city, which have been colorfully illustrated in great detail. The book includes many Spanish phrases that are interwoven with English text. The illustrations depict the diversity of people and culture found in the city.

Where Do We Come From?   Hispanic people represent the second largest and fastest-growing minority group in our country. Spanish-speaking people represent the largest language minority in the United States. Hispanic people represent the population that comes from Spanish-speaking descent in such countries as Colombia, Cuba, the Dominican Republic, Mexico, Puerto Rico, Spain, Ecuador, and Nicaragua. Use your map or globe to locate some of these countries. If any children in the classroom come from a Hispanic family, find the country of their origin.

Grandma.   Rosalba calls her grandma Abuela. Some children call their grandma Nana. There are many words to represent that special relative. Discuss with the children that a grandmother is the mother of their mother or father. Encourage the children to tell about their grandmothers and what special names they might use for her. The children can draw pictures of their grandmothers and label them with their names. Ask the parents to send photographs of grandmothers to be displayed along with the illustrations.

Grandmother Books.   The children can make books about their grandmothers. Include pages for them to tell about and illustrate their grandmother's favorite food, activity, thing to wear, recipe, and saying. Invite grandmothers to the class for a visit. The children will enjoy playing with them and sharing their school environment. The children can present the books to their grandmothers at this time.

Spanish-English Song.   Sing this simple song that translates Spanish words to English. The tune is simple and repetitive, skipping up and down the musical scale.

Pollito—chicken, *gallina*—hen, *lapiz*—pencil, *pluma*—pen.
Ventana—window, *puerta*—door, *maestra*—teacher, *piso*—floor.

Fact/Fantasy.   Although *Abuela* tells an imaginary tale, much of it is real. Children are amused by statements of fantasy. Play a game called "Could It Be?" After the children are familiar with the story, reread it one page at a time. At the end of each page or anecdote, ask the children if it could really happen. As you play the game, discuss the sights that Rosalba and Abuela see; ask the children to share their similar experiences.

Fancy Fabrics.   The illustrations show people wearing colorful and lively clothing. Small fabric remnants can be purchased at a fabric store. Prepare pairs of cards by gluing a matching fabric swatch on each of two cards. Mix up the cards; the children can sort through them to find the matching pairs.

Fly Away.   Ask the children to pretend that they are Rosalba and Abuela, flying above your city or town. List all the familiar sights they will fly over. Use building blocks, dolls, toy cars, and other items to build your city. Label the buildings, parks, rivers, lakes, and other familiar places using the words recorded from the children's flight. Ask older children to compare the city or town in which they live to New York City.

Banana Plants.   Banana plants grow in the land where Abuela grew up. Reproduce ten copies of the black line master of the banana plant. Color, cut, and mount the trees on tagboard. Label each plant with a numeral from 1 to 10; then laminate. Cut out 55 additional banana shapes. The children can count the bananas and "hang" them on the corresponding plant. Teach the children to count from one to ten in Spanish: *uno, dos, tres, cuatro, cinco, seis, siete, ocho, nueve, diez.*

Far-Away Fruits.   Mangoes, papayas, and bananas come from the land where Abuela grew up. Other tropical fruits that come from the same land include coconuts, pineapples, and guavas. Purchase a variety of tropical fruits at the supermarket. Allow the children to touch and smell them. Encourage discussion about the fruits; compare and contrast them; talk about color, size, and texture. Serve the fruit for snacks.

Tempting Tostadas.   Tostadas, a Mexican appetizer, are as popular as hot dogs and hamburgers. The children can prepare their own tostadas for snack. Cover the bottom of an electric frying pan with an inch of oil, heat it, and fry tortillas (can be purchased in the refrigerator section of the grocery store) until they are light brown. Remove the tortillas and drain on a paper towel. Each child can make his or her own tostada by topping the tortilla with chili con carne, grated cheddar cheese, and shredded lettuce. Serve with *limonada* (lemonade).

Banana Buena

4 ripe but firm bananas	¼ cup brown sugar
¼ cup butter	lemon juice

Preheat oven to 450 degrees. Peel the bananas and cut them in half lengthwise. Melt the butter in a baking dish. Add bananas. Sprinkle with brown sugar and bake until sugar melts, about 10 minutes. Sprinkle with lemon juice. Serve with vanilla ice cream.

Statue of Liberty. Rosalba and Abuela flew over the Statue of Liberty. Abuela is reminded of when she first came to this country. Talk with the children about the Statue of Liberty. Facts they might enjoy learning include the statue was a gift from France to the United States way back in 1884; she wears a crown with seven spikes, which shine on the seven seas and seven continents (count them on the map); she holds a glowing torch in her right hand and a tablet in her left hand; and there are 142 steps that lead from the base to the observation deck in the crown.

Statue Games

- Play music for the children while they move their bodies about freely. When the music stops, they are to freeze in their position and stand very still like a statue. When the music starts, they move again.
- Have the children pose like the Statue of Liberty.
- Choose one child to be the statue builder. He or she poses in a certain position; the classmates must assume the same position as the statue builder and stand like statues. The children can take turns being the statue builder.
- The children can get an idea of how tall the Statue of Liberty is by climbing stairs. Over the course of a day or two, climb 142 stairs!

Statue Building. Prepare cornstarch dough according to the recipe. The children can use it to mold their own statues.

```
1  part cornstarch (you may need to add more if consistency is too loose)
3  parts salt
1  part water
```

Heat the water and salt for a few minutes, then slowly add the cornstarch, stirring until well mixed. Knead the dough and add more water if necessary. The dough should dry without cracking.

Cloud Sculptures. Rosalba and Abuela flew through *las nubes,* the clouds. The clouds looked like familiar objects: *un gato*—a cat, *un oso*—a bear, and *una silla*—a chair. Give the children cotton balls to manipulate and use for sculpting their own clouds.

Cityscapes. As Abuela and Rosalba flew over the city, they looked down and saw buildings and skyscrapers of different sizes, shapes, and colors. Provide the children with paper in a variety of colors, designs, and textures. Use construction paper, wrapping paper, and wallpaper from old wallpaper books. The children can cut or tear the paper into different lengths and shapes and glue them on paper to create a cityscape similar to the one illustrated in *Abuela*. Complete the picture by dipping cotton balls into white tempera paint and dabbing clouds onto the paper.

Statue of Liberty Hats. The children can make their own Statue of Liberty hats by cutting seven triangles, making a 1-inch fold on the bottom and stapling the fold onto a band cut and stapled to the correct head size.

City Tour. Rosalba and Abuela began their adventure on the city bus. Plan to tour your city by bus. The children will enjoy paying their own fares and taking in familiar sights on this field trip around the city. You could plan a destination such as a local park where you can enjoy a picnic lunch, feed left-over bread scraps to the birds, and play. The city tour could also be the goal of the trip.

Bus Play. Convert your dramatic play area into a bus. Set up rows of chairs. Supply toy money and a fare box. The children can put numbers on the seats and make tickets with matching numbers. When they pay their fare, the driver can hand out tickets. The children can find the seat that matches the numeral on their tickets. The children can take turns playing the role of the bus driver. Fortunately, the bus is big enough to accommodate as many passengers as would like to ride. The children can brainstorm destinations and routes. Be sure to teach the song "The Wheels on the Bus."

Los Pollitos. This song is a familiar Puerto Rican lullaby that many Spanish-speaking children will recognize. Sing it softly and melodically.

> *Los pollitos,*
> *Los pollitos desen pio, pio, pio.*
> *Cuando tienen hambre.*
> *Cuando tienen frio.*
> *La gallina busca el maiz y trigo*
> *Le da la comida y le presta abrigo.*

Translation:

> The chicks,
> The chicks say peep, peep, peep.
> When they are hungry.
> When they are cold.
> The hen gets corn and wheat.
> She gives them food and lends them warmth.

Head, Shoulders Song. Teach the familiar song, "Head and Shoulders, Knees and Toes," in English and in Spanish. Point to each body part as it is said. Repeat the song, singing it faster each time.

> *Cabeza, hombros, rodillas y dedos, rodillas y dedos.*
> *Cabeza, hombros, rodillas y dedos, rodillas y dedos.*

Ojos y orejas y boca y nariz.
Cabeza, hombros, rodillas y dedos, rodillas y dedos.

Translation:

Head, shoulders, knees and toes, knees and toes.
Head, shoulders, knees and toes, knees and toes.
Eyes and ears and mouth and nose.
Head, shoulders, knees and toes, knees and toes.

Suggested Home Activities. Send home a synopsis of *Abuela.* Inform the parents of some of the activities in which their children are involved. Suggest to parents that this is a good time to talk about family roots and traditions. The children will be interested to know where their family originated. They might want to look at old family photos together. If a second language is spoken in the home or in grandparents' homes, parents or grandparents might want to come into the classroom and teach the children words or songs in that language.

Related Literature

Keats, Ezra Jack. *My Dog Is Lost.*
Volkmer, Jane Anne. *La Musica de la Chirimia.*

1. Cut ten plants and label each with a numeral from 1 to 10.
2. Cut banana shapes from construction paper.
3. Children attach the corresponding number of bananas to each plant.

Banana Plants Activity

Science/Stories About the Earth

CAPS, HATS, SOCKS, AND MITTENS
by
Louise Borden

Developmental Activities Chart	Language & Cognitive Development	Fine Motor Art	Gross Motor	Perception	Social Skills	Math	Dramatic Play	Cooking Snack	Science	Music, Fingerplays, Poems
1 Swift Seasons	X			X					X	
2 Sock Sorting				X		X				
3 Mitten Old Maid	X			X	X					
4 Winter Hats		X		X						
5 Snowmen	X	X				X				
6 Weather Wheel	X	X							X	
7 Snowflakes		X								
8 Easel Fun		X								
9 Dress-up Days	X						X			
10 Classroom Gardens	X								X	
11 Clouds and Rain									X	
12 Raindrop Words	X									
13 Picnics	X				X		X			
14 Opening Day			X							
15 Making Rainbows		X							X	
16 Fishing Hole	X	X		X		X				
17 Exploration Table				X					X	
18 Marshmallows	X			X		X		X		
19 Pigs in a Blanket								X		
20 Pumpkin Cookies								X		
21 Fall Soccer			X	X						
22 Nut Sorting		X		X		X		X		
23 Fall Favorites	X	X		X		X			X	X
24 Leaf Lacing		X								
25 Season Song										X
26 Suggested Home Activities				X		X				
27										
28										
29										
30										

CAPS, HATS, SOCKS, AND MITTENS
by Louise Borden
Scholastic, 1989

This book about the four seasons takes young readers on a guided tour around the calendar, beginning and ending with winter. The seasons are represented with pictures and text to which children can easily relate.

Swift Seasons. *Caps, Hats, Socks, and Mittens* lends itself to enjoyable seasonal activities throughout the year. For a change, try converting the classroom into the different seasons in a short span of time. It is particularly exciting for children to enjoy summer activities in the middle of winter or cold winter activities in the hot days of summer. The season can change every day or two, proceeding in sequence. Choose a few activities from each season that will be particularly interesting to the group of children, while taking into account the local climate. For children with special needs, choose activities that utilize their strengths, while developing weaker areas. Children will enjoy "dressing for the weather" during the "swift seasons."

Sock Sorting. Provide the children with a basket of socks to pair. Vary the difficulty of the task depending on age and developmental level. Children can match socks by color, pattern and design, texture, and size. Children can problem solve by predicting which family member would wear the different socks. The matched socks can be classified by family member. It is helpful to use dolls depicting the various family members as a visual clue.

Mitten Old Maid. Using the mitten pattern provided, make a set of cards. Copy and cut the mitten pattern and decorate pairs of mittens. The number of pairs will depend on the size of the group that will play. A group of four children will play with up to 20 cards. Make one mitten that doesn't have a pair. The mittens can be laminated or mounted on tagboard. Children take turns trying to match their mittens by describing the mitten or showing the mitten they are trying to match. Teachers of children who are delayed in language development might encourage the children to describe the mittens, while students who need to strengthen skills in the visual channel might try to match the mittens visually. Memory skills are strengthened when the children try to remember who has the mitten they need. Younger children can simply try and match mittens from a basket or table top.

Winter Hats. Hats can be made by folding paper using the diagram and directions provided. Depending on the children's age and developmental level, they can make the hats by following the teacher's auditory directions and visual clues, or the teacher can fold the hats for younger students. The hats can be decorated with crayons, markers, and colored chalk or by using pieces of fabric, ribbon, colored paper, and glue.

Snowmen.   Provide the children with a small, medium, and large white circle. Ask the children to put them in order from the largest on the bottom to the smallest on the top. Use the terms "small," "medium," and "large"; "first," "second," and "third"; "bottom," "middle," and "top." The children can decorate the snowman.

Weather Wheel.   Children can predict and record the weather each day with their own weather wheel. Divide a paper plate into four sections. Decorate each section with different weather conditions (e.g., sun, cloud, raindrop, snowflake). Attach an arrow, cut from heavy colored paper, to the center of the plate using a brad fastener. Each day the children can record today's weather, predict tomorrow's weather, and talk about yesterday's weather.

Snowflakes.   Children can cut snowflakes to hang from the ceiling. Have them fold thin white paper into four squares. Designs can be cut into the folds of the paper and around the edges. When the paper is unfolded, a beautiful snowflake appears. Point out the symmetry of the design to the children. What is cut in one place shows up on all four sides of the snowflake.

Easel Fun.   As the seasons rotate in the classroom, the paper shape provided at the easel for painting and drawing can reflect the season. Examples might include: caps, hats, socks, mittens, raindrops, umbrellas, fish, pumpkins, and leaves.

Dress-up Days.   Designate one day for favorite hats, another for special socks, and another for marvelous mittens. Younger children can review what body part is covered.

Classroom Gardens.   Seeds can be planted in milk cartons or pots filled with potting soil. An alternate method for planting seeds is to line a jar or a plastic zipper bag with paper towel. Place seeds (peas and lima beans also work well) between the bag or glass and the paper towel. Keep the paper towel moist and the bag or jar in a warm place. Watch the seeds sprout and grow.

Clouds and Rain.   This activity shows children how clouds and rain are formed. Heat a small amount of water until it forms a little cloud. Hold a small mirror next to the cloud and observe the mirror. Ask the children to describe what they see. Next hold a pan of cold water near the cloud; large drops of water will form and fall. When clouds are cooled, rain falls.

Raindrop Words.   Ask the children to tell everything they can about rainy days. Write their words and phrases on raindrop shapes and display them under an umbrella. Children will enjoy "reading" their own words and phrases.

Picnics.   Have the children help plan and prepare for a picnic. They can brainstorm what they will eat, what utensils they will need to pack, and where to have the picnic. Picnics set up on a blanket on the floor can be quite an adventure for young children. If the weather is pleasant the children will enjoy walking to a nearby park or simply having a picnic on the school grounds. The children can work cooperatively to make sandwiches and pack the basket.

Opening Day.   Opening day for baseball traditionally marks the beginning of spring. Using an oversize bat and a large lightweight ball, have a class baseball game. Younger children and children with weaknesses in visual perception and/or gross motor skills will benefit from using a batting tee. Running skills will be strengthened as children run the bases. The game can be simplified by decreasing the number of bases. Younger children can simply hit and catch the ball.

Making Rainbows.   Fill a jar with water and let it sit overnight so the impurities settle. Using an eyedropper, squeeze one drop each of red, yellow, and blue food coloring into the jar and watch the colors combine to produce the colors of a rainbow.

Fishing Hole.   Set up a fishing hole in the classroom. For an authentic feel, bring in a wading pool. Cut fish shapes out of colored construction paper, laminate the fish, and place a paper clip on them. Tie a string onto a dowel rod, then tie a magnet on the end of the string to make a fishing pole. Besides fishing for "fun," readiness concepts can be strengthened by having the children fish for a certain color, shape, or size. Concept fish can be created by drawing shapes, numbers, or letters on them, or they can be made in different sizes. Challenge the children to try and catch only large or small fish, a triangle fish, or a blue fish. Children can count their fish and sort them according to specific attributes.

Exploration Table.   It is through the different senses that children fully experience their environment. The exploration table provides a natural opportunity to celebrate the four seasons. In the winter it can be filled with snow. In the summer, the beach and sandbox can be imitated by filling it with sand and sand toys. In the fall, crunchy leaves and nuts with various textures prove to be an interesting sensory experience. Trying to imitate the seasons in the exploration table takes a bit more ingenuity and advance planning, but it is possible. Snowballs can be saved from the winter to be used in the spring and summer, or ice can be crushed to imitate snow. Fall leaves, nuts, and seeds can be saved for use at a later time. Warm water and sand are always accessible. Children can use dolls and other toys for imaginative play.

Marshmallows.   Colored miniature marshmallows and large marshmallows can be used as math manipulatives as well as providing a wonderful summertime snack when roasted. The marshmallows can be placed on skewers and roasted over an electric hot plate or over the flames of a small gas burner. The children can make up patterns on their skewers using the different colors and sizes of marshmallows (large, large, small, small; or pink, green, yellow, pink, green, yellow). Children will also enjoy measuring with the marshmallows. Classroom objects can be measured, and length can be compared. Children can predict item length and width in terms of large and small marshmallows. Marshmallows can be used in the winter—try measuring winter objects such as mittens and socks. Use the marshmallows in hot chocolate when celebrating winter. Have children predict how long it will take for the marshmallows to melt.

Pigs in a Blanket.   Each child can prepare his or her own snack using this simple recipe. The only necessary ingredients are refrigerator crescent rolls and hot dogs. Preheat oven to 375 degrees. Have each child place a hot dog on the wide end of a triangle shaped piece of dough and roll it up. Place hot dogs on a cookie sheet seam side down and bake for 10 to 15 minutes until the dough is golden in color and the meat is warm.

Pumpkin Cookies

2	cups flour	1	cup brown sugar
1	cup uncooked oatmeal	1	cup sugar
1	teaspoon baking soda	1	egg
1	teaspoon cinnamon	½	teaspoon vanilla
½	teaspoon salt	½	can pumpkin (16-ounce size)
¾	cup margarine	½	cup chocolate chips

Preheat oven to 350 degrees. Combine dry ingredients and set aside. Cream butter, add sugars. Beat well. Add egg and vanilla, mix. Add dry ingredients and pumpkin alternately, mixing well after each addition. Stir in chocolate chips. Spoon dough onto greased cookie sheet, add a dough stem. Bake approximately 20 minutes or until cookies are firm and lightly browned. Frost with peanut butter, cream cheese, or cream cheese frosting. Decorate with candies, raisins, or nuts. Makes 36 to 48 cookies.

Fall Soccer.   Just as baseball marks the beginning of spring, soccer marks the coming of autumn. The game can be simplified by playing in a small area, which requires less running. The children can simply dribble the soccer ball or attempt to kick it over the other team's goal line. Remind the children to keep their hands off the ball.

Nut Sorting.   Children can classify and sort various nuts in the shell, such as walnuts, almonds, hazelnuts, and pecans. Use a muffin tin, an egg carton or separate berry baskets. To encourage the use of the tactile sense, the children can close their eyes and sort nuts by the way they feel and by their size. Extend the activity by having children make sets of nuts. Label the separate compartments with a numeral, and children can put the correct number of nuts in them. Children can crack the nuts using a nutcracker and eat them for a healthy snack.

Fall Favorites.   Many favorite fall activities require advance planning or need to be done in the fall. Children can collect leaves and sort them by shape, color, and size. Leaf rubbings can be made by placing a leaf between two sheets of paper and rubbing the side of a crayon (with the wrapper removed) over the top paper. Gourds can be sorted by type. They can be left to dry, painted, and used to make music by shaking them. Pumpkins can be painted or carved.

Leaf Lacing. Cut different leaf shapes out of green, yellow, orange, and red construction paper. Laminate the shapes and punch holes around the edges. Cut lengths of yarn, tape the ends, and have the children lace around the edges.

Season Song. Sing this song to the tune of "The Wheels on the Bus."

> The seasons of the year go round and round.
> Round and round.
> Round and round.
> The seasons of the year go round and round.
> All day long.
> The snow in the winter falls down, down, down.
> Down, down, down.
> Down, down, down.
> The snow in the winter falls down, down, down.
> All day long.
> The grass in the spring turns green, green, green.
> Green, green, green.
> Green, green, green.
> The grass in the spring turns green, green, green.
> All day long.
> The weather in the summer is hot, hot, hot.
> Hot, hot, hot.
> Hot, hot, hot.
> The weather in the summer is hot, hot, hot.
> All day long.
> The leaves in the fall turn orange and yellow.
> Orange and yellow.
> Orange and yellow.
> The leaves in the fall turn orange and yellow.
> All day long.

Have the children make up additional verses for each season.

Suggested Home Activities. Send home a synopsis of *Caps, Hats, Socks, and Mittens,* and inform parents about the activities in which their children are involved. Parents will be happy to have their children help them sort socks on laundry day. The socks can be sorted by color, matched in pairs, and placed in designated piles according to family member.

Related Literature

Bennett, David. *Seasons.*
Dabcovich, Lydia. *Sleepy Bear.*
Gibbons, Gail. *The Seasons of Arnold's Apple Tree.*
Miller, Jane. *Seasons on the Farm.*

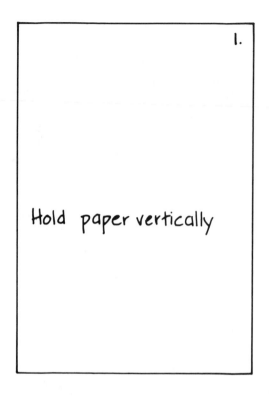

1.

Hold paper vertically

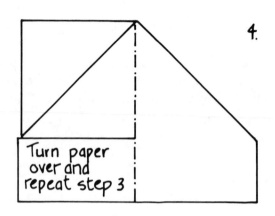

4.

Turn paper over and repeat step 3

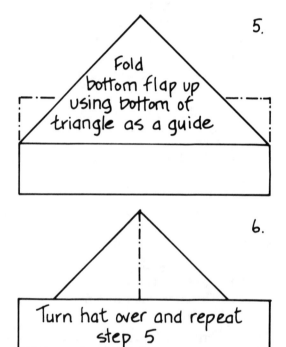

5.

Fold bottom flap up using bottom of triangle as a guide

2.

Fold in half from top to bottom

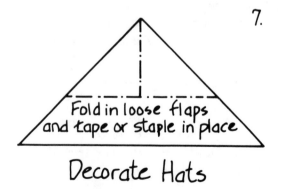

6.

Turn hat over and repeat step 5

3.

fold top left corner to center

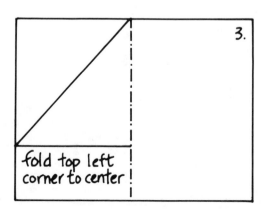

7.

Fold in loose flaps and tape or staple in place

Decorate Hats

Winter Hats Activity

Mitten Old Maid Pattern

FEATHERS FOR LUNCH
by
Lois Ehlert

Developmental Activities Chart

Activity	Language & Cognitive Development	Fine Motor Art	Gross Motor	Perception	Social Skills	Math	Dramatic Play	Cooking Snack	Science	Music, Fingerplays, Poems
1 Bird Walk	X				X	X			X	
2 Nature Collage	X	X								
3 Antipollution Walk	X	X			X					
4 Bird Feeders	X	X			X				X	
5 Close-ups	X	X		X					X	
6 Seed Science				X					X	
7 Birds of a Feather				X		X				
8 Worms						X				
9 Flowers and Seeds						X			X	
10 Jingle Bells		X		X		X				
11 Story Dramatization							X			
12 Cats and Birds			X				X			
13 Obstacle Course	X		X							
14 Feather Art	X	X								
15 Feather Relay			X							
16 Cat Puppets		X								
17 Maze		X		X						
18 Bleeding Hearts		X								
19 What's to Eat?	X								X	
20 Snacks	X	X		X		X		X		
21 Poppy Seed Cake								X		
22 Fingerplay										X
23 Suggested Home Activities									X	
24										
25										
26										
27										
28										
29										
30										

FEATHERS FOR LUNCH
by Lois Ehlert
Harcourt Brace Jovanovich, 1990

A hungry cat sneaks out a crack in the door and goes on an excursion to find a bird. The 12 different varieties of birds he encounters on his way leave him only "feathers for lunch." The colorful illustrations are life size, and the birds, bird calls, and plants are labeled. Children and adults who desire additional information on the birds will find it in the glossary of the book.

Bird Walk. Go for a walk in the neighborhood and look for birds. Each child can be given the responsibility of recording the sightings of a specific variety of bird. The teacher can make up record sheets for each child so that he or she can simply record a sighting with a tally mark. Look for birds that are common to your locality. Your class may want to look for other wildlife such as squirrels and butterflies. Upon returning to the classroom, make a graph of what the children saw by putting tally marks under pictures of the birds. Talk about what birds were seen the most, the least, or not at all. The tally marks can be added up and labeled with a numeral. The concept of zero can be discussed when talking about birds not sighted.

Nature Collage. Go for a walk around the school or neighborhood and look for interesting signs of nature. Each child can carry his or her own bag for individual collections. Examples are nuts, seeds, leaves, interesting weeds, feathers, egg shells, and twigs. Upon returning to the room, the children can tell each other about their collections. Collages can be made by gluing the items on cardboard, or on Styrofoam™ trays, or plates.

Antipollution Walk. In addition to nature walks, children will be proud to take an antipollution walk to help clean up their environment. When discussing *Feathers for Lunch,* talk about where birds and many animals live, and the importance of keeping their environment clean and safe. Compare pollution and litter to poison for birds. Give each child a bag labeled with a Mr. Yuk sad face. The children can pick up garbage and other visible signs of pollution. Upon returning to the classroom, talk about what was found. Glue some of it on a large sheet of cardboard to make a class "Stop Pollution" poster.

Bird Feeders. Children will enjoy observing birds while they dine on birdseed. Simply coat a pine cone or toilet paper tube with peanut butter and then roll it in birdseed. If possible, hang the feeder in a visible place. Binoculars will enhance the children's ability to study the birds. Children might enjoy predicting how long it will take for the birdseed to disappear.

Close-ups.   Display some of the items collected on walks around the neighborhood at the science table. Provide children with a magnifying glass with which to study the items. Discuss how the items change in appearance when seen through a magnifying glass. Use comparative terms such as larger than, smaller than. The children can trace around objects and then use the magnifying glass to observe the change in size.

Seed Science.   Fill the exploration table with a variety of birdseed. Provide containers, measuring cups and spoons, a funnel, a balance scale, and other interesting utensils for the children to use when experimenting with the birdseed.

Birds of a Feather.   Cut bird shapes out of various colors of construction paper. Cut feathers or purchase feathers of different colors at a craft store. Children can match feathers to the corresponding color bird. Expand the activity by labeling the birds with a numeral. Children can put the corresponding number of feathers on the birds.

Worms.   Cut worm shapes out of construction paper. Use the worms to "feed the birds." Using construction paper birds with a numeral or pictorial set printed on them, have children match the corresponding number of worms to the birds. The worms can also be used as a measuring device. Children can measure the birds in the book *Feathers for Lunch* with the worms. Challenge them to estimate how many worms long each bird will be. Talk about which birds are longer/shorter, and how many worms long each bird is. The children can measure classroom objects with the worms. Examples are the snack table, the coat rack, the magnifying glass, or even each other. A large graph can be created by drawing a simple picture of the object measured (or use the real object) and then gluing on the number of worms it took to measure.

Flowers and Seeds.   Plant sunflower seeds in Styrofoam™ cups. Expand the activity by labeling each cup with a numeral or pictorial set. Fill the pot with soil and the number of seeds represented on each cup. Observe how many of the seeds come up. Challenge older children with more advanced math concepts. If five seeds were planted and only two came up, how many didn't come up? Children can use seeds as a math manipulative to solve the problems.

Jingle Bells.   Purchase silver and multicolored bells at the craft store. Give each child a piece of yarn with the end taped. The children can thread the string through the bells to make jingle bracelets. Children can make multicolored bell patterns for their bracelet "collars."

Story Dramatization.   The children can use their bracelet "collars" while dramatizing the story. They can take turns being the cat and the different varieties of birds. The birds can hide while the "cat" tries to find them. The birds can whistle, sing, or talk like birds, while the cat meows and jingles.

Cats and Birds. The children can fly like birds and creep like cats. One child can be the trainer and give the directions "fly," "creep," and "freeze." One goal line can be the tree and another, the house. The object is to get from the tree to the house and back again.

Obstacle Course. Set up an obstacle course in the classroom, gym, or outside. The children can fly over chairs, under tables, around poles. The obstacles can represent puddles, hills, and trees. Stress the directional and positional words.

Feather Art

- Use feathers for painting at the art table or at the easel.
- Provide children with feather shapes, and have them fringe the sides by snipping the paper. This activity is particularly helpful for children who have delayed fine motor skills or no experience with scissors.
- Make a collage out of different colors of feathers. Have the children brainstorm words to describe the way feathers feel.

Feather Relay. The children stand behind a line, scoop up a feather with a spoon, carry the feather to the opposite line, and deposit the feather on a cutout bird shape. Challenge the children to do this without holding the feather in place on the spoon. The children will need to problem solve to figure out how to move so the feather stays in place.

Cat Puppets. The children can create cat puppets out of lunch-size paper bags. Have the children snip paper ears and whiskers to glue on the bag. They can draw eyes, a nose, and a mouth on the cat. Have them thread one bell onto a piece of yarn to make a collar for the cat. Cutting thin strips of paper for whiskers and the triangle shape corners off of construction paper for ears is an excellent activity for children with delayed fine motor skills.

Maze. Reproduce the black line master of the maze which is provided. The children can help the cat find the bird, or they might choose to lead him to the dead end. The children can go through the maze with their finger before deciding which route to take with a pencil, crayon, or marker.

Bleeding Hearts. One of the many plants labeled in the book is the bleeding heart plant. This plant can be made by the children and displayed around the room. Give the children 4" × 4" pieces of pink construction paper, and have them fold the paper in half. Trace half a heart shape on the fold of the paper and have the children cut on the line. When they open the paper, a heart will appear. Some children will be able to cut heart shapes without having the teacher draw the pattern. Stems can be made from yarn, pipe cleaners, or construction paper. The children can tape the hearts on the stems. Leaves can be drawn or glued on.

What's to Eat? After reading the story and looking through the glossary, have the children brainstorm what the cat and the various birds would choose for their favorite meals. Write their ideas on large sheets of paper cut into bird and cat shapes. Children who have birds and cats for pets will enjoy sharing information about their pet's diet.

Snacks

Fruits with Seeds

Serve fruits that contain visible seeds. Examples are apples, oranges, tangerines, grapes, and pears. Availability of fruits will vary depending on the time of year. Collect the seeds and talk about the size, color, shape, and texture of the fruits and seeds.

Sunflower Seeds

Children can strengthen the small muscles in their fingers when they crack open sunflower seeds to eat them. The seeds can also be used as math manipulatives and as devices to measure objects.

Poppy Seed Cake

1½	cups sugar	⅓	cup poppy seeds
1	cup butter or margarine	2½	cups flour
4	eggs separated	2½	teaspoons baking powder
1	teaspoon lemon extract	1	teaspoon baking soda
1	cup buttermilk	½	teaspoon salt

Preheat oven to 350 degrees. Soak poppy seeds in buttermilk. Cream butter and sugar. Add egg yolks. Sift dry ingredients and add alternately with poppy seed mixture and creamed mixture. Beat egg whites and fold into batter. Pour into greased Bundt™ pan. Bake for 1 hour.

Fingerplay

Along came the cat, and what did he see?   [Hold hand above brow and look
   around.]
Five little birds, sitting in a tree.   [Hold up five fingers.]
The woodpecker said, "tap, tap, tap."   [Hold up thumb.]
The blackbird said, "okalee."   [Hold up index finger.]
The house sparrow said, "chirp cheep, chirp cheep."   [Hold up middle finger.]
The goldfinch said, "suwee, suwee."   [Hold up ring finger.]
The morning dove said, "who, who, who."   [Hold up pinky.]
The hungry cat said, "it's only me."
Away flew the birds in a great big bunch, and all that was left was feathers
   for lunch.   [Fly fingers away.]

Suggested Home Activities.   Send home a synopsis of *Feathers for Lunch* and inform parents about some of the activities in which the children are involved. Parents can reinforce the concepts by looking for birds in their yard and neighborhood. Suggest to parents that they look for fruits at the grocery store that contain seeds. The children can make up seed collections at home. If any of the children have a pet cat or bird, they might enjoy having their parent bring it to the class for a visit.

Related Literature

Ehlert, Lois. *Eating the Alphabet.*
————. *Growing Vegetable Soup.*
————. *Planting a Rainbow.*
Fleming, Denise. *In the Tall, Tall Grass.*

Maze Activity

THIS YEAR'S GARDEN
by
Cynthia Rylant

Developmental Activities Chart

	Language & Cognitive Development	Fine Motor Art	Gross Motor	Perception	Social Skills	Math	Dramatic Play	Cooking Snack	Science	Music, Fingerplays, Poems
1 Seed Catalogs	X							X		
2 Vegetable Garden									X	
3 All Season Tree	X	X							X	
4 Fingerplay Rhyme	X	X			X					X
5 Cornucopia		X								
6 Corn Toss		X								
7 Family in the Field									X	
8 Gardener Game				X						X
9 Indoor Garden	X	X			X			X		
10 Seed Activities	X	X		X	X					
11 Vegetable Snack 'n Math	X	X		X		X		X	X	
12 Measure Up	X					X				
13 Where Do They Grow?	X								X	
14 Seasons	X	X							X	
15 Tools	X	X				X			X	
16 Potato Activities	X		X		X				X	
17 Vegetable Market	X	X			X		X			
18 Garden Mural	X	X			X				X	
19 Grow and Show	X	X							X	
20 Favorite Vegetables	X				X					
21 Vegetable Pizza	X	X						X		
22 Rain										X
23 Suggested Home Activities	X	X						X	X	
24										
25										
26										
27										
28										
29										
30										

THIS YEAR'S GARDEN
by Cynthia Rylant
Bradbury Press, 1984

This story depicts the anticipation, planning, and hard work that goes into a large rural family's garden. *This Year's Garden* follows the four seasons of the year, looking at the remains of a garden after winter to the bountiful harvest of autumn. The beauty of winter, spring, summer, and autumn are shown in the colorful illustrations.

Seed Catalogs. Uncle Dean and Uncle Joe discussed what they would plant while they waited for the last frost. They planned their garden crops and probably selected seeds from seed catalogs. The class can send for seed catalogs from seed houses. The children can plan an indoor garden and order some seeds for planting.

R. H. Shumway Seedsman
628 Cedar Street
Rockford, Illinois 61101

Burgess Seeds
Box 3000
Galesburg, Michigan 49053

Grace's Gardens
Autumn Lane
Hackettstown, New Jersey 07840

W. Atlee Burpee & Company
300 Park Avenue
Warminster, Pennsylvania 18974

Vegetable Garden (to the tune of "Are You Sleeping?")

Vegetable garden, vegetable garden.
Planting time, planting time.
Make straight rows and drop the seeds,
Thin the plants and pull the weeds.
We work hard! We work hard!

Vegetable garden, vegetable garden.
Harvest time, harvest time.
Shucking corn and snapping beans,
Stew tomatoes, split the peas.
Veggies taste good. Veggies taste good!

All Season Tree. The illustrations show nature's changes occurring in all four seasons. Give each child a large piece of paper. Demonstrate how to fold the paper so that there are four sections. Look at the illustrations again and talk about the appearance of the trees in each season. Using crayons, markers, or watercolors, have children draw a picture of what a tree would look like in winter, spring, summer, and autumn.

Fingerplay Rhyme.   Use the black line master pattern to make objects for telling the rhyme on the flannel board. Children can help recite the words and hold up the correct number of fingers.

> Five big blackbirds pecking all around,
> Sat in the brown stalks on the cold ground.
> One heard the men walk out the back door.
> He flew away and then there were four.
>
> Four big blackbirds pecking all around,
> Sat in the brown stalks on the cold ground.
> One saw some seeds near a faraway tree.
> He flew away and then there were three.
>
> Three big blackbirds pecking all around,
> Sat in the brown stalks on the cold ground.
> One ate his fill where the garden grew.
> He flew away and then there were two.
>
> Two big blackbirds pecking all around,
> Sat in the brown stalks on the cold ground.
> One saw a tomcat asleep in the sun.
> He flew away and then there was one.
>
> One big blackbird pecking all around,
> Sat in the brown stalks on the cold ground.
> One saw the beagle starting to run.
> He flew away and then there were none.

Cornucopia.   Make a large cone-shaped horn of plenty or large harvest basket out of kraft paper. Provide children with grocery advertisements and magazines. Children cut and glue vegetable pictures for the cornucopia.

Corn Toss.   Get several pieces of dried field corn and pull the husks back. Children hold the corn as a dart and toss it into a garbage can or laundry basket.

Family in the Field (to the tune of "Farmer in the Dell")

> The family in the field,
> The family in the field.
> Hi, ho the derry-o,
> The family in the field.

Add these verses and others that children suggest:

> The family buys the seeds.
> The family plants the seeds.

The family picks the weeds.
The family thins the plants.
The family pulls up carrots.   [radishes, etc.]
The family picks the corn.   [beans, etc.]
The family works together.

Gardener Game.   Play a version of the circle game "The Farmer in the Dell," using the words "the gardener in the field." Each child in the circle holds a picture of a different vegetable. The gardener in the center "takes, picks or digs" a vegetable and the child holding that vegetable goes into the center. The game continues when that gardener chooses another vegetable to go into the center.

Indoor Garden.   Many vegetables can be grown inside the classroom in sunny locations on a ledge or window sill. Seeds can be planted in clay pots or milk cartons or bleach containers in which the tops have been cut. Make holes for drainage and place stones or pebbles on the bottom. Place the containers on a tray to collect excess water. Children can mix potting soil and vermiculite in which to plant their seeds. Cherry tomatoes, green peppers, radishes, lettuce, and baby carrots grow well. After planting the seeds, children can observe the growth of their vegetables. How long does it take for growth to appear? How long will it take for the first leaf to appear? Children can compare how the plants look the same and how they look different. They can measure the height of the plants. A chart can be made to show children's estimates/predictions. Later, the actual answer which was observed or discovered can be recorded.

Seed Activities

- Provide seeds for children to sort, graph, and count. Children can compare how the seeds are the same and how they are different. Squash, bean, pea, corn, pumpkin, green pepper, and cucumber seeds are some of the larger seeds little fingers can handle.

- Have children pattern various seeds, such as bean, pea, corn, and so on.

- Cut various shapes from tagboard or cardboard. Have children glue seeds on the shape and attach yarn to make a harvest necklace.

Vegetable Snack 'n Math.   Provide a variety of fresh vegetables such as red and green peppers, cucumbers, zucchini, celery, carrots, broccoli, and cauliflower. Have children compare the color, shape, size, and length of the vegetables. The vegetables can be ordered from shortest to longest. Children should assist in washing, scraping, peeling, cutting, and slicing the vegetables for snack. Children can compare the seeds found inside some of the vegetables. Serve with dip.

8	ounces softened cream cheese	1	tablespoon chopped green pepper
1	cup mayonnaise	1	tablespoon lemon juice
2	medium cucumbers, peeled, seeded, and chopped	½	teaspoon dill weed

Beat cream cheese until smooth. Stir in remaining ingredients until well mixed. Chill.

Measure Up

- Children use a balance scale to find out how many baby carrots weigh the same as a green pepper. Or how many radishes weigh the same as a potato.
- Children use a carrot, cucumber, and other vegetables to measure how long a desk is. The comparison-measurement possibilities are limitless.

Where Do They Grow?   Use the black line master patterns to make vegetables from felt. Set up the flannel board to represent a garden. Place a piece of masking tape or brown felt across the board to show the soil line. A yellow sun, black clouds, and raindrops can be placed at the top. Talk about what the vegetables need to grow—soil, sun, and water. Children place the vegetables above or below the soil line to show where they grow.

Seasons.   Reread the story and talk about the four seasons depicted in the illustrations. Children can talk about the family's activities throughout the year. Children cut out pictures of clothing worn and people engaged in various activities throughout the year to make a season mural.

Tools.   The family used tools like a hoe, rake, spade, shovel, and dibber for preparing the dirt, planting seeds, and caring for their garden. Exhibit real tools or pictures of tools used by gardeners and talk about what they were used for. Put dirt in the sensory table or work in the dirt outside. Children can use miniature tools to represent those used by farmers or gardeners and plant real seeds or little pebbles.

> **Dibber**—A planting stick for poking holes in the soil for seeds. Children can use a pencil or Popsicle™ stick.
>
> **Rake**—A tool that levels and loosens topsoil and removes rocks. Children can use a fork.
>
> **Hoe**—A tool that opens up soil, breaks up clumps, and is used for weeding. Children can use a bent metal spoon or fork.
>
> **Shovel and spade**—A tool used for digging deep into the soil and moving soil. Children can use a spoon or shoe horn.

Potato Activities

- Place white, russet, and red potatoes in a bag. Children estimate the number of potatoes in the bag. Count and compare with the actual amount.
- Children sort, graph, and count the different kinds of potatoes.
- Children weigh the potatoes.
- Potatoes can be arranged from smallest to largest.
- Show a potato and have children estimate the circumference of the potato. Cut a piece of string or yarn to represent their prediction. Lengths can be compared to the actual circumference—which are too long, too short, or just right?

Vegetable Market.   Provide different colors of play dough. Children make a variety of vegetables to sell at a vegetable market. Provide play money, a scale, cash register, bags, a money apron or a fanny pack, fruit baskets/containers for the vegetables, paper and crayons to make signs, and so on. Children can take turns being the sellers and customers.

Garden Mural.   Section off different areas on a large piece of kraft paper to represent a variety of plots where vegetables are planted in a garden. Supply paint in small margarine containers. Cut vegetables, like cucumbers, potatoes, carrots, celery, beets, and zucchini. Children dip vegetables in paint and print vegetables in rows in the designated garden plots. Children can add weeds by making green fingerprints among the growing "plants." Brown fingerprint bugs can also be added to the mural.

Grow and Show.   Children can try these experiments to help them understand the growth process of plants.

- Children fill clear plastic cups with moistened paper towels. They put dried lima beans or red beans inside next to the cup. Keep the glasses in a warm place, making certain that the paper towels stay moist. Children can observe the growth of roots and leaves.
- Plants need water. Children can observe how plants take in water to grow. Place a stalk of celery (cut off the end) in water colored with a few drops of food dye for several hours or overnight. Children observe the change in color of the celery.

Favorite Vegetables.   Talk about how vegetables are used in different ways/forms to make some favorite dishes. Children can vote for their favorite vegetable.

Favorite potato—baked, french fries, potato chips, or mashed potatoes

Favorite corn—corn on the cob, popcorn, canned, or frozen corn

Vegetable Pizza.   Children can prepare this version of pizza.

    2 (8-ounce) packages crescent rolls
    2 (8-ounce) packages cream cheese with chives or add 1 tablespoon of dill
         weed to plain cream cheese
    ¼ cup mayonnaise
    assorted chopped vegetables (cucumbers, tomatoes, broccoli, cauliflower,
         carrots, radishes, etc.)
    shredded cheddar cheese

Preheat oven to 400 degrees. Unroll and place crescent rolls on a slightly greased 11" × 16" pan. Pinch the seams together; make a pizza edge. Bake for 10 minutes. Cool. Mix cream cheese and mayonnaise until smooth. Spread on crust. Top with favorite raw vegetables and shredded cheddar cheese. Cut into small squares.

Rain. The children looked out the window at the falling rain and walked in the spring rains. Teach children a version of the familiar chant "Rain, Rain, Go Away."

> Spring rain go away.
> Come again another day,
> To help our summer garden grow.

Suggested Home Activities. Send home a synopsis of the story *This Year's Garden,* and tell parents about some of the activities their children will be doing at school. Encourage parents to support their young gardeners by helping their child plant some flower or vegetable seeds in egg cartons. The little plants can later be transplanted in larger containers indoors or outside. Suggest that parents introduce new and interesting vegetables to their child in a positive manner. Many children prefer raw vegetables to those that are cooked. Send home a simple, colorful recipe that children can help prepare with a parent.

Cold Vegetable Salad

Salad
1 can whole kernel white corn, drained
1 can small baby peas, drained
1 can French-style green beans, drained
1 cup celery, diced fine
1 cup chopped red or green peppers

Dressing

1	cup sugar	3/4	cup vinegar
1/2	cup oil	1	teaspoon salt
1/4	teaspoon pepper	1	tablespoon water

Combine ingredients for dressing in a saucepan and bring to a boil. Cool. Combine vegetables and pour dressing over all and refrigerate several hours or overnight.

Related Literature

Carle, Eric. *The Tiny Seed.*
Caseley, Judith. *Grandpa's Garden Lunch.*
Ehlert, Lois. *Growing Vegetable Soup.*
McMillan, Bruce. *Growing Colors.*

Fingerplay Rhyme Patterns

Where Do They Grow? Vegetable Patterns

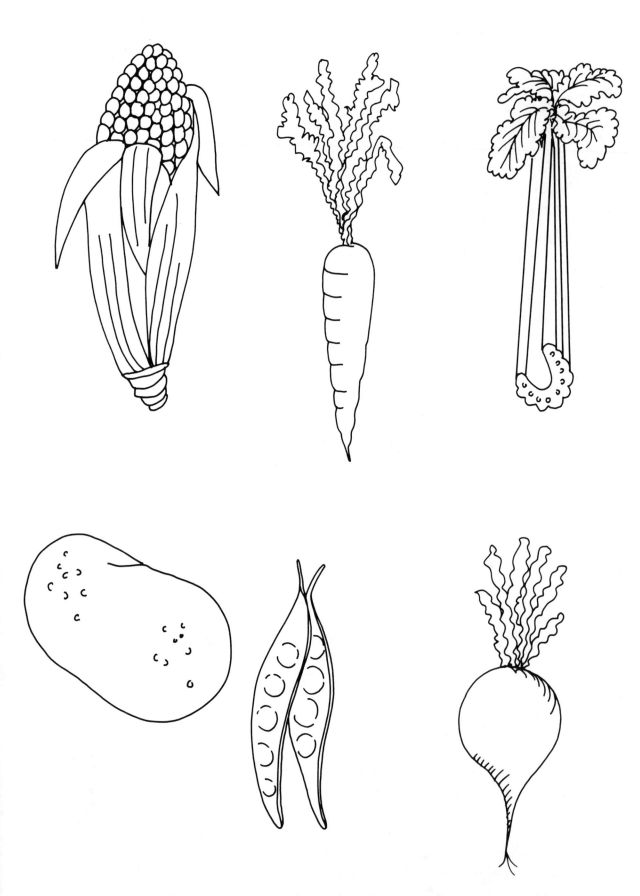

Where Do They Grow? Vegetable Patterns

BONES, BONES, DINOSAUR BONES

by
Byron Barton

Developmental Activities Chart	Language & Cognitive Development	Fine Motor Art	Gross Motor	Perception	Social Skills	Math	Dramatic Play	Cooking Snack	Science	Music, Fingerplays, Poems
1 Dinosaur Dig	X	X		X					X	
2 Tools		X								
3 Dino Drama	X				X		X			
4 Dinosaur Skeleton		X			X					
5 Field Trips	X								X	
6 Fossils	X	X		X					X	
7 Dinosaur Rock										X
8 Five Enormous Dinosaurs		X								X
9 Dinosaur Facts	X					X			X	
10 Tyrannosaurus Teeth	X	X			X	X			X	
11 Just How Long?	X				X	X			X	
12 Walnut Brain!		X					X			
13 The Bones									X	X
14 Dino Dining								X		X
15 Dinosaur Creations	X	X				X			X	
16 Dinosaur Eggs		X			X			X	X	
17 Dinosaur Moves			X			X				
18 How Big?	X			X		X				
19 Dino Path Tracing		X								
20 Prehistoric Puzzle				X						
21 Suggested Home Activities	X							X	X	
22										
23										
24										
25										
26										
27										
28										
29										
30										

BONES, BONES, DINOSAUR BONES
by Byron Barton
Thomas Y. Crowell, 1990

This simple and chantable introductory book about the giants of long ago begins with the search for dinosaur bones and ends with the bones being carefully put together at a museum.

Dinosaur Dig. Introduce the activity by telling children about the work of a paleontologist, a scientist who studies plants and animals of long ago. Place Styrofoam™ pieces, plastic dinosaurs, or cleaned chicken bones (boil chicken bones thoroughly, remove all meat particles, place in a bleach/water solution, drain, and allow to dry) in the sensory table. Cover "dinosaur bones" with sand or cornmeal. Using only small spoons or tongue depressors as their tools, children search for the bones. They can wrap them in tissue paper or waxed paper and then carefully place them in a box.

Tools. Children can make tools for a dinosaur dig. Supply long gift wrapping tubes for the handle, and shovel and pick shapes cut from tagboard or cardboard. Children can decorate the handles with crayons or markers, and cover the precut shape with aluminum foil. Assist children in stapling the handle to the tip with a heavy-duty stapler.

Dino Drama. The simplicity of the story easily lends itself to dramatization. Children can wear hats, tote backpacks, and carry their homemade tools as they chant the words of the story, "Bones, bones, we look for bones." Wooden blocks can be used as bones, and doll blankets or old towels can be used to wrap the "bones" in. Provide boxes and a wagon as children get bones ready to transport to a museum.

Dinosaur Skeleton. Small groups of children can draw their own version of a dinosaur skeleton on large pieces of craft or butcher paper. Children work as paleontologists and complete their dinosaur by gluing on Styrofoam™ pieces.

Field Trips. Visit a museum where dinosaurs are displayed. Visit a local library and select puzzles, books, and tapes that children can use to learn more about dinosaurs.

Fossils. Purchase a set of plastic dinosaurs at a teacher supply store, a museum gift store, or a store that sells birthday favors. Explain to children that a fossil is what remains of an animal or plant that has died. The impression or picture that remains eventually turns to hard rock. Children make fossils by pressing the plastic dinosaur into a piece of play dough. After carefully removing the play dough, the dinosaur imprint remains.

Dinosaur Rock   (to the tune of "Jingle Bells")

> Dinosaurs, dinosaurs.
> Lived so long ago.
> Some ate meat and some ate plants,
> Their teeth were big and strong.
> Dinosaurs, dinosaurs.
> Moved fast or very slow.
> They ruled the land so long ago,
> Now they are dead and gone.

Five Enormous Dinosaurs.   Use this verse as a flannel story by cutting out five dinosaur shapes or as a fingerplay.

> Five enormous dinosaurs, hear how they could roar!
> One stomped away, and then there were four.
> Four enormous dinosaurs, eating a green tree.
> One trudged away, and then there were three.
> Three enormous dinosaurs, in the air they flew!
> One soared away, and then there were two.
> Two enormous dinosaurs, not having any fun.
> One raced away, and then there was one.
> One enormous dinosaur in the blazing sun,
> He went away, and now there are none!

Dinosaur Facts.   Children will enjoy hearing facts about the dinosaurs mentioned in the book. Several activities follow to help children understand the awesome characteristics of dinosaurs.

Tyrannosaurus Rex
- Largest meat-eating dinosaur
- About 50 feet from nose to tail
- Weighed up to 7 tons
- Tall as a telephone pole
- 4-foot jaw, with 60 sharp teeth
- Each tooth was 6 inches long

Apatosaurus
- Used to be called Brontosaurus
- Ate tall vegetation all the time
- Had a long neck
- Waded in marshy swamps
- About 70 feet long
- Weighed about 30 tons
- Had 24 weak, peg-shaped teeth

Stegosaurus
- Ate soft plants, like grass and ferns
- Had a double row of bony plates on its back
- Had four spikes at the end of its tail

- Had a small head and a walnut-size brain
- About 20 feet long
- Weighed about 1½ tons

Ankylosaurus
- Ate plants
- Bony plates covered its body, like armor
- Its head was bone covered, like a helmet
- Had a bony knob at the end of its tail
- Was as long as a car
- Weighed as much as an elephant

Parasaurolophus
- Ate pine needles and leaves
- 30 feet long, 16 feet tall
- Weighed 3 to 4 tons
- Walked on two legs (bipedal)
- Hands were webbed
- Had a duck bill with a hollow 5-foot tube that extended over its shoulder

Gallimimus
- Ate small animals, eggs, and plants
- Resembled a bird, like an ostrich
- 20 feet long, from snout to tail
- Small head, with a long toothless, beak-like jaw
- Ran on two strong legs, three-toed feet with sharp claws
- Short arms with three-fingered hands

Thecodontosaurus
- Probably ate both meat and plants
- 10 feet long, slightly built
- Small head, slender legs and feet, long neck and tail
- Serrated teeth—front teeth were cone shaped and back teeth were flat

Triceratops
- Ate tough plants
- Three horns on its head: one over each eye and one on its nose
- Head ended in a parrotlike beak
- Shield of bone around its head
- About 25 feet long
- Weighed about 5 to 6 tons
- Had a leathery hide

Tyrannosaurus Teeth. Help children understand why Tyrannosaurus Rex was considered the fiercest dinosaur. Make a jaw out of tagboard about 4 feet long. Children glue on Styrofoam™ pieces to represent teeth. Since each tooth was about 6 inches long, children can see how many Styrofoam™ pieces are needed to represent the length of one tooth.

Just How Long? Make several foot-shaped steps out of tagboard or cardboard that are 12 inches long. In a large open area, children can work together and place feet heel to toe to measure out the length of some of the dinosaurs. They can compare which was the longest and which was the shortest. This activity will help children to somewhat comprehend the size of these long-gone creatures.

Walnut Brain!   Remind children that Stegosaurus had a brain the size of a walnut! Children can crack walnuts and eat the meat as a snack.

The Bones   (to the tune of the spiritual "Dem Bones")

> The bones, the bones, the dinosaur bones.
> The bones, the bones, the dinosaur bones.
> The bones, the bones, the dinosaur bones.
> We dig for dinosaur bones!
>
> The claws are connected to the foot bones.
> The foot bones connected to the leg bones.
> The tail bones connected to the end bones.
> The rib bones connected to the back bones.
> The head bones connected to the neck bones.
> We dig for dinosaur bones! [Children can add other parts.]

Dino Dining.   Remind children that meat eaters had sharp teeth for tearing and biting, and plant eaters had flat teeth for chewing. Have children brainstorm foods the meat eaters and plant eaters may have eaten. Serve cocktail hot dogs and broccoli florets at snack and ask children to decide which dinosaur may have eaten each item.

Dinosaur Creations.   Individual children or the entire class can dictate a story about a dinosaur they imagine. Make certain children address such questions as: How big? How tall? How long? What special features does it have (wings, horns, spikes)? What did it eat? How did it move? Children can draw and paint their dinosaur.

Dinosaur Eggs.   Tell children that dinosaurs were thought to be like reptiles. Their babies hatched from eggs just like snakes, lizards, and turtles do. The teacher places a plastic dinosaur in a large balloon and blows it up. Children papier-mâché all around the "egg" using strips of newspaper or plain newsprint and a flour-water paste mixture. They can paint the egg when it has dried (it make take several days). Children care for the egg, making sure to keep it in a warm place in the classroom. Plan a special coming-out party for the dinosaur and serve dinosaur-shaped commercial snacks.

Paste Recipe

   ½   cup flour
   1   heaping tablespoon salt
   1   cup warm water

Mix the flour and salt in a large bowl. Add the warm water and mix with hands. The mixture should be thick and creamy. If necessary, use more flour to thicken the mixture, or more water to thin it.

Dinosaur Moves.   Children move, walk, or run like dinosaurs. Children can stomp with feet wide apart, run with feet wide apart, and walk on all fours. Children can take a certain number of giant steps.

How Big?   Have children brainstorm a list of the largest animals and things they have ever seen. Then play a comparison activity game.

> What's bigger, a dinosaur or a giraffe?
>
> What's bigger, a bike or a car?
>
> What's bigger, an elephant or a gorilla?
>
> What's bigger, a bush or a tree?

Dino Path Tracing.   Children complete the dinosaur path tracing activities by staying within the lines. Two sample black line masters are included.

Prehistoric Puzzle.   Children color a picture of their favorite dinosaur and mount it on a piece of construction paper. The teacher laminates the pictures, cuts them into pieces, and returns them to the children in an envelope. Children can practice assembling their dinosaur puzzle and then trade puzzles with their peers.

Suggested Home Activities.   Send home a synopsis of the story *Bones, Bones, Dinosaur Bones,* and inform parents about some of the activities their children will be doing at school. Be sure to include information about Gallimimus. Families can prepare a meal fit for the dinosaur by scrambling eggs and adding bits of meat and chopped green pepper, broccoli bits, or chopped spinach. Parents can also plan a trip to a local museum where dinosaurs are displayed. If possible, try to visit the museum gift shop—many have a children's section offering affordable souvenirs of their visit.

Related Literature

Aliki. *Digging Up Dinosaurs.*

———. *Dinosaur Bones.*

———. *My Visit to the Dinosaurs.*

Barton, Byron. *Dinosaurs, Dinosaurs.*

Creatures of Long Ago: National Geographic Action Book, published by National Geographic Society, 1988.

Parish, Peggy. *Dinosaur Time.*

Tyrannosaurus Rex eats meat. Trace the path to help him find food.

Triceratops eats plants. Trace the path to help him find food.

BEAR SHADOW
by
Frank Asch

Developmental Activities Chart	Language & Cognitive Development	Fine Motor Art	Gross Motor	Perception	Social Skills	Math	Dramatic Play	Cooking Snack	Science	Music, Fingerplays, Poems
1 Shadow Defined	X								X	
2 Shadow Portraits	X	X							X	
3 Shadow Tag			X						X	
4 Shadow Animals	X		X	X	X		X		X	
5 Bear's Obstacle Course	X		X							
6 Indoor Shadows		X		X					X	
7 Shadow Guess				X					X	
8 Silhouettes on the Wall		X							X	
9 Did You Ever See a Shadow?			X							X
10 Shadow Partners			X							
11 Bear Punchouts		X								
12 Bear's Keys				X						
13 Nail by Number		X				X				
14 A Can of Worms	X			X		X				
15 Shadow Prints		X								
16 Pudding Picture Bears	X	X				X		X		
17 Bear Snacks								X		
18 Bear Rubbings		X								
19 Positions of the Sun	X	X							X	
20 Earth and Sun									X	
21 Suggested Home Activity	X			X					X	
22										
23										
24										
25										
26										
27										
28										
29										
30										

BEAR SHADOW
by Frank Asch
Prentice Hall, 1985

While fishing, Bear is disturbed by his shadow who is scaring the fish away. Bear tries many different solutions, including running away, hiding from, and burying his shadow. Finally, he reasons with Shadow by suggesting a cooperative solution.

Shadow Defined.   Explain to the children that a shadow is a dark area created by an object when it prevents light from shining on a surface. The darkened area is the shape of the object that is blocking the sun or other light. A shadow falls on the side of the object that is opposite the light source. As Bear discovered at midday, his body did not cast a shadow. On a sunny day, take the children outside at different intervals. Tell the children to stand in the same place each time and notice how the shadow moves even though they don't.

Shadow Portraits.   Take the children outside on a sunny day. Have them pose to create shadows. Trace the shadow with chalk, naming body parts as they are traced. Provide the children with colored chalk for coloring in their portraits.

Shadow Tag.   This game of tag should be played outside on a sunny day. One person is chosen to be "It." "It" tries to tag another child's shadow while the children run away from "It." When "It" succeeds, he or she yells "tagged" and the child who is tagged becomes "It."

Shadow Animals.   The children can cooperate, as Bear and Shadow did, to make shadow animals. The children should choose one or two partners. Together they pose in different positions to make shadow animals. The children can experiment with poses or they can try these.

- Stand in a line, back to front, backs to the sun. Experiment with holding heads in different positions, to opposite sides, straight up, or a combination. Experiment with holding arms out to the sides, down to the sides, or up in the air. Together, move like an animal.
- Stand in a line, back to front, crouching on hands and knees. One child stands at the front of the line with arms outstretched, moving slowly while the other children follow behind. Experiment with long and short lines of children.

Bear's Obstacle Course.   When Bear was trying to run away from Shadow, he ran around the pond, through a field of flowers, he jumped over a brook, he hid behind a tree, and he finally climbed up a cliff. Set up an obstacle course outside, representing the obstacles Bear encountered. An example might include running around a small field or group of trees pretending it is a pond, through tall grass or flowers, up and down a jungle gym or slide, or through rungs of a ladder placed flat on the ground. On a sunny day, ask the children to observe their shadows. Is it possible to lose them?

Indoor Shadows. Shadows can be created indoors. Darken the room and turn on an electric light or a large beamed flashlight. Direct the light toward the wall or screen. Any object that stands between the light source and the wall will create a shadow. Children can experiment with hand and finger shadows, by holding up and moving only hands and fingers. A rabbit can be formed by holding up the index and middle fingers while making a circle out of the thumb, ring, and pinky fingers. Encourage the children to experiment with their hands and fingers to make silly shadows.

Shadow Guess. Using an indoor light, the teacher holds a familiar object in front of the light source without letting the children see the object. The children try to guess what the object is by looking at the shadow it creates.

Silhouettes on the Wall. Direct an indoor light toward construction paper that is taped on the wall. One child at a time can sit or stand sideways between the light and the wall. The teacher traces the child's silhouette onto the paper. Children can color in their own silhouettes.

Did You Ever See a Shadow? Sing to the tune of "Did You Ever See a Lassie?" Simply substitute the word "shadow" for the word "lassie." One child at a time is chosen to be the leader. The other children mimic the leader's actions, pretending to be a shadow.

> Did you ever see a shadow? A shadow? A shadow?
> Did you ever see a shadow go this way and that?
> Go this way and that way. Go this way and that way?
> Did you ever see a shadow go this way and that?

Shadow Partners. Divide the children into pairs or ask each child to find a partner. The children can take turns being the leader and the shadow. The leader performs an action while the shadow mimics it as a shadow would.

Bear Punchouts. Use the bear stencil provided. Trace it onto the center of a piece of construction paper. Secure the paper to a carpet square or other soft flat surface. Just as Bear tried to nail his shadow to the ground, the children can hammer a nail around the bear form. As the child taps in a nail and removes it, using a child-size hammer and a flat head nail, small holes will form. When holes have been created around the entire bear, the child can punch out the bear. The negative space form that is left in the construction paper can be used as Bear's shadow.

Bear's Keys. After Bear's nap, Shadow reappeared. Bear quickly got up, ran outside, and tried to lock Shadow in the house. Children can match the keys that Bear might use to lock Shadow in the house. Find 15 to 20 old keys. Trace the key outlines on tagboard, and laminate the tagboard to preserve it. Place the keys in a box or on a tray. Children can match the real key to its outline.

Nail by Number.   Label ten blocks of wood with a numeral from 1 to 10. Provide flat head nails, a child-size hammer, and safety goggles. The children can pound the appropriate number of nails into the blocks of wood, just as Bear tried to nail his shadow to the ground.

A Can of Worms.   Bear used worms from a can to catch a fish. Cover cans with various colors of Con-Tact® paper. Cut wiggly worms out of construction paper in colors that correspond with those of the cans. The children can sort the worms and place them in the corresponding colored can. Increase the difficulty level of the activity by labeling each can with a numeral. Children place the correct number of colored worms in each can.

Shadow Prints.   Fold a piece of construction paper in half. Children can paint a picture on one-half of the page. When the picture is complete, tell them to fold the paper to create a shadow of the picture on the opposite half of the page.

Pudding Picture Bears.   Cut bear shapes out of waxed paper using the stencil provided. Place the waxed paper bears on a plastic tablecloth or on plastic placemats. Mix up a batch of instant chocolate pudding following the directions on the package. Allow the children to do the pouring, measuring, and stirring. Give each child enough pudding to finger paint on their bear. They will enjoy the activity of finger painting as well as licking their fingers clean.

Bear Snacks.   Serve bear-shaped snacks such as Teddy Grahams™ or Bearwiches™. You can also use a bear-shaped cookie cutter to cut toast, bread, and sandwiches. Use spreads such as peanut butter, butter and cinnamon sugar, and honey.

Bear Rubbings.   Cut bears out of tagboard using the bear stencil provided. The children can place a piece of lightweight paper over the stencil and rub over the bear using the side of a crayon. The bears can be cut out and decorated with crayons or markers. Some children might want to punch a hole in the bear, attach a string, and wear the bears around their necks.

Positions of the Sun.   The position of an object in relation to the sun determines where a shadow will fall. This activity will help children visualize how the sun appears to change position in the sky during the course of the day. Use a 12" × 18" sheet of construction paper. Cut a narrow slit across the top of the paper about 2 inches from the top of the paper. Leave a 1-inch border on either side of the paper. Have the children trace and cut a sun which is about 2 inches in diameter, or provide them with a predrawn or precut sun. Attach a string to the back of the sun and secure it in place with tape. Place the string through the slit. Using the string, the children can move the sun along the paper, showing the position of the sun relative to the position of the earth. Ask the children to draw a picture of Bear on the construction paper.

Earth and Sun.   Use a large ball and a smaller ball or globe to illustrate how the sun stays in one place while the earth slowly revolves causing day and night. Explain to the children that night time occurs when part of the ball (the earth) is facing away from the sun. Daytime occurs when that part of the ball (the earth) is facing toward the sun. The concept of the earth revolving around the sun can be illustrated by having the children form a circle. One child stands in the center pretending to be the sun. The children slowly move around the sun just as the earth does.

Suggested Home Activity. Send home a synopsis of *Bear Shadow* and tell the parents about the kinds of activities the children are doing at school. Bedtime can be a difficult time for preschoolers. Parents can talk with their children about what causes shadows on the walls in the bedroom. Tell them to place objects in the path of light, creating shadows of familiar objects. The children will be interested to see that even small familiar items can cast large, sometimes scarey-looking shadows on the wall.

Related Literature

Asch, Frank. *Bear's Bargain.*
————. *Happy Birthday Moon.*
————. *Mooncake.*
————. *SkyFire.*

Bear Punchouts/Pudding Picture Bears/Bear Rubbings Activities

Personal Experience Books

MEATBALL
by
Phyllis Hoffman

Developmental Activities Chart	Language & Cognitive Development	Fine Motor Art	Gross Motor	Perception	Social Skills	Math	Dramatic Play	Cooking Snack	Science	Music, Fingerplays, Poems
1 School Comparison	X					X				
2 Occupations	X									
3 Occupation Graph	X	X				X				
4 Nicknames	X	X		X	X					
5 Class Helpers	X				X					
6 Name Recognition	X	X		X						
7 Class Tree	X	X			X				X	
8 My Day	X	X				X				
9 Favorite Activity Memory Game	X			X	X					
10 Jump Rope	X		X		X					
11 Time to . . .	X					X				
12 Calendar Activities	X			X	X	X				
13 What's the Weather?	X								X	
14 Counting	X				X	X				
15 Role Play	X				X		X			
16 Career Play					X		X			
17 Cooking and Snack Recipes	X	X			X	X		X	X	
18 Class Pets					X				X	
19 Mary Wore a Red Dress					X					X
20 My Mommy Is a . . .	X				X					X
21 Suggested Home Activities	X				X					
22										
23										
24										
25										
26										
27										
28										
29										
30										

MEATBALL
by Phyllis Hoffman
HarperCollins, 1991

Marilyn, nicknamed Meatball by her teacher, attends a day care center with many children. A typical day is represented from the time the children arrive and must separate from their parents until the end of the day. Young children will be able to relate to the range of emotions exhibited by the children as well as the typical school day that is represented. The book lends itself to discussion and activities related to day/night care, the school experience, separation, parent occupations, and being an important member of a group.

School Comparison. Read *Meatball* and discuss with the children the similarities and differences between the day care center that Meatball attends and their school or day care. Make a chart with the headings "Same" and "Different" and record the children's observations. The children can compare schools and count to determine if there are more similarities or differences.

Occupations. Talk about parent occupations. Children can share what they know about where their parents work and what they do at work. Encourage parents to come to the classroom, or write a letter to the class when job schedules don't permit enough time to get away. They can describe their occupation and the responsibilities involved in it. Pictures and/or job-related objects add to the discussion.

Occupation Graph. Prepare a graph with parent occupations listed at the top. If possible, use pictures to represent the occupations. Children can draw pictures of themselves under the occupation category of their parents. Categories of occupations can be used instead of actual job titles. Consider using categories such as working in an office, wearing a uniform to work, day or night work, hospital work, restaurant work, and so on. Children can compare categories on the graph in terms of most/least and more than/less than.

Nicknames. Meatball is a nickname that Julia gave to Marilyn because she is round and yummy. Ask the children about nicknames they may have or nicknames of their family members. Trace around each child on a large sheet of kraft paper, and have the children color themselves and cut out the forms. Write each child's nickname on the body tracings and display them in the classroom. An alternative to the body tracings might be to have the children make self-portraits and label them with their nickname.

Class Helpers. Children's jobs can be compared to parents' work inside and outside of the home. In Meatball's day care center, there was a job for everyone. The jobs were represented pictorially on a "job chart." Have the children brainstorm a list of classroom jobs. Make a chart, listing jobs with picture words. Prepare a name card for each child to display next to the job that he or she is responsible for that day or week. Classroom responsibility helps children to realize that they are a contributing and important member of the group.

Name Recognition. Prepare a name card for each child like those illustrated in the book. Children can use this name card on the job chart and for other classroom activities. Younger children and children with developmental delays may need a pictorial cue next to the name. Either glue a picture of the child on the card, or have the child draw a picture of himself or herself on the card.

Class Tree. Meatball loves her mother, her teacher, and her friend. This can be explained in terms of belonging to special groups of people (family, friends, school). Talk with children about the special groups of people who are important in their lives. In the book, a picture of a tree hangs on the school wall. Make a special class tree. Make the outline of a trunk and branches on a large sheet of paper. The children can make unique leaves by pressing their thumbs and fingers in paint and then on the paper. Explain to the children that each person has unique and special fingerprints. The class tree illustrates they are unique and important members of the class "group." Small photographs of each child can also be used as leaves on the class tree.

My Day. The children can write a book to take home and share with their family and friends. Choose a typical school day. After each activity, ask the children to draw a picture showing what they did. Have them dictate a sentence or two about each picture activity. At the end of the day help the children sequence the activity pictures by reviewing the day. Assemble the pictures into book form.

Favorite Activity Memory Game. Have the children sit in a circle. One child starts the game by saying his or her name and favorite school activity. The next child repeats what the first child said and then adds his or her own name and favorite activity; the game continues until everyone has had a turn. The teacher or friends can help when the list gets long and children have difficulty remembering. The activity can be simplified for younger children and children with auditory memory weaknesses by reducing the number of children in the circle. Another way to simplify the activity is to ask the children to tell about only one other child from the group (e.g., "His name is Pat and he likes the exploration table the best.")

Jump Rope. A favorite outside activity at the day care center is jump rope. Play different games using a jump rope. Jump ropes can be used in a variety of ways depending on the age, physical abilities, and physical limitations of children.

1. Have two children hold the ends of the rope while the other children walk, jump with two feet, or hop with one foot, over and under the rope. Reinforce the positional concepts of high/low, over/under.
2. Give each child a jump rope. Children can step or jump over the rope, experimenting with speed.

3. Using a smooth jump rope, have a tug of war. Draw a line and each team of children tries to be the last to go over the line.

4. Place the jump rope on the ground in the form of a circle. Play music and have children walk, jump, hop, crawl, and tiptoe around the circle. Have the children move fast and slow. Tell the children to go *in* and *out* of the circle.

Directional and positional concepts can be reinforced while playing the various games. Children who are limited by wheelchairs can play many of the games by adapting the directions and movements.

Time to . . .   At the day care center there is a special time for many activities. The schedule includes time to play, work, share, eat, nap, read, and so on. The schedule helps children know what to expect next. They also know what time their parents will come for them. Introduce the concept of time with an activity clock. Cut a clock out of construction paper or tagboard. Mark the hours with pictures depicting a sample activity, typical of that time. Use clip art, pictures cut from magazines, or teacher-made illustrations. The children can look at the clock to predict what comes next. Older children, and those children with more developed temporal and number concepts will benefit from matching numerals with the pictures.

Calendar Activities.   The calendar time offers a wonderful opportunity to include concept development in a variety of areas. Children can count days; match numerals to days; predict what comes next; sequence days, weeks, and numbers; talk about the concepts of yesterday, today, and tomorrow; and follow picture and color patterns. Looking at and discussing the calendar helps children develop a sense and understanding of time. Special days, such as birthdays, field trips, and holidays can be introduced and illustrated using the calendar. Children can visualize and count how many days until the special day. Calendar time also offers children a relaxed time to talk about upcoming or past events and activities that are important to them.

What's the Weather?   At the day care center children talked about and described the weather each day. The children enjoyed thinking up different weather words. Make a weather chart depicting different kinds and combinations of weather. Children can display the day's weather, and adjust it during the day if there is a change in weather. It is interesting for children to note changes in weather and describe the weather in a combination of terms (cold and sunny; part sun, part clouds; rainy and cold; or rainy and warm). Have the children dictate a sentence or more to describe the weather; encourage them to use creative terms like those used at the day care center. Display the weather description for all to see.

Counting.   At lunchtime in the day care center the children clap and count for each other. They count in different languages, thereby celebrating their cultural diversity. Counting is a natural activity in the classroom. Count the days of the week; the months of the year; the children in the class; the number of plates, napkins, and cups on the table; and so on. Count in English, Spanish, French, and Japanese. Send a note to parents encouraging them to share words from languages spoken at home or in homes of friends and relatives. Children will be proud to teach each other the new words and numbers. It is especially important to introduce the concept of cultural diversity in classrooms and schools that tend to be more homogeneous. Sensitivity should be nourished from an early age.

Role Play.   One way young children learn to express and deal with feelings is through creative play. Set up the dramatic play area as a day care center. Children can take turns pretending to be parents, teachers, and each other. Feelings that deal with separation anxieties can be discussed, acted out, and worked through using play as the vehicle. Many of the same kind of anxieties occur when children are left at home with a babysitter. Children can role play parents who are dressed up for work or an evening out, the babysitter who arrives, and the children who are left at home with the babysitter. Provide props for the children, such as dress-up clothes, briefcases, purses, pens and paper (for babysitter instructions), and other items the children might need.

Career Play.   Children will enjoy pretending to be their parents when they go to work. Provide props that represent the occupations and workplaces of parents. An office can be created with a desk, phone, paper and pencils, and so on. Uniforms that are worn by hospital or restaurant workers, firefighters, and police officers can be provided. Most parents will be happy to share props that represent their careers and occupations.

Cooking and Snack Recipes.   Many children eat one or two of their meals at the day care center, as well as snacks. Even though meals are generally prepared for the children, occasionally they enjoy preparing their own food. Cooking with children reinforces many language as well as fine motor, math, and science concepts, including sequencing, pouring, measuring, stirring, observing changes in matter, and experimenting with hot and cold. Children will enjoy preparing these simple recipes for breakfast, lunch, and dinner, and they will be very proud of their accomplishment. Before eating, exchange common pleasantries from different languages, such as *salut* and *bon appetit.*

French Toast

Each child can prepare his or her own serving of french toast. Have each child crack one egg into a large bowl. Add milk (approximately ¼ cup for every two eggs). Whisk together. Heat griddle or frying pan to a medium-high setting; add butter or coat with a nonstick spray. Have each child dip a slice of bread into the egg/milk mixture and place in pan. Fry until golden brown on each side. Serve with syrup, fruit or fruit juice, and milk.

Grilled Cheese Sandwich

Most children enjoy eating grilled cheese—it is a simple lunch that they can prepare individually. Give each child two slices of bread, two slices of American cheese, two pats of butter or margarine, and a dull knife. Have them spread margarine or butter on each slice of bread. Place the cheese between the two unbuttered sides. Preheat a griddle or frying pan to a medium-high setting.

Add the sandwiches buttered side down and cook until golden brown on both sides. The sandwiches can be individualized by shaping and cutting them with a large cookie cutter prior to spreading the butter. Serve with carrot and celery sticks, apple slices, and milk.

Pizza

Children will enjoy preparing their very own individual pizzas for dinner. They might also wish to share and sample their friends' creations. Purchase pre-made 6-inch Italian bread shells and canned pizza sauce. Provide children with various toppings including shredded mozzarella cheese, cooked sausage, pepperoni, chopped green pepper, mushrooms, and chopped onions. Preheat oven to 425 degrees. Give each child a spoon for adding and spreading sauce on their crust. Have them choose the toppings they desire, cover toppings with cheese. Bake for about 10 minutes or until the cheese melts. Cut into triangles. Serve with sliced fruit, cut-up raw vegetables, and milk.

Class Pets. Adding a pet to the classroom helps to bring children together as a group since they can all share in the responsibility and caregiving a pet requires. Choice of a class pet is often dictated by school policy and health department codes. Typical class pets include fish, birds, guinea pigs, hamsters, and gerbils. Pet store owners are able to make suggestions regarding what type of pet is suitable for a particular group's needs. The care of a class pet provides an ongoing science experiment. Children will learn how much and when to feed and water the pet and how to clean up after it. If it is a pet that can be held, they will learn how to hold it appropriately. Children can observe how the pet responds to certain noise and activity levels and changes in temperature, and how the pet adapts to the change of seasons. Some pets need care on weekends and holidays. Families may volunteer to offer temporary care and shelter for the pet, giving their child another opportunity to share the school experience with the family.

Mary Wore a Red Dress. The children at the day care center sang this old familiar song. Each day Julia held up each child's name card, and the children would tell something about what they were wearing. This gives the children the opportunity to recognize their own names and the names of their friends. It also gives children a chance to really observe what they are wearing. All children love to hear their own name in a song:

> Mary wore a red dress, red dress, red dress.
> Mary wore a red dress all day long.

Repeat for each child giving him or her the chance to choose the verse. For example,

> Sascha wore a dinosaur shirt, dinosaur shirt, dinosaur shirt.
> Sascha wore a dinosaur shirt all day long.

My Mommy Is a . . . (to the tune of "Farmer in the Dell"). Sing about parents' occupations:

> My mommy is a firefighter, my mommy is a firefighter, my mommy is a
> firefighter all day long.

My daddy drives a truck, my daddy drives a truck, my daddy drives a big
   truck all night long.

You may wish to substitute children's names for the word "my" or sing the song
as a guessing game. Challenge the children to guess whose parent you are
singing about.

Suggested Home Activities.   Send home a synopsis of *Meatball*. Inform parents of the kinds of activities in which their children are involved. Encourage parents to visit the class to discuss what they do at work. Suggest to parents that
young children can perform simple jobs at home, such as picking up toys, putting
spoons away, and making the bed. This helps to reinforce the concept that there is
work to be done at home, away from home, and at school. Parents can help their
children understand that all family members must work together as a unit. Parents go to work or work at home while children go to day care or school for their
"work."

Related Literature

Oxenbury, Helen. *First Day of School.*
Rogers, Fred. *Going to Day Care.*
Tyler, Linda Wagner. *Waiting for Mom.*
Wolde, Gunilla. *Betsy's First Day at Nursery School.*

A CHAIR FOR MY MOTHER
by
Vera B. Williams

Developmental Activities Chart	Language & Cognitive Development	Fine Motor Art	Gross Motor	Perception	Social Skills	Math	Dramatic Play	Cooking Snack	Science	Music, Fingerplays, Poems
1 Squeeze Painting		X								
2 Blue Tile		X		X		X				
3 Too Tired	X				X					
4 Special Chairs		X		X						
5 Coin Count and Sort				X		X				
6 Choice Chairs	X	X		X		X				
7 Fire Safety	X		X							
8 Fire Safety Song										X
9 Stop, Drop, Roll	X		X							
10 Crawl Under Smoke and Flames			X							
11 Meet the Firefighter	X				X					
12 Down at the Fire Station										X
13 Fire Hose Fun	X		X	X		X				
14 Hose Painting		X								
15 Play Dough Fun		X		X						
16 Ladder Climbing			X				X			
17 Fire Play							X			
18 Boot Relays			X		X					
19 Noodle Hoses		X								
20 Hat Sequence						X				
21 Cooperative Coloring		X			X					
22 Target Practice			X	X						
23 Fire Station Breakfast								X		
24 Suggested Home Activities	X				X	X				
25										
26										
27										
28										
29										
30										

A CHAIR FOR MY MOTHER
by Vera B. Williams
Mulberry Books, 1982

A young girl tells the story of how she, her grandmother, and mother worked to save coins to purchase a comfortable new chair. After a fire destroys their belongings, many friends donated necessary items. The one item still missing was a comfortable chair in which to relax.

Squeeze Painting. The girl in the story sometimes helps her mother at the Blue Tile Diner. One of her jobs is filling ketchup bottles. Fill squeezable ketchup bottles with fingerpaint. The children squeeze the paint onto fingerpainting paper to make pictures. The children can use their fingers and hands to spread the paint.

Blue Tile. The girl's mother works as a waitress at the Blue Tile Diner. The diner was probably given that name because of its blue tile decor. Cut 2" × 2" squares out of blue construction paper. The children can make tile designs and patterns by gluing the "tile" on paper.

Too Tired. The girl's mother was so tired after work some days that she would fall asleep on a kitchen chair. Occasionally, all children observe exhausted parents. All parents feel the stress of too much work and too little relaxation time at one time or another. Begin a discussion by asking the children why the girl's mother fell asleep on a hard kitchen chair. As a group, the children can brainstorm things they can do to help when "Mom" and "Dad" are tired after working all day. Even young children can help set and clear the table, pick up toys, put on pajamas, and brush teeth, with very little help.

Special Chairs. The girl, her mother, and grandmother knew exactly what their special chair would look and feel like. Reproduce the black line master of the chair for each child. Provide them with fabric swatches in various colors and textures (corduroy, velvet, satin, fur, and so forth). The children can upholster their special chair with the fabric(s) of their choice.

Coin Sort and Count. Save coins until you have an assortment of the various denominations, or use play money. Label five containers with a picture of a penny, nickel, dime, quarter, or half dollar. The children can sort through the coins and put them into the appropriate container. When the containers are full, the children can estimate how many coins are in each container. Help them count the coins and check their estimates with the actual number.

Choice Chairs.   Provide the children with an assortment of old magazines, catalogs, and newspaper advertisements. Tell the children to look for and cut out any chair pictures they find. Glue the chairs on heavy paper or tagboard and laminate them. Ask the children to sort the pictures in as many different ways as they can. Attributes for sorting might include color, size, covering, or the room of the house in which it would go. After sorting and classifying the pictures, the children can count the chairs in the various categories. Prepare a graph by making a pictorial representation of the category at the top of the page; fill in the correct number of squares under the pictures of each category.

Fire Safety.   The girl and her mother lost their chair along with many other belongings to a fire. Children need to know what they can do to prevent fires from occurring and what to do in the event a fire starts.

1. Always give matches and lighters to a grown up. Never try to light a match or a lighter.
2. Never play near a hot stove, oven, iron, or fireplace.
3. Clean up trash in the basement.
4. Plan a fire escape route with parents.
5. If there is a fire in the house, leave immediately. Don't go back for anything.
6. Learn to dial 911 (or other appropriate telephone number) to ask for help.
7. Learn how to stop, drop, and roll in case your clothes catch fire. Teach the technique to a friend.
8. Practice crawling low in smoke.
9. Talk with firefighters about how they help you and how you can help them.
10. Never hide from a fire. If you can't get out of a room, the firefighter needs to be able to find you.

Fire Safety Song (to the tune of "Do You Know the Muffin Man?")

Do you know the firefighter? The firefighter? The firefighter?
Do you know the firefighter?
She is a friend to us.

Learn to dial 911. 911. 911.
Learn to dial 911.
If your house has a fire.

Learn to stop and drop and roll. Stop, drop, and roll. Stop, drop, and roll.
Learn to stop and drop and roll.
If your clothes catch on fire.

Learn to crawl under smoke and flames. Smoke and flames. Smoke and flames.
Learn to crawl under smoke and flames.
So you will be safe.

Never play with matches or lighters. Matches or lighters. Matches or
    lighters.
Never play with matches or lighters.
Because it could start a fire.

Give matches to a grown-up. A grown-up. A grown-up.
Give matches to a grown-up.
So you will stay safe.

Encourage children to make up additional verses.

Stop, Drop, Roll.   Teach the children what to do if their clothes catch on fire.
All children should practice this drill. Stop in your tracks. Drop to the floor. Roll
back and forth to put out the flames.

Crawl Under Smoke and Flames.   Explain to the children that heat rises so
the safest place to be in a smoke-filled room is on the floor. Practice crawling under smoke and flames by setting up an obstacle course in the classroom for children to crawl through. Children can crawl under a course made up of chairs,
tables, desks, and other items.

Meet the Firefighter.   Children need to know that firefighters are community
helpers. When firefighters are dressed in full gear, they can be quite frightening.
Take a field trip to the fire station or ask a firefighter to visit the classroom. Ask
the firefighter to show the firefighter clothes to the children and allow them to
watch while putting the gear on piece by piece. Some children might be interested
in trying on the clothes, helmet, and face mask. When children understand that
there is a friendly person underneath all the gear, they are less likely to hide from
the firefighter in the event of a fire.

Down at the Fire Station (to the tune of "Down at the Station")
    Down at the fire station early in the morning.
    The firefighters wait to get a call.
    When a fire call comes.
    They all slide down the fire pole.
    Ding, ding, ding, ding, off they go.

    First they check the house out.
    For people and their pets.
    Then they put the ladder way up high.
    Soon the water squirts out of the fire hose.
    Squirt, squirt, squirt, squirt, out the fire goes.

Fire Hose Fun.   Cut an old garden hose into graduated lengths just as firefighters use hoses of varying lengths. The children can sequence the fire hoses from
longest to shortest and shortest to longest. The hoses can also be used to play
games such as jumping or hopping over the hose, crawling under the hose, and
walking between the hoses.

Hose Painting.   Provide the children with tempera paint, paper, and straws to
be used as hoses. Place a spoonful of paint on the paper. The children can blow
through the fire hose to spread the paint around the paper.

Play Dough Fun.   Children can manipulate play dough to make fire theme objects.

- Roll dough into lengths of fire hose.
- Roll dough into two long lengths and into many shorter lengths to make a firefighter's ladder.
- Roll dough or shape dough into circles, squares, and rectangles. Assemble them in the shape of a fire truck or house.

Ladder Climbing.   Firefighters must climb up ladders to put out many fires. Children can pretend to be firefighters when climbing up the slide ladder and then sliding down the pole (slide). If a climbing structure with a pole is available, children will be able to climb the ladder and slide down the pole. A short collapsible-type A-frame ladder can be used indoors. Children can climb up and down the rungs while an adult holds the ladder steady. A long ladder can be placed on the floor. Children can practice climbing through the rungs.

Fire Play.   Set up a fire station in the dramatic play area. Provide old rubber rain coats, rubber boots, lengths of garden hose, and fire helmets. These items can often be obtained from the local fire station. The children can pretend to eat and sleep at the fire station in between fire calls.

Boot Relays.   Borrow old fire boots from the local fire station or provide old rubber rain boots. Divide the children into teams of four or five children. Use masking tape or chalk to make a starting line and goal line. At the sound of the fire bell, the first child from each team runs to the goal line and back to the starting line wearing fire boots. He or she removes the boots and gives them to the next child in line who puts on the boots and runs the same course. When the runner returns, he or she sits down at the back of the line. When the entire team is sitting, the race is over. The relay can be played in a noncompetitive way by not determining which team won or lost.

Noodle Hoses.   Children can make fire hoses by stringing manicotti noodles. Provide children with different lengths of string or yarn. Tie a knot in one end and wrap masking tape around the other end to make stringing easier. When the hose is complete, tie a knot to hold the noodles in place.

Hat Sequence.   Firefighter hats are identified by number. Reproduce ten copies of the fire hat black line master. Cut out and color the hats. Label each hat with a numeral from 1 to 10. The children can sequence the hats in numerical order.

Cooperative Coloring.   The girl in the story worked cooperatively with her mother and grandmother to save money for a new chair. The children can work cooperatively to color a large fire engine to display in the classroom. On a large sheet of kraft paper, make the outline of a fire engine. It can be as simple as a large rectangle with circles for wheels. Provide the children with plenty of red or yellow crayons, markers, or paint. Together they can work to color in the fire engine.

Target Practice.   Firefighters must know how to aim the fire hose at the source of the fire. Children will enjoy using empty squirt bottles to shoot water at a target. Place a target in the exploration table, sink, large bucket, or outside. Children squirt water, trying to hit the target. The target can be a simple object such as a plastic ball or block.

Fire Station Breakfast.   Firefighters must eat a good breakfast to provide the energy they will need to fight fires. Children can help prepare this healthy breakfast to eat at the fire station.

Firefighter Pancakes

1	egg	½	teaspoon baking soda
2	tablespoons oil	½	teaspoon salt
1	teaspoon honey	1¾	cups flour
½	teaspoon baking soda	1½	cups buttermilk

Blend ingredients together. Fry on a hot griddle. Yields 12 regular-size pancakes or 24 small pancakes.

Serve with Firefighter Fizzy Drink:

2	10-ounce packages frozen strawberries
1	cup orange juice
2	bananas
20	ounces lemon-lime soda

Combine berries, banana, and juice. Blend until smooth, stir in soda.

Suggested Home Activities.   Send home a synopsis of *A Chair for My Mother.* Inform parents of the kinds of activities their children are doing at school. Parents can reinforce the concepts of saving money and fire safety at home.

- Suggest to parents that the entire family save change in a jar. Together, the family can decide on a special purchase or activity for which to save. All family members will be surprised to see how quickly the pennies can add up. Saving for something special helps children appreciate the value of saving money at an early age.

- Encourage parents to install and/or check smoke detectors on a regular basis. It is suggested that a battery check be done at least once a month.

- Every family should have a fire escape route with which all family members are familiar. Local firefighters will be happy to help a family determine the most efficient escape route. Firefighters also can help families with fire safety checks in the home.

- Parents should review with their child fire safety rules and procedures to follow in case of a fire.

Related Literature

Maass, Robert. *Fire Fighters.*
Smith, Maggie. *My Grandma's Chair.*

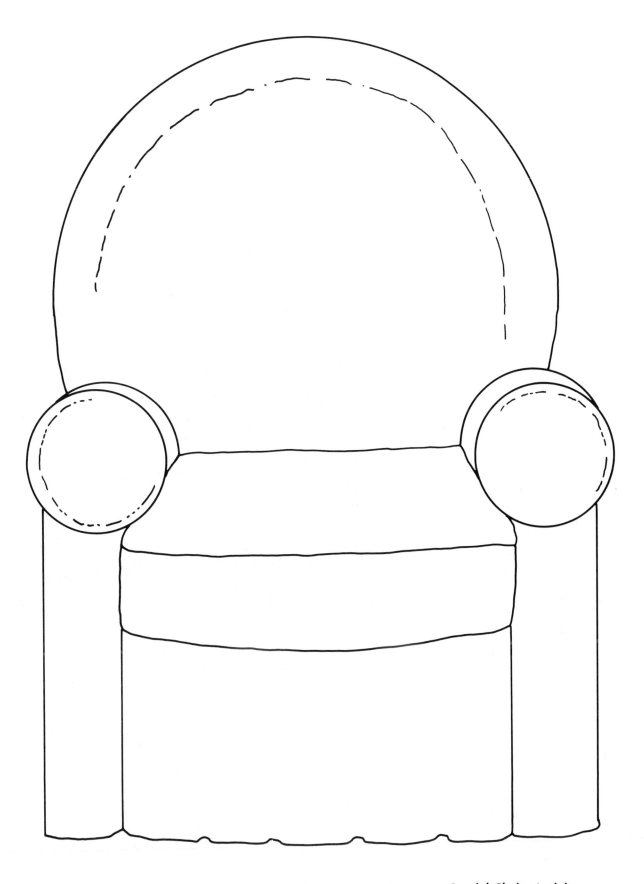

Special Chairs Activity

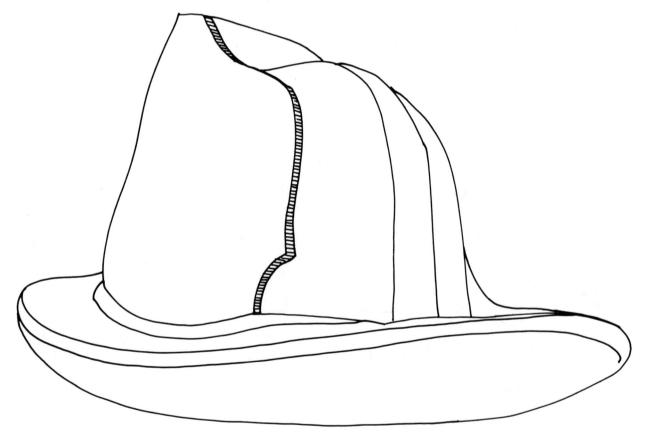

Hat Sequence Activity

GOODBYE HOUSE
by
Frank Asch

Developmental Activities Chart	Language & Cognitive Development	Fine Motor Art	Gross Motor	Perception	Social Skills	Math	Dramatic Play	Cooking Snack	Science	Music, Fingerplays, Poems
1 Moving Day	X									
2 Home Memories	X									
3 Home Sweet Home	X	X			X					
4 Family Memories	X									
5 Furniture Grouping	X					X				
6 Dream House		X		X						
7 Carpet Maze Relay			X		X					
8 Pack It Up!		X			X		X			
9 My New Block										X
10 My House		X								X
11 Construction Site	X	X			X		X			
12 Carpenter's Tools	X						X			
13 Cracker House		X								
14 My Special Place	X	X								
15 What's It Made Of?	X			X						
16 New Friends	X	X			X					
17 Neighborhood Walk			X			X				
18 Household Tracing		X		X						
19 Empty-Full	X		·	X		X				
20 Cookie Jar	X	X			X	X		X		
21 Suggested Home Activities	X	X			X					
22										
23										
24										
25										
26										
27										
28										
29										
30										

GOODBYE HOUSE
by Frank Asch
Prentice Hall, 1986

Moving can be a difficult experience for anyone, including Little Bear. After the moving van is loaded and the family is ready to move to their new house, Little Bear is not quite ready to leave. He takes one last look at all his favorite places in and around the house, remembering how it looked before, and says goodbye to each room.

Moving Day. Little Bear, Papa, and Mama packed their belongings in the moving van. Play a memory game where children remember two to six items packed in the van. Challenge the children to repeat the items in order. For example, Papa put a chair, two lamps, and a dresser in the van. What did Papa put in the van?

Home Memories. The bear family walked through the house and remembered everything that was once in its now-empty rooms. Have children brainstorm furniture and household items that could go in each room—dining room, kitchen, living room, bedroom, bathroom, attic, cellar/basement.

Home Sweet Home. The teacher can sketch a cutaway home, with all the rooms included, on a large piece of craft paper. Divide the children into cooperative groups. Each group would be responsible for completely furnishing a room of the house. Provide magazines, catalogs, and lots of glue as children get the house ready for move-in day.

Family Memories. Memories are more than the furnishings of a home, they are made from the day-to-day activities and special events each family shares and experiences. The teacher names an activity, and children name where the activity occurs in their home. Remind children that there are no incorrect responses, since all families are different.

In your family, where do you open birthday presents, listen to stories, read the newspaper, clean the paintbrushes, follow a recipe, frost a cake, fold the laundry, roast marshmallows, store boxes and old toys, get weighed, pack a picnic lunch, rake the leaves, make the bed, put puzzles together, fix a bike? The list is unlimited.

Furniture Grouping.   Using the house that the children "furnished" in their groups, graph furniture found, for example, chairs, tables, beds, dressers, and nightstands. Children count the number of each item found in the house, graph, and compare the results. Which item has the most, which item has the least?

Dream House.   Precut pieces of cardboard and ridged packing materials that are difficult for children to cut themselves. Provide construction paper, sandpaper, waxed paper, aluminum foil, and varied materials so that children can cut out squares, triangles, rectangles, octagons, and circles of different sizes and textures. Children glue pieces on tagboard to represent the walls, windows, doors, roof, and other parts of their dream house. Demonstrate to children how a roofer overlaps shingles for the house. They can try overlapping their paper pieces to get a shingle effect.

Carpet Maze Relay.   Set up a maze/course in the gym using carpet squares. One child from each of two teams completes the maze by moving scooter boards behind, between, in front of, and around the carpet squares. The first team to finish wins. Children can propel their scooter boards in a prone, kneeling, or sitting position.

Pack It Up!   The housekeeping corner can be the site for a move to a new location. Provide different-sized boxes, newspapers, Styrofoam™ pieces, tape, and markers to "label" the contents of each box. Children carefully wrap all the items and place them in boxes. Ask children how and why the Styrofoam™ pieces are used by movers. A wagon can serve as the moving van.

My New Block (to the tune of "Home on the Range")

>Home, home on my new block.
>Where the fun and friends never stop!
>Sharing secrets and toys
>With the girls and the boys.
>And our smiles show we're happy all day!

My House (fingerplay)

>I'm going to build a little house,   [Fingers form roof.]
>With windows big and bright.   [Hold up two index fingers and
>   thumb.]
>With chimney tall and curling smoke,   [Stand with arms up in the air.]
>Drifting out of sight.
>In winter when the snowflakes fall,   [Hands flutter down.]
>Or when I hear a storm,   [Hand cupped to ear.]
>I'll go sit in my little house,   [Sit down.]
>Where I'll be snug and warm.   [Cross arms over chest.]

Construction Site.   The woodworking area of the classroom can be turned into a construction site where children become carpenters building a new home. Provide wood scraps (free of splinters), cardboard, sandpaper, hammers, nails, screws, screwdrivers, a hand drill, wood glue, and aprons for the carpenters to wear. Children can use pencils, paper, and rulers for drawing plans before they begin construction. They use problem-solving skills as they experiment with the concepts of size, balance, and spatial relationships. Tempera paint can be provided to add the final touch to their house.

Carpenter's Tools.   Use the black line master provided. Children name each item pictured and circle only those used by carpenters. They tell how each item is used or pantomime how each is used so the other children can guess the tool.

Cracker House.   Graham crackers can be used to build a house. Rectangular pieces can be carefully scored and gently broken at the line to make square- or triangular-shaped pieces. The work surface should be covered with a large piece of waxed paper. Place one graham cracker square on the paper for the bottom of the house. Start building by using ready-made frosting as the mortar that holds the walls together and the roof in place. Patient adult volunteers can assist children in holding the pieces together until the frosting is firm. Wait several hours until the house becomes sturdy before decorating. Licorice ropes and other candy can be used to form the doors and windows.

My Special Place.   Children draw a picture of their favorite place in their home. They dictate a story about why it is a special place.

What's It Made Of?   A house and its furnishings are made of many different things. Take a walk in the neighborhood and in the school building; touch and describe how various objects feel. Children can tally and record things made of brick, wood, plastic, leather, and metal.

New Friends.   Children need to make new friends when they move into a new home and neighborhood, and attend a new school. Brainstorm a list of games and activities children like to do with their friends. Compose a class letter telling an imaginary new friend things they will be doing together. Students cut out pictures of children engaged in various play activities to make a friendship collage.

Neighborhood Walk.   Take a walking field trip around the school neighborhood. Children can count doors, windows, mailboxes, swing sets, garbage cans, garden hoses, and so on. Have children guess which of the homes may have children living in them and ask how they can tell.

Household Tracing.   Children trace around a variety of household items on a large piece of kraft paper. Then they can take turns matching the actual object to its traced silhouette.

Empty-Full.   Baby Bear walked through the empty house and for a moment he remembered when each room was full.

- Brainstorm things that could fill an empty mailbox, refrigerator, tool box, closet, medicine cabinet, toy chest, and so on.
- Fill the sensory table with sand, water, or rice. Provide a variety of containers for pouring, filling, and emptying.

Cookie Jar. Welcome a new family into the neighborhood with a plate of cookies, or share cookies with friends old and new. Children recite the verse and then make cookies.

> A house should have a cookie jar.
> To welcome friends both near and far.

Nutty Pecan Bars

½ cup butter
½ cup margarine
½ cup white sugar

Preheat oven to 350 degrees. Cook the ingredients and stir constantly until the mixture comes to a rolling boil. Let stand for 2 minutes. Line a large jelly roll pan with 48 Waverly™ or Club™ crackers. Pour sugar mixture over crackers and sprinkle 1 cup finely chopped pecans on top. Bake for 10 minutes. Cool and break apart. Remove bars from pan while still warm.

Suggested Home Activities. Send home a synopsis of the story *Goodbye House* and inform parents of some of the activities the children will be doing at school. This would be a perfect time to reinforce to parents the importance of giving their child simple household jobs and responsibilities. Putting toys away, making their bed, or setting the table are jobs that will help children feel like valued family members. Stress the importance of helping their child learn his or her home address. Send home a copy of the black line master. Parents and child can have fun "moving into the empty house." The activity reinforces fine motor skills and vocabulary.

Related Literature

Aliki. *We Are Best Friends.*
Komaiko, Leah. *Annie Bananie.*
Malone, Nola Langner. *A Home.*
Tsutsui, Yoriko. *Anna's Secret Friend.*

Name each object; then circle all the tools a carpenter would use. Tell how each tool is used.

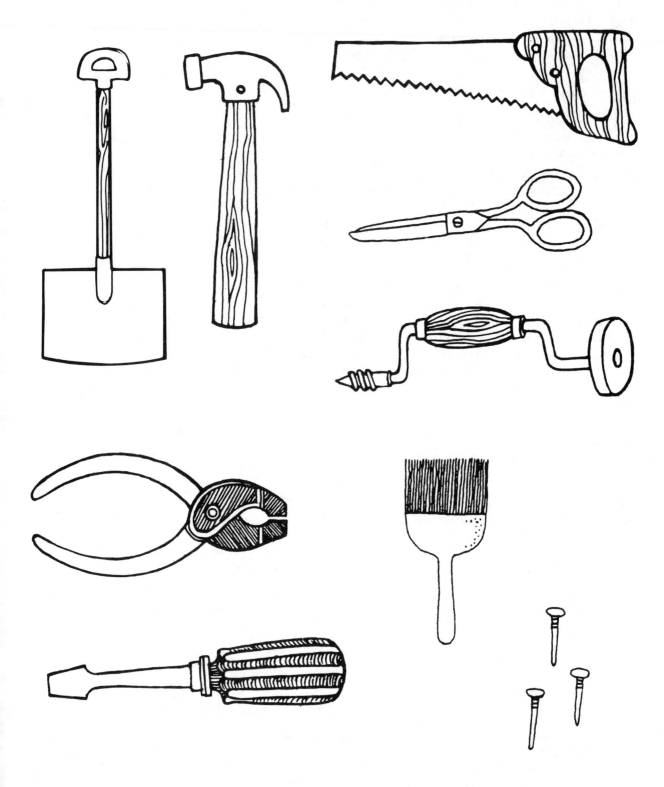

Carpenter's Tools Activity

Draw a picture or cut out a magazine picture of something that could go in each room of the house.

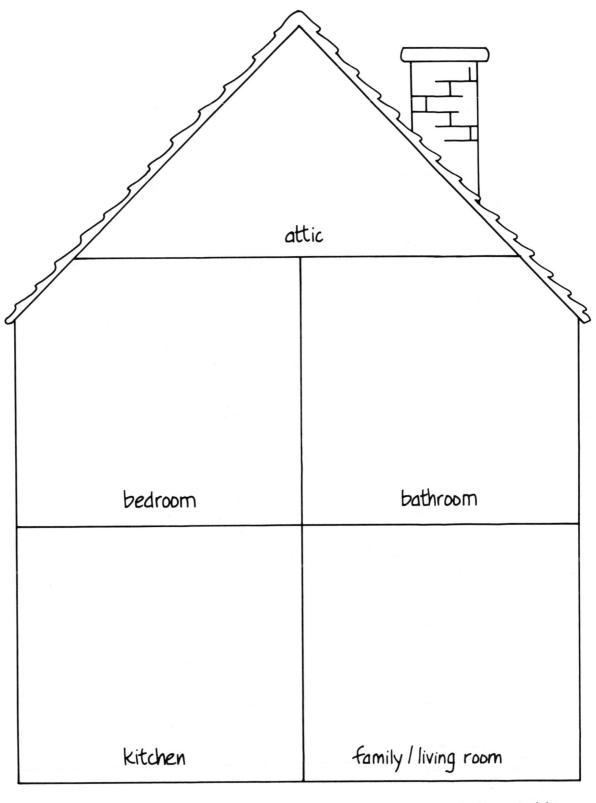

Home Activity

PETER'S CHAIR
by
Ezra Jack Keats

Developmental Activities Chart

	Language & Cognitive Development	Fine Motor Art	Gross Motor	Perception	Social Skills	Math	Dramatic Play	Cooking Snack	Science	Music, Fingerplays, Poems
1 Look at Me Now	X				X					
2 Picture Match-ups	X			X	X					
3 Flannel Board Families	X				X					
4 Toys	X			X		X				
5 Babies Are People	X				X	X				
6 Watch Me Grow	X				X	X			X	
7 Me Dolls		X		X						
8 Sound Toys		X		X						
9 Texture Books	X	X		X					X	
10 Family Graph	X					X				
11 Family Albums	X				X					
12 Baby Blankets		X								
13 Look What I Eat	X	X							X	
14 Dress the Baby		X								
15 Dramatic Play					X		X			
16 Exploration Table							X	X		
17 Baby Moves			X							
18 Snacks								X		
19 Poem										X
20 The Family										X
21 Suggested Home Activities	X				X					
22										
23										
24										
25										
26										
27										
28										
29										
30										

PETER'S CHAIR
by Ezra Jack Keats
Harper & Row, 1967

Peter feels displaced when his parents paint his baby furniture pink for his new sister Susie. He decides to run away and brings along his special chair, his only baby item that hasn't been painted. Upon sitting in his chair he finds that he has grown and no longer fits in it. This Reading Rainbow selection touches on many feelings that are familiar to children when a new sibling arrives. The book lends itself to activities and discussion related to a new baby, family, and individual growth.

Look at Me Now. Ask parents to send in a baby picture and a recent photograph of their child. Display the photographs in a special area. The children can tell about what they could do when they were a baby (cry, eat, sleep) and what they can do now (play, sing, climb).

Picture Match-ups. Use the baby pictures and current photographs. They can be placed in a small plastic bag if they are pictures that parents want to preserve. Have children try and match the baby picture to the corresponding "big kid" picture.

Flannel Board Families. Provide a variety of flannel board people shapes including women, men, boys, girls, and boy and girl babies. Give each child the opportunity to select and tell about their family members. Some children might want to include extended family members who live in the same house. Provide enough cutouts for children who have families and step-families who live separately.

Toys. Preschool and primary-aged children enjoy exploring baby toys, but lose interest fairly quickly when more age-appropriate toys are available. Display a variety of baby toys and "big kid" toys for the children to explore. After giving the children ample time with the toys, place the toys in a "feely bag" or large pillowcase. Ask the children to identify a toy using only their sense of touch. When the toy has been identified, ask the child to classify it as a baby toy or a "big kid" toy. Label two toy boxes, one for each group of toys. The children may decide that some toys are appropriate for either group; in that case, provide a third toy box.

Babies Are People. Many children have never seen a baby close up. Help children to realize that babies are just small people. Use a realistic looking doll to compare baby bodies with children bodies. Baby bodies are the same, just smaller. Have the children measure the "baby" with string, ribbon, unifix™

cubes, blocks, and other common items. Children can measure the baby's arms, legs, head, and trunk. Next have the children measure each other and the teacher. Children will be aware that we all have the same body parts (arms, legs, a head), but in different sizes. If possible, invite a parent with a baby to visit.

Watch Me Grow. Create a growth chart from a large sheet of kraft paper, or purchase a ready-made growth chart. Measure the children monthly so they can watch themselves grow. If possible, bring a scale into the classroom for weighing children at the same times. Keep a graph of the children's height and weight near the growth chart for recording the children's growth. Children can compare tallest, shortest, heaviest, and lightest and who weighs more and less. Keep track of who grew the most in a month, who stayed the same, and so on. Stress that babies, children, and adults come in different shapes, sizes, and colors and also that we all grow at different rates. Ask parents for the children's birth size and talk with the children about how much they have grown since they were born.

Me Dolls. Use the pattern provided to make dolls for the children to decorate and dress to represent themselves. Cut the body pieces out of tagboard and attach them with brad fasteners. The bodies can move just as the children do. The dolls can be dressed and decorated with markers, colored paper, or fabric and yarn.

Sound Toys. Babies listen to sound and turn toward it. The children can make sound toys for their new sibling or another baby. Have the children put a handful of dried beans or rice in a small margarine container and secure the lid. Cover the container with brightly colored Con-Tact® paper. This will make the sound toy visually stimulating and also keep the lid permanently in place.

Texture Books. Babies and young children enjoy touching and feeling a variety of textures. The children can create a texture book to share with a younger sibling or relative. Children can glue shapes that have been cut from different textures on the pages of a book. Books can be bound with yarn. Provide a variety of textures such as sandpaper, satin, corduroy, sticky paper (the back side of Con-Tact® paper), bumpy crumbled foil, and shiny smooth foil. Cut the textures into a variety of shapes and glue one on each page. The children can write a word or two labeling each textured shape. Stress to the children that the baby will need to be closely supervised by a parent or big brother or sister, so he or she doesn't place the book in his or her mouth.

Family Graph. Prepare a graph with pictorial representations of family members across the top; include men, women, boys, and girls. Down the left-hand side of the paper put pictorial representations of the class members. Illustrate under family members how many of each are in the children's families. Children can compare families in terms of most/least boys and girls, most children, least children, most members, and least members.

Family Albums. Designate a day for each child to bring a picture album to school. The children can share pictures and stories that explain the pictures to their classmates. Parents can help their child make up a special album with pictures of their child taken at different times such as vacations, birthdays, and special holidays.

Baby Blankets.   The children can make baby blankets for their new sibling or favorite doll. Provide pieces of soft fabric large enough to cover a doll or newborn baby. The children can use scissors to snip and fringe around the outside of the fabric for decoration.

Look What I Eat.   Older siblings appreciate their role as a "big kid" when they have the opportunity to compare the delicious food and snacks they eat with what the new baby eats. Talk with the children about the function of their teeth. Have them look in the mirror and count their teeth. Compare their teeth to those of a newborn or older baby. The children will then understand why they get to eat fun foods such as apples, ice cream, popcorn, hamburgers, and pizza. Talk about new babies only being able to drink warm milk, and older babies needing soft, mushy food. Give the children magazines in which to look for their favorite foods. Have them cut out the foods and mount them on construction paper or body tracings of themselves. Ask the children to try and find baby foods to mount separately.

Dress the Baby.   Provide the children with an assortment of dolls and doll clothes. The children will enjoy dressing and undressing the dolls while they practice their buttoning, zipping, snapping, and tying skills.

Dramatic Play.   Set up the dramatic play area as a nursery. Provide dolls, a crib, a high chair, a baby seat, a variety of baby clothes, bibs, diapers (old cut up sheets work well), and blankets. The children can make a sign that says, "Shh, Baby Sleeping!" If a rocking chair is available, the children can rock their babies to sleep. Children express feelings through play. Using dramatic play as the vehicle, many children can work through their new feelings regarding their new role in the family in a safe environment.

Exploration Table.   Water play can be tied into the new baby theme. The children can practice bathing their babies and washing baby bottles, diapers, and clothes. Stock the water table with dolls, baby soap and shampoo, "dirty" baby clothes and bottles, and plenty of towels.

Baby Moves.   Children can pretend they are babies when they move like babies. Discuss with the children the stages babies go through when learning to be mobile. They lie on their tummies and hold up their heads. They roll from front to back, then back to front. They creep on their tummies and then crawl on their knees. They pull themselves up on furniture and then learn to walk, one step at a time. Finally, they learn to run, jump, hop, gallop, and skip. The children can practice the movements. Contrast "baby moves" with favorite "big kid" games such as tag; "Duck, Duck, Goose"; and kickball.

Snacks.   Serve snacks that are smooth and can be eaten by older babies, as well as fun foods that only "big kids" eat. Sample baby snacks that might include apple sauce, bananas, single Cheerios™, cooked carrots, and mashed sweet potatoes.

Serve favorite snack foods to contrast the difference between what babies and "big kids" can eat. Examples are popcorn, ice cream, crackers, raisins, cut-up vegetables and dip, muffins, and toast with favorite spreads.

Poem

Before I was big   [Stand up tall.]
I was very, very small.   [Crouch down.]
Then I was short.   [Stay down.]
But now I'm TALL!   [Pop up.]

The Family

This is my father.   [Hold up thumb.]
This is my mother.   [Hold up index finger.]
This is my brother tall.   [Hold up middle finger.]
This is my sister.   [Hold up ring finger.]
This is the baby.   [Hold up pinky.]
Oh, how we love them all.   [Squeeze fingers with other hand to give a hug.]

Suggested Home Activities.   Send home a synopsis of *Peter's Chair,* and inform parents of the kinds of activities in which their children are involved. Parents who have a new baby or are expecting one soon can employ their older child's help. The older child can help babyproof the house by looking for small objects, moving soaps and detergents, and making sure that all electrical outlets have safety covers. The older child can also help by looking for outgrown baby items and clothes that the new baby will be able to use. The older child can help clean the items and ready them for use. All families, including those without a new baby, will enjoy looking back over family picture albums together and remembering their older children as newborns and babies, as well as reminiscing over past times. Ask parents to help their child prepare a simple family tree. Send home the outline of a tree trunk. The parents can fill in the family members with names, pictures, or both.

Related Literature

Alexander, Martha. *Nobody Asked Me If I Wanted a Baby Sister.*
Greenfield, Eloise. *She Come Bringing Me That Little Baby Girl.*
Henkes, Kevin. *The Baby of the World.*
Viorst, Judith. *I'll Fix Anthony.*

ME DOLL PATTERN

1. Trace pieces onto tagboard.
2. Attach pieces with brad fasteners.
3. Decorate dolls.

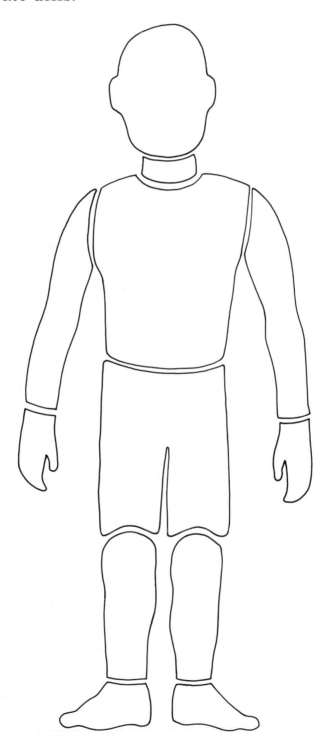

Me Dolls Activity

SOMEONE SPECIAL, JUST LIKE YOU
by
Tricia Brown

Developmental Activities Chart	Language & Cognitive Development	Fine Motor Art	Gross Motor	Perception	Social Skills	Math	Dramatic Play	Cooking Snack	Science	Music, Fingerplays, Poems
1 The World Around Me	X			X						
2 Hands to See	X			X						
3 Feely Can	X			X						
4 Braille	X	X		X						
5 Seeing	X			X						
6 Can You Hear?	X			X						
7 Listen to the Story	X			X						
8 Wheels to Move			X							
9 Touch and Sort	X			X						
10 Sound Game			X	X						
11 Texture Collage		X								
12 Invisible Picture	X	X								
13 Touch and Count	X				X	X				
14 Hear and Count	X			X		X				
15 Learn to Listen	X	X		X	X					
16 I Can't, I Can		X								X
17 Classroom Visitor	X				X					
18 Body Parts I Use	X						X		X	
19 I Am Me										X
20 Signing	X	X								
21 Classifying	X									
22 Suggested Home Activities	X									
23										
24										
25										
26										
27										
28										
29										
30										

SOMEONE SPECIAL, JUST LIKE YOU
by Tricia Brown
Holt, Rinehart and Winston, 1982

Photographs of preschoolers show children doing things like singing, going down slides, eating ice cream, and engaging in many other typical early childhood activities that help young children learn about the world around them. The children shown are physically, mentally, and sensorily challenged. The simple text and pictures depicted help children and adults focus on the similarities, rather than the differences, between handicapped children and their nonhandicapped peers.

The World Around Me. Have children brainstorm a list of things they like to see/look at, hear/listen to, and ways they move. Introduce the concept of special needs by telling children that not everyone enjoys and experiences the world like they do. Some people wear glasses, some can't see at all, some people wear hearing aids or can't hear at all, and some people need braces, crutches, or wheelchairs to help them move. Encourage children to share any experiences they may have had with handicapped people.

Things to see/look at—sun, snow, people, flowers, mountains, birthday cake, animals, clouds, and books.

Things to hear/listen to—record player, TV, train whistle, instruments, lawn mower, clock ticking, telephone ringing, and whispers.

Ways to move—run, walk forward and backward, gallop, skip, roll, leap, jump, and hop.

Hands to See. People who have difficulty seeing can do most of the same things sighted people can do. They use their ears, hands, and memory to help them. Make simple yarn pictures of shapes, toys, and letters on heavy tagboard. Children use their sense of touch to feel around the yarn picture and try to name/identify it.

Feely Can. Cover a large container that has a plastic rim (the 18-ounce size container of Quaker Oats™ works well) with a stretchy sock. Place small objects, toys, and shapes inside the canister. Children reach inside and try to identify the object by touch, finding one that is the same as a sample, one that is different, and so on. Auditory clues or riddles can be used if needed.

Braille. People who can't see are blind and don't learn to read the same way as other children. They learn to read a code of dots called Braille. Each letter of the alphabet is made from different combinations of raised dots that are "read" with fingers. Children can be given one or more copies of the Braille black line master. They can find the letters in their name, try to print their name with the Braille dots, or cut and paste the sheets to spell their name in Braille.

Seeing.   Demonstrate to children how objects look to a person with limited eyesight. Hang up a large piece of crumpled waxed paper or a frosted shower curtain liner in the classroom. Children sit on one side and try to identify objects on the other side. Children will see light and the outline of objects, but details will be difficult to see.

Can You Hear?   Help children understand that one way we learn is by hearing. Try these activities with children.

- Whisper something into one child's ear and he or she whispers what was heard to the next child, and so on. The last person shares what was heard. Compare that statement to the original thing shared/whispered by the teacher. Discuss what happened when it was difficult to hear what was being said.

- Children listen to and describe sounds heard in their environment while wearing earphones. Encourage children to share their feelings about these experiences and why hearing is important when trying to learn.

Listen to the Story.   There are many different degrees and kinds of hearing loss. This activity will help illustrate how difficult it is to be hearing impaired. Read a story into a tape recorder. Play the tape for the children and keep the volume very low. At the end of the story, ask a variety of "who," "what," "where," "when," and "why" questions. The children are likely to have missed some important details. This activity demonstrates how hard one must listen and what close attention must be given when a hearing impaired person is trying to listen to something. After a while, this kind of listening becomes very tiring.

Wheels to Move.   Many physically challenged people are unable to use their legs because they are paralyzed or too weak. If possible, give children the opportunity to use a wheelchair. They will probably find that it is fun for a while, but not all the time. If a wheelchair is not available, have children move around by propelling themselves on a scooter board, using only their arms, not their legs. Children will quickly discover that it takes strength to maneuver and that it is difficult to get to many places they want to go.

Touch and Sort.   Some children are unable to touch and feel things with their hands. Talk about other parts of our bodies that we can feel with, such as face, feet, legs, and arms. Provide a variety of objects and textures for children to touch somewhere on their body. Sort things into categories—rough, smooth, soft, hard, sticky, hot, cold, sharp, prickly, and slippery. Talk about the easiest way to feel things.

Sound Game.   One child is chosen to be "It." "It" closes his or her eyes while the other children scatter or form a circle around "It." One child calls "It's" name. "It" tries to listen carefully and walk toward and find the child calling his or her name. Give every child a chance to be "It." Talk about the game experience. Was it easy/hard to find someone you couldn't see? How did it make you feel?

Texture Collage. Children make a collage of objects with various textures. Interesting items to touch and include are pieces of corrugated cardboard, cotton balls, fabric scraps, buttons, beans, seeds, eggshells, different kinds of pasta, sandpaper, and leaves.

Invisible Picture. Each child traces around a familiar object or stencil using a white crayon. Have other children try to identify the picture. Next, each child puts a watercolor or tempera paint wash over his or her picture. Ask children to try to identify the picture now. What made it easier to name the picture?

Touch and Count. Children work in pairs. One child will touch and count objects in a small container or on the tabletop with eyes closed. The partner can touch and count the objects to check for accuracy, with eyes open. Compare results.

Hear and Count. One child sits behind a screen. The other children take turns bouncing a ball, stamping feet, clapping, ringing a bell, and so on. The child behind the screen must listen and count the number of sounds heard.

Learn to Listen. Attempt to teach children something that is developmentally above their level of readiness, such as tying shoelaces, subtracting, and remembering a long series of numbers. Repeat the activity over and over again. Ask children to tell how they felt about trying hard and not mastering the task. Explain to children that learning is difficult for some people no matter how hard they try.

I Can't, I Can (movement verse)

> I can't hear the popcorn jumping.   [Point to ears.]
> But it sure tastes good!   [Rub stomach.]
> I can't run or move too fast.   [Run fingers quickly over open hand.]
> But I'll catch up with you.
> I can't see the morning sun.   [Point to eyes.]
> But it warms me with its glow.   [Hug self.]
> I can't be heard when I talk.   [Point to mouth.]
> But my signs tell all.   [Move fingers.]
> We are different.
> We're the same.
> What makes me special,   [Point to self.]
> Makes you special, too!   [Point to someone.]

Classroom Visitor. Invite a handicapped person to visit the class. To minimize any fears, prepare children in advance by talking about what they might see. Encourage children to ask questions, talk, and interact with the visitor. Have children write or dictate a classroom story after the visit to share what they learned and how they felt about the handicapped visitor.

Body Parts I Use. Have children brainstorm a list of activities they enjoy, such as playing catch, painting, watching TV, and riding a bike. Then go through the list and have children identify all the body parts needed to perform the activity. If necessary, children can demonstrate the activity as a visual cue.

I Am Me (to the tune of "This Old Man")

> I'm so glad, I am me.
> See how happy I will be
> When I learn something new,
> Even when it's hard.
> I'll feel special, just like you!

Signing.   Explain to children that people who are deaf have a difficult time talking because they are unable to hear sounds and words spoken by others. Many deaf people learn to speak by talking with their hands: this is called sign language. Get a beginning book from the library and teach children some simple words to sign. Some excellent books are

Bahan, Ben and Joe Dannis. *Signs for Me, Basic Sign Vocabulary for Children.* Dawn Sign Press, 1990. The signed vocabulary is divided into parts of speech—verbs, adjectives, nouns, and pronouns—and number signs.

Chaplin, Susan Gibbons. *I Can Sign My ABC's.* Kendall Green, 1986. Each letter of the alphabet includes the capital letter, the sign for the letter, a picture of an object beginning with that sound, and the printed word.

Flodin, Mickey. *Signing for Kids.* G. P. Putnam, 1991.

Gillen, Patricia Bellan. *My Signing Book of Numbers.* Kendall Green, 1988.

Rankin, Laura. *The Handmade Alphabet.* Dial Books, 1991. Each signed alphabet letter is accompanied by an object beginning with that sound. The illustrations are delicate.

Sesame Street Sign Language ABC with Linda Bove. Random House, 1985. The book shows every letter of the alphabet with several words in sign language for each.

Classifying.   Children classify sights, sounds, and actions. Do you see, hear, or move?

music playing	hopping	letters on the chalkboard
bells ringing	a flower	a bird's nest
clouds	galloping	voices whispering
thunder	coughing	walking
a magazine	a siren	a green light

Suggested Home Activities.   Send home a synopsis of the story *Someone Special, Just Like You,* and inform parents about some of the activities their children will be doing at school. Encourage parents to visit the library and select some books they can read and talk about with their child. Children are curious and afraid of things they don't understand, so parents should be prepared to answer questions about handicapped people they see.

Related Literature

Burns, Kay. *Our Mom.* Franklin Watts, 1989. Four children in a busy family describe their wheelchair-bound mom.

MacLachlen, Patricia. *Through Grandpa's Eyes.* Harper & Row, 1980. John's blind and loving grandpa teaches him a way of seeing with his fingers, ears, and heart.

Peterson, Jeanne Whitehouse. *I Have a Sister, My Sister Is Deaf.* Harper & Row, 1977. An older sister plays with her younger deaf sister. The strengths and accomplishments as well as the compensations she must make are described.

Prall, Jo. *My Sister's Special.* Children's Press, 1985. A young boy describes his brain-damaged sister.

Rabe, Berniece. *The Balancing Girl.* E. A. Dutton, 1981. Wheelchair and crutches bound, Margaret proves her balancing talents and causes a sensation at the school carnival.

Braille letters of the alphabet.

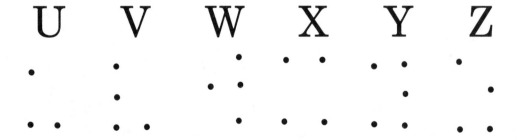

Braille Activity

Winning
Picture Books

GINGER JUMPS
by
Lisa Campbell Ernst

Developmental Activities Chart	Language & Cognitive Development	Fine Motor Art	Gross Motor	Perception	Social Skills	Math	Dramatic Play	Cooking Snack	Science	Music, Fingerplays, Poems
1 Circus Performers	X	X								
2 Circus Acts						X				
3 Face Painting		X			X					
4 Circus Dogs		X					X			X
5 Circus Day	X	X	X		X		X			X
6 Carmel Corn	X				X			X		
7 Circus Song										X
8 Sugared Peanuts	X				X			X		
9 Tightrope Walker			X							
10 Circus Jugglers			X	X						
11 Puppy Trampoline			X		X	X				
12 Popcorn Math		X			X	X				
13 Pet Performer	X									
14 Balloon Math	X					X				
15 Circus Practice	X		X			X				
16 Balloon Magic!	X								X	
17 Feelings	X				X					
18 Animal Parade			X							
19 Circus Animals	X					X				
20 Suggested Home Activities	X	X	X							
21										
22										
23										
24										
25										
26										
27										
28										
29										
30										

GINGER JUMPS
by Lisa Campbell Ernst
Bradbury Press, 1990

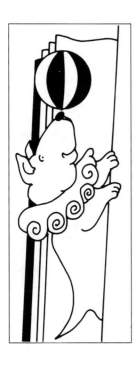

Ginger is a lonely circus puppy who spends her days practicing for performances and dreaming of someone who has time to play with her. When a prissy poodle fails to perform a daredevil stunt, Ginger races to the sound of the drum roll and makes her dream come true.

Circus Performers.   Ginger had to learn new tricks to perform in front of the audience. Children can dictate individual stories to answer the question, "If you could be a circus performer, what would you like to be?" Children can illustrate their stories.

Circus Acts.   Children graph their favorite circus act—elephant rider, unicyclist, tightrope walker, juggler, clown, acrobat, aerialist, daredevil dog, and so on. Compare results.

Face Painting.   Clowns are a special circus delight! Provide mirrors and allow children to experiment with painting their own clown face or that of a friend. Before trying this activity, inform parents in advance of the face paint ingredients to be assured it is safe for tender faces.

Mix together:

    ¼   cup Johnson's Baby Lotion™
    ½   teaspoon powdered tempera paint
    2   squirts Ivory™ dishwashing liquid

Circus Dogs.   Children can act out this verse or do it as a fingerplay.

> Five frisky circus dogs performing in the ring.
> One got a biscuit, oh, how she could sing!
> Four frisky circus dogs, skating all around.
> One raced away, without making a sound.
> Three frisky circus dogs, jumping through a hoop.
> One learned a new trick and danced in a loop.
> Two frisky circus dogs, balanced a big ball.
> One limped away when he took a giant fall.
> One frisky circus dog, practiced all day long.
> She fell asleep without making a sound.
> No little circus dogs performing in the ring.
> Wait for a new day and watch the smiles they bring!

Circus Day.   Have children plan and prepare for a circus day. After talking about costumes worn by circus performers, children can wear costumes or funny clothes to school. They can decorate old hats with yarn, streamers, plastic flowers, ribbon, glitter, buttons, fabric scraps, and pipe cleaners. Children can transform shoe boxes into colorful circus wagons by decorating them with paint, paper, or streamers. The teacher can attach long lengths of yarn for handles. Children place a favorite stuffed animal in the "circus wagons" and parade them around a circus ring made in the center of an open space. Children then take turns performing in the ring or being part of the audience. Provide such things as balls, hoops, balance beams, and balloons. The children will enjoy making tickets for circus day. Provide a special popcorn treat. Consider inviting parents for this special event.

Caramel Corn.   Children will enjoy preparing this circus treat.

6	quarts of lightly salted popped corn		

Syrup:

2	sticks butter or margarine	½	cup white corn syrup
1	cup white sugar	⅛	teaspoon cream of tartar
1	cup light brown sugar	⅛	teaspoon baking soda

Preheat oven to 225 degrees. Combine first five ingredients and boil for 5 minutes. Remove from heat and add baking soda. Pour over popped corn and stir. Place popcorn on a large, greased cookie sheet and bake for 1 hour, stirring every 10 to 15 minutes.

Circus Song (to the tune of "Mary Had a Little Lamb")

Silly clowns are doing tricks, doing tricks, doing tricks.
Silly clowns are doing tricks all around the ring.

Big striped tigers jump through hoops, jump through hoops, jump through
    hoops.
Big striped tigers jump through hoops when the trainer shouts!

Elephants parade around, parade around, parade around.
Elephants parade around, then balance on one foot.

Circus jugglers toss the balls, toss the balls, toss the balls.
Circus jugglers toss the balls and never let them drop.

Ginger is a jumping dog, jumping dog, jumping dog.
Ginger is a jumping dog and jumps to find a home!

Sugared Peanuts (from the kitchen of Jo Anne Skiera).   Circus elephants *and* children will enjoy this peanut recipe!

2	cups raw peanuts
1	cup sugar
½	cup water
	salt

Preheat oven to 300 degrees. Combine peanuts, sugar, and water. Cook until sugar crystalizes and coats the peanuts, about 10 minutes. Spread in a greased

11" × 14" baking pan and sprinkle with salt. Bake for 15 minutes. Turn peanuts, sprinkle with salt, and bake 15 minutes longer. Cool before eating.

Tightrope Walker.   Use colored chalk or masking tape to make several 6-foot lines. Children jump, hop, or walk heel-toe along the "tightrope." A balance beam with a mat underneath it can also be used.

Circus Jugglers.   Demonstrate how to keep a balloon in the air by gently tapping it with fingers. After children practice with one balloon, give them another balloon to juggle. Children can also try keeping the balloons in the air by using other body parts such as heads, elbows, or toes.

Puppy Trampoline.   Children form a circle and hold an old sheet like a trampoline. Place a stuffed dog in the center and have children work together raising and lowering the sheet to make the puppy "jump" a certain number of times.

Popcorn Math.   Children transform white paper bags into popcorn bags by decorating them with red paint, construction paper, or markers. Prepare bowls of popcorn and place them in front of the children. Children take turns rolling one or two die. They count and say the number, then fill their bags with the correct number of popcorn pieces. After the game is over, children eat the popcorn in their bags.

Pet Performer.   Invite parents and students to bring in family pets that can do some simple tricks for the class. Remind students that they need to be a good audience.

Balloon Math

- Children sort and graph small water balloons by color. Compare the results—which color has the most? Which color has the least? Do any of the colors have the same number? Give each child his or her favorite colored balloon to take home.

- Cut several sets of multicolored balloons from construction paper. Number half the balloons with the numerals 1 to 10 and the others with colored dots from 1 to 10. Laminate the balloon shapes and tie on a short string. Children match the numeral balloon with its corresponding dot balloon.

- Give each child a small handful of balloons and lengths of string or yarn. Children practice one-to-one correspondence by matching a string to each balloon.

Circus Practice.   Make large shapes (square, circle, triangle, rectangle, and diamond) with chalk or masking tape on the floor in an open area. Children follow oral directions which will help to develop language skills, gross motor, and math skills.

Example:

Hop to the diamond.

Jump 4 times in the square.

Balance on 1 foot inside the triangle.

Put 1 foot and 1 hand inside the rectangle.

Stand in front of the circle and bend at your waist.

Balloon Magic!   Pour ¼ cup of vinegar into an 8- to 10-ounce soda bottle that has a bottle cap rather than a twist-off top. Using a small funnel, put 2 teaspoons of baking soda inside a balloon. Quickly and carefully, put the open end of the balloon over the soda bottle. Children will watch in awe as the vinegar–baking soda combination forms a gas to fill the balloon.

Feelings.   Have children retell the important events of the story and focus on how Ginger's feelings changed in the story. Children can share personal experiences about times they have felt lonely, scared, tired, and happy.

Animal Parade.   Children can practice moving like some animals seen in the circus: *elephant*—bend forward at the waist, allow arms to hang limp, take lumbering steps swaying from side to side—and *prancing horse*—stand with arms folded across the chest, throw head upward and back, prance around, lifting feet high and pointing toes.

Circus Animals.   Make copies of the black line circus animal patterns. Color the pictures with crayons or markers, cut them out, and laminate the pieces.

- Children can practice one-to-one correspondence by giving one collar to every dog.
- Give each child a round hoop or long piece of yarn to represent the circus ring. Children can count and place a certain number of prancing horses in the ring. Children can arrange horses in ordinal positions according to their appearance, for example, the brown horse is first, the gray horse is second, and so on.

Suggested Home Activities.   Send home a synopsis of the story *Ginger Jumps,* and inform parents of some of the activities the children will be doing at school. Encourage parents to take their child to a real circus when it comes to town. While waiting for this special event, parents and children can also enjoy balloon fun such as balloon volleyball or balloon badminton. Paddles can be made by pulling a hanger into a circular shape and covering it with a panty hose. The top part of the hanger can be squeezed together and covered with electrical tape to form a safe handle.

Related Literature

Crews, Donald. *Carousel.*
Crockett, Johnson. *Harold's Circus.*
Ehlert, Lois. *Circus.*

Circus Animal Patterns

THE TUB PEOPLE
by
Pam Conrad

Developmental Activities Chart	Language & Cognitive Development	Fine Motor Art	Gross Motor	Perception	Social Skills	Math	Dramatic Play	Cooking Snack	Science	Music, Fingerplays, Poems
1 The Plumber	X									
2 Plumber's Rescue									X	
3 Plumbing Play		X		X	X					
4 Pipe Detectives	X								X	
5 Drip, Drip, Drip	X					X			X	
6 Bathroom Collage		X			X					
7 Toolbox Memory	X									
8 Bathtub Rafts	X			X					X	
9 Creative Writing	X									
10 Bath Bubbles		X		X					X	
11 Line Up!	X					X				
12 Clean Up	X					X				
13 Busy Bathroom	X									
14 Ode to a Plumber										X
15 Sink or Float	X								X	
16 Water Play		X		X					X	
17 Bathroom Charades	X				X		X			
18 Soap Sculptures		X								
19 What's in the Bag?	X			X			X			
20 Bathroom Safety	X	X								
21 Suggested Home Activities	X	X		X						
22										
23										
24										
25										
26										
27										
28										
29										
30										

THE TUB PEOPLE
by Pam Conrad
Harper & Row, 1989

The Tub People is a bath-time tale of the little wooden tub people who live on the ledge of the bathtub. One day their water play turns into tragedy, but an unusual chain of events brings smiles to their small wooden faces.

The Plumber.　Have children brainstorm all the ways they think a plumber helps us. If necessary, explain that a plumber connects and repairs pipes that bring water into our homes, schools, stores, and other buildings. A plumber can unplug a drain in the sink or fix a leaking pipe with his or her tools. The tools that he or she uses may include a plunger, wrenches, pipe wrenches, pliers, and special wire "snakes" for jiggling. If possible, show some tools.

Plumber's Rescue (to the tune of "Clementine")

> Call the plumber, call the plumber.
> Call the plumber for the tub.
> He can help us in the bathroom,
> Rescue Tub Child, pretty quick!

Plumbing Play.　Make a wooden base as the foundation for "plumbing works." Provide PVC pipes cut in varying lengths, connectors and elbows, couplings, and fittings for children to make different pipe configurations. Materials can be purchased at any home center or hardware store.

Base: Use six 1¼-inch drill screws to secure two ¾-inch pieces of 12-inch plywood square together. Screw a steel floor flange into the center of the base and screw in a female plastic adapter.

Plumbing Works:

4	T fittings	12	90-degree elbows
6	couplings	3	45-degree elbows
3	end caps	2	90-degree street elbows

and 4 10-foot lengths of 1- or 1½-inch plastic pipe, cut to lengths ranging from 6 to 12 inches.

Pipe Detectives.　Walk around the school building so that children can search for pipes in the bathroom, kitchen, basement, boiler room, and so on. Look for pipes of all different sizes and lengths. Ask children where they think the pipes lead and what they contain. Explain that the pipes they see are connected to other pipes that carry water under the ground.

Drip, Drip, Drip.　Turn on a faucet in the classroom or kitchen area so that it has a slow drip. Place a cup under the leaking faucet. Have children watch for a while and then predict how much water will drip during a specified amount of time (the length of playtime, the length of story time, etc.). Children fill small, clear plastic cups with their predictions and then compare with the actual amount that has dripped out. This is a good time to talk about the importance of conserving and not wasting water. Children use thinking skills to make a list of ways they can save water at home and school.

Bathroom Collage.   Provide children with catalogs and magazines to find pictures of things found in the bathroom, ranging from toys and towels to rugs and toothpaste. Children cut out the pictures and glue them on paper to make an individual or class collage.

Toolbox Memory.   Place three to eight tools or bathroom items inside a toolbox. Use pictures or actual objects. Children name all the items that were placed in the box. Another activity is to have children watch as objects are placed in the toolbox. One object is removed when they close their eyes. Children name the missing object.

Bathtub Rafts.   Fill the sensory table with water. Talk about what the Tub People used as rafts in the story. Have children guess what raft will hold Tub Child afloat longer—a washcloth, a sponge, or a bar of Ivory™ soap. Record guesses. Experiment by placing one Fisher-Price® person on a sponge, one on a washcloth, and one on a bar of soap. Children observe and watch for the results.

Creative Writing.   Children write or dictate a story about the new adventures of the Tub People in the bedroom.

Bath Bubbles.   Fill the sensory table with water and add liquid dish soap. Children use egg beaters and wire wisks to make frothy bubbles. Drops of food coloring or tempera paint can be added to make colored bubbles.

Line Up!   The Tub People always lined up in the same order on the bathtub ledge. Line up Fisher-Price® people to represent the Tub People. Review ordinal positions by asking children who is first, last, second, third, fourth, in the middle, and so on. Move figures around and try again. In addition, children can follow oral directions by placing the figures in a certain position—"Put the policeman in the middle" or "Put the dog second."

Clean Up.   Make a graph of what children like better, taking a bath or a shower. Children should explain why they like one better than the other. Compare results.

Busy Bathroom.   Have children brainstorm all the activities that occur in the bathroom—wash hands, get weighed, shave whiskers, put on Band-Aids™, take a shower, and so on. Children name all the items needed for each activity and sequence the events in the correct order.

Ode to a Plumber.   Children can recite this poem.

I want to be a plumber.
I'll check pipes and every sink.
My tools will help me fix things,
Working quicker than a wink!

Sink or Float. Provide objects such as Styrofoam™, feather, marble, penny, cotton ball, rock, straw, plastic spoon, leaf, and nutshell. Ask children to predict if each object will sink or float in water. Tally predictions in a sink or float column. Children take turns placing objects in the water to test their predictions.

Water Play. Play with wooden Tub People, like Fisher-Price® characters, in the sensory table. Place sponges, plastic containers, wooden blocks, and some travel-size bars of soap in the water. Children can have the Tub People float, dive, race, slide off the bars of soap, and play in the water like the people in the story.

Bathroom Charades. One child acts out an activity that occurs in the bathroom, such as taking a shower, curling hair, washing hands, and shaving. The other children guess what the person is doing and then name all the things needed to perform the activity.

Soap Sculptures. Provide a travel-size bar of soap for each child. With supervision, the children can sculpt the bar into different shapes by using dull plastic knives and potato peelers.

What's in the Bag? Place a familiar bathroom object in a feely bag or pillowcase. Each child can reach inside, feel the object, and try to name it. Include a sponge, a bar of soap, an ear swab, a comb, brush, tub toys, toothbrush, and other bathroom objects. If the child is unable to name the item, ask the child to demonstrate how it can be used.

Bathroom Safety. Brainstorm a list of bathroom safety rules with the children. Make a Xerox™ copy for each child to take home. Children can draw a picture to illustrate one of the rules. Suggested rules might include:

- Walk in the bathroom—the floor might be slippery.
- Sit in the bathtub so that you won't slip.
- Stay away from mom and dad's razors—they can cut.
- Let mom or dad help you with the hair dryer or curling iron—they can burn skin.
- Don't take medicine, use lotions, or open other products that are found in the bathroom unless an adult is supervising.
- Check the bathtub water before getting in—it may be too hot!
- Don't bring a radio, curling iron, telephone, or hair dryer near the water—it can hurt you.

Suggested Home Activities. Send home a synopsis of the story *The Tub People* and inform parents of some of the activities the children will be doing at school. Encourage parents to review the list of bathroom safety rules that were sent home and add others that are appropriate for their family. Suggest that parents take the time to check their bathroom cabinets and make certain that they are childproof.

Encourage parents to provide a variety of water toys children can play with in the tub. Imagination, creativity, and language skills can be encouraged as the child interacts with the toys and his or her parents. Parents might also consider putting shaving cream on the shower wall so that children can make faces, shapes, and designs in the foam. It washes off easily with a sponge. The experience is bound to leave a smile on each child's face, just like the Tub People in the story! Send home a copy of the black line master. Parents can help their child draw a picture of their favorite tub toy. Each child could also dictate a sentence story about their toy. Completed pictures/stories may be sent to school and shared with classmates.

Related Literature

Cole, Brock. *No More Baths.*
Hughes, Shirley. *An Evening at Alfie's.*
Pomerantz, Charlotte. *The Piggy in the Puddle.*

Draw a picture of your favorite tub toys.

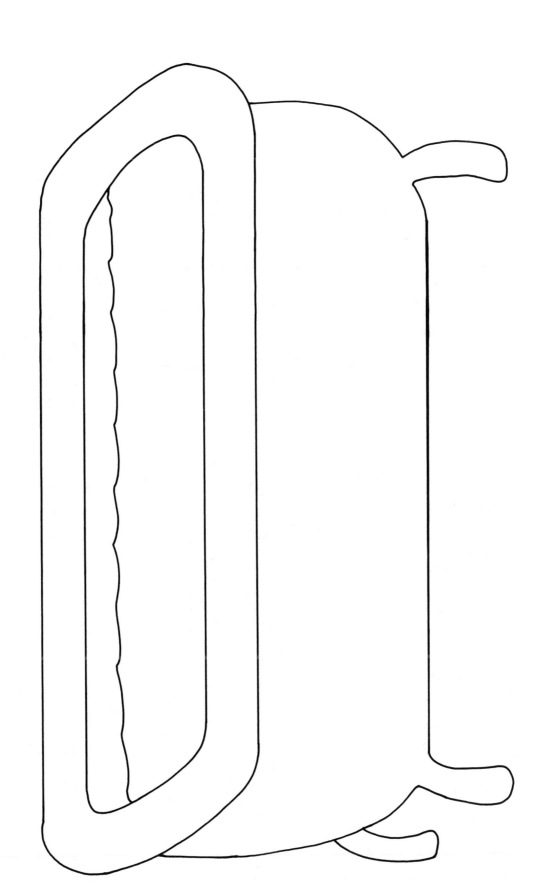

Suggested Home Activity

CHRYSANTHEMUM
by
Kevin Henkes

Developmental Activities Chart	Language & Cognitive Development	Fine Motor Art	Gross Motor	Perception	Social Skills	Math	Dramatic Play	Cooking Snack	Science	Music, Fingerplays, Poems
1 Name Graphing	X				X	X				
2 A Flower Is a Flower	X									
3 Name Collages	X	X								
4 Birthday Chant	X									X
5 Name Scramble	X	X								
6 Name Ball			X		X					
7 Sensory Names		X		X						
8 Pick a Name	X									
9 Initial Pancakes	X	X						X		
10 Me Flag	X	X	X		X					
11 Song About Me!										X
12 Prized Possessions	X	X			X					
13 Same and Different	X				X	X				
14 Me Puppet		X		X						
15 Sticks and Stones	X				X					X
16 Name Buddy	X				X					
17 I Have Grown	X								X	
18 Read My Name	X			X						
19 Friendship Recipe	X				X		X			
20 Partner Faces	X	X	·	X	X					
21 Suggested Home Activity	X				X					
22										
23										
24										
25										
26										
27										
28										
29										
30										

CHRYSANTHEMUM
by Kevin Henkes
Greenwillow Books, 1991

A delicate and absolutely perfect little mouse loves her name until she goes to school. She is tormented by her classmates because of her long, flowery name. Chrysanthemum withers from their cruel remarks until she meets Mrs. Twinkle, the new music teacher.

Name Graphing.   Chrysanthemum had the longest name in her class. Make a graph to compare the length of students' names. Place a small picture of each child (photo or child drawn) along the left side of a large piece of butcher or kraft paper. Children count the letters in their first and/or last name and make a horizontal bar graph by gluing a 2-inch square of construction paper for each letter in their name. Compare results of the name graph: Who has the longest name, the shortest name, and the same number of letters in their name?

A Flower Is a Flower.   Chrysanthemum was named after a flower. Bring in a picture book of flowers and help children brainstorm a list of other flower-derived names, for example, Rose, Lily, Daisy, Dahlia, Iris, Violet, and Delphinium. Tally which name children like the best. Ask children to find out how and why their name was chosen and report back to the class.

Name Collages.   Names are as individual as each person. Print each child's first name on a large piece of paper or tagboard. Provide colored, plain, and sugared cereal; sequins; cotton balls; toothpicks; macaroni; and so on. Children choose one item from the variety of collage materials and glue it on their name. Ask children to select a collage item that best describes them. Help children fill in the sentence written at the bottom of their name collage: I am _____ (sweet, soft, strong, etc.).

Birthday Chant.   Birthdays are special. Help children remember theirs by reinforcing the date with this clap-and-chant activity.

> January, February, March, April, May, June, July,
> August, September, October, November, December.
> Cookies, candy,
> Treats and gum.
> Tell me when your birthday comes!

The teacher then points to a child to tell his or her birthdate and repeats the rhythmic part before asking another child. If a child is unable to say the date, the teacher can tell him or her.

Name Scramble.   Put the letters of each child's name in a small zip-style bag. (Post Alpha-bits™ cereal works well.) Children will shake the bag, pour out the letters, and spell their name from memory or copy the letters from a sample. If possible, have magnetic letters available so that children can spell their names.

Name Ball.   Children form a large circle in an open area. The child with the longest name is selected to be in the center. That child says the name of a classmate and rolls, bounces, or throws the ball to him or her. If the child catches the ball, he or she goes in the center. If not, the child in the center gets another turn. This is a good activity to help children learn each other's names.

Sensory Names.   Chrysanthemum practiced writing her name over and over again because it made her feel good. Provide a variety of different mediums children can print their names in and with—shaving cream, pudding, sand, squeeze icing, crayons, markers, pencils, chalk, and paint.

Pick a Name.   Since people don't have the opportunity to choose their own names, pick a day when children can select a nickname or new name to be used for the entire day. Bring in a baby name book from the library and share unusual and common names with the children. Many books provide the meaning of names; this information might help children make a choice.

Initial Pancakes.   Make pancake batter from a mix or use a batter that has been commercially prepared. Pour the mix in a squeeze container, like that used for mustard or ketchup. Children squeeze the batter-filled container and form their initials on a griddle. Provide butter and syrup to sweeten the experience.

Me Flag.   Give each child a triangular-shaped piece of tagboard. Children select and cut out pictures from magazines that show their favorite meal, dessert, pet, game, color, and so on, to glue on their flag. Flags can be taped to paper towel or wrapping paper tubes. Children parade around the room with their flags, increasing their awareness of self and others.

Song About Me! (to the tune of "This Old Man")

> Look at me!
> I'm carefree.
> Moving every way I please.
> With a jump, a hop, and a dance across the floor.
> Move, be happy just like me!

Prized Possessions.   Chrysanthemum prepared herself for another difficult day at school by carrying her most prized possessions and good luck charms in her pockets. Children can prepare for a *good* day at school by decorating a shoe box or brown bag and filling it with things that are important to them. Everyone gets a chance to share their prized possessions.

Same and Different.   Children build self-confidence by learning more about themselves and others when they complete this graphing activity. The teacher prepares a grid on large butcher or kraft paper. Children's names are written along the left side, and characteristics are depicted along the top. Characteristics to compare might include eye and hair color, pets, and number of brothers and sisters. Children cut pieces of construction paper to show their eye and hair color, magazine pictures to show their pet, and blue or pink paper snips to show the number of brothers and sisters they have. Talk about the ways children are the same and how they are different.

Me Puppet.   Provide each child with a white, lunch-size paper bag to make a puppet. Children can color the "face" to show their skin color. Supply felt, fabric scraps, and yarn to make facial features and hair. Arms and legs cut from construction paper can be glued or stapled on. Fabric scraps and old buttons can be glued on for clothes.

Sticks and Stones.   Teach children this verse and talk about what it means.

   Sticks and stones may hurt my bones.
   And unkind words can hurt me.

Talk about how Chrysanthemum was treated by her classmates. Brainstorm a list of ways children can be kind or helpful to each other or to someone who is different.

Name Buddy.   Each child pulls the name/picture of a classmate out of a box. That child becomes his or her special buddy for the day. Remind children of ways to be kind or helpful, and ask them to do or say nice things to their buddy.

I Have Grown.   Show children the pictures of Chrysanthemum as she grew and grew. Ask parents to send three or four pictures to school that show their child at different ages, doing different things. Children sequence their pictures from birth to the present. Encourage children to talk about what they can do now that they couldn't do when they were babies.

Read My Name.   Make two pocket charts using cardboard, tagboard, and strapping tape or use purchased charts. Place one chart outside the classroom and one somewhere in the room. Prepare tagboard name cards for each child and laminate first and last names separately. Children find their name(s) upon entering the classroom and place it in the pocket chart in the classroom. Children will need help to understand the correct positions of their first and last name in the pocket chart.

Friendship Recipe.   Decorate a large piece of paper to look like a recipe card. Children brainstorm a list of ingredients that make a friend. Example: "Mix 3 hugs, 2 smiles, and a handshake. Stir in a happy hello." The recipe will serve the number of students in the class. Children can also act out the recipe ingredients.

Partner Faces.   Each child is paired with a partner and the pair receives a copy of the black line master. One child draws and colors a face. His or her partner tries to make a face that looks exactly the same, by matching eye, hair, and skin colors. Children then reverse roles; one draws and colors the face and his or her partner tries to make it match.

Suggested Home Activity.   Send home a synopsis of the story *Chrysanthemum*, and inform parents of some of the activities their children will be doing at school.

Chrysanthemum was loved very much by her parents. Suggest that parents plan a special day for their child. Prepare his or her favorite meal, read a favorite story, play a favorite game, and give lots of hugs and kisses. Cuddle and look at a family photo album together.

Related Literature

Lester, Helen. *A Porcupine Named Fluffy.*
Mosel, Arlene. *Tikki Tikki Tembo.*
Pinkwater, Daniel. *The Wuggie Norple Story.*

Draw a face. Have your partner color a face that looks **just the same.** Your partner draws a face. You color a face that looks **just the same.**

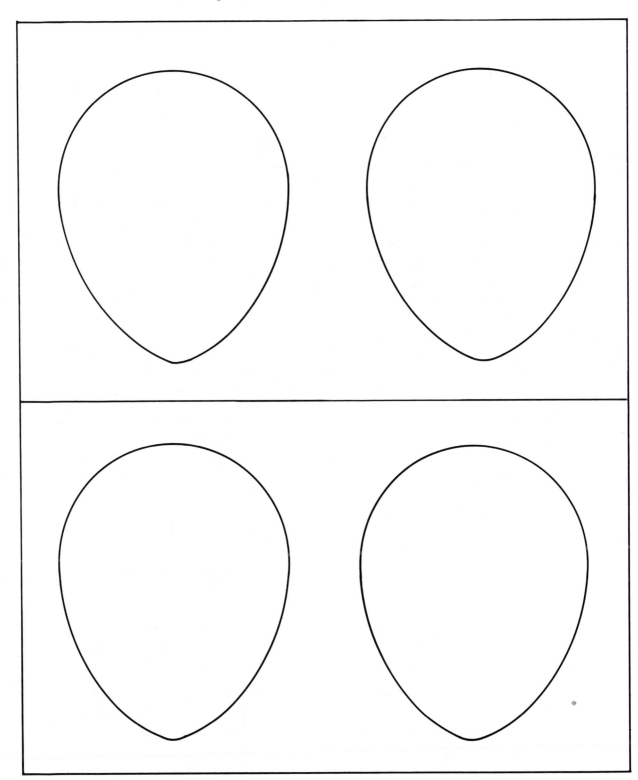

Partner Faces Activity

THE GIRL WHO LOVED WILD HORSES
by
Paul Goble

Developmental Activities Chart	Language & Cognitive Development	Fine Motor Art	Gross Motor	Perception	Social Skills	Math	Dramatic Play	Cooking Snack	Science	Music, Fingerplays, Poems
1 Unique Interests	X			X						
2 Horse Facts	X	X							X	
3 Tipis		X								
4 Dramatic Play							X			
5 Hand Games	X			X	X	X				
6 Maize								X		
7 Corn Cob Prints		X								
8 New Names	X				X					
9 Moccasin Game	X				X	X				
10 Concho Belt		X								
11 Clay Pots		X								
12 Sign Language	X									
13 Native American Foods								X		
14 Toss Ball			X							
15 On the Mark			X							
16 Bowl Games			X							
17 Foot Races			X							
18 Kickball			X							
19 Texture Tubs		X		X		X		X		
20 Kachinas		X								
21 Bead Stringing		X		X		X				
22 Weaving		X								
23 Rattles		X		X						X
24 Buffalo		X								X
25 Suggested Home Activities		X			X					
26										
27										
28										
29										
30										

THE GIRL WHO LOVED WILD HORSES
by Paul Goble
Bradbury Press, 1978

This is the story of a young Native American girl who had a special relationship with horses. The people in her village understood this and allowed her to care for the horses of her village. She was always careful not to wander out of sight, but one day a terrible storm blew in, frightening the horses. The girl was carried off to a new life, living among the horses. The brilliant illustrations depict the love of nature, the clothing, lodging, and artwork indigenous to this nation of Native Americans.

Four to five hundred years ago North America was inhabited by numerous nations of Native Americans. Their food, clothing, lodging, and life-styles were very different depending on the area in which they lived. It is likely that this book represents the Plains Indians who lived in tipis and hunted buffalo, following them with their horses. Some of the activities presented in this unit may not be specific to the Plains Indians, but are representative of other Indian cultures instead. This unit uses the term "Native Americans" to refer to the people who have been referred to as Indians. The name "Indian" was given by Columbus when he first discovered North America, thinking he was in India. The term "Indian" is considered to be a misnomer by the Native Americans. The present Native American population descended from the numerous nations of Native American ancestors referred to in this book.

Unique Interests.   The girl in this story loves horses and has a special understanding of them. Most children, beginning at an early age, have a unique interest or collection. Examples might include cars, airplanes, musical instruments, insects, dolls, and sports. Many unique interests can be observed in the classroom; if not, parents can add valuable insight. Talk about the children's interests and collections. Encourage them to bring in items to share which depict their special interest.

Horse Facts.   Many children have never had the opportunity to see or ride a horse. If possible, visit a farm or petting zoo where the children can look at and touch the horses. Look at the pictures of horses in the book and share information about horses with the children.

- Point out the different parts including the mane, tail, and hooves. Define and show the stallion, mare, and colt.
- Tell the children that the horses eat natural vegetation such as grass, weeds, and flowers.
- The Spaniards brought horses with them when they came to North America. Prior to that the Native Americans traveled and hunted on foot.
- The horses were used to pull their belongings, including tipis, from place to place.
- Horses were very special and important to the Native American people, especially to the people of the western plains who used them to round up and hunt buffalo. The people had great respect for horses.

Distribute copies of the black line master for children to identify the different parts of a horse. Children can color and cut out the horse to use in small group discussions and to reinforce newly learned concepts.

Tipis.   Plains Indians lived in a tentlike structure called a tipi. Tipis were made with tall wooden poles shaped like a cone and covered with buffalo hides. The outside of the tipi was covered with designs or pictures, often representing nature or great deeds. Tipis were arranged in a circle. The children can make tipis with sticks they find outside, dowel rods, pencils, pick-up sticks, and similar materials. Secure ten sticks at the top with a rubber band or string. The bottom of the sticks can be placed in play dough or clay that has been patted into a circular shape. Cut an old white sheet into circles large enough to fit over the sticks. The children can use chalk or fabric paint to decorate the cloth outer covering of the tipi. The sticks can be covered by cutting a small hole in the center of the cloth, placing the cloth over the sticks, and securing it at the bottom by placing pushpins, tacks, staples or pegs made from toothpicks, through the cloth and into the clay or play dough. Arrange the tipis in a circle.

Dramatic Play.   Set up a freestanding tent or make one by draping blankets over a table. Follow the custom of having the door face the east toward the rising sun. Young Native American children's play prepared them for their role in adult life. Daily life was centered on providing food, clothing, and shelter. Boys learned to make weapons and developed skills that prepared them to be good hunters. Girls helped their mothers set up the tipis, gather berries, and prepare food. Boys and girls ran races and played games with balls. The entire family slept in one room. Each person slept on a buffalo or deer skin hide, depending on the season.

After sharing this background, the children can play, pretending to be Native American children in the 1600s.

Hand Games.   Native Americans enjoyed playing guessing games. A common game was called the hand game. Specially marked sticks were hidden in the hand or under a blanket. The opponent tried to find a specific stick. Try these simple guessing games.

- Place three to five different-colored chips or markers in front of the children. After giving them a chance to look at the markers, ask them to close their eyes. Remove one or more of the chips or markers and close your hand around it. The children will guess which one(s) are missing. The number of markers displayed and removed will depend on the age and developmental level of the children.

- You will need five to ten small chips or marbles and cards containing a numeral from 1 to 5 or 10 to do this activity. Children sit in a circle, one child at a time "It" draws a numeral card, reads the card, and takes the appropriate number of chips or marbles from the center of the circle while classmates close their eyes. "It" holds his or her hands out in front with fists closed. The classmates try to guess how many chips or marbles are in "Its" hands. The correct guesser becomes "It."

- Children sit in a circle. One small classroom object is chosen for children to hide in closed hands. One child "It" closes his or her eyes while another child is quietly chosen to hide the object in his or her hands. All the children sit with their hands closed in front of them to confuse "It." The teacher or another child gives clues to "It," who then tries to guess who is holding the object. Sample clues might include, "It's a girl." "She is wearing blue." "She is wearing sneakers."

Maize.   The Plains people did not plant gardens because they were constantly moving, following the buffalo. Maize, the Native American word for corn, was extremely important to some Native American nations. The word *maize* means "our life."

Try this recipe.

Sweet Corn Bread Muffins

1 cup cornmeal	1 teaspoon salt
1 cup flour	1 cup milk
1 tablespoon baking powder	3 tablespoons melted butter
1 tablespoon sugar	1 egg

Preheat oven to 375 degrees. Line a muffin tin with paper liners. Combine dry ingredients in a large bowl. Combine remaining ingredients in another bowl. Add to dry ingredients and mix until moistened. Pour into muffin tin. Bake about 15 to 20 minutes or until tester comes out clean. Yields 12 muffins or 24 mini muffins.

Corn Cob Prints.   Fill Styrofoam™ meat trays or other shallow pans with colored tempera paint. Have the children roll corn cobs in the paint and then onto paper to make interesting pictures.

New Names.   Names that were given to Native American children were chosen after the child's birth and were given much consideration. Names were often based on a physical characteristic or a particular attribute. Nature was highly revered, and names often reflected this. The girl in the story was not referred to by name. If she had a name, it probably would refer to her special relationship with horses, such as "Girl Who Lives with Horses." Ask the children to brainstorm other names for her. The children can then brainstorm names for each other, taking into account unique interests or physical characteristics. A child who loves to run might be called "Running Legs." A teacher might be named "Tall Teacher." The new names can be written on paper, illustrated by the children, and bound into book form to add to the class library.

Moccasin Game.   In this game pebbles were hidden inside one of three moccasins. Shoeless children can play a variation of this game by hiding marbles or other counters in a shoe belonging to a classmate. Clues can be given by a selected child called "It" while classmates try to guess whose shoe contains the counters. Math concepts can be reinforced by hiding a particular number of marbles and having children guess how many. Color concepts can be reinforced by guessing the color. The teacher may need to help "It" think of appropriate clues.

Concho Belt.   Native Americans in the Southwest made concho belts that were worn by both men and women. The belts are still popular today. Concho belts are made from decorated pieces of silver attached to a leather belt or held together with silver links. Children can make simplified concho belts to wear for play by cutting shapes out of aluminum foil. The shapes can be decorated with pencils and permanent markers. Staple the decorated pieces onto a belt made out of construction paper, heavy yarn, or fabric. Fasten with a paper clip or safety pin, or simply by tying the ends in a knot.

Clay Pots.   Clay pots were used for cooking and eating. Pots were made by rolling a long "snake" of clay and forming it into a bowl shape by making a continuous coil starting at the bottom of the bowl. Once the bowl was formed, the coils were smoothed out using moistened fingers. Use the following clay recipe or a commercially prepared clay. Children can make their own pots. When the clay is dried, the children can paint designs on the bowl with tempera paint.

Clay Recipe

Combine
1 cup salt	2 tablespoons vegetable oil
½ cup water	2 cups flour

Knead and shape the dough. Bake at 250 degrees until hardened. Approximately 2–3 hours.

Sign Language.   Many different languages were spoken by the Native Americans, even among the different groups of the Plains people. Therefore, many Native Americans communicated with each other using sign language. The word "friend" was signed by holding up the middle and index fingers, while closing the thumb over the fourth and fifth fingers. The word "tipi" was signed by making a triangle shape out of the left and right index fingers. The word "walk" was signed by holding hands palm down, moving one hand and then the other as though walking. The word "woman" was signed by pretending to comb hair with curved fingers from top of head to shoulders. The word "you" was signed by pointing the index finger at the other person. The word "see" was signed by holding the index and middle finger in front of the eyes, and pointing in the appropriate direction. The word "man" was signed with the index finger pointing up, palm toward face, and then raising hand in front of the face. Teach some of these signs to the children. They can also make up their own signs for words that are important to them. As a class, brainstorm what common words might look like in sign language.

Native American Foods.   There were many different nations of Native Americans, each with its own culture. The food, clothing and shelter of the different nations depended on their geographic location. Nations who remained in one area grew gardens. Corn and potatoes were grown, among other vegetables. Native Americans who hunted buffalo, such as the Plains people, followed the herd. Their diet consisted of foods they could hunt or gather, including buffalo meat, wild game and fowl, roots, berries, and herbs. Most of the meat and berries were dried to preserve them. For a snack, try serving foods that different groups of Native Americans might have eaten. Ideas include beef jerky, raspberries, blueberries, strawberries, corn products (popcorn, corn on the cob, corn meal bread and muffins, creamed corn, corn chips, tortillas), potatoes, and potato products.

Toss Ball.   Young children and adults enjoyed games of skill. In this game the participants laid down on their backs and tossed a ball behind them. The winner was the person who could throw the ball the farthest. The point of the first bounce marks the distance. Variations of this game can be made up for young children to enjoy. Children can practice throwing balls backward and forward from a standing, kneeling, and lying position.

On the Mark.   Games of skill that prepared children and young adults for hunting were popular. In one game arrows were shot at a target similar to a bull's-eye game. Hitting the inside of the circle was worth the most points; point value decreased toward the outer circle. A variation of this game can be played with young children. Prepare a target with a red circle in the center, followed by a yellow circle, green circle, and blue circle. Tape the target to the wall. Children can throw a tennis ball and try to hit the various colored circles. (Colors can be substituted.)

Bowl Games.   In this game of skill, participants threw a decorated rock or peach pit into the air with one hand and tried to catch it in a bowl held in the other hand. Point value was determined by the design that was face up when the target landed in the bowl. Use a large, lightweight plastic bowl and a Ping-Pong™ ball to play a young child's variation of this game.

Foot Races.   Running races were another popular pastime. Young children enjoy running races as long as the race course is short. Set up a race course between two trees, cones, or other markers. Make the race noncompetitive by timing each child. When they run the race the second and third times, they can try to do it even faster than they did it the first time.

Kickball.   Races were run with participants kicking a ball in front of them. Set up a kickball course with cones. Children can move around the cones dribbling a ball with their foot. Use a large ball and encourage the children to use short, soft kicks, to best control the ball.

Texture Tub.   Fill the exploration table or dress boxes with corn meal or sand. Children can measure and pour, form designs, and write letters and numerals in the substances.

Kachinas.   The Hopi Nation of the Southwest presented young girls with *kachinas* at the end of ceremonies. The dolls were designed like the masks and costumes worn in ceremonies honoring nature. The dolls were carved; had arms, legs, and faces; and were decorated with feathers and painted designs. Young children can make kachinas by attaching a head, body, arms, and legs, cut from cardboard, to a tongue depressor. They can decorate their kachinas with markers, tempera paint, and feathers. Kachinas can also be made from empty spools. Glue three empty spools together, and draw a face, arms, and legs. Decorate with paint and feathers.

Bead Stringing.   Brightly colored beads were made and worn by the Native Americans. Beads can be made by forming clay into small balls and inserting a wire through the center while they dry. Once dry, the beads can be painted. Children can make their own beads or use beads which have been purchased, to make necklaces. The children can pattern the beads by color or design (red-red-yellow-yellow or solid-stripe-solid-stripe).

Weaving.   Warm blankets were made by weaving fibers. Children can learn the basic over/under weaving pattern using paper. Cut slits in a 12" × 18" sheet of construction paper, leaving a 2-inch border intact. Cut 12" × 1" strips to weave through the slits. Demonstrate to children how to go over and under the slits. Secure the ends with tape or glue. The children can form patterns in their weaving by alternating the colors of the stripes. The finished product can be used as a placemat or doll blanket.

Rattles.   Rattles were used in ceremonies, along with drums, to create the beat. Rattles were made from dried gourds, carved wood, turtle shells, hides, and other materials found in nature. Make simple rattles by filling margarine containers with beans, dry pasta, wood chips, gravel, unpopped popcorn, and rice. Tape the lids onto the containers. The children can shake the containers to produce different sounds and rhythms. Challenge the children by shaking a rattle behind a screen or other barrier. They try to guess what substance is making the shaking sound.

Buffalo.   The buffalo was not only respected, but was sacred to the Plains people. It was used to sustain life. The meat and fat were used for food. The buffalo hide was used for shelter, clothing, and warmth. Cooking and storage utensils also came from the buffalo. The people hunted only as much buffalo as was needed for food, shelter, and daily living. Many children have never seen a buffalo. Look for pictures in the library to display. The children can color their own buffalo using the black line master provided. Teach this simple poem that could have been recited by a young Native American about buffalo. Make up a rhythm with the rattles to go with it.

> The buffalo keeps us warm.
> The buffalo gives us food.
> The buffalo is our friend.
> The buffalo is good.

Suggested Home Activities.   Send home a synopsis of *The Girl Who Loved Wild Horses.* Inform parents of the kinds of activities in which the children are involved. Suggest to parents that they go with their child to the library and look for Native American picture books (see related literature). Like this book, most of the picture books are based on legends and revolve around nature. Children and parents can read the books and discuss the meaning of the legend. Many of the legends explain how things in nature came to be. Parents can compare the spiritual meanings with their own spiritual beliefs at a level their young child can comprehend. Beginning at a very young age, children can be taught respect and tolerance for beliefs that are different from their own.

Related Literature

Aliki. *Corn Is Maize, the Gift of the Indians.*
de Paola, Tomie. *The Legend of Indian Paint Brush.*
Goble, Paul. *Buffalo Woman.*
———. *The Gift of the Sacred Dog.*
———. *The Great Race of the Birds and Animals.*
———. *Star Boy.*
Grossman, Virginia and Sylvia Long. *Ten Little Rabbits.*
Jeffers, Susan. *Brother Eagle, Sister Sky.*
Martin, Bill, Jr., and John Archambault. *Knots on a Counting Rope.*
Medearis, Angela. *Dancing with Indians.*
Olighton, Jerrie. *How the Stars Fell into the Sky.*
Osofsky, Audrey. *Dream Catcher.*

Horse Facts Activity

Buffalo Activity

IS THIS A HOUSE FOR HERMIT CRAB?
by
Megan McDonald

Developmental Activities Chart	Language & Cognitive Development	Fine Motor Art	Gross Motor	Perception	Social Skills	Math	Dramatic Play	Cooking Snack	Science	Music, Fingerplays, Poems
1 Animal Home Match-ups	X								X	
2 Legs, Legs, Legs	X				X				X	
3 Shell Collections	X			X					X	
4 Shell Graphing	X			X		X				
5 Shell Tracing		X							X	
6 Sand Pictures		X								
7 Colored Sand		X							X	
8 Digging for Shells		X		X						
9 Sand and Water	X			X						
10 Touch and Make		X		X						
11 Underwater Imagination	X	X							X	
12 Water Activities	X									
13 The Aquarium	X								X	
14 Colors of the Ocean	X								X	
15 Hermit Crab Song										X
16 Crab Cakes						X		X		
17 Find-a-Home Maze		X		X						
18 Crab Moves			X							
19 Pet Shop	X								X	
20 Suggested Home Activities	X			X						
21										
22										
23										
24										
25										
26										
27										
28										
29										
30										

IS THIS A HOUSE FOR HERMIT CRAB?
by Megan McDonald
Orchard Books, 1990

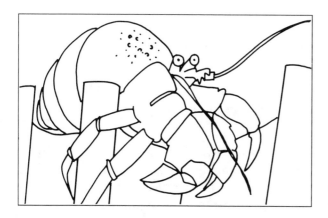

Hermit Crab needs to find a new home because he has outgrown his brown spotted one. A new home will also keep him safe from the dreaded pricklepine fish. Hermit Crab exhausts many possibilities before he finally finds the perfect home.

Animal Home Match-ups. Hermit crabs have soft skin and need to protect themselves from birds, fish, or other crabs by moving into hard, discarded sea shells. Talk about other animals and why their homes are just right for them. Examples to include—bird-nest, squirrel-tree, bear-cave, fox-den, beaver-lodge, gopher-burrow, and so forth. Pictures for this activity could be teacher prepared or bought commercially.

Legs, Legs, Legs. A hermit crab has four pair of legs. He keeps two pair inside the shell that help hold the shell in place. The other two pair of strong, walking legs outside the shell help the crab move around carrying its heavy shell. Brainstorm a list of familiar animals and insects, and make a simple graph comparing how many legs each has. Which has the most legs, which has the least?

Shell Collections. Explain to children that many different animals live inside seashells. People often collect the shells after the animals inside have died and their shells are washed up along the seashore. If possible, have an assortment of shells for the children to look at, touch, and compare. Children can compare the shells by size, color, and texture. They can use words like rough, sharp, prickly, and striped.

Shell Graphing. After children have had enough time to look at, touch, and compare the shells, they can make a real graph on a large piece of butcher paper. Children can count and compare which shell variety has the most, the least, or the same number.

Shell Tracing. Clams, mussels, oysters, and scallops live inside two flatter-type shells (bivalves) that are kept closed by a strong muscle. When found on the seashore, these shells are usually separated and can be used to trace around, creating the familiar fanlike shell appearance. After tracing around the shells, children can draw on the curved and straight lines found on the surface of the shell.

Sand Pictures.   Children squeeze craft glue on heavy paper or tagboard, creating interesting lines or patterns. Then they sprinkle sand on top of the glue. Allow some time for the glue to set before shaking the excess off.

Colored Sand.   Children will enjoy the process and end product of coloring sand. Place a small amount of sand and one drop of food coloring into a margarine tub. After putting the lid on, children shake the mixture until it is well blended. Experiment with the amount of food coloring to get the desired color. Place the containers in a sunny location to dry.

Digging for Shells.   Place shells at the bottom of the sensory table and cover with sand. Allow children to dig in the sand with their hands or small beach shovels and uncover the shells.

Sand and Water.   Provide a small container of water at the sand-filled sensory table. Place a variety of plastic containers, funnels, strainers, and measuring spoons in the sand. Children can experiment pouring, mixing, and molding the sand-water mixture. When talking with the children about what they have done, be sure to reinforce the concepts of empty-full and wet-dry.

Touch and Make.   Line the bottoms of several sturdy shirt boxes with sand. Children can take turns making letters, numbers, faces, shapes, and designs in the sand. Consider using slightly moistened sand. This multisensory activity is excellent to do with special needs children.

Underwater Imagination.   Show children pictures of some creatures that live in the sea, like jellyfish, electric eels, seaweed, sea sponges, crabs, seahorses, and octopi. Let children draw or paint their own version of a sea creature, and then name it and tell about it. Their pictures and dictated stories can be displayed around the room.

Water Activities.   Reinforce how many plants and animals need their water environment to survive. Brainstorm ways that people need and use water too. Include a discussion about water-related activities such as swimming, scuba diving, fishing, taking boat rides, water skiing, surfing, and playing by beaches.

The Aquarium.   If possible, take a field trip to an aquarium and enjoy underwater life firsthand. Write an experience story upon returning.

Colors of the Ocean.   After a trip to an aquarium, ask children what color the water was. It is likely that children will say that some of the water looked blue, some greenish, some gray, and so on. Do a simple experiment with children to show them how the water reflects the color of the plants in the water and the sky above. You will need:

> 1 glass of water (use a plain glass with no design)
> a hand-held mirror
> construction paper: 1 piece of green, 1 blue, 1 gray, 1 black

Place the glass of water on the mirror so that all the children can see. Have children take turns holding the different colors of construction paper over the glass. Ask children to tell what happens to the color of the water as they change the color of the construction paper. Ask why they think this is happening. Explain that the ocean is like a mirror reflecting the color of the plants in the ocean and of the changing colors of the sky above it. Provide time for the children to explore this phenomenon; they may want to see if it occurs with other colors, too!

Hermit Crab Song (to the tune of "The Wheels on the Bus")

> The crab in the sand moves scritch, scratch, scritch,
> Scritch, scratch, scritch, scritch, scratch, scritch.
> The crab in the sand moves scritch, scratch, scritch.
> All along the shore.

Other verses to sing:

> The crab in the sand eats plants and bugs.
> The crab in the sand looks for a home.
> The crab in the sand finds a new shell.

Repeat the first verse.

Crab Cakes

1 8-ounce package softened cream cheese	1 tablespoon lemon juice
1 6-ounce can crabmeat	Dash of Worcestershire sauce
¼ cup mayonnaise	Dash of pepper

Preheat oven to 350 degrees. Beat the cream cheese until smooth. Stir in the remaining ingredients and thoroughly combine. Bake for about 20 minutes until hot and bubbly. Serve between fish-shaped crackers.

Find-a-Home Maze.   The teacher should make enough copies of the maze that is included with the story. Children complete the hermit crab-shell maze by first tracing a path with their finger and then using a crayon or pencil.

Crab Moves.   Have children move like hermit crabs. They start by sitting on the ground with hands behind them pointing out and with feet in front of them flat on the ground. Their bodies should form a capital "M." Children raise their bottoms off the ground, and they are ready to move their hands and feet in opposition. They can move slowly, repeating the words "scritch-scratch, scritch-scratch." They can move quickly like the hermit crab, repeating the words, "scritch-scritch, scritch-scritch." Have children practice moving forward and backward. Modify the move for younger students and those with low muscle tone and strength by allowing them to drag their bottoms along the floor.

Pet Shop.   Call ahead to a local pet store to see if they have any hermit crabs. If they do, take a field trip there to see and learn more about hermit crabs. Consider purchasing one as a classroom pet, since they are easy to care for and can be handled by young children.

Suggested Home Activities.   Send home a synopsis of the story *Is This a House for Hermit Crab?* and inform parents about some of the activities the children will be doing at school. Hermit Crab searched a long time for a new home because some were too deep, some were too heavy, too dark, too noisy, or too crowded. Ask parents to provide an assortment of objects found around the house and boxes or containers that will hold the items. Initially, they can allow their child to estimate visually if the object will fit inside the container. Then, their child can experiment making the perfect fit. Encourage parents to reinforce concepts such as larger than, smaller than, middle or medium sized, and so on.

Related Literature

Carle, Eric. *A House for a Hermit Crab.*

Help Hermit Crab find a new home in the maze.

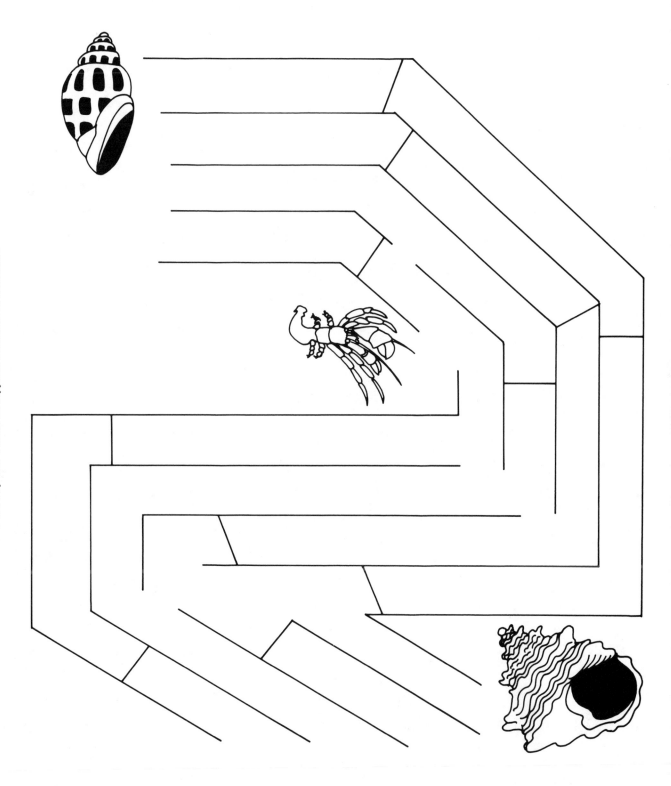

Find a Home Maze Activity

Folk and Fairy Tales

STREGA NONA
by
Tomie dePaola

Developmental Activities Chart	Language & Cognitive Development	Fine Motor Art	Gross Motor	Perception	Social Skills	Math	Dramatic Play	Cooking Snack	Science	Music, Fingerplays, Poems
1 Sort and Pattern	X			X		X				
2 Cook and Watch	X					X			X	
3 Pasta Sauce	X	X				X		X		
4 Lace Pasta		X								
5 Measure and Compare	X					X				
6 Pasta Science	X					X			X	
7 Pasta Weigh-in	X					X				
8 Pasta Song										X
9 Magic Pot	X	X								
10 Dramatize	X				X		X			
11 Pasta for All					X	X				
12 Magic Memory	X									
13 Pasta Factory		X								
14 Pasta Mosaics		X								
15 Numbers and Letters	X	X		X		X				
16 Pot Match-ups				X						
17 Pasta Moves			X							
18 Pasta Pictures	X			X		X				
19 The Tale of Strega Nona and Big Anthony										X
20 Dyeing Pasta		X								
21 Design Copying		X		X						
22 Suggested Home Activities	X	X				X		X		
23										
24										
25										
26										
27										
28										
29										
30										

STREGA NONA
by Tomie dePaola
Prentice Hall, 1975

Big Anthony disobeys Strega Nona's warning never to touch her valuable pasta pot. When Strega Nona leaves to visit her friend in another town, Big Anthony tries to make her magic pot work for him and then can't make it stop. Soon the whole town is filled with pasta. Only Strega Nona can save the day, and Big Anthony learns a lesson.

Sort and Pattern.   Provide children with a bag or box of colored, vegetable-flavored pasta and cooking pots like the one Strega Nona might have used to cook her pasta. Children can sort the pasta into the pots by color. The class can also graph the colored pasta and compare the results: which color has the most, which color has the least, and so on. Next, children can be challenged to create as many multicolored patterns with the pasta as they can think of, such as green-green-orange, green-plain-orange, and orange-orange-green. Glue all the pasta patterns on tagboard strips. Later, children can be given a pasta pattern card and asked to continue the pattern.

Cook and Watch.   Using a hot plate, cook pasta in the classroom. Children can predict how many minutes it will take for the pasta to cook. Record predictions. The children can observe how the pasta gets larger as it cooks. Have children recite Strega Nona's rhyme as the pasta cooks. Compare actual cooking time with the children's predictions. Top with a favorite sauce. Eat and enjoy.

Pasta Sauce.   Children can measure, pour, and stir to make pasta sauce. Be sure to review health and safety rules before cooking.

2	6-ounce cans tomato paste	1	tablespoon basil
1	1-pound can tomatoes	1½	teaspoon salt
1	tablespoon parsley flakes		

Mix all ingredients. Bring to a boil. Simmer uncovered until thick, about 45 minutes. Stir occasionally.

Lace Pasta.   Children can use heavy string or yarn to lace pasta such as manicotti and nuggetlike radiatore.

Measure and Compare.   Pasta can be used in a variety of measurement activities. For example, measure and compare which pasta is longer, manicotti or spaghetti. Measure and compare which pasta is shorter, shells or bows. Pasta can be used to measure the length of familiar classroom objects. Ask how many shells long is the sensory table, how many linguines long is the wagon. The types of pasta used and the objects measured are unlimited.

Pasta Science.   Have children carefully measure out two 1-cup portions of pasta such as elbow macaroni, shells, or bows. Cook a 1-cup portion and compare it with the uncooked pasta. Children can observe, compare, and brainstorm to answer a variety of questions: What happened to the pasta that was cooked? How did it change? What made it change? Does it weigh the same as the uncooked pasta? Did the number of pieces change or are they still the same? Which pasta tastes better?

Pasta Weigh-in.   Place various kinds of pasta at the science center such as shells, rotini, elbows, manicotti, cavatelli, bows, radiatore, mafalda, ziti, and rigati. Children can sort the various kinds of pasta. Using a primary balance scale, children count and compare how many pasta bows weigh the same as five manicotti or five shells, and so on.

Pasta Song (to the tune of "The Wheels on the Bus")

Cook pasta in the pot then bubble, boil, stir.
Bubble, boil, stir.
Bubble, boil, stir.
Cook pasta in the pot then rinse, rinse, scoop.
Pasta's good to eat.

Magic Pot.   Provide children with paper cut into the shape of Strega Nona's magic pot. Children can write or dictate a story about what they would cook if they had a magic pot. They can draw a picture or cut pictures from a magazine to illustrate their individual stories. Stories can be combined to make a class book. As a class, children can brainstorm the magic words that would be said to make their magic pots begin cooking. This can be included in the class book.

Dramatize.   Encourage children to dramatize the story about Strega Nona by providing pots, spoons, and pasta in the housekeeping center.

Pasta for All.   In the story, Big Anthony told all the townspeople to bring forks, plates, bowls, and platters to eat their pasta. Children can practice one-to-one correspondence by setting the table with forks, plates, bowls, cups, napkins, and so on.

Magic Memory.   Cover a wooden cooking spoon with aluminum foil and use a large cooking pot to play a memory game. Children watch and name as the teacher places two to five objects in the cooking pot. The teacher stirs the objects while all say the magic words: "Abracadabra. Stir, stir, gone!" Children close their eyes when hearing the word "gone" and the teacher removes one object from the pot. Objects from the pot are displayed and children identify which thing is missing.

Pasta Factory.   The play dough center can be turned into a pasta factory. Children can form pasta pots or bowls. Play dough can be rolled into thin snakes to make spaghetti or linguine. Play dough snakes can be cut and twisted to make rotini. Children can experiment making other kinds of pasta.

Pasta Mosaics.   Children can make a pasta mosaic by gluing various colored and shaped pasta on tagboard scraps or foam meat trays.

Numbers and Letters.   Using cooked and uncooked spaghetti, children can cut or break the spaghetti pieces to form numbers and letters. Extend the activity by having children make their name with spaghetti or make sets representing the numerals they have formed.

Pot Match-ups.   Bring in various pots of different sizes that have lids. Children can brainstorm different foods that would fit inside the pots. Children can match the correct lid to fit each pot.

Pasta Moves.   Pretend that a jump rope is an extra long piece of Strega Nona's pasta. Children can jump over the "pasta" held at various heights and move under it in creative ways. The "pasta" can be wiggled on the floor as children attempt to jump over it without slipping on it.

Pasta Pictures.   The teacher can make a variety of pasta pictures on the copy machine using different kinds of pasta. Children can match the pasta pictures or use the picture as a sample to copy one of their own. This is an excellent time to introduce or reinforce directional-positional concepts such as above and below, beside, between, and next to. The ordinal positions of first, second, next, and last can be reinforced when children work on reproducing pasta pictures.

The Tale of Strega Nona and Big Anthony (to the tune of "She'll Be Coming Around the Mountain")

> He cooked a lot of pasta when she left.
> Yes, he cooked a lot of pasta when she left.
> Oh, the pot just wouldn't stop.
> No, the pot just wouldn't stop.
> Yes, he cooked a lot of pasta when she left.
>
> Strega Nona said the magic, yes she did.
> Strega Nona said the magic, yes she did.
> She stopped the pasta cooking pot,
> She saved the town from pasta hot.
> Strega Nona said the magic, yes she did.

Dyeing Pasta.   Children will enjoy dyeing pasta that can be used for many of the suggested activities. Each child will need a small plastic margarine tub with a lid. Assist children in combining 2 tablespoons of rubbing alcohol with 4 drops of food coloring (add more or fewer drops of food coloring depending on the intensity of the color desired) in their tub. Add small amounts of pasta—small pasta such as elbow macaroni and bows work the best. Shake the pasta in the closed container. Remove the pasta from the container and allow to dry thoroughly on paper toweling.

Design Copying.   Prewriting can be practiced and reinforced using spaghetti or linguine. Children can break the pasta to make vertical, horizontal, and diagonal lines, "V" stroke, "T," "H," and shapes such as triangles, squares, and rectangles. This is a good sensory experience for children who have difficulties in the area of perceptual motor development. This activity could provide an extra challenge for some children as they are encouraged to produce shapes such as octagons, hexagons, and others.

Suggested Home Activities.   Send home a synopsis of the story *Strega Nona,* and inform parents about some of the activities their children will be doing at school. Invite parents to plan, prepare, and cook a favorite hot pasta dish or cold pasta salad with their child. Parents can bring the pasta item to school, and everyone can create a new version of the story. Then enjoy eating the pasta as the townspeople did in the story!

Related Literature

dePaola, Tomie. *Big Anthony and the Magic Ring.*
———. *Strega Nona's Magic Lessons.*
Galdone, Paul. *The Magic Porridge Pot.*
Hines, Anna Grossnickle. *Daddy Makes the Best Spaghetti.*

THE MITTEN
by
Alvin Tresselt

Developmental Activities Chart	Language & Cognitive Development	Fine Motor Art	Gross Motor	Perception	Social Skills	Math	Dramatic Play	Cooking Snack	Science	Music, Fingerplays, Poems
1 Color of Life	X	X								
2 Folk Dance			X							X
3 What to Wear?		X								
4 Grandparents' Day	X				X					
5 Traditional Snack								X		
6 Keeping Warm		X			X		X			
7 Winter Scene		X								
8 Path Tracing		X								
9 Mitten Relay			X		X					
10 Mitten Weather										X
11 Retelling the Story	X						X			
12 Mitten Math						X				
13 I'm Thinking of . . .	X			X						
14 Winter Cold		X								
15 Mitten Song										X
16 Ukranian Cookies	X	X				X		X		
17 Story Moves			X							
18 Snowdrift		X			X					
19 Suggested Home Activities	X	X	X						X	
20										
21										
22										
23										
24										
25										
26										
27										
28										
29										
30										

THE MITTEN
by Alvin Tresselt
Lothrop, Lee & Shepard, 1964

The Mitten is an old Ukranian folktale of a little boy's mitten lost in the snow as he gathers firewood for his grandmother. One by one, the animals of the forest crowd into the boy's mitten to keep warm.

Color of Life.   The little boy in the story wore a red coat, hat, scarf, and boots. Red was a popular color for the people of the Ukraine because it was considered to be the color of life. Have a red day at school. Children can wear red clothing; use red paint, and red markers; string with red beads; build with red 1-inch blocks; and cut magazine and catalog pictures of red objects to glue on paper to make a collage.

Folk Dance.   Ukranian people love to dance. Teach children a simple heel-toe, heel-toe movement. They can move in place to lively music and practice the step. As they become proficient, they can move around in a circle, heel-toe, heel-toe, with their hands at their waist. The children might also wave red scarves or crepe paper streamers as they dance.

What to Wear?   The animals in the story all wore special-looking clothing. In the Ukraine, color and design is very important. Clothing is decorated with many different kinds of embroidery or stitching. Cross-stitching [XXXX] is popular. Black, red, or multicolored threads are used. Cut out a long rectangular piece of kraft paper and make a vest for each child to decorate and wear. Cut out a circular opening for the head in the center of the rectangle, and cut up the front of one of the long sides. Staple pieces of yarn under the arms on both sides and tie to hold the vest securely in place when worn by the children. Children can use black crayons or markers to make XXXXXX's on their vest. Also provide red, black, and multicolored yarn for them to use in decorating their vest.

Grandparents' Day.   In the story, the boy's grandma was knitting him a new pair of mittens. In the Ukraine, families helped each other and enjoyed spending time together. Often grandparents would read stories to their grandchildren. Invite grandparents to visit the class for a day. If a grandparent is unable to visit, children can ask another family member to come or bring pictures of a special family member. Grandparents can read stories to the children, share a craft or hobby they enjoy, or just spend time with their grandchild. After the experience, the children can each finish the sentence, "I love my grandma/grandpa because _____." Sentence stories and a picture can be given or sent to their grandparents as a remembrance of their special day.

Traditional Snack.   On cold days, the boy and his grandma probably enjoyed a snack together. Consider serving a traditional Ukranian snack on "Grandparents' Day." Sweet buns, like doughnuts filled with jam or apple, were eaten. Serve bismarks and tea with a spoonful of black currant jam, a slice of lemon, or sugar.

Keeping Warm.   Bundle up on a cold day and have students walk around the schoolyard and neighborhood gathering sticks to put in a wagon. Inside at the block center, children can role play and stack their blocks in the wagon, making certain they are balanced and won't fall.

Winter Scene.   The illustrations of the story depict the stark cold winter weather. Children can use white paint to sponge snow on a 12" × 18" piece of blue paper. They can glue some small sticks, collected on their walk, on the snowy background to represent trees.

Path Tracing.   Children can complete the path tracing black line master provided. Follow the path and take the animals to the lost mitten.

Mitten Relay.   Divide children into teams. Everyone on the team wears mittens as they perform a variety of tasks, for example, carry a potato or several cotton balls on a spoon, bounce and catch a ball. The team to complete all the tasks first wins.

Mitten Weather (verse to recite)

> Thumbs in the thumb place, fingers all together.
> This is the song we sing in mitten weather.
> Doesn't matter whether they're made of wool or leather.
> Thumbs in the thumb place, fingers all together.

Retelling the Story.   Make a mitten out of felt. Cut out the shape for each of the animals. Children can retell the story on the flannel board. Another version is to make a large mitten out of kraft paper. Children sit in a circle around the mitten. Each child can tell a part of the story and place his or her stuffed animal in the mitten. The end result will be the same as in the story!

Mitten Math

- Children can sort mittens by color, size, and other attributes they decide upon.
- Vote on the favorite pair of mittens.

• Cut 11 pairs of mittens from construction paper. On one mitten write a numeral from 0 to 10; on the mitten partner, draw the corresponding number of snowflakes. Laminate the mittens. Children match the numeral to the correct number of snowflakes to make a pair.

I'm Thinking of . . . .   Place all of the children's mittens on a large piece of white paper to represent snow. A crumpled piece can be added to make a snowdrift. Children sit around the snow pile in a circle. Depending on the abilities of the students, the teacher or children can take turns describing a mitten for the other children to find. For example,

I'm thinking of a mitten.
It's red on the outside.
It has fur on the inside.
Which mitten is it?

Winter Cold.   The little boy trudged through the snow on the coldest day of winter. Provide catalogs and magazines, and have children cut out clothing they would wear, from head to toe, on a *very* cold day. Pictures can be glued on a mitten-shaped piece of construction paper.

Mitten Song (to the tune of "The Farmer in the Dell")

The mitten in the snow.
The mitten in the snow.
Help us please,
So we won't freeze.
The mitten in the snow.

A _____ squeezes in. [Supply animal name, one per verse.]
A _____ squeezes in.
Help us please,
So we won't freeze.
The mitten in the snow.

The mitten in the snow.
The mitten in the snow.
With a rip and a snap,
It split in half!
The mitten in the snow.

Ukranian Cookies

8	ounces butter		2	eggs
6	ounces sugar		2	egg yolks
1½	cups flour		½	cup chopped almonds

Preheat oven to 375 degrees. Lightly beat together the butter and sugar until creamy. Beat in the eggs; then lightly stir in the flour to make a dough. Divide the dough and press into two greased 7-inch pie pans. Brush the top with the beaten egg yolks and sprinkle with chopped almonds. Bake for 15 minutes until golden.

Story Moves.   Have children move like the boy and the animals in the story—trudge in the snow like the boy, scurry like the mouse, hop like the rabbit and the cricket, fly like the owl, run like the boar and the wolf, trot like the fox, lumber like the bear, and leap like the frog.

Snowdrift.   The boy in the story dropped his mitten in a snowdrift. Provide children with white styrofoam pieces. Challenge small groups of children to create a snowdrift by gluing small pieces and large packing pieces together.

Suggested Home Activities.   Send home a synopsis of the folktale *The Mitten,* and inform parents of some of the activities the children will be doing at school. If you live in a region that experiences cold, snowy weather, suggest that parents and children play in the snow together, making snowballs, snowmen, and angels in the snow. Warm up by enjoying hot chocolate and cookies together (send home the Ukranian cookie recipe). This is a good time to encourage parents to work with their child to strengthen dressing skills and reinforce what goes on first, next, and last. If you live in an area that is not cold and snowy, suggest parents visit the library and select more books about snowy winter weather.

Related Literature

Brett, Jan. *The Mitten.*
Rogers, Jean. *Runaway Mittens.*

Trace each path and help the animals find the mitten.

Path Tracing Activity

GOLDILOCKS AND
THE THREE BEARS
by
James Marshall

Developmental Activities Chart	Language & Cognitive Development	Fine Motor Art	Gross Motor	Perception	Social Skills	Math	Dramatic Play	Cooking Snack	Science	Music, Fingerplays, Poems
1 Reading the Story	X									
2 Problem Solving	X				X					
3 Stranger Danger	X				X					
4 Rooms of the House	X	X								
5 Small, Medium, and Large	X			X		X				
6 Size Sequencing	X			X		X				
7 Matching	X			X		X				
8 Groups of Three	X					X				
9 Measuring						X				
10 Ordinals	X					X				
11 Bears' Feely Bag	X			X						
12 Hot or Cold?	X			X						
13 Hard or Soft?	X			X						
14 Textured Bears	X	X		X						
15 Laced Bears		X								
16 Hot to Cold						X			X	
17 Forest Path		X		X						
18 Hot Porridge			X		X					
19 Obstacle Course	X		X	X						
20 Story Dramatization					X		X			
21 Bears' Cottage		X			X		X			
22 Bear Puppets					X		X			
23 Safe Acting					X		X			
24 Porridge Snack								X		
25 Oatmeal Cookies								X		
26 Three Bears' Fingerplay									X	
27 Three Bears' Song									X	
28 Suggested Home Activities	X				X	X				
29										
30										

GOLDILOCKS AND THE THREE BEARS
retold and illustrated by James Marshall
Dial Books for Young Readers, 1988

The expressive text and delightfully humorous illustrations add a new charm to the age-old tale of *Goldilocks and the Three Bears*. On her way to buy muffins, Goldilocks broke the promise she made to her mother and took the shortcut through the woods. The three bears who were off riding bikes while the porridge was cooling left their cottage open and unattended. Anyone can guess what happens next in this favorite fairy tale.

Reading the Story.   Children enjoy hearing this story over and over; they feel successful in their ability to predict what will happen next. Read the story a few different times. Stop to look at the pictures and define some of the new expressions used in this version, such as "patooie," "scalding," and "smashed to smithereens." Ask the children to retell the story in sequence using only the pictures as cues. Finally, read the story leaving out familiar words and phrases for the children to fill in.

Problem Solving.   Discuss Goldilocks' behavior with the children. Ask open-ended questions such as, "What do you think about what Goldilocks did?" "Was it a good idea to go into someone's house?" "What else could she have done when she saw that nobody was home?" "Why do you think she went in?" "Do you think she'll go into another empty house?" Ask questions that require more than a yes/no response. Concentrate on asking "wh" questions (who, what, where, when, what if). Children can brainstorm what Goldilocks could have done differently and what the consequences would have been. Using the children's ideas, write a new story or a new ending for the story about Goldilocks and the three bears. Each class will have a different story to tell depending on the problem-solving and brainstorming responses.

Stranger Danger.   Discuss with the children some of the basic stranger danger rules. The depth of discussion will depend on the age of the children. Very young children need to know that they shouldn't talk to strangers or take any gifts from somebody they don't know. They should also know what to do in case they get lost (stop their feet, look for another mom with children or store worker, and ask for help). Older children need to know not to answer the door for someone they don't know and the correct way to answer the phone. Good and bad touch can be taught at different levels. Stranger danger rules that are discussed in class should be shared with parents for the sake of consistency.

Rooms of the House. Goldilocks made herself at home in all the rooms of the house: the kitchen, the parlor, and the bedroom. Each room is identifiable by the furnishings of the room. Use a dollhouse with removable furnishings or a large outline of the inside of a house and pictures cut from magazines. Children can identify the room furnishings (or pictures of them) and place or glue them in the appropriate room. Include not only furniture, but items that are typically found in the room.

Small, Medium, and Large. The story of Goldilocks and the three bears naturally lends itself to the concept of small, medium, and large. Find like objects that come in three different sizes, such as bowls, spoons, bottles, jars, plates, socks, mittens, crackers, pencils and crayons, books, and balls. Label each of three containers with the words "Small," "Medium," or "Large." The children can sort the objects according to size. They will need to compare all three of the like objects to classify them properly.

Size Sequencing. As in the previous activity, use like objects that come in three sizes. Have the children arrange them largest to smallest or smallest to largest. The children can try to trick their friends by asking them to guess in which order the objects are arranged. Have the children work from left to right, a skill that is prerequisite to reading and writing.

Matching. Cut simple shapes for use with the flannel board representing the three bears, their bowls, spoons, chairs, and beds. The children can match the bear with its own belongings according to size (small, medium, or large).

Groups of Three. Mostly everything at the three bears' cottage came in a group of three. The children can look around the classroom, playground, and their homes to find other groups of three. Any group of three the children make is acceptable (3 books, 3 tissues, 3 crayons, 3 bicycles, and so on). Designate a special area of the classroom for displaying the groups of three. The children will be proud to tell about their groups of three.

Measuring. One way to determine the size of an object is to measure it. Children can measure classroom objects to determine if they are small, medium, or large. Encourage children to measure items with different units, such as unifix™ cubes, blocks, erasers, and books. Compare like items, and suggest ways for children to discover that no matter what unit of measurement is used, large items will require more units of measurement than will medium or small items and that medium items require more units than small items.

Ordinals. The terms "first," "second," and "third" can be used during many three bears' activities. The terms can be used and reinforced when measuring and sequencing. Line the children up and talk about who is first, second, third, and so forth. Rearrange the children so that everyone has a chance to be first, last, and somewhere in the middle. Look at the bears on the bicycles: Who is first, second, third? Whose bed was slept in first? Whose porridge was tasted second? Whose chair was sat in third/last? As children become familiar with the terms, they will use them in their own discoveries.

Bears' Feely Bag. Fill a pillowcase with items that could be found in the three bears' cottage. Include bowls, spoons, cups, books, and toys. The children can take turns feeling for objects and identifying them using only their sense of touch.

Hot or Cold? The bears went for a ride because their porridge was too hot. When Goldilocks arrived, one bowl of porridge was too hot and another, too cold. Expose the children to the concept of hot and cold using real objects and pictures. When real objects are used, close teacher supervision must be exercised. Compare a cup of hot water with a cup of cold water by looking at the steam and touching the outside of the cup only. Children can compare a warm iron with a cold iron. Compare hot cereal or pudding with cold cereal or pudding. Compare cold ice cream with hot chocolate. After the children have been exposed to real objects, use pictures cut from magazines. Children can look at the pictures, predict if the item is hot or cold, and classify them accordingly.

Hard or Soft? Goldilocks didn't like Papa Bear's chair because it was too hard. Mama Bear's chair was too soft. Children can compare items that could be hard or soft and classify them according to those attributes. Compare sitting in a bean-bag chair or large pillow to sitting on the hard floor. Compare items such as soft Jell-O™ with hard pretzels; soft fresh play dough with hardened play dough; soft, furry slippers to hard leather shoes; and a soft cloth-covered book with a hard cardboard book.

Textured Bears. Provide the children with simple small, medium, and large bear shapes that have been cut from cardboard (see pattern). Bears of different textures can be created by covering the bears with a variety of collage materials. Examples are coffee grounds, sand, brown rice, furry fabric, cotton balls, corduroy fabric, satin fabric, tin foil pieces, and crumpled leaves. The children can compare the textures. Use the bears to play a touch-and-tell game. Place one or two bears behind a screen or in a covered box with a hand hole cut in it. The children can guess with what the bear has been covered.

Laced Bears. Cut simple bear shapes from cardboard, or use construction paper which has been laminated or covered with clear Con-Tact® paper. Punch holes around the bears. Give children yarn to lace through the holes.

Hot to Cold. Children can experiment with how a substance changes from hot to cold. Prepare hot chocolate or breakfast cereal. When the substance is cooked, children will know that it is too hot to eat or drink. Talk about what the bears did while their breakfast was cooling. Ask the class to brainstorm what the bears could have done to help their breakfast cool. The children might suggest adding cold water or ice or putting the substance in the refrigerator or freezer. They might think of other activities to do while the substance cools. Experiment with their ideas. Ask the children to predict if the substance will cool faster by adding ice or by playing a favorite game while it cools. Encourage the children to predict how long it will take the substance to cool by the different methods. Use a clock to verify their predictions.

Forest Path.   The children can help Goldilocks follow the path through the woods to the three bears' cottage. Reproduce a copy of the path for each child. Encourage them to use their finger and then a crayon, pencil, or marker. The children might want to help Goldilocks escape by starting the path at the cottage and helping her find her way out of the woods.

Hot Porridge.   Play this game like "hot potato." Have the children sit in a circle on the floor. Play favorite music on the tape player or piano, while children pass a small bowl around the circle. When the music stops, the person holding the hot bowl of porridge is "out." Allow the children who are "out" to help start and stop the music.

Obstacle Course.   Goldilocks took the shortcut through the woods despite her mother's warning and the signs posted along the way. Set up a course with obstacles similar to those Goldilocks might have encountered on her trip through the forest, for example, a wide river to jump over (made out of masking tape), a log to balance and walk on (balance beam), a tree to climb (a ladder placed flat on the floor), a dark tunnel to crawl through (an empty carton), and a large trap to run through (a falling parachute or sheet). Put up some of the signs that were posted at the entrance to the forest.

Story Dramatization.   Dramatize the story using props and dress-up clothes. Allow the children to try playing different roles. If possible, videotape the dramatization so the children can watch themselves on the television.

Bears' Cottage.   Set up the dramatic play area like the bears' cottage. Provide kitchen utensils, chairs, and sleeping bags for beds. Since the characters in the story wore colorful costumes and hats, provide a variety of dress-up clothes and hats for the children to wear.

Bear Puppets.   Provide the children with brown lunch-size paper bags. The bags can be decorated like a bear or like Goldilocks. Use markers and small pieces of construction paper or other collage materials for ears, buttons, bows, hats, and vests. Some children may choose to make all the characters, others may want to make only one. They can use the puppets to dramatize the story.

Safe Acting.   Role play with the children the safe response in the following situations.

- They go to a friend or neighbor's house when there is nobody at home.
- Somebody comes to their house when parents' are unable to open the door.

Porridge Snack.   Porridge is a soft breakfast food. For a snack, prepare a hot oat or wheat cereal. Flavor it with brown sugar, cinnamon, or honey. Allow the children to help measure, pour, and mix the ingredients.

Oatmeal Cookies

2	cups margarine or shortening	1	teaspoon baking soda
2	cups sugar	¼	teaspoon salt
1	egg	4	cups 1-minute oats
2	cups flour		

Preheat oven to 350 degrees. Cream shortening, sugar, and egg. Add dry ingredients. Mix well. Drop by the teaspoon on an ungreased cookie sheet. Flatten with a fork dipped in cold water. Bake for 8 to 10 minutes. When cool, sift powdered sugar on top. Yield 4 dozen cookies.

Three Bears Fingerplay

The three bears lived together as a happy family.   [Hold up middle finger, ring finger and pinky.]
The papa was the largest of the three.   [Point to middle finger with opposite hand.]
The mama's size was medium.   [Point to ring finger with opposite hand.]
The baby bear was small.   [Point to pinky with opposite hand.]
They lived in a forest cottage one and all.   [Make a triangle out of thumbs and index fingers.]

Three Bears Song (to the tune of "Farmer in the Dell")

The papa bear is large.
The baby bear is small.
The mama bear is medium, she isn't large or small.

The porridge was too hot.
It burned their tongues a lot.
So off they went a riding
To their favorite spot.

But when they came back home
They found they weren't alone.
Goldilocks was fast asleep.
She came in on her own.

Suggested Home Activities.   Send home a synopsis of *Goldilocks and the Three Bears*. Inform the parents of the kinds of activities their children are involved in at school.

- The three bears' favorite breakfast is porridge. Ask the parents to help their children prepare a list of their favorite foods to send to school. At school, the responses can be listed on a picture graph. Children can compare their favorite foods and count how many children like the same foods.

• Send home an explanation of the stranger danger activities that were done and the rules that were discussed. Encourage the parents to reinforce this at home.

Related Literature

Brett, Jan. *Goldilocks and the Three Bears.*
Cauley, Lorinda Bryan. *Goldilocks and the Three Bears.*
Galdone, Paul. *Goldilocks and the Three Bears.*

Textured Bears Pattern

Textured Bears Patterns (continued)

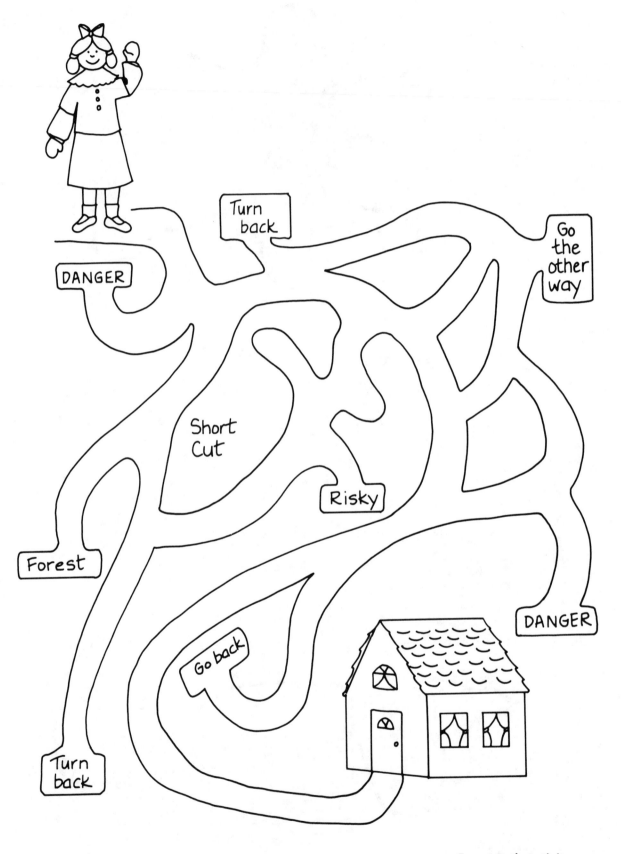

Forest Path Activity

SEVEN BLIND MICE
by
Ed Young

Developmental Activities Chart	Language & Cognitive Development	Fine Motor Art	Gross Motor	Perception	Social Skills	Math	Dramatic Play	Cooking Snack	Science	Music, Fingerplays, Poems
1 Blindfold				X						
2 A Strange Something				X						
3 Calendar	X					X				
4 Puzzler				X						
5 Ordinal Numbers	X					X				
6 Mouse Parade	X	X				X				
7 Role Play							X			
8 Crayon Melting	X	X							X	
9 Puzzles		X		X						
10 Days of the Week Song	X					X				X
11 Paper Animals		X								
12 Seven Little Mice Song										X
13 Mouse Toast								X		
14 Picture Puzzles		X			X					
15 Oily Animals		X		X				X	X	
16 Matching Tails				X						
17 Climb to the Top			X							
18 Mouse Moves			X	X						
19 Paper Fans		X								
20 Peanutty Snacks								X		
21 Visual Closure	X			X						
22 Suggested Home Activity				X						
23										
24										
25										
26										
27										
28										
29										
30										

252 Folk and Fairy Tales

SEVEN BLIND MICE
by Ed Young
Philomel Books, 1992

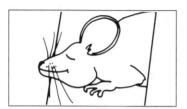 *Seven Blind Mice* is an adaptation of the fable from India entitled "The Blind Men and the Elephant." The story is about seven blind mice who discover a strange "something" by their pond. Each day a different mouse goes to the strange something trying to figure out what it is. The story exemplifies the moral: "Knowing in part may make a fine tale, but wisdom comes from seeing the whole."

Blindfold. The story is about seven blind mice trying to figure out what an unfamiliar object might be. Children will better understand their dilemma if they understand what it is like to be blind. If the children are willing, blindfold them one at a time and hand them a familiar object from the classroom. Ask them to describe and identify the object without using their sense of sight. If the children hesitate to wear a blindfold, ask them to close their eyes.

A Strange Something. After reading the story to the children, ask them how the mice knew there was a strange something by the pond. The children can brainstorm answers. Provide firsthand experience by taking children with blindfolds or closed eyes for a walk around the classroom. Place a strange something where children would not expect it to be. Children can try to guess what the strange something might be.

Calendar. Each day a different-colored mouse went to the pond to try to figure out what the strange something might be. The red mouse went Monday, followed by the green mouse, the yellow mouse, the purple mouse, the orange mouse, the blue mouse, and finally the white mouse. Cut colored mice out of construction paper using the black line master as a pattern. Cover each day on the calendar with the appropriately colored mouse. Children can predict what color comes next. As the month continues, the children will notice a color pattern associated with the days of the week.

Puzzler. Each day one of the mice discovered a different part of the whole. Find an interesting picture of an animal or object; mount it on heavy cardboard. Cut the picture into seven parts. Each day present the children with a different part of the picture. The children will discover you can't always determine the whole from one of the parts.

Ordinal Numbers. Tell the children that they can count objects by saying first, second, third, and so on just as they can count by saying 1, 2, 3. Count the days on the calendar using ordinal numbers. Line the children up and count them using ordinal numbers. The children can line up toys and count their order.

Mouse Parade.   Use the black line master of the mouse provided. Make seven mice for each child to color and cut out. They can line up their mice when complete and count them using the ordinal positions first, second, third, fourth, fifth, sixth, and seventh.

Role Play.   When the children are familiar with the story, have them take parts and role play *Seven Blind Mice*. Cut mouse ears and tails out of red, green, yellow, purple, orange, blue, and white paper. The ears can be attached to a band that fits around each child's head. The tails can be pinned or taped on. Cut an elephant's trunk out of gray construction paper. Attach it to yarn that can be tied around the "elephant's head." The children can alternate roles.

Crayon Melting.   The seven mice are boldly colored. Children will enjoy coloring mice as well as other pictures with crayons that have been melted into a different shape. Place broken chunks of crayons in sections of a cupcake tin that has been coated with a nonstick spray. Colors can be kept separate or they can be combined for a different effect. Place the pan in a 300-degree oven. Remove when the wax has melted. Let cool. Remove the new crayons from the pan.

Puzzles.   Puzzles are a wonderful activity for reinforcing the concept of part/whole. Provide the children with a variety of puzzles to complete. When choosing puzzles for the children, consider the different developmental levels of puzzle play:

1. Look at the picture.
2. Remove the pieces.
3. Organize the pieces.
4. Complete single-piece form boards and puzzles.
5. Complete inset puzzles with an increasing number of pieces.
6. Complete interlocking puzzles with an increasing number of pieces.

Days of the Week Song (to the tune of "Allouette")

Sunday, Monday, Tuesday, Wednesday, Thursday, Friday, Saturday.
A week has seven days.

Paper Animals.   The illustration of the elephant appears to be made from torn paper. Provide the children with scraps of colored paper for tearing and gluing. The children can create a real or imaginary animal. If the animals are imaginary, ask the children to think of names for them.

Seven Little Mice (to the tune of "Six Little Ducks")

Seven little mice went out one day.
Over to the pond where they liked to play.
When they were there they saw something strange.
To find out what it was, it took them seven days.

Mouse Toast.   Children will have fun creating toast that looks like a mouse. Cut toast, which has been spread with peanut butter into a circle shape with a glass or cookie cutter. Peel a long carrot strip with a vegetable peeler, coil it with fingers, and use it as a tail. Attach marshmallow ears, raisin eyes, nose, and feet, and strings of coconut for whiskers. Ask the children to think of ways to create an elephant using toast as the base.

Picture Puzzles.   Children can make puzzles to take home. Provide magazines with interesting pictures. Each child can choose a picture to glue on tagboard. The tagboard picture can be cut into puzzle pieces. Store the pieces in individual zip-close bags. Encourage the children to cut an appropriate number of puzzle pieces to match their own developmental levels.

Oily Animals.   Try this recipe for oily dough. The children can form the elephant parts that the mice discovered and put them together to make a whole elephant. They can also make mice with long squiggly tails.

    4 cups flour
    1 cup oil mixed with 6 cups water and food coloring

Knead and add more flour if necessary. The dough is meant to be quite oily.

Matching Tails.   Cut seven mice (red, green, yellow, purple, orange, blue, and white) using the black line master. Cut a set of seven tails in corresponding colors. Laminate the pieces. The children can match the tail to the mouse.

Climb to the Top.   The mice had a long way to climb to get to the top of the elephant. Place a ladder on the floor. The children can pretend they are mice climbing up the elephant as they move between the rungs and balance and walk on the side rails. Visit the playground or a neighborhood park. Children can climb on the jungle gym and pretend it's an elephant.

Mouse Moves.   The children can lumber like elephants and scamper like little mice. Talk about the quiet and loud sounds made by mice and elephants. Beat a drum slowly and loudly to imitate the sound of a lumbering elephant. Beat it quickly and softly to imitate the sound of scampering mice. Children will move to the sound of the drum. Children will enjoy beating the drum while their classmates move like the animals.

Paper Fans.   The orange mouse discovered the end of the elephant's tail and thought he had found a fan. Show the children how to make a paper fan by folding paper backward and forward. Hold the end of the fan in place with a paper clip. The children can fan themselves and create a breeze like an elephant's tail does when it swishes back and forth.

Peanutty Snacks.   Both elephants and mice like to eat peanuts. Serve peanuts in the shell for snacks. Children will strengthen the small muscles of the fingers as they crack the shell and pick out the peanuts.

Visual Closure.   Visual closure activities reinforce visual perception and the ability to see part-whole relationships. Find pictures with which the children are familiar, like animals, people, and toys. Cover the pictures with construction paper cut to the same size as the picture. Attach the construction paper with paper clips at the top. Prepare the construction paper by cutting four to six strips from the bottom to within a 1-inch border at the top. Lift the paper one strip at a time, revealing only one part of the picture at a time. Children can guess what the picture is by looking at parts of the whole. See black line master for the visual closure pattern.

Suggested Home Activity.   Send home a synopsis of *Seven Blind Mice,* and inform parents of the kinds of activities the children are involved in at school. Tell parents the "mouse moral": "Knowing in part may make a fine tale, but wisdom comes from seeing the whole." Parents can reinforce this concept at home by preparing a feely bag game. They can put a familiar household item or toy in a box or pillowcase. Tell them to have their child feel the item and try to guess what it is using only the sense of touch.

Related Literature

Kraus, Robert. *Whose Mouse Are You?*
Lionni, Leo. *Matthew's Dream.*
Schories, Pat. *Mouse Around.*

Calendar/Mouse Parade Activities

Cut on the vertical lines.

Visual Closure Activity

THE LITTLE RED HEN
by
Margo Zemach

Developmental Activities Chart	Language & Cognitive Development	Fine Motor Art	Gross Motor	Perception	Social Skills	Math	Dramatic Play	Cooking Snack	Science	Music, Fingerplays, Poems
1 Red Hen and Her Chicks			X	X						
2 Tale of the Red Hen			X							X
3 Planting Wheat									X	X
4 Path Tracing		X								
5 From Grain to Bread Sequencing	X	X							X	
6 Card Games	X		X		X	X				
7 More with Cards	X				X	X				
8 Yeast Science	X								X	
9 Little Red Hen's Quick Bread	X	X				X		X		
10 Bread and _____?	X					X		X		
11 Little Red Hen's Whole Wheat Pancakes	X	X				X		X		
12 Wheat Snacks								X		
13 Wheat Cereal Math	X			X		X				
14 Wheat Cereal Mosaic		X								
15 Cereal Patterns		X		X						
16 Working Hard	X				X					
17 Sensory Table		X		X						
18 Red Hen	X	X								
19 Story Characters		X					X			
20 The Bakery Trip	X							X		
21 The Bakery	X	X			X		X			
22 Machines	X									X
23 Suggested Home Activities	X	X			X	X			X	
24										
25										
26										
27										
28										
29										
30										

THE LITTLE RED HEN
by Margot Zemach
Farrar, Straus, Giroux, 1983

A resourceful little red hen makes bread from scratch without the help of her three lazy friends—the goose, the pig, and the cat. When the loaf of bread is ready, the lazy friends come running, only to meet with some disappointing results. Children love the repetitive lines "Not I" and "Then I'll do it myself" throughout this old folktale. Other popular versions are written by Paul Galdone and Janina Domanska.

Red Hen and Her Chicks. A mother hen is a busy and devoted mom who always recognizes her own baby chicks. The chicks learn fast by watching and imitating her. Mother hens, just like the little red hen, often take their chicks out on walks around the barnyard. Play a hen and chick game. One child is selected to be the little red hen, all the other children are baby chicks. The baby chicks watch and imitate all the movements made by the red hen (run, hop, strut, flap arms). The body movements imitated are unlimited.

Tale of the Red Hen (to the tune of "My Bonnie Lies Over the Ocean")

No, her friends did not wa-ant to help her.
The red hen did all the hard work.
She planted, cut wheat, and she threshed it.
With flour, red hen baked some bread!
Warm bread! Warm bread!
Cat, goose, and pig ran to e-eat it!
Warm bread! Warm bread!
Red hen and her chicks ate it all!

Planting Wheat (to the tune of "Here We Go 'Round the Mulberry Bush")

First the red hen plows the ground,
Plows the ground, plows the ground,
First the red hen plows the ground,
Then she plants the seeds.   [Children bend to plant.]

This is the way she plants the seeds,   [Children crouch down.]
So that they will grow.

The rain and sun will help them grow,   [Children spread arms open and
Right up through the ground.   begin to rise.]

Now the red hen picks the wheat,   [Pick wheat.]
So she'll have bread to eat.

Path Tracing.   Children complete the black line path tracing activity. Children first use their finger to trace the dotted lines and then use a pencil or crayon to take the red hen and her hungry friends to the loaf of bread.

From Grain to Bread Sequencing.   Use the black line master patterns to make felt pieces for the flannel board. Show the step-by-step sequence, beginning with planting wheat seeds and ending with a loaf of fresh bread. When children understand the process, they cut the pictures apart and glue them on paper in the correct sequence. The pictures can also be stapled together to make a small book.

Card Games.   In the story, the red hen's lazy friends were seen playing cards. Teach children a variety of card games to strengthen math and thinking skills. (Remove the face cards for all the games.)

- Put three cards on a table with the middle card face down. Give clues:

  I'm more than 3, but less than 5.

  What number am I?

  I'm less than 7, but more than 5.

  What number am I?

- Two or three children can play a card game similar to "Go Fish." Start with two suits of number pairs 1 through 10. Pass out four cards per player. The rest of the cards are placed in the middle. Children find number matches in their hand and put them on the table. Then children take turns trying to make a number match by asking another player, "Do you have a ____?" If the player does not have the card, the child picks a card from the pile in the middle. Play continues until someone matches all his or her cards.

- Play a concentration game with cards. Put two to four number pairs face down on a table. Each player takes a turn and tries to find a pair of numbers that match by turning over two cards. If a match is not made, the two cards are turned over, and the next player takes a turn.

- Each child picks a card and reads the numeral. He or she must clap, jump, hop, skip, tap, or gallop the correct number of times.

More with Cards.   Remove the face cards for all the activities.

- Sort cards by suit, by color, or by number.
- Children sequence the cards 1 to 10, frontward and backward.
- Place the cards 1 to 10 on the table in order. Children close their eyes while the teacher removes one to three cards. Children tell what cards are missing.
- Place a card on the table. Ask children what number comes before it and what number comes after it.
- Show a card. Ask children to name a smaller number or a bigger number. Ask children to name a number that is more than or less than the number shown.

• Have children make sets 1 to 10 to correspond to the cards. Use blocks, buttons, beads, and other easy-to-count materials.

Yeast Science. Yeast is an interesting foodstuff for children to smell and to watch in action. The little red hen used flour and other ingredients to make a "lovely loaf of bread." To make her bread rise, and not be flat like a pancake, she had to use yeast. Children will enjoy watching this simple experiment to show how yeast can blow up a balloon.

Add 1 teaspoon of dry yeast and ¼ cup of sugar to 1 cup of very warm water. Stir to dissolve. Pour the mixture into a quart-size soda bottle. Soften a balloon by blowing it up several times. Put the balloon over the top of the bottle. Keep it in place with a rubber band, piece of string, or twist tie. Fill a large pot half full of very warm water. Place the soda bottle in the warm water. In about one hour, bubbles from the yeast will fill the balloon and slowly blow up the balloon.

Little Red Hen's Quick Bread

3	cups warm water	9	or 10 cups flour
3	cakes/packages yeast	5	teaspoons salt
¼	cup sugar *or* honey	5	tablespoons oil

Preheat oven to 400 degrees. Combine water, yeast, sugar, or honey. Stir until yeast dissolves. Add half the flour and salt. Beat hard with a spoon until batter is smooth. Add remaining flour and salt and blend well. Pour oil over the dough and knead for 3 minutes. Cover bowl, let rise until doubled in size, about 45 minutes. Punch down and turn out on a lightly floured board and knead slightly. Shape into loaves (two large or three small). Place in buttered pans. Cover and let rise about 30 minutes. Bake for 30 minutes.

Bread and _____? Have children brainstorm a list of things they could put on their warm bread. Tally responses to determine what topping is the class favorite. Provide several of the most favored toppings to serve with the bread.

Little Red Hen's Whole Wheat Pancakes

1	cup whole wheat flour	1	cup milk
1	tablespoon sugar	2	egg yolks
4	teaspoons baking powder	2	tablespoons oil
½	teaspoon salt	2	beaten egg whites (stiff)

Beat egg whites. In a separate bowl, mix all the ingredients. Fold in egg whites and grill pancakes until brown and fluffy.

Wheat Snacks. Select wheat cereals and/or crackers to serve at snacktime. Look for favorite cereals at the store that are low in sugar.

Ralston Wheat Chex™
Post Golden Crisp™
General Mills Lucky Charms™

Quaker Puffed Wheat™
General Mills Cheerios™
Honey Nut Cheerios™

General Mills Cinnamon Toast Crunch™   Nabisco Shredded Wheat™
                                                                 Original or Spoon Size
Nabisco Crackers Premium™   Nabisco Wheat Thins™
Nabisco Graham Crackers™   Keebler Wheatables™

Wheat Cereal Math.   Not all wheat becomes white or whole wheat flour; much of it is turned into wheat breakfast cereal. Divide the class into groups of two to four children. Provide each group with a small bowl filled with a variety of wheat cereals, such as Ralston Wheat Chex™, Post Golden Crisp™, General Mills Cheerios™, and so on. The children sort the cereal by shape or size, graph the different varieties, and compare the amounts—which type of cereal has the most pieces, the least, or the same amount.

Wheat Cereal Mosaic.   Provide children with a variety of wheat breakfast cereals. Children glue the cereal on sturdy paper, a paper plate, or a Styrofoam™ plate to make a mosaic.

Cereal Patterns.   Children make simple or complex patterns with the different varieties of wheat cereal.

Working Hard.   The little red hen worked hard to provide the loaf of bread for herself and the chicks, because her lazy friends refused to help. Encourage a discussion about the behavior of the goose, the pig, and the cat. Brainstorm a list of ways children help at home and at school, so that one person doesn't have all the work to do. Set up a situation in the classroom where one child cleans up the block or kitchen area alone, the next day several children help to clean up the same area. Lead a discussion in which children can talk about which way was better and more fair.

Sensory Table.   Put kernels of wheat or flour in the sensory table. Provide children with measuring spoons, measuring cups, bowls, funnels, a hand sifter, a wire whisk, and other items to pour, measure, stir, sift, and so on.

Red Hen.   Trace each child's hand on white construction paper. The thumb is the head of the hen, fingers are the tail feathers, the palm is the body, and the wrist is the legs. Children glue red craft feathers, or feathers cut from construction paper or felt on the hen. Add a yellow beak and a red comb. The teacher can make a hen using a solid-colored garden glove, covering it with craft feathers. This red hen could be used to tell "her story."

Story Characters.   Use paper plates or paper bags to make puppets for each character in the story. Provide children with felt, fake fur, feathers, construction paper, wiggly eyes, and pipe cleaners. Staple paper plate puppets on tongue depressors. The puppets can be used to retell the story or for dramatic play.

The Bakery Trip.   Take a field trip to a bakery shop or the bakery department of a large grocery store. Be sure to point out the different varieties of bread—pita bread, French bread, sourdough bread, wheat bread, rye bread, pumpernickle bread, raisin bread, and others. Talk about how the loaves of bread look the same and how they look different. Perhaps children could sample some bread.

The Bakery.   Set up a bakery in the housekeeping corner. Children can bake breads, muffins, cakes, cookies, and rolls using play dough. Provide aprons, baker's hats, baking pans, bowls, spoons, dull knives, rolling pins, cookie cutters, a cash register, play money, paper and pencils, bags, and a balance scale. Children can take turns being bakers or customers.

Machines.   The little red hen did all the work herself. Today, farmers use machines to help them get hard jobs done easier and quicker. Select some books from the library that show pictures of the farm machinery used by wheat farmers.

- A plow or disk turns and loosens the soil and kills the young weed plants that have started to grow.
- A harrow, with many fine teeth, breaks up lumps of dirt and leaves a smooth surface for planting.
- A grain drill plants seeds.
- A combine cuts the wheat (called reaping) and separates the grain from husks and stems (called threshing).
- A milling machine cleans the wheat grains and grinds the grain into flour.

Brainstorm a list of familiar, simple machines, such as a pencil sharpener, toaster, a mixer, a vacuum cleaner, and others. Talk about what each machine does and how it helps us do jobs easier.

Suggested Home Activities.   Send home a synopsis of the story *The Little Red Hen,* and inform parents about some of the activities children will be doing at school. Send home a list of some of the card game ideas. Number concepts, memory, and turn-taking skills can be reinforced at home. Children will enjoy spreading various toppings on bread to make sandwiches.

Related Literature

Cauley, Lorinda Bryan. *The Cock, the Mouse and the Little Red Hen.*
Galdone, Paul. *Henny Penny.*
———. *Little Red Hen.*
Heller, Ruth. *Chickens Aren't the Only Ones.*
Morris, Ann. *Bread, Bread, Bread.*

Follow the lines and take the little red hen and her
friends to the bread.

Path Tracing Activity

Cut the pictures apart and put them into the correct order.

From Grain to Bread Sequencing Activity

Books About Holidays and Special Occasions

CRANBERRY THANKSGIVING
by
Wendy and Harry Devlin

Developmental Activities Chart	Language & Cognitive Development	Fine Motor Art	Gross Motor	Perception	Social Skills	Math	Dramatic Play	Cooking Snack	Science	Music, Fingerplays, Poems
1 Thanksgiving	X									
2 Friends	X									
3 Something to Share	X			X	X					
4 Chores	X				X					
5 Thanksgiving Aprons		X								
6 Cranberry Decorations		X		X		X				
7 Placemats	X	X								
8 Cranberry Math						X				
9 Feather Math						X				
10 Musical Turkeys			X			X				X
11 Gobble Gobble Turkey			X							
12 Nosey Noses				X		X			X	
13 Thanksgiving Manners	X				X					
14 Friendship Snack					X			X		
15 Invite a Friend					X					
16 Set the Table					X	X				
17 Washing Dishes					X					
18 Dramatic Play					X		X			
19 Turkey Dinner Song										X
20 Grandmother's Famous Bread								X		
21 Homemade Butter								X		X
22 Suggested Home Activities	X							X		
23										
24										
25										
26										
27										
28										
29										
30										

CRANBERRY THANKSGIVING
by Wendy and Harry Devlin
Parents Magazine Press, 1971

Grandmother learns an important lesson as she and Maggie celebrate Thanksgiving in their New England cranberry bog. According to tradition, they each invite someone who is poor or lonely to Thanksgiving dinner. Grandmother prepares a mouthwatering meal, including her famous cranberry bread. Children experience an important lesson on the meaning of the Thanksgiving holiday throughout the pages of this book.

Thanksgiving.   The Thanksgiving holiday provides a perfect opportunity for talking with children about the things for which they are thankful. Younger children can understand the concept in terms of who and what makes them happy. Have the children brainstorm their ideas. Record the group's responses on a large sheet of chart paper or in a class book. Individual ideas can be recorded on a body tracing of each child.

Friends.   The meaning of friendship and sharing is explored in *Cranberry Thanksgiving*. Sit in a circle and play music while children pass a ball around. When the music stops, the child holding the ball gets to tell "how to be a friend" or what he or she likes about a special friend or family member. Ideas include sharing, saying nice things, having someone over to play, or just being nice.

Something to Share.   Ask the children to bring in an item with which to play or share with a friend. Before the children take their items home, try playing this memory game. Display three to five toys on a tabletop or tray. The number of items can be adjusted—children with visual memory problems will require fewer items. Have the children look at the items. Ask the children to close or cover their eyes, while one item is removed. When the children open their eyes, they try to guess what is missing. The difficulty level of the activity can be increased by removing more than one item at a time.

Chores.   Maggie and her grandmother each have chores to do on the cranberry farm. Discuss with the children the concept of helping each other with chores so that the work is shared. Brainstorm with the children common household and school chores. Make a list of classroom chores and let children choose how they would like to help. Children can "share" the chores and work with a friend if there aren't enough chores to go around. Examples are setting the table for snack, pushing in chairs, putting away toys, and so on. Chores can be alternated daily or weekly.

Thanksgiving Aprons.   Cut child-size apron shapes from old sheets; attach ties with a glue gun or fabric glue. The aprons can be decorated using fabric crayons or paint. Consider decorating the aprons with turkeys made out of children's hand-prints. Trace each child's hand down to the wrist. The thumb is the turkey's head, the fingers are feathers and the wrist is the feet. (See black line master pattern.)

Cranberry Decorations.   Using large needles and heavy thread (such as coat thread), children can string cranberries to use as decorations for the classroom. Vary the activity by providing the children with miniature marshmallows and cranberries; they can make up patterns for their decorations.

Placemats.   Children can strengthen their fine motor skills by snipping the edges of a large piece of construction paper. Have the children look through magazines to find and cut pictures of things they can share. They can glue the pictures on their placemats. Cover the placemats with clear Con-Tact® paper, leaving the fringe uncovered.

Cranberry Math.   Use cranberries as a math manipulative. Children can count cranberries and make sets for their friends to count. Label small containers with a numeral and have the children count out cranberries to match the numeral. The numerals and sets used will depend on each child's understanding and concept of number. The children can use the cranberries as units of measurement to measure classroom objects such as books and toys. Take a vote on favorite Thanksgiving foods, and have the children graph the results with cranberries. The children can use the cranberries combined with marshmallows (see "Cranberry Decorations") for making patterns. The children can count the cranberries and marshmallows in the patterns they make. Compare the patterns in terms of which is longer/shorter? Which has the most/least cranberries/marshmallows? How many cranberries all together? The children will enjoy being creative with the cranberries.

Feather Math.   Provide children with turkey shapes and cutout or purchased feathers. Write a numeral from 0 to 10 on each turkey, and have the children glue on the appropriate number of feathers. The children can place the completed turkeys in numerical order.

Musical Turkeys.   Use the turkeys the children created in "Feather Math," or cut out another set of turkeys. The number of turkeys should correspond to the number of children playing. Place the turkeys in a circle on the floor. Play music; when the music stops, have the children try to find a turkey on which to stand. Expand on the game by asking the children to say the number that is written on the turkey. The game can be played like musical chairs: remove one turkey before stopping the music so the children must try to stand on a remaining turkey. Each time the music stops, the child without a turkey to stand on is "out." Give the children who are "out" a turn to remove the next turkey or to stop the music.

Gobble, Gobble, Turkey.   Play this game like "Duck, Duck, Goose," but substitute the words "gobble, gobble, turkey." Children sit in a circle on the floor, one child is "It." He or she walks around the circle touching children on the head and saying "gobble." Finally, "It" says "turkey" to someone. That person chases "It" around the circle until "It" sits down in the empty space. The person who was picked as "Turkey" is now "It."

Nosey Noses. On Thanksgiving, Mr. Horace arrived smelling of lavender and Mr. Whiskers came smelling of clams and seaweed. Make up smelling jars for the children. Baby food jars work well as do small margarine containers. Put lavender in one container and clam juice in another. The children can take turns smelling the containers. Try covering the containers and ask the children to guess which one smelled like Mr. Whiskers or Mr. Horace. The activity can be expanded by using more "smelly jars." Examples to include in the jars are cinnamon sticks, coffee, vinegar, perfume, garlic, and extracts such as lemon, peppermint, chocolate, and vanilla. The children can describe the odors and decide which ones they like the most and the least. Graph the results.

Thanksgiving Manners. Integral to the celebration of Thanksgiving is the enjoyment of the meal. Discuss with the children the meaning of good manners. Have them brainstorm their ideas and record them on large chart paper. Use picture words where possible. Post it near the snack table.

Friendship Snack. All the children can contribute to this special snack. Take a vote to decide if the children prefer fruit salad or vegetable soup, or try making both on different days. Each child brings in a fruit for the friendship salad or a vegetable for the friendship soup. Children might enjoy bringing an item that starts with the same letter as his or her first or last name. Salad ingredients can simply be cut up and combined in a large bowl. Vegetables for the soup should be cut up and combined in a large pot with chicken or beef broth and a large can of tomatoes. Add enough liquid to cover all of the vegetables. Season with a little salt, pepper, and favorite herbs. Bring to a boil and then simmer until the vegetables are soft.

Invite a Friend. Just as Maggie and her grandmother each invited a friend to Thanksgiving dinner, talk with the children about who they would like to invite to snack. You may decide to limit invitations to people in the school or to parents, siblings, or grandparents. Some classes have the unique opportunity to be involved with senior citizen groups; if this possibility exists, the children may want to invite these special friends. The children can make invitations and hand deliver or mail them.

Set the Table. The children can set the table for snack each day as well as for their special Thanksgiving celebration. The concept of one-to-one correspondence will be strengthened as children realize that each person gets one cup, one bowl, one napkin, one spoon, and so on. Fine motor development is strengthened as children fold and crease napkins. Social skills are reinforced as children cooperate to complete the task.

Washing Dishes. Fill the exploration table with warm soapy water and plastic dishes; the children can practice washing dishes for fun. Children take turns washing and drying. Following daily snack and the special feast, provide children with wash and rinse tubs. They can wash, rinse, and dry the dishes. The concept of cooperation and job sharing will be enhanced.

Dramatic Play.   Create a kitchen in the dramatic play area. Decorate the area for Thanksgiving. Provide plenty of dishes, pots and pans for cooking, empty food boxes, aprons, recipe cards, and cookbooks. The children might enjoy dressing up as Mr. Whiskers, Mr. Horace, Maggie, and grandmother. Provide them with dress-up clothes and shoes. Whiskers can be made by fringing black construction paper and attaching string to hold on the whiskers.

Turkey Dinner Song (to the tune of "Are You Sleeping?").   Make a drumstick by tracing the black line master onto construction paper. Laminate it. Pass it around as the first verse is sung.

> Turkey dinner, turkey dinner, gather round, gather round.
> Who will get the drumstick? Yummy, yummy, yum stick.
> All sit down, all sit down.

> Corn bread muffin, chestnut stuffin', pudding pie one foot high.
> I was so much thinner, before I came to dinner.
> Me oh my! Me oh my!

Grandmother's Famous Cranberry Bread.   Make cranberry bread with the children. Use the recipe for "Grandmother's Famous Cranberry Bread" given in the book. Serve it with fresh home-made butter.

Home-made Butter.   Children can shake their own butter to spread on warm cranberry bread. Pour a container of heavy cream into a jar with a tightly fitting lid. Children can take turns vigorously shaking the cream until butter forms in the jar. The remaining liquid is buttermilk. The children might enjoy reciting this simple verse as they shake the butter:

> Shake butter shake, shake butter shake.
> Soon you'll be butter, that we can spread,
> On Grandmother's famous, cranberry bread.

Suggested Home Activities.   Send home a synopsis of *Cranberry Thanksgiving*. Inform parents of the kinds of activities their children are doing at school. Ask the parents to share a special family tradition or recipe with the class. A class Thanksgiving book can be compiled and added to the class library.

Related Literature

Brown, Marc. *Arthur's Thanksgiving*.
Bunting, Eve. *How Many Days to America?*
Stock, Catherine. *Thanksgiving Treat*.

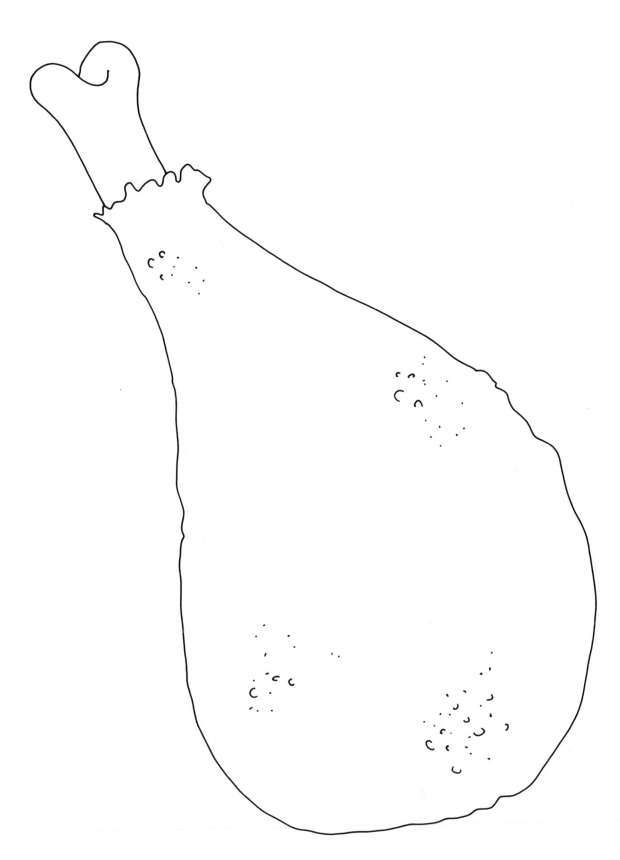

"Turkey Dinner" Song Activity

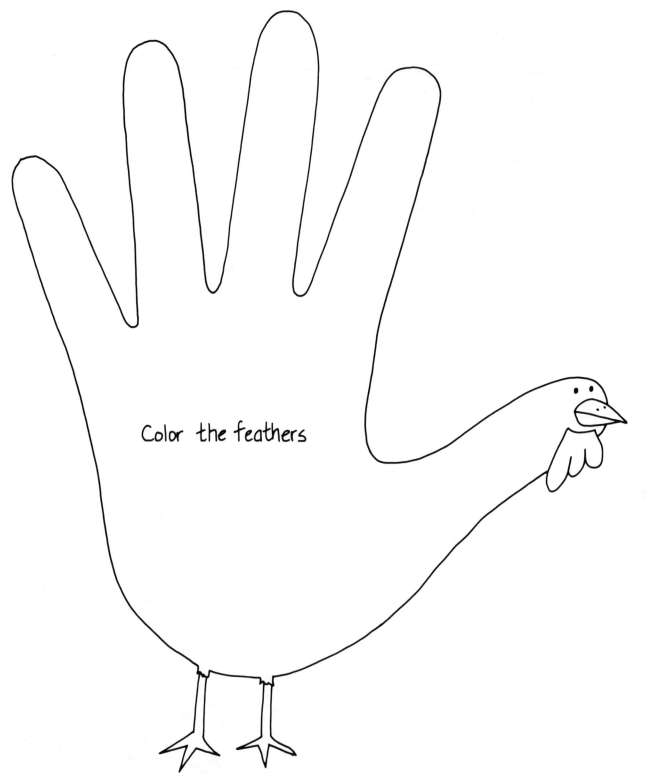

Color the feathers

Thanksgiving Aprons Activity

APPLES AND PUMPKINS
by
Anne Rockwell

Developmental Activities Chart	Language & Cognitive Development	Fine Motor Art	Gross Motor	Perception	Social Skills	Math	Dramatic Play	Cooking Snack	Science	Music, Fingerplays, Poems
1 Harvest Necklace		X		X		X				
2 Pumpkin Sequence	X	X						X		
3 Trick or Treating										X
4 Seed Count	X					X				
5 Apple-Pumpkin Snacks	X	X						X		
6 Apple Harvest										X
7 Few or Many	X					X			X	
8 Apple Chew Roll-ups		X						X		
9 Same and Different	X			X					X	
10 Apple Roll			X							
11 Halloween Dress-up					X		X			
12 Pumpkin Seeds	X	X						X		
13 Harvest Bag		X								
14 Pumpkin Pictures		X								
15 Pumpkin Math	X					X				
16 Pumpkin Slush		X		X						
17 Pumpkin Face	X	X		X						
18 Harvest Science	X								X	
19 Fall Trip	X								X	
20 Fun with Leaves		X	X							X
21 Just Imagine!	X			X						
22 Suggested Home Activities	X	X		X						
23										
24										
25										
26										
27										
28										
29										
30										

APPLES AND PUMPKINS
by Anne Rockwell
Macmillan, 1989

In preparation for Halloween night, a family spends a beautiful fall day at Mr. Comstock's farm. They enjoy the multicolored fall leaves and the animals that walk with them to the orchard. There they all pick apples to fill their basket. The little girl finds the best pumpkin in the field for her father to cut from the vine and bring home for carving a jack-o'-lantern.

Harvest Necklace. Children make a necklace to celebrate fall. Cut apples and a small pumpkin into little pieces. Give each child a dull craft needle threaded with heavy-duty coat thread. Children carefully pull the threaded needle through apple and pumpkin pieces, whole cranberries, and brown and golden raisins. Some children may want to pattern the items on their necklace. Let the necklace dry thoroughly (about one week) and tie the ends together.

Pumpkin Sequence. Flannel pieces can be used to talk about the growth of a pumpkin and how it changes in size and appearance over time. Use the black line master to have children sequence its growth from seed to jack-o'-lantern. Children color the pictures, cut them apart, and arrange them in order from left to right.

Trick or Treating (to the tune of "Are You Sleeping?"). This simple song reinforces some basic safety rules for Halloween trick or treating.

Trick or treating, trick or treating.
Bring a light, make it bright.
Check out all your candy,
Make sure it's fine and dandy.
Let's be safe, let's be safe!

Seed Count. Cut 11 large apples out of red felt and number them from 0 to 10. Cut out at least 55 seeds from black felt. Children place the correct number of seeds on each apple. Children can also order the apples from 0 to 10. This activity can be made using construction paper. Laminate the pieces.

Apple-Pumpkin Snacks. Have children brainstorm a list of foods made from apples and pumpkins. Children can vote to decide which snacks they would like to try at school. Items to consider are apple pie, applesauce, apple butter, apple jelly, apple juice, apple crisp, apple pizza, baked apples, apple chew roll-ups (recipe included), pumpkin pie, pumpkin pudding, pumpkin bread, pumpkin muffins, and pumpkin seeds.

Cut bread with an apple-shaped cookie cutter; top with peanut butter or soft cream cheese and thinly sliced apples.

Melt ½ pound of vanilla caramels with 2 tablespoons of milk. Children dip apple slices in the caramel and then in chopped nuts.

Apple Harvest (to the tune of "Paw, Paw Patch")

Picking red apples, put 'em in a basket.
Picking red apples, put 'em in a basket.
Picking red apples, put 'em in a basket.
Carryin' them home, it's harvest time.

Cut red apples, put 'em in a pie shell.
Cut red apples, put 'em in a pie shell.
Cut red apples, put 'em in a pie shell.
We'll eat apple pie, it's harvest time.

Dipping red apples, swirl 'em in the caramel.
Dipping red apples, swirl 'em in the caramel.
Dipping red apples, swirl 'em in the caramel.
Roll 'em in some nuts, it's harvest time.

Few or Many. Does a small apple have just a few seeds and a large apple have many seeds? Bring in two apples, one very large apple and one very small apple, to test predictions. Have children estimate the number of seeds in each. With adult assistance, children carefully remove the seeds from each apple. Make a graph on construction paper and compare results to check predictions.

Apple Chew Roll-ups

2 cups applesauce
vegetable oil

Preheat oven to 400 degrees. Pour applesauce onto a greased jelly roll pan. Spread to ⅛-inch thickness. Put pan in oven and immediately lower the temperature to 180 degrees. Cook for 3 to 3½ hours or until the apple chew can be peeled from the pan. Children cut it with scissors and roll it before eating.

Same and Different. Place several different varieties of apples and several pumpkins on the science table for children to look at and touch. Children compare their characteristics. Consider the number and color of seeds, where they each grow, their color inside and outside, size, outside texture, and mass (solid versus hollow). Chart similarities and differences.

Apple Roll. Roll apples outside on the grass. See who can roll their apple the farthest. Children follow directions and tiptoe to their apple, jump over it, hop to it, gallop around it, and so on.

Halloween Dress-up. Supply a large variety of costumes and clothing children can use for dress-up in the dramatic play area. Provide one bag for each child. They can role play and practice trick or treating, substituting small blocks or beads as their "treat."

Pumpkin Seeds. Thoroughly wash and clean the pumpkin seeds. Drain them well on paper toweling. Generously sprinkle the bottom of a cookie sheet with salt. Arrange the seeds in a single layer on the sheet and sprinkle them again with salt. Place the cookie sheet in a moderately low oven, 300 degrees, for 40 to 45 minutes, until lightly browned. Cool and enjoy.

Harvest Bag. Children decorate large brown grocery bags with fall leaves, tissue or construction paper, felt, feathers, pipe cleaners, and so on. They can also use leaf-shaped cookie cutters or sponges to print or paint their bags. Staple on a laminated construction paper handle. Bags can be used to collect fall leaves and artifacts or for trick or treating.

Pumpkin Pictures. Collect and clean pumpkin seeds. Make designs on orange or black construction paper. Another option is to give children a predrawn fall/ Halloween shape. Children glue the seeds on the outline of their picture.

Pumpkin Math

- Make sets using pumpkin seeds, count seeds, or make ten cups with seeds.
- Vote for a favorite jack-o'-lantern face before carving one in class.
- Estimate the number of seeds inside the pumpkin or the number of creases on the outside of the pumpkin. Check predictions.
- Estimate how many pounds the class pumpkin is. Weigh pumpkin.
- Estimate the circumference of the pumpkin. Children cut lengths of yarn to match their guess. Each child then compares the length with the actual pumpkin. Which predictions were too short, too long, or just right?

Pumpkin Slush. Put pumpkin seeds and threads in the sensory table for children to handle. How does it feel? How does it smell?

Pumpkin Face. Provide children with a precut pumpkin. They cut shapes (circle, rectangle, diamond, triangle, and square) to make a face on their pumpkin. Challenge the children to make a jack-o'-lantern that is different from everyone else's. Each child dictates a story to describe unique original pumpkin.

Harvest Science. Place a pumpkin, ear of corn, an apple, seeds, and gourds near a container filled with water. Have children predict if each object will sink or float. Check predictions.

Fall Trip. Visit an apple orchard and/or pumpkin patch. Children will delight in picking apples high in the trees or down low on the ground. Observe pumpkins growing in the field; are they all the same, how are they different? Look for changes in the color and shape of pumpkins as they lay on the ground. Write a class story upon returning from the trip.

Fun with Leaves. Playing in the leaves is a wonderful sensory experience for children. They can rake or pile leaves, jump and roll in them, and fill bags and baskets with fall leaves. Act out the words to this action rhyme inside or outside.

> I like to rake the leaves in fall,
> And pile them in a clump.
> Then step back a little way,
> Bend my knees, and JUMP!

Just Imagine!   Have children sit in a circle on the rug and close their eyes. The teacher tells them the tale of a little field mouse who finds refuge from the fall wind and rain, and winter snow inside a discarded jack-o'-lantern. Ask children to pretend they are that field mouse. They can stretch their arms to "touch" and describe how it feels inside the pumpkin. Remind children to keep their eyes closed as they brainstorm feelings and thoughts about their "home."

Suggested Home Activities.   Send home a synopsis of the story *Apples and Pumpkins,* and inform parents about some of the activities children will be doing in school. Together they can make a fall collage by collecting artifacts in their neighborhood or by cutting out pictures of fall clothing, foods, and activities from old catalogs and magazines. Objects and/or pictures can be glued on a paper plate. Send home the fall black line master for parents to use with their child. Include the following ideas and directions.

Same and Different

Cut the fall objects apart after your child has named them. Place three pictures on a table. Ask which two are the same and which one is different.

Memory Game

Place the three pairs of matching objects face down on a table. Turn over two pictures at a time to try and make a match. If a match is not made, turn cards over again. The next person gets a turn to make a match. Continue until the three pairs are matched.

Related Literature

Gibbons, Gail. *The Seasons of Arnold's Apple Tree.*
Ryder, Joanne. *Chipmunk Song.*

Sequence the story of a seed.

Watch it grow.

Plant the seed.

Carve a jack-o'-lantern.

See the pumpkin vine.

Pumpkin Sequence Activity

Suggested Home Activity—Same and Different, and Memory Game

HANUKKAH CAT
by
Chaya Burstein

Developmental Activities Chart	Language & Cognitive Development	Fine Motor Art	Gross Motor	Perception	Social Skills	Math	Dramatic Play	Cooking Snack	Science	Music, Fingerplays, Poems
1 Eight Days of Hanukkah	X					X				
2 Hanukkah Surprise	X	X								
3 Surprise Hunt	X									
4 Dreidel		X			X	X				
5 More, Less, or the Same						X				
6 Milk Carton Dreidels		X			X	X				
7 Hanukkah Candles	X					X				
8 Window Menorah		X								
9 Wishing Dreidels		X								
10 Colorful Candles		X								
11 Beanbag Dreidel			X							
12 Match the Dreidels				X						
13 Shining Lights		X				X				
14 One-to-One Matching						X				
15 Count the Candles						X				
16 Easel Shapes		X								
17 Geoboard Stars		X		X		X				
18 Dot to Dot		X				X				
19 Potato Latkes								X		
20 Jelly Doughnuts								X		
21 The Dreidel Song										X
22 Hanukkah Candles Song										X
23 Suggested Home Activity	X	X								
24										
25										
26										
27										
28										
29										
30										

HANUKKAH CAT
by Chaya Burstein
Kar-Ben Copies, 1985

The Hanukkah cat appeared at Lenny's window on the first night of Hanukkah. His parents agreed that Lenny could keep the cat for the eight days and nights of Hanukkah. The Hanukkah story and the traditions of the holiday are nicely woven into the story of Lenny and the cat that he wants to keep forever. Divided into eight short chapters, one for each night of Hanukkah, *Hanukkah Cat* can be read all at one time or a chapter can be read each day of Hanukkah.

Eight Days of Hanukkah.   Hanukkah lasts for eight days and nights. The days are marked by the lighting of candles on the Hanukkah menorah (candelabra). The first night one candle is lit, the second night two candles are lit, until the eighth night when all eight candles are lit. The candles are lit with a helper candle called the *shamash*. The shamash has a special place on the menorah, and it burns along with the candles each night. Display a menorah on the flannel board or on the bulletin board, or use a real menorah. Each day have the children add a candle to the menorah to mark the passing of the days. Talk about which day it is using ordinal terms (first, second, third, etc.). Count how many more days are left. Have children predict how many candles there will be the next day.

Hanukkah Surprise.   It is traditional for boys and girls to receive a gift after lighting the candles each night. Wrap a box for each day of Hanukkah. Place the items necessary for a special activity in the box. The activity might be a game, art project, cooking project, or a book. The children can unwrap the box to discover the special activity for each day.

Surprise Hunt.   Add fun and suspense to the Hanukkah surprise by having the children find the box by following clues. The clues can be written or verbal; they can be simple or complicated depending on the age and language skills of the group. Younger children and children with delays in language development will require one- or two-step directions and clues. Older children with higher-level language and problem-solving skills can be given more complicated directions with more steps.

Dreidel.   Dreidel is a traditional game of Hanukkah. It is played with a four-sided top, each side displaying a different Hebrew letter. Children can play with pennies, counters, small candies, nuts, or raisins. The players sit in a circle and put a counter into the pot (pile in the middle of the circle). The players take turns spinning the dreidel. The letter showing when the dreidel drops tells the player what to do. The Hebrew letters are gimmel ג , heh ה , shin ש , and nun נ . If the dreidel lands on gimmel, the player gets everything in the pot and all the players add another counter. If the dreidel lands on heh, the player gets half (the small half) of the pot. If the dreidel lands on shin, the player must add a counter to the pot. If the dreidel lands on nun, the player gets or loses nothing. When the pot gets very small, all players add a counter. Younger children and children with delays in fine motor development will be challenged just trying to spin the dreidel. Leave the dreidels in an accessible place since spinning practice helps to develop the small muscles of the hand. Dreidels come in many colors and sizes. They can be purchased in specialty gift or toy stores. Many local synagogues carry them in their gift shops, or they can be ordered from a catalog.

More, Less, or the Same.   When the children are finished playing dreidel, have them count their pennies, candies, or other manipulatives. Children can see who has more than them or less than them. They can look for someone with the same number. They can determine who in the class has the same, most, and least.

Milk Carton Dreidels.   Dreidels can be made with a half-pint milk carton and an unsharpened pencil. Cover the milk carton with Con-Tact® or construction paper. Write a Hebrew letter gimmel ג , heh ה , shin ש , and nun נ on each side of the dreidel. Insert a pencil up through the center of the carton, eraser at the bottom. Play dreidel as described.

Hanukkah Candles.   Each box of Hanukkah candles comes with colored candles. If using a real menorah, children can make patterns with the candles. They may choose to use all one color or alternate colors. Hanukkah candles can be purchased in supermarkets or through a local synagogue. If using paper or felt menorahs, cut candles of various colors for the children to use as they would real candles. If patterning candle colors, challenge the children to predict what color they will use the next day. The children can use the candles in a color classification activity: have them put all the blues, yellows, greens, and reds in groups. The candles can also be used as math manipulatives: they are suitable as counters and units of measurement and for color patterning activities.

Window Menorahs.   Children can make a menorah to hang in the window using this simple negative space pattern. Using the black line master, trace the menorah pattern onto construction paper and cut out the menorah shape leaving the remainder of the paper intact. Provide the children with various colors of cellophane and clear tape. They can cover each candle and flame with their favorite colors or color patterns.

Wishing Dreidels.   The children can decorate dreidels cut from heavy paper with pictures of toys they would like to receive for a Hanukkah gift. Provide them with old magazines and catalogs as a source for toy pictures.

Colorful Candles.   Provide each child with a toilet paper tube. Have them paint it or roll it in a shallow container with a layer of paint at the bottom. When the tube dries, they can crumple up different colors of tissue paper and stick the paper in the tops of the tube to resemble the flame.

Beanbag Dreidel.   Play a variation of the dreidel game. Print a Hebrew letter gimmel ג , heh ה , shin ש , and nun נ on pieces of construction paper. Turn the papers letter-side down on the floor. Give children pieces of candy, nuts, raisins, pennies, or other counters. Play the game following the rules for dreidel, but instead of spinning the dreidel, have the children toss a beanbag. The Hebrew letter that the beanbag lands on will determine if the child gets the whole "pot" or half, or if he or she adds to the "pot" or gets or gives nothing.

Match the Dreidels.   Make a set of 8, 12, or 16 dreidels using the black line master and colored construction paper. Make an equal number of dreidels with each of the four Hebrew letters, gimmel ג , heh ה , shin ש , nun נ . Laminate the dreidels to preserve them. The children can look for the matching dreidels. The dreidels can also be used to play the game "Concentration." Put the dreidels face down in rows. The children turn over two cards at a time. If the cards match, the player keeps the cards and takes another turn. If the cards don't match, they are turned back over and the play goes on. The game can be simplified for younger children by making simple designs on the dreidels instead of Hebrew letters.

Shining Lights.   Using the black line master, the children can make a menorah by gluing rectangular strips onto paper. Glue one long rectangle shape horizontally and nine smaller strips vertically. The ninth candle is the helper candle (shamash). It should be taller than the other eight candles and placed in the middle. Have the children squeeze a drop of glue above each candle; then sprinkle glitter on the glue.

One-to-One Matching.   Reinforce the concept of one-to-one correspondence by matching eight candles to the eight candle holders on the menorah; then match one flame to each of the candles.

Count the Candles.   The children can practice their counting skills while making sets to match a numeral. Use the flannel board or a real menorah and candles. Show the children a numeral from 1 to 8 and have them place the corresponding number of candles on the menorah. Ask the children to guess which day of Hanukkah it is by counting the candles on the menorah. Have the children estimate and then count how many more days are left of Hanukkah.

Easel Shapes.   Draw Hanukkah shapes at the easel for the children to paint. Make large stencils by cutting shapes out of easel-size paper. Place the paper with the cut-out stencil on top of the paper on which the children will paint. The children can use brushes or sponges to fill in the shape.

Geoboard Stars.   Six-sided stars (star of David) are common decorations on menorahs. The children can make these six-sided stars on geoboards by making a triangle, then covering it with an inverted triangle. See the black line master pattern.

Dot to Dot.   The children can make dot-to-dot Hanukkah pictures using the black line masters. Have them follow the numbers to connect the dots; then color the pictures.

Potato Latkes.   Potato latkes (pancakes) are a traditional Hanukkah food. They can be served with applesauce or sour cream.

8 large potatoes	1 tablespoon salt
1 large onion	1 teaspoon pepper
2 eggs, separated	vegetable oil for frying
2 tablespoons flour	

Grate potatoes and onions; strain to remove the liquid. Combine potatoes and onion with egg yolks, flour, salt, and pepper. Beat and gently fold in the egg whites. Heat oil. Fry on one side; turn when golden brown and crisp. Makes 24 small pancakes.

Jelly Doughnuts. Jelly-filled doughnuts are a traditional Hanukkah snack in Israel. The Israeli word for them is *sufganiyot.*

The Dreidel Song (to the tune of "I Have a Little Shadow")

I have a little dreidel
I made it out of clay.
And when it's dry and ready
Then dreidel I shall play.

Chorus:

Oh dreidel, dreidel, dreidel
I made it out of clay.
And when it's dry and ready
Then dreidel I shall play.

Hanukkah Candles Song (to the tune of "Twinkle, Twinkle Little Star")

Hanukkah candles burning bright.
Light up the house on Hanukkah night.
Playing dreidel is such fun.
Gimmel, you get all.
Shin, you put in one.
Heh, you get half.
Nun, you get none.
Hanukkah is eight nights of fun.

Suggested Home Activity. Send home a synopsis of the *Hanukkah Cat* and an explanation of some of the activities the children are doing at school. Include a short explanation of the two miracles of Hanukkah as Lenny explained them to Hanukkah Cat. (1) The small army (Maccabees) defeated a large army who took over the Jewish temple and tried to force the people to worship idols. (2) When the Maccabees recaptured their temple, there was only enough oil to last one day, but it burned for eight days. Send home a chart with the explanation of the dreidel game and the children's milk carton dreidels. The children will be proud to teach their families how to play the game.

Related Literature

Hyman, Trina Schart. *Hershel and the Hanukkah Goblins.*
Manushkin, Fran. *Latkes and Applesauce: A Hanukkah Story.*
Zalben, Jane Breskin. *Beni's First Chanukah.*

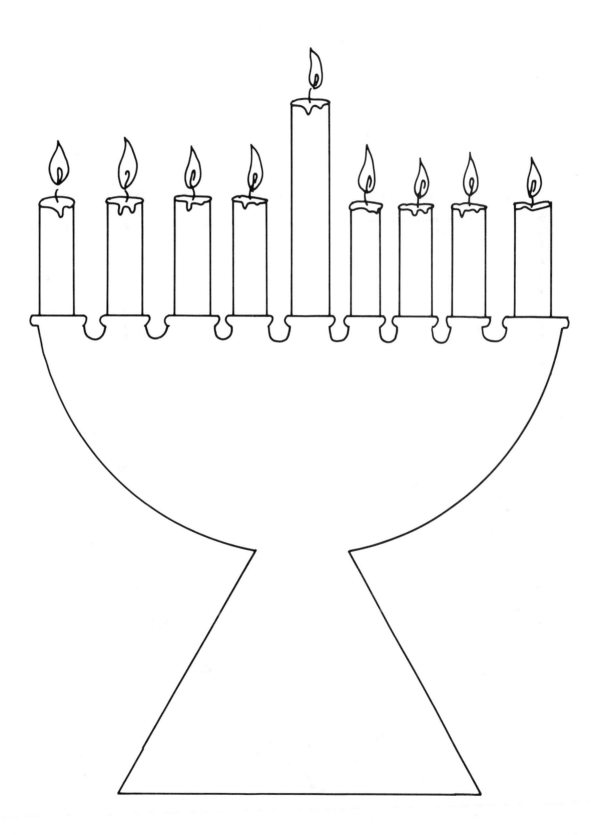

Window Menorah Activity

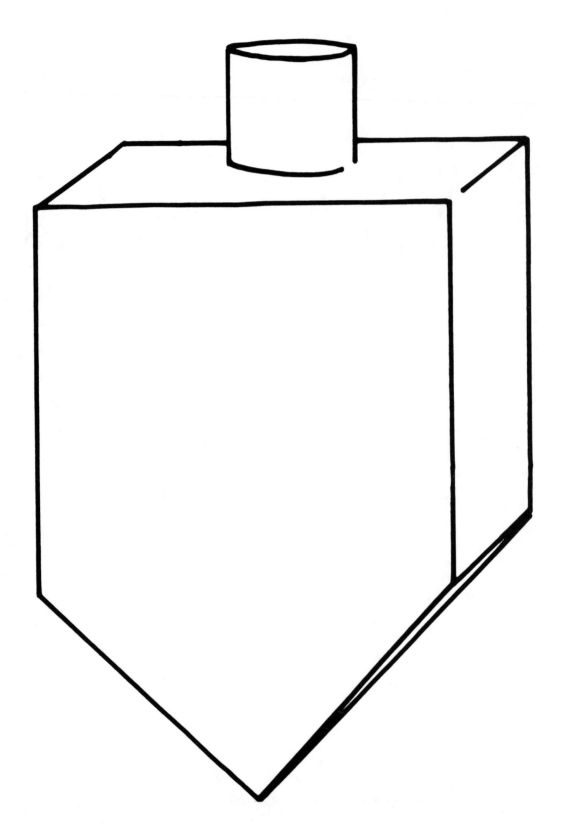

Match the Dreidels Activity

Geoboard Stars Activity

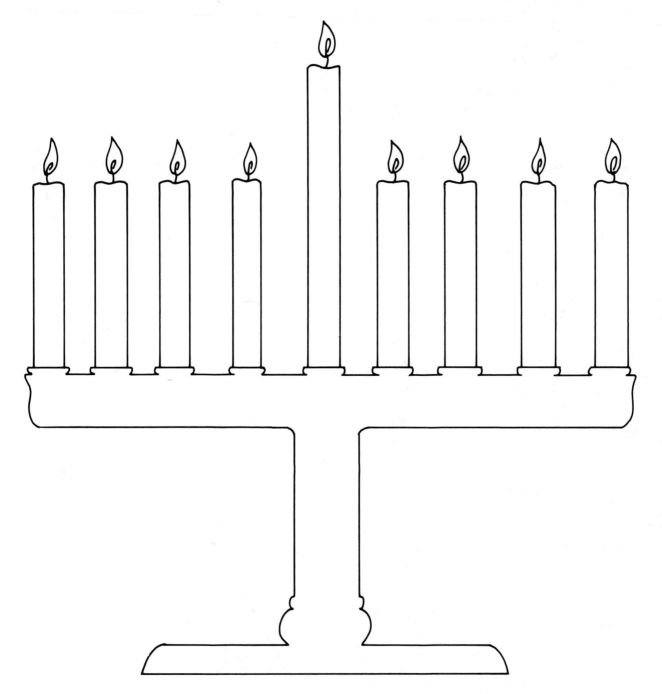

Shining Lights Activity

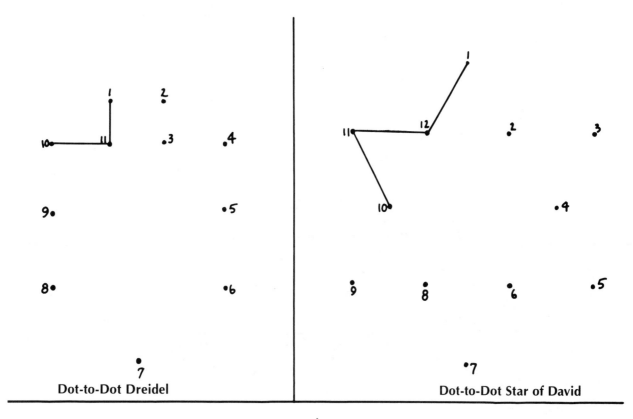

Dot-to-Dot Dreidel

Dot-to-Dot Star of David

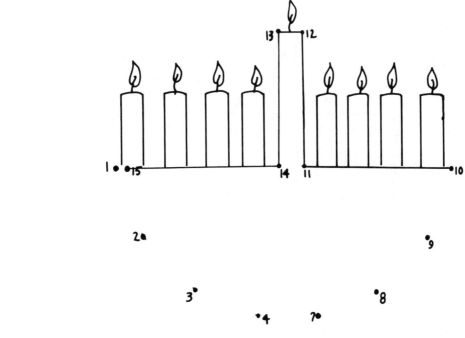

Dot-to-Dot Menorah

gimmel – gets all

heh – gets half

shin – put in one

nun – get nothing

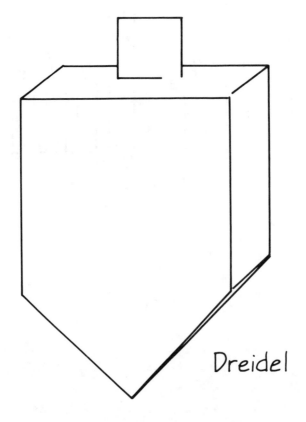

Dreidel

Suggested Home Activity—Dreidel Game Chart

KEEPING A CHRISTMAS SECRET

by
Phyllis Reynolds Naylor

Developmental Activities Chart	Language & Cognitive Development	Fine Motor Art	Gross Motor	Perception	Social Skills	Math	Dramatic Play	Cooking Snack	Science	Music, Fingerplays, Poems
1 Gift Giving	X	X			X					
2 Christmas										X
3 Wreath		X								
4 Christmas Tree Math		X			X	X				
5 Christmas Books	X	X								
6 Christmas Around the World	X				X					
7 Stained Glass Ornament		X								
8 Candy Cane Patterning		X		X						
9 Toy Book	X	X				X				
10 Christmas Tree		X						X		
11 Sledding										X
12 Something New	X	X			X					
13 Smell the Season		X						X		
14 Gift Boxes	X			X						
15 Toys	X			X		X				
16 Wrap It Up!		X								
17 Wrapping Center		X								
18 Egg Nog	X	X						X		
19 Painted Holiday Cookies		X						X		
20 Shopper's Paradise	X				X	X	X			
21 Before Christmas Morn										X
22 Rope Activities			X							
23 Christmas Science	X								X	
24 Suggested Home Activities	X	X		X	X			X		
25										
26										
27										
28										
29										
30										

KEEPING A CHRISTMAS SECRET
by Phyllis Reynolds Naylor
Atheneum, 1989

Two days before Christmas, Michael and his family choose a special gift for dad. Michael assures everyone that he can keep it a secret. Much to the disappointment of everyone, Michael slips and lets dad know that his present is a sled. Michael redeems himself and saves their Christmas day family activity when he presents dad with a much-needed secret gift.

Gift Giving.   Giving gifts is more than wrapping paper and bows; it is a special way of showing love for someone. Michael and his family shopped until they could find the perfect gift for dad. Each child can write or dictate a list of Christmas presents they would like to give friends and family members. Lists can be illustrated. Children can also look through catalogs to find special gifts they would like to give. They cut pictures out and mount them on a construction paper list.

Christmas   (to the tune of "Are You Sleeping?")

   Christmas secrets, Christmas secrets, hard to keep, mustn't peek!
   Don't give clues I'm warning. Wait till Christmas morning.
   What's inside? What's inside?

   Christmas morning, Christmas morning, will it come? So much fun!
   Wrapping all the presents. Eating tasty cookies.
   Yum, yum, yum. Yum, yum, yum.

   Sleighbells ringing, children singing, in the night, oh so bright!
   I can't wait for Santa, jolly, jolly fat man.
   Ho, ho, ho! Ho, ho, ho!

Wreath.   Michael's family decorated their door with a Christmas wreath. Give each child a paper plate that has the center cut out. Children scrunch up precut pieces of green tissue paper and glue the pieces on the plate. Small red pompoms can be glued on to represent holly berries. A red ribbon bow can be added.

Christmas Tree Math.   Give each child a green Christmas tree shape to cut out or one that is precut. A pattern is included. Give each child a margarine tub container that has chocolate chips, raisins, gumdrops, red hots, Nonpareils™, and other small pieces of candy. Provide one or two die, depending on the children's developmental levels. Children take turns shaking the die, counting the dots, and decorating their tree with the correct number of candy "ornaments."

Christmas Books.   Children can make a Christmas storybook by cutting pictures from old Christmas cards and gluing them onto rectangular pieces of construction paper. Children dictate stories about their picture(s). Pages can be assembled and stapled together to make individual books or a class book.

Christmas Around the World.   Michael and his family celebrated the Christmas season by shopping, wrapping gifts, decorating their home, opening presents Christmas morning, and sledding together Christmas day. Give children an opportunity to share their family holiday traditions with the class. Children from different cultures should be encouraged to share how they celebrate. Invite parents to visit class to share the decorations, music, costumes, foods, and other customs of their country.

Stained Glass Ornament.   Children glue small multicolored squares of tissue paper on clear coffee or margarine lids. After the tissue has dried, children paint the tissue side of the ornament with a coat of varnish or Mod Podge™ to make it glossy. Punch a hole and string a piece of yarn or ribbon to hang it from a tree.

Candy Cane Patterning.   Give each child a large candy cane cut from tagboard or construction paper. Children can pattern stripes on the candy cane using crayons, markers, snips of construction paper, wrapping paper, and tissue paper.

Toy Book.   Prepare a toy book for each child using plain white paper. Number pages from 1 to 5, or 1 to 10, depending on each child's ability. Add a page for the cover, and staple the pages together. Children look through catalogs and cut and glue the correct number of toys for each page. They can dictate a sentence story about their toy selections on each page, if desired. Children illustrate the cover.

Christmas Tree.   Children can prepare and decorate an edible Christmas tree. Children make butter cream frosting or use ready-to-spread frosting. Mix green food coloring thoroughly into the frosting. Each child frosts a large waffle-style ice cream cone to make the tree. Children trim their tree with M&M's™, red hots, raisins, mini-marshmallows, gumdrops, chocolate chips, and other colorful edibles.

Sledding (to the tune of "A Hunting We Will Go").   Michael and his family enjoy sledding on the new blue-and-silver sled with shiny runners. If possible, take the children sledding at a hill near school. Teach them this sledding song.

> A sledding we will go.
> A sledding we will go.
> We'll hold on tight,
> And sit just right!
> And down the hill we'll go.
> Wheeee!

Something New.   Michael thought of a new way to use an old toy. The old jump rope became a handle for dad's new sled. Small groups of children can use problem-solving skills to think of new ways to use their toys at home or school. Group ideas can be shared with the class. Playtime can incorporate playing with toys the "new way."

Smell the Season.   Make play dough. Add red or green food coloring. Knead cinnamon or mint extract into the dough. Provide rolling pins and a variety of holiday cookie cutters for children. They can roll, pound, flatten, and squeeze the play dough, in addition to making holiday shapes.

Gift Boxes.   Place a variety of different-sized and -shaped boxes, classroom toys, and instruments on a table. Children visually estimate which toy will fit inside each box. Children check their estimates, making certain that every item has a box. After this hands-on activity, children can complete the black line master, matching a gift to the correct box.

Toys.   Children complete a variety of activities by using toys found in the classroom.

- Order toys by size, arranging them from smallest to largest.
- Count the toys.
- Sort toys into categories, such as toys with wheels, stuffed animals, dolls, sound toys, and so on. Children graph the toys and compare which category has the most, the least, or the same amount.
- Place two toys on a table. Brainstorm ways the toys are the same and ways that they are different.
- Place three toys on a table. Children decide which toy does not belong, for example, car–doll–truck, or drum–horn–stuffed animal, and so on.
- Make up riddles about classroom toys. Children name and find the toy after hearing the riddle.

Wrap It Up!   Children decorate white tissue paper or white bags to make Christmas wrap. Provide cookie cutters and sponges cut into holiday shapes. Children dip the cookie cutter or sponge into a paint-lined Styrofoam™ plate, then print or sponge paint designs on the wrap.

Wrapping Center.   Ask parents to donate a variety of new or old wrapping paper. Provide small boxes, tape, yarn, and ribbon. Children can practice wrapping boxes and tying knots.

Egg Nog.   Children will enjoy this traditional Christmas drink.

    4   cups milk
    4   eggs
    2   teaspoons vanilla
    3   tablespoons sugar
    2   cups vanilla ice cream

Measure and pour all the ingredients into a blender. Cover and blend the mixture until smooth.

Painted Holiday Cookies.   Prepare a favorite sugar cookie recipe or use Pillsbury Slice and Bake™ sugar cookies. Before baking cookies, children paint the "cookie paint" on each cookie with a small brush.

  2   egg yolks
  ½   teaspoon water
      food coloring

Mix together the egg yolks and water in a small bowl until well blended. Divide the mixture into small custard-size cups, and add food coloring to each cup. A few drops of water can be added if the paint becomes too thick. Bake cookies as directed.

Shopper's Paradise.   Set up a department or toy store in the dramatic play area. The "Wrapping Center" can be placed close to the store. Children take turns playing the role of shopper, clerk, cashier, or gift wrapper. Children arrange displays of toys, instruments, winter hats, scarves, and mittens, and other items to be sold. Props include play money, a cash register, bags and boxes. Children may want to use the shopping list they made in the "Gift Giving" activity.

Before Christmas Morn   (to the tune of "Here We Go 'Round the Mulberry Bush")

Let's decorate our Christmas tree,
Our Christmas tree, our Christmas tree.
Let's decorate our Christmas tree.
In time for Christmas morn.

Other verses:

String the lights, the tree will shine.
Hang the bulbs and add a star.
Wrap the gifts, and keep a secret.

Rope Activities.   Children can brainstorm ways to use a rope in the gym. For example, children can take turns pulling each other around the gym. One child pulls another who sits on a piece of cardboard or scooter board "sled." Or two children can take hold of a rope and wiggle it on the floor for the other children to jump across. Or children can raise the rope to different heights, and the other children try to move under the rope in a variety of ways without touching it.

Christmas Science.   Take a field trip to a nursery, garden center, or floral shop. Children can look at the different types of evergreen trees—fir, spruce, pine, and hemlock. They can compare the length and color of the needles, and the smell of the branches. Talk about how evergreen trees are the same as/different from deciduous trees—leaves versus needles, color, length of time leaves/needles remain on the tree, need for sunlight and water, presence of a trunk, and so on. With adult supervision, children can look at traditional Christmas plants. Examples to include are holly with its glossy leaves and bright red berries (berries are poisonous), mistletoe with its thickly clustered leaves and tiny white berries, Christmas cactus, and the poinsettia plant with its red leaves (leaves are poisonous) resembling a star with a yellow center. If the class is unable to take a field trip, the teacher can call a local nursery or flower shop and request a donation of branches from various evergreen trees and some Christmas plants. In the classroom, children can more closely observe the branches and plants under large magnifying glasses.

Suggested Home Activities.   Send home a synopsis of the story, *Keeping a Christmas Secret,* and inform parents of some of the activities the children are doing at school. Encourage families to enjoy the sights, sounds, and smells of the holiday season. Remind parents to include children in as many holiday preparations as possible, including shopping, wrapping gifts, baking, decorating and even keeping Christmas secrets! Families can walk or drive around the neighborhood to enjoy the lights, trees, wreaths, and 3D figures that decorate homes. If possible, parents can accompany a group of children caroling in the neighborhood.

Related Literature

Keller, Holly. *A Bear for Christmas.*
Quinlan, Patricia. *Anna's Red Sled.*

Christmas Tree Math Activity

Name each toy. Draw a line to match the gift with the best fitting box.

Gift Boxes Activity

Name each toy or instrument. Draw a line to match the gift with the best fitting box.

Gift Boxes Activity (cont'd.)

HURRAY FOR THE FOURTH OF JULY

by
Wendy Watson

Developmental Activities Chart	Language & Cognitive Development	Fine Motor Art	Gross Motor	Perception	Social Skills	Math	Dramatic Play	Cooking Snack	Science	Music, Fingerplays, Poems
1 Star Spangled Banner	X					X				
2 Flag Form Puzzle				X		X				
3 Coloring		X		X						
4 Flag Game				X	X	X				
5 T-shirts		X								
6 Sparkle Pictures		X								
7 Play Safe	X				X				X	
8 Safety Song										X
9 Picnic Baskets		X								
10 Number Banners						X				
11 Patriotic Jell-O™								X		
12 Class Parade and Picnic	X				X	X	X			
13 Frisbees		X	X							
14 Boat Races									X	
15 Happy Birthday, America				X		X				
16 Colored Chips		X		X		X				
17 Bell Ringing		X		X						X
18 Kazoos		X								X
19 Marching			X	X						X
20 Painted Rocks		X							X	
21 Suggested Home Activities	X							X		
22										
23										
24										
25										
26										
27										
28										
29										
30										

HURRAY FOR THE FOURTH OF JULY
by Wendy Watson
Clarion Books, 1992

A small town celebrates the Fourth of July in the traditional way. The residents gather together for a parade, picnic, family games, and fireworks. In addition to the simple text of the story, familiar patriotic songs and rhymes are woven into the illustrations.

Star Spangled Banner.   The star spangled banner is another name for the flag of the United States. The Fourth of July is the birthday of the nation, and the flag (also known as a banner) is the symbol of the nation. Explain to the children this is the reason that flags are displayed on this day. The children will be interested to know that the 50 stars stand for the 50 states. There are 13 stripes, which symbolize the first 13 colonies. Count the stars and the stripes together. Look at a map of the United States and count the states.

Flag Form Puzzle.   Draw the outline of the American flag on a large piece of tagboard. Include the outline for the 13 red and white stripes, the blue background (the canton), and the 50 stars. Make corresponding cutouts of 7 red and 6 white stripes, 50 white stars, and the blue star background. The children can assemble the flag using the outline as a guide.

Coloring.   Reproduce copies of the black line master of the American flag. Provide the children with red, white, and blue crayons; chalk; or markers. Children can color the flag using a visual model. The developmental level of each child should be considered. Some children will have the interest and ability to color the flag as it appears. Younger children and those with developmental delays may not have the interest or the ability to color the flag as it appears. The developmental level and interest level of each child should be accepted and respected. Completed flags can be affixed to a small dowel stick. Children can carry them in a class parade.

Flag Game.   Reproduce the black line master of the flag to play this game. Give all players a picture of the whole flag and a small bag containing the individual pieces of the flag (13 stripes, 50 stars, and the canton) cut from the black line master so that the size of the pieces correspond to the size of the whole picture. The pieces can be colored and laminated. Children take turns shaking one die or two dice. They place the number of flag pieces onto the outline which corresponds to the number they shook. The object of the game is to complete each flag. The game can be played cooperatively in a shorter amount of time when all players try to complete one flag together.

T-shirts.   Ask parents to send a plain white T-shirt to school. Purchase fabric paint. Children can decorate their T-shirts using red, white, and blue paint.

Sparkle Pictures.   Children can create glowing pictures of Fourth of July fireworks. Provide an assortment of colored glitter, stars, sequins, metallic ribbon, and tinsel. The children squeeze glue onto dark paper and cover the glue with the shiny decorations.

Play Safe.   Safety rules regarding Fourth of July fun should be discussed at school and reinforced at home. Safe play with fireworks is a must; rules to include are:

1. If you find matches or lighters, give them to an adult. *Do not* try to use them.
2. Fireworks and sparklers are not toys. Although fireworks and sparklers are fun to watch, children *should not* play with them. They are very hot, they can burn people, and start fires. The people who are in charge of firework displays are usually professional firefighters. They are trained to put out fires if one should start.
3. If you find sparklers or fireworks, give them to an adult.
4. Water safety rules should also be stressed at this time of year. The primary rule for young children to remember is to stay out of the water unless they are with an adult in the water.

Safety Song   (to the tune of "If You're Happy and You Know It")
If you're safe and you know it, shout hurray.
If you're safe and you know it, shout hurray.
If you're safe and you know it,
All your friends and you should show it.
If you're safe and you know it, shout hurray.

Always give matches to an adult.
Always give matches to an adult.
If you're safe and you know it,
All your friends and you should show it.
Always give matches to an adult.

Always give sparklers to an adult.
Always give sparklers to an adult.
If you're safe and you know it,
All your friends and you should show it.
Always give sparklers to an adult.

Only go in water with an adult.
Only go in water with an adult.
If you're safe and you know it,
All your friends and you should show it.
Only go in water with an adult.

Children can make up additional verses.

Picnic Baskets. Children can decorate baskets and fill them with Fourth of July treats. Provide each child with a strawberry basket and red, white, and blue lengths of heavy yarn long enough for the children to weave in and out through the spaces in the baskets. Children can pattern the colors, weaving in and out until the basket is decorated to their liking. Create a handle out of a pipe cleaner. The basket can be filled with bubbles and blowers; red, white, and blue balloons; healthy treats; and other items that would be fun to take along on a picnic.

Number Banners. Cut triangle-shaped banners from construction paper. Label the banners with a numeral from 1 to 10. Children can decorate the banners by gluing on the appropriate number of items. Items to consider for decorations are stars, magazine pictures that depict Fourth of July activities, Fourth of July picture stickers, or cutouts of flags.

Patriotic Jell-O ™. Children will enjoy making this special treat to eat on their Fourth of July picnic. Prepare red Jell-O™ and blue Jell-O™ according to the directions on the package. Purchase clear plastic drinking cups. Each child fills his or her cup ⅓ full of blue Jell-O™. Refrigerate until almost firm. Children add red Jell-O™ until the cup is ⅔ full. Refrigerate until the Jell-O™ is set. Top off the treat with whipping cream. Enjoy the red, white, and blue treat.

Class Parade and Picnic. Plan a class picnic. If it isn't actually the Fourth of July, the children will have fun pretending it is the special day. The children can brainstorm what they want to eat at the picnic. Each child can be responsible for bringing one item. Be sure to include enough napkins, forks, spoons, and cups for everyone. The children can help pack the picnic basket with all the necessities, counting to make sure there is enough for each class member. Plan to have the picnic at a nearby park or playground; if you are pretending to celebrate the Fourth of July in the winter, the picnic can be held in a gymnasium. The children can march in a parade on the way to the park. Wagons and bikes can be decorated with crepe paper streamers and banners.

Frisbees. Children can make frisbees by cutting the center section out of a dinner-size paper plate. Frisbees can be decorated with paint, markers, or shiny glitter. The children can play with the frisbees at the picnic.

Boat Races. The children can make boats out of empty milk cartons. The pouring end of the carton is the front end of the boat (bow), and the bottom end of the milk carton is the tail end (the stern). Use a sharp object to push a hole through the stern, close to the bottom of the boat. Poke another hole through the front of the boat at the top. Place a straw through both holes. Attach a balloon to the end of the straw near the front of the boat. Hold the balloon in place with a rubber band. Inflate the balloon through the straw and then pinch the straw shut so the air stays in the balloon until the boat is set in the water. At the sound of a whistle children can let their boats go. Experiment with the placement of the straw in the water. Boats can be raced in a wading pool or in the classroom exploration table.

Happy Birthday, America.   Explain to the children that the Fourth of July is the celebration of our country's birthday. The country is officially more than 200 years old. Make a birthday cake shape from Styrofoam™ and purchase red, white, and blue golf tees. The children can make patterns in the Styrofoam™ with the different-colored golf tees. The cakes could be labeled with numerals. Children would then place the corresponding number of tees in the cake.

Colored Chips.   Children can use red, white, and blue poker chips in various ways.

1. Mix chips altogether; have children sort them according to color.
2. Children make up color patterns with the chips, such as red, red, white, white, blue, blue.
3. Label containers with numerals from 0 to 10; have children place the appropriate number of chips in the container.
4. Use one chip to flip another chip into a shallow container. Use one chip to press on the edge of another chip forcing it to flip away.
5. Stack chips to make towers. Sequence the towers according to height, shortest to tallest or tallest to shortest. A game board can be prepared for this by tracing around the chips. Label the center of each circle with a numeral, increasing in size from left to right. Children will discover that the towers grow progressively taller or shorter going from left to right/right to left.

Bell Ringing.   The Fourth of July is often celebrated with the ringing of bells. Children can make a bell instrument by stringing bells on a piece of yarn or string or by gluing bells onto a tongue depressor. Children will strengthen auditory memory skills when they listen to the teacher ring a bell and then copy the bell-ringing pattern.

Kazoos.   Children can make kazoos to play while marching in a parade. Provide each child with an empty spool from toilet paper or paper towel, a square of waxed paper, and a rubber band. The children secure the waxed paper over one end of the empty spool with the rubber band. Music is made by humming into the other end of the spool. The kazoos can be decorated for the Fourth of July with glitter, ribbon, stars, sequins, and tinsel. Teach the children familiar tunes, such as "Yankee Doodle Dandy" and "Star Spangled Banner," to play while marching in the parade.

Marching.   Teach the children how to march lifting their knees up high. Children can march to the beat of a drum. They will need to listen and step with each drum beat. Provide different tempos. Children stop when the drum stops, and they go when they hear the drum beat. The children can take turns beating the drum for their classmates. The children can use the marching step while marching in a Fourth of July parade.

Painted Rocks.   While picnicking, children can collect rocks and stones. Upon returning to the classroom they can wash their rocks in soapy water and set them in the sun to dry. Rocks can be painted with red, white, and blue or with shiny gold and silver paint. Younger children can paint rocks with fingerpaints. School-aged students can use tempera or poster paints with a paintbrush. They can paint color patterns on the rocks, or they can paint over stencils to create a special picture. A Fourth of July star stencil can be made by cutting a star shape out of a piece of waxed paper, leaving the paper intact. Place the paper over the rock and fill in the negative star space with paint.

Suggested Home Activities.   Send home a synopsis of *Hurray for the Fourth of July.* Inform parents of the kinds of activities their children are doing at school. Parents can talk with their children about special family traditions that are observed in their home on the Fourth of July. Together they can write a paragraph telling how they celebrate the day. Children can bring their paragraphs to school and share them with the class. Parents may want to try making ice cream using the following recipe with their children:

Mix 1 pint of whipping cream with 1 teaspoon of vanilla in a clean 2-pound coffee can. Crush ice with a hammer or in a blender and place it in a plastic bin. Shake a generous amount of salt in with the ice. Secure the lid on the coffee can with masking tape. Place the coffee can in the bin and surround it with the ice and salt mixture. Take turns shaking the bin until ice cream forms in the can. Enjoy the ice cream plain or with a favorite topping.

Related Literature

Lasky, Kathryn. *Fourth of July Bear.*

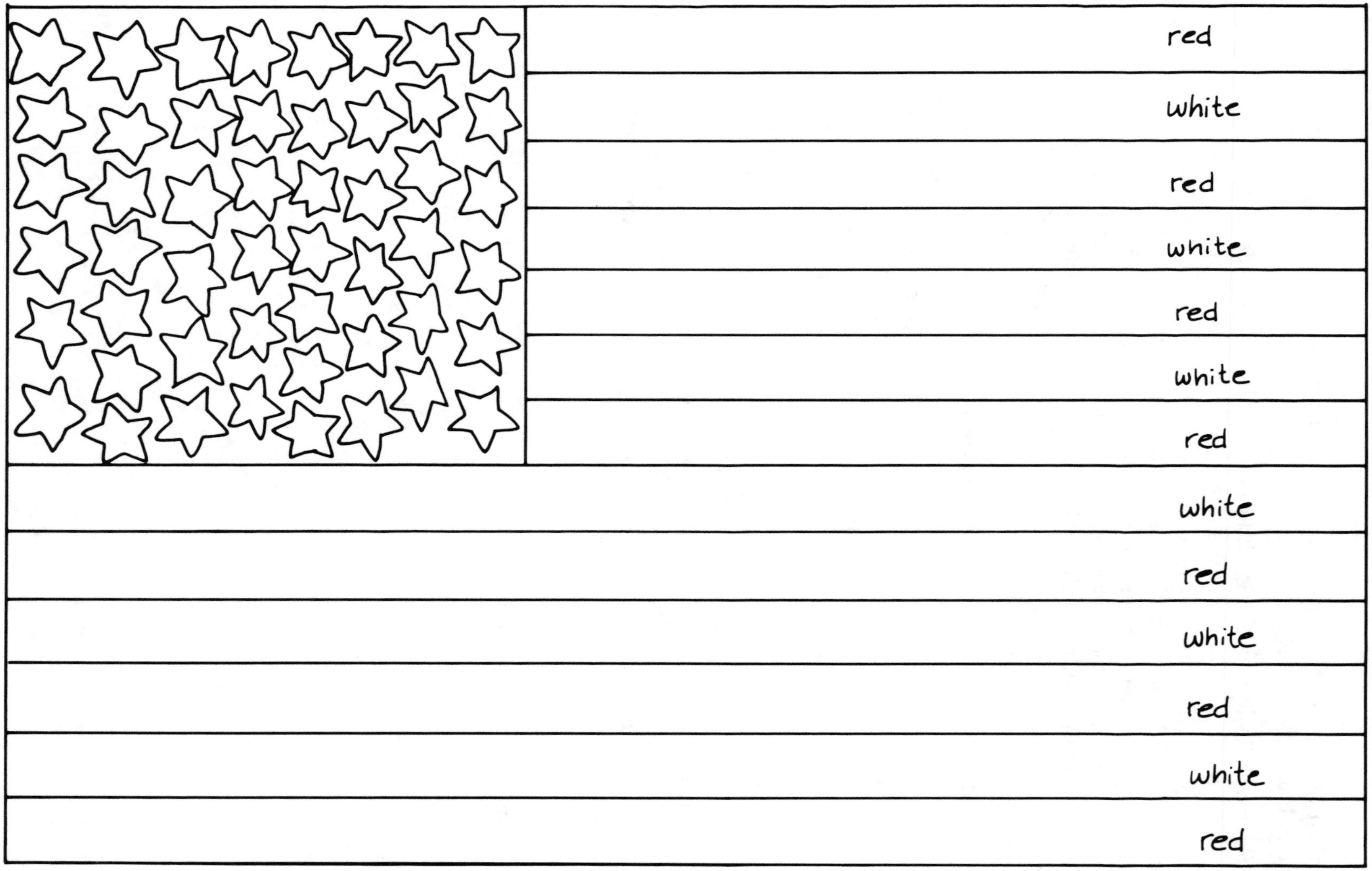

red

white

red

white

red

white

red

white

red

white

red

white

red

Coloring Activity/Flag Game Activity

All Time Favorite Books

CORDUROY
by
Don Freeman

Developmental Activities Chart	Language & Cognitive Development	Fine Motor Art	Gross Motor	Perception	Social Skills	Math	Dramatic Play	Cooking Snack	Science	Music, Fingerplays, Poems
1 Button Sorting	X			X	X	X				
2 Button Problem Solving	X				X					
3 Same or Different?	X			X						
4 Dramatic Play	X	X			X	X	X			
5 Shopping Spree	X				X	X				
6 Touch Time	X			X						
7 Feelie Can				X						
8 Button Brainstorming	X	X								
9 Button Factory		X								
10 Button Hunt	X									
11 Corduroy's Adventure			X							
12 Button Jump		X				X				
13 Teddy Bear Measurement	X					X				
14 Action Rhyme			X							X
15 Teddy Bear Paws	X	X						X		
16 Bear Lacing		X								
17 Texture Bear		X								
18 Find the Different Button		X		X						
19 Suggested Home Activities		X		X						
20										
21										
22										
23										
24										
25										
26										
27										
28										
29										
30										

CORDUROY
by Don Freeman
Viking Press, 1968

Corduroy is a stuffed teddy bear who lives in the toy department of a big store. One day he almost finds a home when a little girl wants to buy him, but one of his buttons is missing. Although Corduroy goes through an evening of adventure searching for his lost button, he is unable to find it. The little girl returns to buy Corduroy, brings him home, sews on a button, and finds lasting friendship.

Button Sorting.   Collect a variety of buttons and give children an opportunity to manipulate and explore the assortment. Divide children into small groups and have them sort the buttons into various categories, including color, shape, size, texture, shanked and shankless, number of holes, and any other category the children determine.

Button Problem Solving.   Place an assortment of six to ten buttons in front of a group of children. Play the game "I'm Thinking of a Button." The teacher selects one button to be "It" and gives children clues that will eliminate all the buttons except "It." For example, "I'm thinking of a button that is *not* black." Children remove all the buttons that are black. "I'm thinking of a button that has two holes." Children remove all the buttons that have more than or fewer than two holes. Continue until "It" has been discovered.

Same or Different?   Place three buttons in front of the children. Talk about the characteristics of each button. Have children compare and tell how the buttons are the same and how they are different.

Dramatic Play.   Set up a toy store in your classroom, like the one where Corduroy lived. Gather a variety of dolls, trucks, stuffed animals, books, games, blocks, and other items, and place them in a large area. Ask children to help you set up a store by putting all the toys that are the same together. Provide children with paper, blank price stickers, pencils, markers, play money, and a cash register. Let children price the toys (assist them in pricing items from one cent to ten cents) and take turns being clerks and shoppers.

Shopping Spree.   Structure the toy store dramatic play area into a fun math lesson. Give each child ten real or pretend pennies. The children can take turns going to the toy store to select one or more toys. Provide assistance in counting and making change.

Touch Time.   Corduroy wore overalls that were made of corduroy fabric. Collect a variety of fabrics (rough, smooth, bumpy, scratchy, soft, slippery, etc.) and place them in the sensory table. Give children the opportunity to touch, compare, and describe what they feel.

Feelie Can.   Make several pairs of texture cards (two cards with wool, two cards with corduroy, two cards with satin, and so on) by gluing a variety of fabrics on small pieces of tagboard. Separate the cards into two sets, one set for the teacher and one set for the children. The teacher puts one fabric card into a feelie can or box. Children take turns reaching inside to touch the fabric and then identify a fabric sample that is the exact match from their set of cards.

Button Brainstorming.   Draw a large button on a piece of copier paper. Gather children around you and talk about things in the story that had buttons on them (Corduroy's overalls and the mattress). Brainstorm other things that could have buttons and record children's responses (pillows, sweaters, chairs, shirts, etc.), around the picture of the button. Reproduce the completed list so that each child has a copy. Children can then color or decorate the button before bringing it home. Encourage children to add to the list of button items with family members.

Button Factory.   Create a button factory in your classroom. Provide children with modeling clay or play dough, dull knives, small cookie cutters, rolling pins, and straws to make button holes. Let children create different buttons.

Button Hunt.   The teacher hides a button somewhere in the classroom and gives children clues to find it. Be sure to take advantage of reinforcing directional-positional concepts such as in, on, over, under, beside, between, next to, above, and below, just to name a few. Directions can be tailor made to meet the individual levels of students' needs and abilities.

Corduroy's Adventure.   While searching for his button, Corduroy moved up an escalator, through rows of furniture, over beds, and under the covers. Set up an obstacle course in an open area of the classroom or gym where children can move and climb in search of Corduroy's button. The teacher can place a real button or one made of construction paper or tagboard at the end of the obstacle course.

Button Jump.   Give each child a large, flat button and several smaller ones. Children place a small button on a smooth, hard surface and snap the small button with the large button to make the small one "jump." When children get proficient, they can compare the distances that their buttons have jumped.

Teddy Bear Measurement.   Ask children to bring a teddy bear to school. Children can measure classroom objects or their peers and determine how many teddy bears tall or how many teddy bears long each item is.

Action Rhyme.   Recite this rhyme with the children and demonstrate actions for each line.

     Teddy bear, teddy bear turn around.
     Teddy bear, teddy bear touch the ground.
     Teddy bear, teddy bear hop, hop, hop.

Teddy bear, teddy bear stomp, stomp, stomp.
Teddy bear, teddy bear reach for the stars.
Teddy bear, teddy bear fill honey jars.
Teddy bear, teddy bear climb the stair.
Teddy bear, teddy bear make a pair.   [Join hands with a friend.]
Add additional verses with suggestions from the children.

Teddy Bear Paws.   Children will enjoy making a teddy bear paw to eat at snack time.

> 1 refrigerator biscuit per child
> melted margarine
> cinnamon sugar

Preheat oven to 450 degrees. Children form their biscuit into the shape of a bear paw. Using the dull edge of a knife, they can draw lines or perforations to create the effects of a paw. Brush paw with melted margarine and sprinkle with cinnamon sugar mixture. Place paws on a baking sheet and cook according to package directions.

Bear Lacing.   Cut several simple bear shapes out of heavy cardboard or tagboard. Laminate the pieces and punch holes at equal intervals around the edges of each bear. Have children sew or lace around a bear.

Texture Bear.   Give each child a precut shape of a bear cut from heavy paper. Provide dried coffee grounds, fabric scraps, buttons, and glue for the children to create their own Corduroy.

Find the Different Button.   Give each child a copy of the black line master. Children find and color the button that is different from the first button.

Suggested Home Activities.   Send home a synopsis of the story *Corduroy,* and inform parents about some of the activities the children will be doing at school. This is a perfect time to encourage parents to provide opportunities for their child to strengthen the self-help skill of buttoning. Remind them to give their child opportunities to practice buttoning on a flat surface as well as on clothing they are wearing. Both require different skills in perception and motor planning.

Related Literature

Butler, Dorothy. *My Brown Bear Barney.*
Carlstrom, Nancy White. *Jesse Bear, What Will You Wear?*
Degan, Bruce. *Jamberry.*
Freeman, Don. *A Pocket for Corduroy.*
Hissy, Jane. *Little Bear's Trousers.*
———. *Old Bear.*

Color the button that is *different* from the first button.

Find the Different Button Activity

CAPS FOR SALE
by
Esphyr Slobodkina

Developmental Activities Chart	Language & Cognitive Development	Fine Motor Art	Gross Motor	Perception	Social Skills	Math	Dramatic Play	Cooking Snack	Science	Music, Fingerplays, Poems
1 Monkey Business			X				X			
2 Angry Feelings	X				X					
3 Dramatic Play	X				X		X			
4 Caps for Sale										X
5 Riddles	X									
6 Hide the Hat	X				X					
7 Dramatize	X						X			
8 New Endings	X	X								
9 Monkey Math				X		X				
10 Cap Patterns				X						
11 Caps		X								
12 Memory Game	X									
13 Peddler, Peddler, Cap!			X		X					
14 Monkey Snack								X		
15 Peddler's Tale										X
16 Silly Hat Day		X								
17 Monkey's Banana Nut Bread	X	X				X		X		
18 Suggested Home Activities	X		X						X	
19										
20										
21										
22										
23										
24										
25										
26										
27										
28										
29										
30										

CAPS FOR SALE
by Esphyr Slobodkina
Harper & Row, 1947

Caps for Sale is the classic tale of a peddler, his hats, and some observant monkeys. On a slow day of peddling his wares, the peddler stops to take a nap in the country. He awakens to find that his hats are missing! The humorous story has a surprisingly funny conclusion that children will enjoy.

Monkey Business. Monkeys are known for their ability to copy behavior by observing and imitating. In the story, the monkeys imitated the actions of the peddler, and because of it, he got back his caps. The teacher can be the "peddler" and perform a wide range of actions and movements that the students can copy and imitate. Children can also take turns performing actions for their classmates to copy.

Angry Feelings. In the story the peddler became very angry with the monkeys. He shook his hands, stamped his feet, and shouted at the monkeys. Have children brainstorm a list of things they do when they become angry—cry, yell, punch things, and so on. Next, brainstorm a list of things they can do to help themselves feel better—tell mom, ask for help, go in their room, and so on.

Dramatic Play. Supply a variety of hats in the housekeeping corner. Children can try on and model the hats, acting out the roles of people who would wear that hat. Have a large mirror available so that children can look at and admire themselves. Children will also enjoy opening a hat shop. Provide play money, a cash register, and bags or boxes for the hats that are purchased. Children take turns being cashiers and customers.

Caps for Sale   (to the tune of "Jingle Bells")

    Caps for sale,
    Caps for sale,
    Wear one every day.
    Blue or red
    Let it warm your head
    On a cold and windy day.

Riddles. Show children pictures of various caps and hats, or use those found in the dramatic play area. The caps and hats will serve as visual clues for this auditory lesson. The teacher gives a riddle and the children must decide which person would wear a particular hat. Include riddles for hats worn by a chef, firefighter, witch, baseball player, football player, nurse, pirate, construction worker, police officer, magician, cowboy, bride, king, queen, gardener, farmer, and lifeguard.

Hide the Hat.   Select one child to be a naughty monkey and another child to be the peddler. The monkey hides a cap or hat somewhere in the classroom. The other children give clues using directional and positional concepts such as behind, between, beside, above, and so on, to the peddler to help him or her find the missing cap/hat.

Dramatize.   This is an excellent story for children to dramatize because there can never be too many monkeys in the story! One child is selected to be the peddler (perhaps the children could pick their parts out of a cap), and the other children are the fun-loving monkeys. The peddler and the monkeys can decide upon the actions, noises, and movements they will perform in the story. Children can bring hats from home to wear or they can make hats at home or school for the dramatization.

New Endings.   Children can write or dictate a new ending(s) for the story. What might have happened if the peddler didn't get angry? What might have happened if the monkeys didn't throw the caps back on the ground? The teacher can read all the new story endings. Children can illustrate their stories.

Monkey Math.   Use the black line master as a pattern to cut 11 monkeys out of construction paper. Write a numeral from 0 to 10 on each monkey. Cut out a variety of caps: red, blue, gray, brown, and checkered. Laminate the pieces. Children place the correct number of caps on the monkeys' heads.

- Children can vote for the favorite hat worn by the peddler.
- Children can sort and graph caps/hats by color, size, season, occupation, leisure activity, and any other category they propose. Which set has the most, the least, the same number, and so on.
- Practice one-to-one correspondence with construction paper cutouts of monkeys and colorful caps. Laminate the pieces. Children give each monkey one cap to wear on his or her head.

Cap Patterns.   Use the laminated, construction paper caps prepared for "Monkey Math." Children design, copy, or continue patterns with the caps. Patterns can be simple or complex, such as gray-red/gray-red or blue-blue-checkered-brown/blue-blue-checkered-brown.

Caps.   Call a local paint or hardware store and ask if they could donate enough white painter's caps for the class. Children can decorate their cap like those sold by the peddler or decorate in a more elaborate manner. Provide markers, sequins, fabric and felt scraps, tissue, pompoms, and so on.

Memory Game.   Place pictures of three or four hats on the table, or use hats found in the dramatic play area. Children name and describe each hat, then cover their eyes while the teacher removes one from the table. Children remember which hat is missing by describing it.

Peddler, Peddler, Cap!   Play a version of the familiar game "Duck, Duck, Goose." One child is chosen to be a monkey; he or she walks around the circle of children carrying a cap, touching each child along the way saying, "Peddler, peddler, cap!" When the monkey says "Cap!" he or she drops the cap. The peddler sitting on the floor picks up the cap and chases the monkey around the circle, trying to catch the monkey before he or she reaches the safety of the peddler's seat on the floor.

Monkey Snack.   Children will enjoy preparing and eating a special snack designed to feed hungry monkeys. Mix equal amounts of dried banana chips, dry roasted peanuts, flaked coconut, raisins, and M&M's™ in a large bowl. Stir and eat.

Peddler's Tale   (to the tune of "This Old Man")

Way up high, in a tree
Monkeys wearing caps like me!
So I shook both hands and threw down my checkered cap.
Now I know I'll never nap!

Silly Hat Day.   Send home a note to parents asking them to help their child create a silly cap or hat to wear on Hat Day at school. Children can model their hats, move to music and have a hat parade.

Monkey's Banana Nut Bread

½ cup butter	3 tablespoons sour cream
1 cup sugar	1 teaspoon baking soda
2 eggs	2 cups flour
2 bananas, mashed	1 cup chopped nuts

Preheat oven to 325 degrees. Cream butter and sugar. Then mix in the remaining ingredients in the order given. Bake for 1 hour in a greased loaf pan.

Suggested Home Activities.   Send home a synopsis of the story *Caps for Sale* and inform parents of some of the activities the children will be doing at school. Suggest that parents and child plan to visit the zoo, making sure to spend a long time enjoying the antics of the monkeys, and observing if they imitate one another. Children will also enjoy going to a neighborhood park. With adult supervision, children can climb on the monkey bars.

Related Literature

Geringer, Laura. *A Three Hat Day.*
Keats, Ezra Jack. *Jennie's Hat.*
Miller, Margaret. *Whose Hat?*
Roy, Ron. *Whose Hat Is That?*

Monkey Pattern

Monkey Math Activity

Cap Patterns

Monkey Math Activity

SWIMMY
by
Leo Lionni

Developmental Activities Chart	Language & Cognitive Development	Fine Motor Art	Gross Motor	Perception	Social Skills	Math	Dramatic Play	Cooking Snack	Science	Music, Fingerplays, Poems
1 Little Fish, Big Fish		X		X	X					
2 Move Together			X		X					
3 Fishy Swimming Circle Game			X							
4 Many Fish in the Sea				X						
5 Fish Puzzles		X		X	X					
6 Size Schools	X			X		X				
7 Individual Differences	X			X	X	X				
8 Go Fish	X			X		X				
9 Sponge Painting		X								
10 Ocean Waves									X	
11 Fresh Water, Salt Water									X	
12 Float and Sink	X					X			X	
13 Eggs-periment									X	
14 Five Little Fishies		X				X				X
15 Fish Snacks								X		
16 Shrimpies								X		
17 Collection Table									X	
18 Easel Art		X								
19 Measuring with Fish						X				
20 Field Trip	X								X	
21 Suggested Home Activities					X	X				
22										
23										
24										
25										
26										
27										
28										
29										
30										

SWIMMY
by Leo Lionni
Scholastic, 1963

Swimmy was a small black fish who swam with a school of fish who were just like him in almost every way except that all his brothers and sisters were red. One day a bad tuna fish came along and ate all the red fish. Swimmy escaped because he was such a fast swimmer. Swimmy went off on his own where he discovered the many wonders of undersea life. His undersea adventures led him to a school of small red fish, just like his own family. Through a cooperative effort, Swimmy and his new school of fish were able to swim and play without having to worry about the big fish of the sea.

Little Fish, Big Fish. Swimmy and his new school of fish fooled the larger fish by swimming all together in the formation of one large red fish with a black eye. The children can work together just as the small red fish worked together. On a large sheet of kraft paper, draw a simple outline of a very large fish. Make a fish stencil for children to trace using the black line master provided. The children can trace and cut fish and glue them to the outline of the large fish. Modify the activity for younger children and those with delayed fine motor skills by pretracing and/or precutting the fish. When finished, the children can count how many little fish it took to make one big fish.

Move Together. The children can move together just like the school of fish swam all together in a fish formation. Help the children to organize themselves into a formation. Start with a simple formation such as a circle. When the teacher blows a whistle, children move together while staying in formation. When the whistle blows again, the children stop. The children can move by walking, running, jumping, hopping, marching, skipping, crawling, and swimming.

Fishy Swimming Circle Game. Children sit in a circle. One child is selected to be "It." "It" walks around the circle touching each child on the head, while all the children chant, "Fishy swimming in the sea. You swim so fast but you can't catch me." The child whose head is tapped on the word "me" jumps up and chases "It" around the circle. "It" runs around the circle and sits in the vacant space before being tagged. The child who chases becomes "It."

Many Fish in the Sea. Ocean fish come in a vast assortment of sizes, colors, and designs. There are fish with stripes, polka dots, and many other line and shape patterns. Use the fish black line master provided to cut a set of 20 fish.

Paint or color the fish using a variety of colors and design patterns. Every fish should have a pair that matches it in size and appearance. Laminate the fish to preserve them. Mix up the fish. Children can find the matching pairs.

Fish Puzzles.   Use the fish black line master to cut an assortment of fish. The children can decorate the fish with markers, paint, or crayons. Laminate the fish. They can cut their fish into two to four pieces using zigzag or curved lines. The children will enjoy trading fish puzzles with a friend and assembling each other's puzzles. Store pieces in a zip-close bag.

Size Schools.   Cut a variety of small, medium, and large fish. Children can classify them by size into schools of fish. Schools of fish can range in number from just a few to many fish. Children can estimate the number of fish in each of the schools and then count the fish to check their estimations. Encourage children to use the terms "few" and "many" when referring to the schools. The children can sequence individual fish from smallest to largest and largest to smallest.

Individual Differences.   Swimmy was a black fish living among red fish. He used his difference in appearance to his advantage when he was able to help a school of red fish look like a large fish with a black eye. Children should be aware of and proud of their individual differences. Ask children to name physical attributes of people that can be different. Encourage children to think of hair color, eye color, size, skin tone, handedness, and so on. Make a graph for the different attributes. Count and graph the number of children with brown, black, red, or blond hair. Make another graph for counting and displaying the number of children with blue, brown, green, and hazel eyes. Graphic representations can be made for height, weight, skin tone, and so on. Children can compare the results and note commonalities as well as differences.

Go Fish.   A "Go Fish" card game can be made to reinforce concepts being taught to children at different levels. Prepare a deck of 30 fish-shaped cards. Cards can be labeled with numbers, colors, sizes, shapes, alphabet letters, and so on. The object of the game is to match pairs. Children are each dealt four to six cards. Remaining cards are placed in a pile in the center of the table. Matching pairs are set on the table. On each turn one child asks another for a card that will help to make a pair. If the child does not get the card he or she asked for, he or she draws from the pile of cards in the middle.

Sponge Painting.   Children can make fish that resemble Swimmy. Children first make water by dipping sponges into blue or turquoise paint and then onto construction paper. When the painted water dries, the children can add fish. Cut sponges into fish shapes. Children dip the sponges into different colors of tempera paint and then gently print the fish shapes on construction paper.

Ocean Waves.   Use a bottle with a lid that screws on, such as a one-liter soda bottle. Fill it one-third full of salad oil. Add blue and green food coloring to the oil. Fill the remainder of the bottle with white vinegar. As the bottle is gently rocked, the salad oil forms waves.

Fresh Water, Salt Water.   Explain the difference between fresh water and salt water to the children with this simple experiment. Give each child a container with fresh water and allow the child to taste the fresh water. Each child then pours 2 to 4 tablespoons of salt into the water (depending on the amount of water used.) The child can place a finger into the salt water and then into his or her mouth to taste the difference.

Float and Sink.   Collect a variety of items from the classroom, some that will sink and some that will float. Fill the exploration table or a basin with water. Children can test each item to determine if it floats on the top of the water or sinks to the bottom. The children can group the items accordingly. Add salt to the water. Children can determine if the same items float and sink the same as they did in the fresh water.

Eggs-periment.   Half fill a wide-mouth jar with water. Stir in salt until it will no longer dissolve. Put an egg into the jar and watch it float. Slowly pour fresh water over the egg and observe what happens. Clue—the egg will continue to float over the salt water but under the fresh water. (Salt water is heavier than the egg, so the egg floats on top of it; the egg is heavier than the fresh water, so it sinks in the fresh water.)

Five Little Fishies   (fingerplay)

> Five little fishies on the ocean floor.   [Hold up five fingers.]
> One swam away and then there were four.   [Put one finger down.]
> Four little fishies swimming in the sea.   [Hold up four fingers.]
> One swam away and then there were three.   [Put one finger down.]
> Three little fishies swimming in a school.   [Hold up three fingers.]
> One swam away and then there were two.   [Put one finger down.]
> Two little fishies swimming in the sun.   [Hold up two fingers.]
> One swam away and then there was one.   [Put one finger down.]
> One little fishy looking for a friend.   [Hold up one finger.]
> He found a new fish school.   [Put finger down.]
> And now we've reached the end.

Fish Snacks.   Serve fish-shaped crackers in different flavors, oyster crackers, fish sticks, tuna fish and/or salmon mixed with mayonnaise on crackers, shrimp toast, and fish or clam chowder.

Shrimpies

1 package English muffins	1 tablespoon lemon juice
6–8 ounces shredded cheddar cheese	6-ounce package frozen shrimp finely chopped
1½ cups mayonnaise	

Preheat oven to 325 degrees. Mix ingredients together and spread on quartered English muffins. Bake until bubbly.

Collection Table.   Set up a special area for children to display shells that they can bring in from home. Set out a magnifying glass to help children get a closer look at the shells. Include other ocean items such as sand, fossils, turtle shells, lobster shells, crab shells, starfish, and so on. Set up a goldfish bowl on the table. Children can observe the goldfish and take turns feeding them.

Easel Art. Cut easel paper into fish shapes. Provide a variety of paint colors for children to use on their fish. Fish shapes can be cut using negative space—cut fish shapes in easel paper leaving the easel paper surrounding the fish intact. Children can paint, creatively utilizing the negative space in the paper.

Measuring with Fish. Using any of the black line masters, children can color and cut fish to use for measuring. Children can measure tabletops, chairs, toys, and each other. Encourage them to compare lengths in terms of how many fish long the items are. Which is longer? Which is shorter? Which two are the same? If the children cut enough fish, they can tape them in a vertical line on the wall, illustrating their own and each other's height.

Field Trip. If possible, take the children on a field trip to a pet shop that sells tropical fish. They will be able to observe a variety of colors, sizes, and designs in the fish. Children will also be able to see plants and other marine life. If your local zoo has a fish display or aquarium, children will enjoy visiting it and observing the many varieties of fish. Experts can talk with the children about diet, rest patterns, and schooling habits of the various fish.

Suggested Home Activities. Send home a synopsis of *Swimmy*. Inform the parents of some of the activities in which their children are involved. Explain the various concepts which are reinforced in the story, including individual differences, size, friendship, cooperation, and ocean life. Parents can reinforce the idea of cooperation at home by asking siblings to complete a task together, and then talking with the children about how well they cooperated with each other to get the job done. Parents can talk with their child about individual differences within the family. Prepare a graph for parents and children to fill out together that represents hair and eye color of family members. Just as Swimmy was black and his brothers and sisters were red, many brothers and sisters look very different. The children can bring their graphs back to school and share the results with their classmates.

Related Literature

Lionni, Leo. *Fish Is Fish.*
McDonald, Megan. *Is This a House for a Hermit Crab?*
Oppenheim, Joanne. *Follow That Fish.*

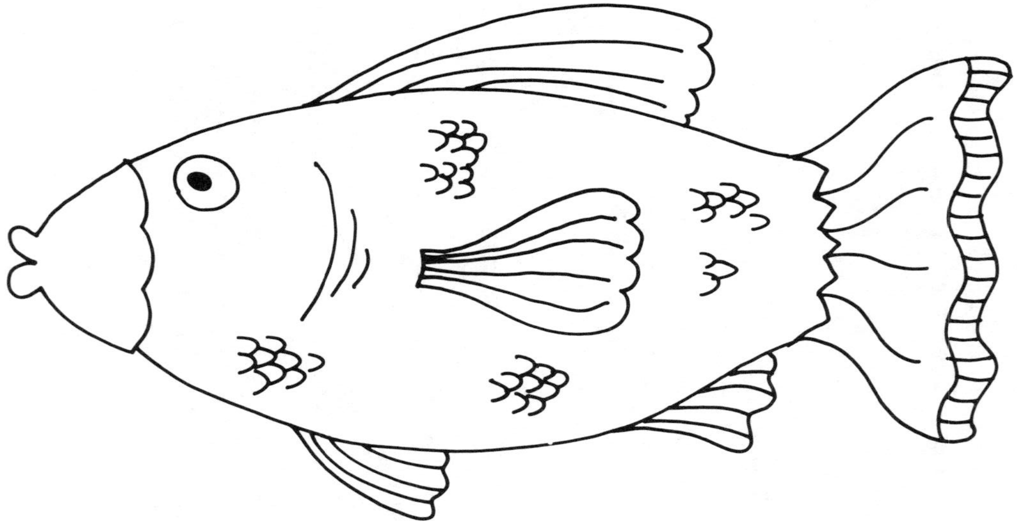

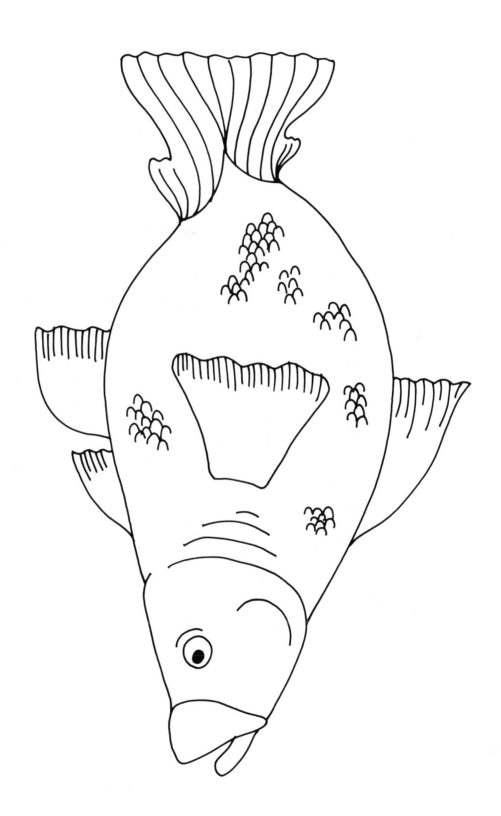

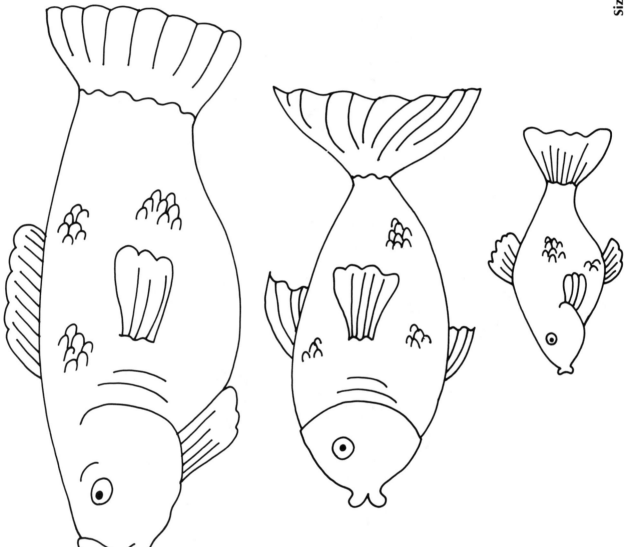

MADELINE'S RESCUE
by
Ludwig Bemelmans

Developmental Activities Chart	Language & Cognitive Development	Fine Motor Art	Gross Motor	Perception	Social Skills	Math	Dramatic Play	Cooking Snack	Science	Music, Fingerplays, Poems
1 Find France	X					X				
2 When in Time	X									
3 Flags	X	X		X		X				
4 Eiffel Tower	X	X		X						
5 Don't Fall in the Water			X							
6 Say It in French	X					X				
7 Twelve Little Girls in Two Straight Lines					X	X				
8 My Favorite Pet	X					X			X	
9 Pet Store	X				X	X	X			
10 Pet Visitors					X				X	
11 Puppy Chow								X		
12 Color Matching	X			X	X					
13 Doggie, Doggie, Where's the Bone?			X		X					
14 Looking High and Low	X	X			X					
15 High, Low, Fast, and Slow	X		X							X
16 A Story in Rhyme	X	X								
17 Pet Songs										X
18 I Can Count in French										X
19 Paper Pups		X								
20 Puppy Prints		X				X				
21 Suggested Home Activities		X						X		
22										
23										
24										
25										
26										
27										
28										
29										
30										

MADELINE'S RESCUE
by Ludwig Bemelmans
Viking Press, 1953

This Caldecott Award-winning book tells the timeless story of young heroine, Madeline, who is rescued from the water by a quick-thinking dog. The dog comes to live at the boarding school with Madeline and her 11 other schoolmates. The humorous story, which is told in rhyme, has continued to charm young audiences for more than 40 years.

Find France. The Madeline stories are set in Paris, France. Look at a map or globe with the children and locate your hometown, state, and country. Then find Paris, France. Tell the children that the color blue denotes water. Talk about what means of transportation the children would need to use to travel to France. Use pieces of string to measure the size of France, the size of your state, and the distance from your home state to France. The children will be eager to share names of distant places where grandparents and other relatives live. Find those places on the map and use string to measure if those places are farther away or closer than France.

When in Time.   The story *Madeline's Rescue* first appeared in *Good Housekeeping* magazine in 1951. It is difficult for most preschoolers to imagine a time before they were born. Many children will be amazed when they realize that this book was written even before many of their parents were born. Talk about how things were different back when this book was written. Girls wore only dresses, television was brand new (black and white only if people had it), there were no videos or Nintendo™, telephones had dials, and so on. Look at the pictures and notice some things that are still the same—swing sets, balloons, bicycles, and so on.

Flags.   The French flag is shown in the street scene pictures of Paris. Explain to the children that every country (and state) has its own special flag. Show them pictures of the French and the American flags. Talk about the similarities between the flags (same colors and shape) and the differences (different color patterns, stars on American). Make a set of American and French flag picture cards for the children to sort. Some children might enjoy coloring the flags from models.

Eiffel Tower.   The Eiffel Tower is a landmark of Paris. It was once the tallest building in the world. Cut tall triangle stencils from cardboard resembling the Eiffel Tower. The children can trace them and cut out the center so they resemble the Eiffel Tower. Have the children look for triangular-shaped objects in the classroom, at home, and in the neighborhood. Set aside a special place for a triangle collection. The children can make tall towers and skyscrapers out of blocks and unifix™ cubes.

Don't Fall in the Water. When Madeline fell in the water while balancing on a wall, she was rescued by a dog which the girls named Miss Genevieve. Set up a balance beam with mats spread underneath. The children can take turns balancing on the beam while walking heel to toe forward and backward.

Say It in French. Explain to the children that people who live in different countries often speak different languages. Teach the children how to count to 12 in French and how to say some basic words. Talk about other languages that are spoken in the children's homes. If any of the parents speak different languages, invite them to the classroom to teach the children simple words and songs:

> One to 12: *un, deux, trois, quatre, cinq, six, sept, huit, neuf, dix, onze, douze.*

Hello—*bonjour*	red—*rouge*	nose—*le nez*
Good bye—*au revoir*	blue—*bleu*	mouth—*la bouche*
Please—*s'il vous plait*	yellow—*jaune*	head—*la tête*
Thank you—*merci*	white—*blanc*	eyes—*les yeux*

Twelve Little Girls in Two Straight Lines. That's how the girls lined up for their daily walk. Challenge 12 children to line themselves up in two straight lines with the same number of children in each line. The children will need to problem solve to accomplish this. If the task is too difficult, they can use blocks, small dolls, or other manipulatives on the floor or tabletop to help them work through the problem. Count the lined-up children in French.

My Favorite Pet. The 12 girls became very attached to their pet dog. Discuss pets that the children own. Make a class graph of the different kinds of pets; count the number of dogs, cats, fish, birds, gerbils, rabbits, and other pets children have. Determine which kind of pet most of the children own. Write a class story about what pets need and how to take care of them. Ask a veterinarian to visit the class to talk about pet care.

Pet Store. Set up a pet store in the dramatic play area. The children can bring in stuffed animals to inhabit the store. The children can classify the pets and keep the different species together. Have the class brainstorm what other things might be sold in a pet store and try to supply those items or furnish substitutes. Assist the children in making signs and price tags to use in the store. Provide play money and a cash register. If possible, visit a pet store.

Pet Visitors. Ask parents to bring pets to the classroom to visit. Before the pet visitors arrive, discuss with the children the proper way to handle animals and how to behave around them. Stress that animals are easily frightened and that the children must not grab at them. The children should wait for the pets to approach them first.

Puppy Chow.   It looks like puppy chow but tastes great.

1	box Quaker Oat Squares™	1	stick butter
1	12-ounce bag chocolate chips	1–2	cups powdered sugar
1	cup creamy peanut butter		

Melt the chocolate chips, butter, and the peanut butter in a sauce pan on low heat. Coat the oat squares with the mixture. Allow to cool. Coat with powdered sugar. (Shake the oat squares together with the sugar in a bag for easy coating.)

Color Matching.   Make copies of the dog and bone black line master, color them in matching pairs, and laminate. For younger children and children with delays in the area of perception, make solid color pairs. For older children and children who are able to notice more intricate details, color the pairs with patterns (stripes, checks, dots, and so on). The children can find the matching dogs and bones. This activity can be done individually or in game format. The children sit in a circle with the dogs and bones evenly distributed. They try to make pairs by describing to other children the bone or dog they need to make a pair.

Doggie, Doggie, Where's the Bone?   One child at a time is chosen to be "It" and another child is "Doggie." The remainder of the children sit in a circle on the floor. "Doggie" covers his or her eyes or leaves the room while "It" secretly gives the bone to a child seated in the circle. When "Doggie" returns or uncovers his or her eyes, the children chant, "Doggie, Doggie, where's the bone? Someone stole it from your home." "Doggie" tries to guess who is holding the bone by walking around the outside of the circle and gently touching children on the head. When he or she touches the correct person, that person ("It") jumps up and chases "Doggie" around the circle. Doggie quickly runs to the empty space in the circle and sits down. "It" becomes "Doggie" and a new "It" is chosen.

Looking High and Low.   When Genevieve was thrown out by the board of trustees, the girls looked high and low to find her. Discuss the concepts of "high and low" with the children. Go for a walk outside and look for things that are up high and down low. Upon returning from your walk prepare a long sheet of kraft paper by drawing a horizontal line through the middle of the paper. Together, the children can create a class mural by drawing pictures of things that were up high on the top half of the paper and things that were down low on the bottom half of the paper. The teacher can label the items.

High, Low, Fast, and Slow.   The children can take turns giving directions in this simple creative movement game. Play music, alternating fast and slow tempos. When the music stops, a child calls out "high" or "low." When the music starts again, the children move according to direction, either high on their tiptoes or low down on their feet, hands and knees, or creeping on their tummies.

A Story in Rhyme.   The story *Madeline's Rescue* is told in rhyme.

- Reread the story, accentuating the rhyming words.
- Make or find pictures of objects that rhyme. Provide opportunities for children to hear the rhyming words.

- Make up a class story using rhyming words. Illustrate the pages and assemble into book form. Add it to the class library.

Pet Songs.   Sing familiar songs about pets such as "How Much Is the Doggie in the Window?" and "Bingo." Substitute the French word *le chien* for the English word "dog."

I Can Count in French   (to the tune of "Are You Sleeping?")

> *Un, deux, trois.*
> *Quatre, cinq, six.*
> *Sept, huit, neuf.*
> *Dix, onze, douze.*
> I can count to twelve.
> I can count in French.
> Count with me.
> *S'il vous plait.*

Paper Pups.   The children can make puppies by tearing pieces of paper and gluing them onto a predrawn puppy shape, or they can create their own puppy shape. Purchase plastic moving eyes at a craft store to glue on or use a different-colored paper for eyes. Let the children decide on the color/breed for their puppy. Have them look through a dog book for ideas.

Puppy Prints.   The story ends happily when Genevieve comes back to school and gives birth to enough puppies "to go all around." Ask the children how many that would be? Have them print that number of puppies by dipping a dog-shaped cookie cutter into tempera paint and then onto construction paper. Children will see the relationship of one puppy for each girl, if the teacher draws 12 simple girl shapes on the construction paper. The children can give each girl a puppy print.

Suggested Home Activities.   Send home a synopsis of the story *Madeline's Rescue*. Inform parents about some of the activities in which the children are involved and the concepts that they are learning about. Parents and children will enjoy using pet-shaped cookie cutters to cut slices of bread to use with simple spreads such as cream cheese, peanut butter, or jelly, or they can use the pet shapes in making buttered toast and sandwiches. If pet-shaped cookie cutters aren't available, they can make a simple puppy face with a circle for the face and triangles for the ears. The facial features can be made with raisins or breakfast cereal. Another simple home activity children will enjoy is building their own Eiffel Tower by stacking cartons and boxes.

Related Literature

Bemelmans, Ludwig. *Madeline.*

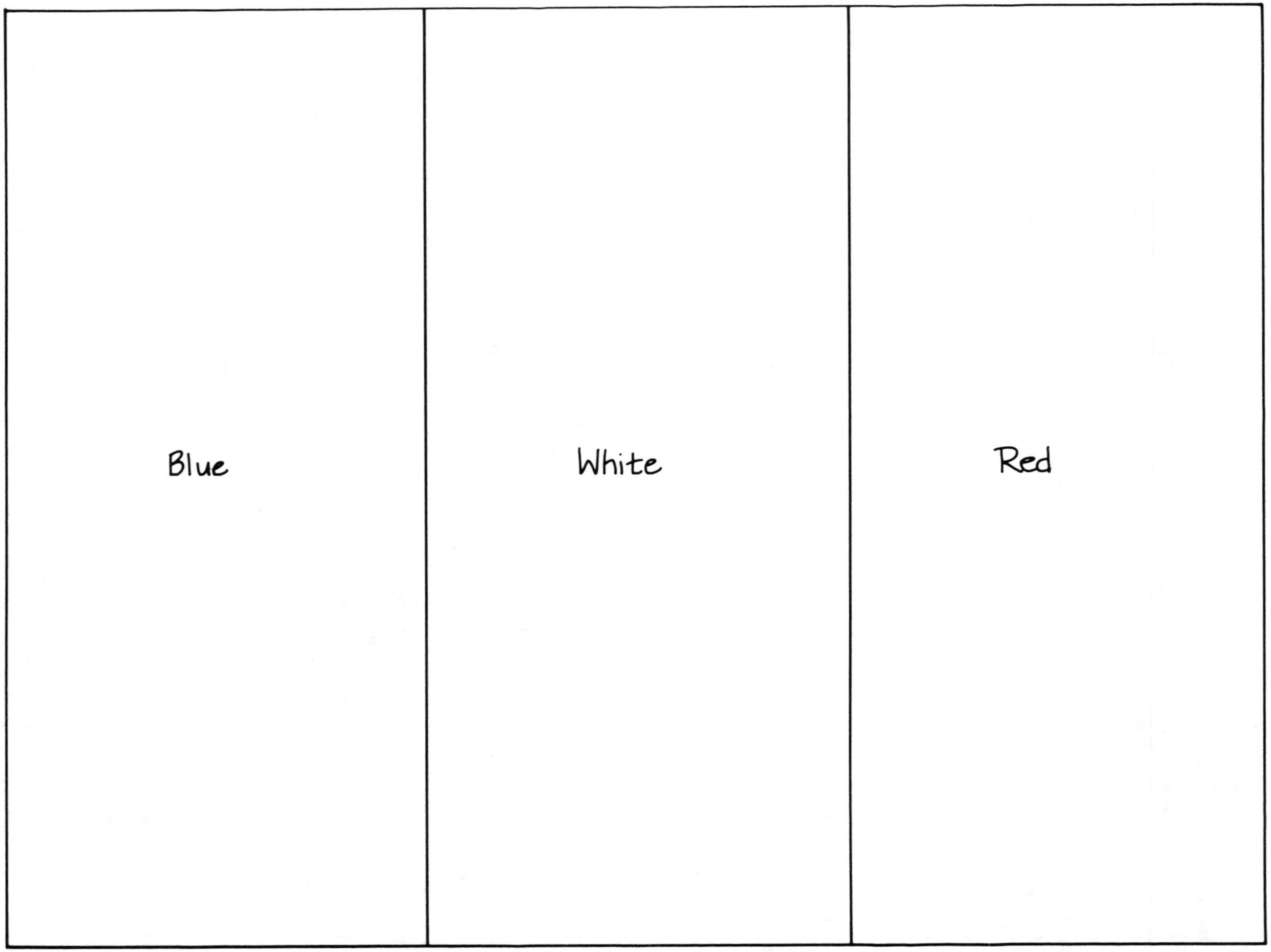

Blue

White

Red

French Flag "Tricolor"

red

white

red

white

red

white

red

white

red

white

red

white

red

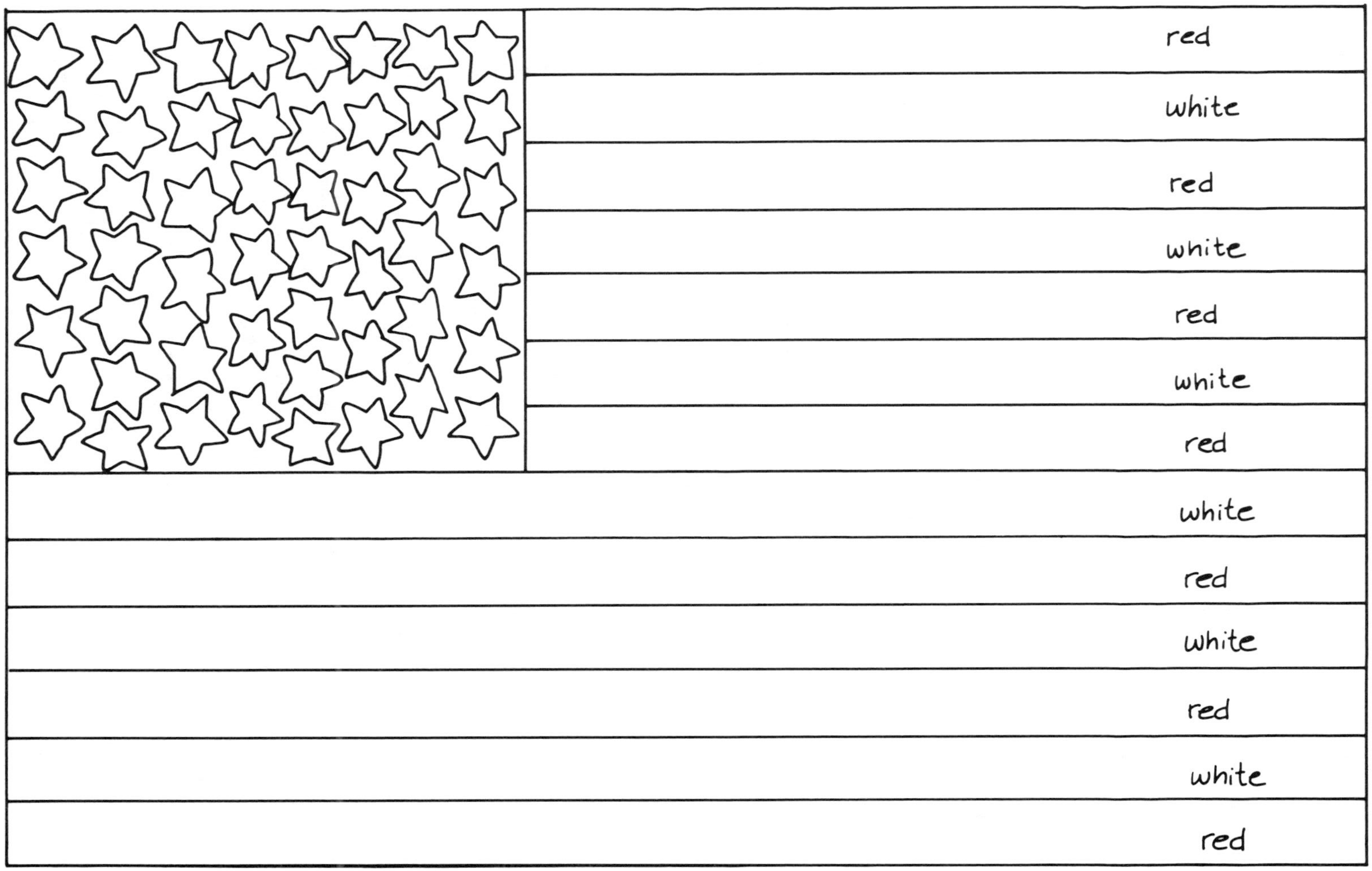

American Flag

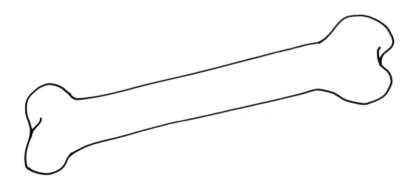

Color Matching Activity

BIG RED BARN
by
Margaret Wise Brown

Developmental Activities Chart

	Language & Cognitive Development	Fine Motor	Art	Gross Motor	Perception	Social Skills	Math	Dramatic Play	Cooking Snack	Science	Music, Fingerplays, Poems
1 Barnyard Friends	X						X			X	
2 Home Near the Barn											X
3 Corn Meal Play Dough		X							X		
4 Egg Relay				X		X					
5 Five Little Pigs		X						X			X
6 The Barnyard											X
7 Day and Night	X	X								X	
8 Farm Recipes	X	X					X			X	X
9 Barnyard Animals	X			X				X		X	
10 Math Activities	X	X				X	X				
11 Farm Collage		X									
12 Sensory Table		X			X						
13 Feather Activities	X			X		X					
14 Cat and Field Mouse				X		X					
15 Butterfly		X									
16 Eggs, Eggs, Eggs					X		X				
17 Hear the Rooster											X
18 Weather Vane	X	X								X	
19 Farm Balance Scales	X						X			X	
20 Mom and Babies	X									X	
21 Big Red Barn	X	X						X			
22 Field Trip	X	X								X	
23 Animal Classification	X									X	
24 Musical Farm Animals	X			X						X	
25 Scarecrow	X	X									
26 Suggested Home Activities	X								X	X	
27											
28											
29											
30											

BIG RED BARN
by Margaret Wise Brown
Harper & Row, 1956

This classic story in rhymed text tells about the different animals that live in the big red barn by night and play in the great green field all day when the children are away. A new colorful edition, illustrated by Felicia Bond, will delight young children. The bright early morning illustrations are in sharp contrast to the darkened illustrations depicted as night falls on the big red barn.

Barnyard Friends.   Have children look at the illustrations and name all the animals. Provide simple pictures of farm animals, or have children draw pictures. Prepare a graph where children place each animal picture under the correct animal body covering—fur, hide, or feathers. Prepare another graph where children pictorially show the animals with two legs and those with four legs. Compare the results.

Home Near the Barn   (to the tune of "Home, Home on the Range")

Home, home near the barn,
Where the pups and the new kittens play.
Where hens lay their eggs,
And stand on one leg.
And the animals play every day.

Home, home near the barn,
Where the rooster crows in the new dawn.
Pink pig learns to squeal.
Brown cow moos for a meal.
And at night, the moon sails on high.

Corn Meal Play Dough.   Children will enjoy preparing and using this rough-textured play dough. Provide rolling pins, dull knives, and animal-shaped cookie cutters.

2½   cups flour
 1   cup cornmeal
 1   tablespoon oil
 1   cup water

Mix the flour and cornmeal together in a large bowl. Gradually add oil and water to the flour mixture. Knead together until well blended. If necessary, add more water to reach desired consistency.

Egg Relay.   Divide the children into two groups of equal size. The first child on each team balances a plastic egg, Styrofoam™ egg, or hard-boiled egg on a large serving-size spoon. Children reach a designated line, turn, and race back to their respective team with the egg. The next child in line takes the spoon and egg. Children cheer teammates until everyone has had a turn.

Five Little Pigs.   Make five pigs out of felt to use on a flannel board as you say the rhyme. Pigs can be pink, black, white, or reddish-brown. Children can hold up five fingers and bend each down as the verse progresses.

> This little pig makes a squealing sound.
> This little pig is fat and round.
> This little pig roots all around,
> With his piggy snout, he digs up the ground.
> This little pig has a curly tail.
> He eats his lunch from a shiny pail.
> This little pig doesn't seem to care
> If any of the other pigs get their share.

The Barnyard.   Make farm animals out of felt to use on a flannel board or staple pictures of farm animals on tongue depressors to hold up as children recite the noisy verse.

> In the barnyard at the end of the day,
> All the animals seem to say,
> "Didn't we have fun today?"
> The cow says, "Moo."
> The pigeon, "Coo."
> The sheep says, "Baa."
> The lamb says "Maa."
> The hen, "Cluck, cluck, cluck."
> "Quack," says the duck.
> The dog, "Bow wow."
> The cat, "Meow."
> The horse says, "Neigh."
> And the donkeys "Bray."
> The goose says, "Honk."
> Pink pig, "Squeal."
> The red barn is closed up tight
> When the sky is dark at night.

Day and Night.   The story begins as the sun rises and ends when darkness covers the barnyard. Talk about the parts of the day—morning, afternoon, and night. Have children brainstorm activities they do at home and school during each part of the day. Each child can dictate a sentence story about their favorite time of day and illustrate their story.

Farm Recipes

Pigs in Blankets

> 1 large package refrigerator   1 package of 8 hot dogs
>   crescent rolls   2 slices of cheese

Preheat oven to 375 degrees. Divide crescent rolls into 8 triangles. Cut each slice of cheese into 4 strips. Cut the hot dogs down the center and place a piece of cheese into each slit. Put a hot dog on the wide end of the triangle dough and roll up. Put on cookie sheet, seam side down. Bake 10 to 15 minutes until golden brown.

Haystacks

> 12-ounce package semisweet chocolate chips or vanilla-flavored bark
>   2 cups Chinese noodles

Melt chocolate chips or vanilla bark. Stir in Chinese noodles. Drop by teaspoonful on waxed paper. Refrigerate; then serve.

Sweet Butter

Pour a half or full pint of whipping cream into a clear glass jar with a tight fitting lid (peanut butter jars work well). Children take turns shaking the jar vigorously. After a while, the cream separates into two parts: butter and whey. Pour off the liquid whey, and allow children to taste the buttermilk. Rinse the butter that remains in very cold water and refrigerate to harden slightly. Serve with crackers.

Barnyard Animals.   Place pictures of farm animals in a box or basket. Each child gets a turn to select an animal picture. The child makes the sound or movement the animal makes or tells a fact about the specific animal (what it eats, the name of its babies, physical characteristics, products we get from the animal, and so on). The other children listen and watch, then name the animal.

Math Activities

- A field mouse was born in a cornfield. Remove the dried kernels from field corn and use them for counting activities. Count kernels of corn from one ear and place them in small plastic or paper cups. Children count ten kernels for each cup. Count how many kernels there are altogether or how many cups were used in all.

- Use a permanent marker to write a number from 1 to 12 in each section of an empty egg carton. Divide children into small groups. Each group sits in a circle with the prepared egg carton and a supply of corn kernels. Each child gets a turn to put one kernel in the carton, shake it, then name the number where the kernel landed. Group members make a set corresponding to the number.

- Children graph their favorite farm animal. Compare results.

- Use the black line master provided and cut several sets of six to eight field mice. Laminate the field mice. Staple tails of different lengths, using heavy yarn, on each field mouse. Children can order their set of mice by the length of their tails, from shortest to longest or longest to shortest.

Farm Collage.   Children make a farm collage by gluing pictures of farm-related objects/foods on paper. Craft feathers, corn kernels, hay, straw, and soft cotton puffs can also be added.

Sensory Table.   Place rice, split peas, dried beans, dried corn, seeds, feathers, soft cotton puffs, hay, straw, and other items in the sensory table. Discuss how the materials look, feel, and smell. Provide small plastic shovels, rakes, hoes, spoons, cups, and buckets for the children to use with the materials.

Feather Activities.   Name the feathered farm animals in the story and try these activities.

- Hold a feather in one hand and touch the body parts named by the teacher or student leader.
- Each child holds a feather above his or her head, arm extended, and drops it. The child follows the falling feather with eyes, finger, and body until it reaches the floor.
- Hold the feather up high, drop it, and try to catch it before it falls to the ground. Children can also try to catch a partner's falling feather.
- Place a feather on the floor and blow it across the room.
- Hold the feather up high, drop it, and try to keep it from reaching the ground by blowing it.

Cat and Field Mouse.   Children hold hands and form a circle. One student is chosen to be the "Cat," and he or she stands outside the circle. Another student is the "Field Mouse" and stands inside the circle. At the beginning of the game the cat and field mouse run anywhere—near the circle, inside, or outside of the circle until the "Cat" tags the "Field Mouse." After the "Field Mouse" is tagged, he or she picks someone new to become the "Cat." The old "Cat" then becomes the new "Field Mouse." The children in the circle help the "Field Mouse" by raising their arms whenever the "Field Mouse" wants to enter or leave the circle.

Butterfly.   Butterflies are shown in the story on the beautiful day the children were away and the animals played. Use the butterfly pattern provided, and cut or have children cut the shape out of construction paper. Children decorate their butterflies in various ways, such as using multicolored tissue squares, dyed and dried eggshell pieces, or multicolored foil or construction paper squares. This will create a mosaic effect. Children can spoon on various colors of tempera paint and blow the colors in interesting patterns on the butterfly. Children can also apply paint on one wing of the butterfly and then fold it over. When opened, the butterfly will have the same "blot" design or pattern on both butterfly wings.

Eggs, Eggs, Eggs.   Place multicolored plastic eggs in a basket. Children estimate how many eggs there are, while the teacher records their estimations on the board. Children count the actual amount and then compare it to their estimates. Colored eggs can also be sorted by color or patterned by color.

Hear the Rooster   (to the tune of "Are You Sleeping?")

> Hear the rooster.
> Hear the rooster.
> Up at dawn,
> Animals yawn.
> Horses, cows, and donkeys.
> Sheep, and goats and field mice,
> All wake up!
> All wake up!

Weather Vane.   The wind blows from all directions, and a weather vane shows which way the wind is blowing. Children can make a simple weather vane or pinwheel, take it outside, and see the direction of the wind.

- Children staple or tape strips of tissue or crepe paper to a tongue depressor.
- Provide children with an 8" × 8" or 10" × 10" square of construction paper, a straight pin, and a pencil with an eraser. Fold the paper in half diagonally; then fold it in half again. Children cut on the fold lines, stopping within about 1 inch of the center point. With assistance, children fold over the four alternating points and hold at the center point, then secure the points on the eraser tip using the straight pin.

Farm Balance Scales.   Supply farm-related items such as eggshells, corn kernels, dried beans, dried peas, feathers, cotton balls, and a hard-boiled egg. Children compare the weight of the hard-boiled egg to the other items. They can determine how much of each item weighs the same as the egg. Children should be encouraged to make comparisons using the words "lighter than" and "heavier than."

Moms and Babies.   Talk about the similarities and differences between mom and baby farm animals. Look at the illustrations in the story and name mom and baby. Extend the activity by having children match up mom and baby farm animals using commercial pictures or plastic pieces (dog-puppy, cat-kitten, goose-gosling, donkey-foal, goat-kid, cow-calf, horse-foal, chicken-chick, pig-piglet, and other mom and baby pairs).

Big Red Barn.   Inform children that farmers need to protect their animals from bad weather. Animals sleep in special houses such as barns, sheds, stables, and coops. Supply children with different-sized boxes and cartons. With assistance, small groups of children can cut doors and windows in their animal shelter. Children can work together to cover the buildings with tempera paint or construction paper. Supply plastic farm animals so that children can set up a farmyard with which to play. Some children may be able to make animal pens and fences using craft Popsicle™ sticks.

Field Trip.   If possible, take the class on a field trip to a farm or visit the farm-in-the-zoo in a nearby community. Upon returning, children can write or dictate a story about the trip and illustrate it.

Animal Classification.   Place plastic animals or pictures of farm animals on the table. Challenge children to sort and group the animals in as many different ways as they can think of—color, shape, size, where they live, what they eat, how they move, body covering, and number of feet.

Musical Farm Animals.   Tape pictures of farm animals on the floor in a large circle. Play lively music as children walk around the circle. When the music stops, each child should be standing on an animal. The children identify the animal and tell a fact about it.

Scarecrow.   Farmers place scarecrows near their gardens to keep birds away from the growing crops. Children color the scarecrow provided or follow the oral directions the teacher gives. For example,

> Color the hat brown.
> Color the pants blue.
> Color the pockets red.
> And so on.

Suggested Home Activities.   Send home a synopsis of the story *Big Red Barn*, and inform parents about some of the activities the children will be doing at school. Encourage parents to visit the library and select books about specific farm animals that interest their child. Children can share the interesting facts they have learned at school. A trip to the grocery store is an excellent place to talk about and learn the foods that come from the farm animals. Encourage children to taste different types of milk, meat, and cheese.

Related Literature

Brown, Margaret Wise. *Baby Animals.*
Gammell, Stephen. *Once Upon McDonald's Farm.*
Pizer, Abigail. *It's a Perfect Day.*
Tafuri, Nancy. *Early Morning in the Barn.*

Butterfly Pattern

Scarecrow Activity

More Picture Books to Enjoy

GARAGE SONG
by
Sarah Wilson

Developmental Activities Chart	Language & Cognitive Development	Fine Motor Art	Gross Motor	Perception	Social Skills	Math	Dramatic Play	Cooking Snack	Science	Music, Fingerplays, Poems
1 Mechanics	X									
2 Garage Trip	X			X						
3 Garage Smells				X		X				
4 Wheels	X					X				
5 Block Center					X		X			
6 Tools of the Trade	X	X								
7 Class Mechanics	X	X								
8 Mechanics' Song										X
9 Wheels 'n Oil	X	X			X	X		X		
10 Tire Fun			X							
11 Tracks		X				X				
12 Sort and Count		X		X		X				
13 Patterns		X		X		X				
14 Home Mechanics	X									
15 Tire Rubbings		X								
16 Garage Problem Solving	X									
17 License Plate Memory	X									
18 Body Wheels			X							
19 Dramatic Play					X		X			
20 Make a Vehicle		X								
21 Wheel Match				X						
22 Suggested Home Activities	X	X			X					
23										
24										
25										
26										
27										
28										
29										
30										

GARAGE SONG
by Sarah Wilson
Simon & Schuster, 1991

From early morning until exactly 10:00 at night, three friendly servicemen work in a small-town garage. In this rhythmic story, realistic pictures show a young boy enjoying the sights, sounds, and smells of this busy place. Wagons, cars, trucks, and even taxis come for gas, tune-ups, and new tires.

Mechanics. After hearing the story, have children brainstorm a list of all the things auto mechanics like Fred, Jim, and Mike do. For example, they put air in tires, fill cars with gas, fix wiper blades, give tune-ups, fix noisy brakes, replace hoses and wires, and so on. If possible, have a mechanic visit the class to talk about his work. Ask children to tell why the job of the mechanic is important.

Garage Trip. Arrange to take in all the sights, sounds, and smells of a local gas station/garage by taking a class field trip. Upon returning, talk about the activities occurring at the gas station/garage compared to their garage at home. Talk about how the two places are the same and how they are different.

Garage Smells. After returning from the field trip, talk about things the children may have smelled at the garage—oil, gasoline, antifreeze, grease, window wash solution, and brake fluid. Make simple yes/no graphs. Did you like the smell of _____, _____, _____? Compare results.

Wheels. Make a list of vehicles that go to a garage for services. Place vehicle names and/or their pictures into categories—vehicles with two wheels, vehicles with four wheels, and vehicles with more than four wheels. Talk about how the vehicles are the same and how they are different. Discuss how specific vehicles are used, such as taxis, police cars, campers, and ambulances.

Block Center. Invite children to create a garage like the one in the story. Different-sized blocks can be used to make the station and the ramps, hoists, and jacks needed for their cars and trucks. Straws can be taped on blocks to create gas pumps.

Tools of the Trade. Mechanics like Fred, Jim, and Mike use many different kinds of tools like wrenches, chisels, pliers, and screwdrivers when they are fixing cars and trucks. Show children a variety of real tools that a mechanic might use. Demonstrate how the tools are used and talk about their safe use. Provide opportunities for children to use screws and screwdrivers, nuts, bolts, and washers.

Sand the edges of a 1-foot 2 × 4. Partially screw in different-sized screws so that they are secure. Children use fine motor skills as they use flat head and Phillips™ screwdrivers to screw fasteners into the wood. Provide various nuts, bolts, and washers for children to put together.

Class Mechanics. Have children dictate a class story about being a car mechanic. They can sequence the events in repairing a car, list the tools they would use, tell what was wrong with the car, and decide upon the cost of the repairs. Children can illustrate their story.

Mechanics' Song (to the tune of "If I Had a Hammer")

> I am a mechanic,
> Repairing in the morning,
> Repairing in the evening,
> Inside my garage.
> I change flat tires.
> I give lots of tune-ups.
> I fix all leaks and squeaks
> Between the front and rear tires.
> A-l-l, all over this town!

Wheels 'n Oil. Help children prepare a lunch fit for a mechanic.

8 ounces racconto (wheel-shaped pasta)	2 tablespoons chopped parsley
1 cup cooked ham cut into small pieces	½ cup vegetable oil
1 cup cheddar cheese shredded or cut into small cubes	¼ cup wine vinegar
	½ teaspoon salt
1 small green pepper, chopped	¼ teaspoon pepper
1 carrot, peeled or scraped, cut into thin wheels	⅛ teaspoon garlic powder
	¼ teaspoon oregano leaves

Prepare wheel-shaped pasta according to package directions; drain. In a large bowl combine pasta and remaining ingredients; mix well. Chill before serving.

A special treat might include having children share cans of soda purchased from the school soda machine.

Tire Fun. Many schools use tires in their physical education programs. If tires are not available, arrange to get tire donations from a local garage or tire store. Place four to eight tires in a straight row one foot apart; have children:

- Walk across the tires—right foot on the back of the first tire, left foot inside of the first tire, right foot on the front of the first tire, left foot on the floor between the first and second tire. Children continue with the pattern.

- Repeat the walk, changing the lead foot.
- Walk across the tires—left foot outside of the tires and the right foot inside.
- Repeat the walk, changing feet.
- Jump from the back to the front of the tires.
- Crawl or creep across the tires.
- Jump across the tires—jump in the center of a tire, jump between tires, jump in the center of a tire, continuing to the end.

Tracks.   Provide small Match Box™–type cars, vans, and trucks. Children dip the wheels into a shallow pan of paint. They "drive" their vehicles on long pieces of kraft paper to make tracks. Compare whose tracks are the longest and whose tracks are the shortest.

Sort and Count.   Provide nuts, bolts, screws, and washers. Children can sort them, graph the pieces on a teacher-prepared grid, count the pieces, and compare the sets.

Patterns.   Provide nuts, bolts, screws, and washers. The teacher makes a pattern with the fasteners and children continue the pattern, for example, nut-nut-washer or washer-screw-nut-washer-screw-nut. The patterns can be simple or complex. Encourage children to create their own patterns.

Home Mechanics.   Have children brainstorm ways any of their family members have been mechanics at home, fixing items large or small. Have children complete the following sentences and think of others:

To fix the fence, mom needs _____.
To fix dinner, dad needs _____.
To fix the torn shirt, grandma needs _____.
To fix the toaster, grandpa needs _____.
To fix the car, my big brother needs _____.
To fix my torn paper, I need _____.

Tire Rubbings.   Touch the treads of a tire and talk about their purpose. Encourage children to compare them to the treads they have on their gym shoes. Children place newsprint on the tire treads and press down firmly as they color with the side of their crayons. Each time they move the paper to a new location, children change the crayon color to get an interesting picture.

Garage Problem Solving.   Children use thinking skills to associate objects and tell how two things are alike. Picture cues can be used.

How are a truck and a car alike?
How are bolts and screws alike?
How are the air hose and gas pump alike?

How are bikes and motorcycles alike?

How are tires and steering wheels alike?

How are hammers and screwdrivers alike?

How are vans and station wagons the same?

How are leaky tires and an air hose the same?

How are wiper blades and washer fluid alike?

License Plate Memory.   When customers bring in a vehicle to be repaired, they give their license plate number to the mechanic to help him identify the vehicle needing repair. Make tagboard cards that are the size of a license plate. Print a set of numbers and letters on each plate and laminate them. The teacher reads the license plates, and the children repeat the number-letter sequences.

Body Wheels.   Children move different body parts to make the circular motion of wheels—arms, hands, legs, feet, and head. Challenge them to move their whole body like a wheel—provide mats for rolling and turning somersaults.

Dramatic Play.   Set up an outside dramatic play area for the garage/gas station theme. Props can include bikes, trikes, wagons, scooters, tools, a cash register, play money, squirt bottles, water, and rags for cleaning the vehicles. Children take turns being customers and mechanics. Customers should test drive their vehicle to make sure repairs have been completed before paying for the work. Mechanics can check the tires, fill vehicles with gas, check the oil, give tune-ups, change flat tires, and clean windshields.

Make a Vehicle.   Provide toilet paper and paper towel tubes, empty spools, plastic milk jug lids, small boxes, aluminum foil, tongue depressors, sticks, glue, and tape. Children can create make-believe or real-looking vehicles.

Wheel Match.   Children match wheels that are the same on the black line master provided.

Suggested Home Activities.   Send home a synopsis of the story *Garage Song,* and inform parents of some of the activities the children will be doing at school. At home, parents and children can wash the car together, clean the windows inside and out, and look under the hood and in the trunk. This is a good time to talk about the importance of wearing seat belts. If possible, let children watch as you change a tire. Children can use a hand pump to add air to the tires.

Related Literature

Miller, Margaret. *Who Uses This?*

Find the wheels that are the same and draw a line to
connect them.

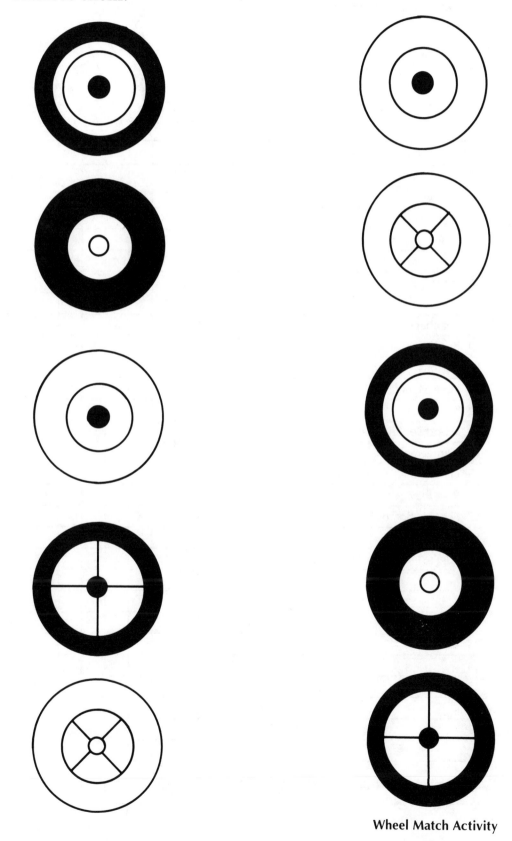

THE OLD RED ROCKING CHAIR

by
Phyllis Root

Developmental Activities Chart	Language & Cognitive Development	Fine Motor Art	Gross Motor	Perception	Social Skills	Math	Dramatic Play	Cooking Snack	Science	Music, Fingerplays, Poems
1 Story Sequencing	X									
2 Making Books	X	X								
3 Captivating Cartons	X	X			X		X			
4 Beautiful Junk		X							X	
5 Woodworking	X	X		X	X	X			X	
6 Tools	X			X						
7 Geoboards		X		X		X				
8 Beanbags		X		X						
9 Beanbag Games	X		X		X	X				
10 Buttons						X				
11 How Many?	X					X				
12 Seasons	X					X			X	
13 Woodworking Math	X	X				X				
14 Garage Sale	X			X	X	X	X			
15 Garage Sale Memory Game	X			X	X					
16 Role Play	X				X		X			
17 Scooter Boards			X		X					
18 Teeter-Totter			X			X			X	X
19 Suggested Home Activities	X						X			
20										
21										
22										
23										
24										
25										
26										
27										
28										
29										
30										

THE OLD RED ROCKING CHAIR
by Phyllis Root
Arcade, 1992

This delightful cumulative tale begins when Martha Jenkins decides to throw her old red rocking chair out with the garbage. The rocking chair is first salvaged by Sam Puckett and his dog Fergie. After changing owners and form many times throughout the story, the chair eventually returns to its original owner.

Story Sequencing. Read the story to the children on a few different occasions until they are familiar with it. Cut a simple rocking chair form out of red construction paper, or use the pattern provided. Have the children retell the story in sequence, using the rocking chair as a visual cue. Alter the rocking chair in sequence: first remove the arms, next the back, and last the rocker. This activity can also be done by using red felt rocking chair pieces on the flannel board.

Making Books. Using the reproducible picture sequence, children can color and cut the pictures. Have them glue the pictures onto paper and staple the paper into book form in proper sequence. The children can dictate words to go with each picture; they will enjoy having a book to take home to share with their family and friends.

Captivating Cartons. The Old Red Rocking Chair stimulates creative thinking by suggesting the many different uses for a single object. Bring in one or more large cartons and have the children brainstorm what the carton could become. Work together as a class to translate their ideas into structures. Examples might include a house, truck, airplane, train, school, and so on. The children will enjoy playing with the carton for days. While they play with the creation, observe the many different ways each child uses it, record the observations, and talk about them at the end of the unit.

Beautiful Junk. Ask parents to donate old items with many parts. Old radios, record players, telephones, and anything else held together by screws work well. Supply the children with assorted screwdrivers, pliers, and other tools, and let them experiment with the items.

Woodworking. Aside from being a favorite activity for many children, woodworking helps to build many skills and concepts. Before children use the woodworking materials, be sure to brainstorm and post picture safety rules for the children to follow. Children should be required to wear safety goggles when working with wood. Include hammers and nails, an assortment of screws and screwdrivers, a hand drill, pliers, wrenches, wood, sandpaper, a small saw, wood, and glue. A small tree stump is a wonderful item in which children can pound nails. It is suggested that the woodworking center be supervised by an adult. If teacher or assistant time isn't available, enlist parent volunteers.

Tools.   Sam Puckett was forced to throw away the old red rocking chair because he didn't know the difference between a hammer and a hammerhead shark. Sharifa Shannon, on the other hand, was handy with pliers and a wrench, so she was able to repair the chair. The children will enjoy identifying the tools they work with. On a large sheet of tagboard, trace around tools, screws, and nails. Include various sizes of pliers, hammers, nails, screwdrivers, and so on. The children can match the actual tools to the outlines. The number of items can be adjusted for younger children and children with delays in visual perception.

Geoboards.   The children can create their own geoboards. Supply them with a piece of wood that is approximately 8" × 8". Have them pound four rows of nails with four nails in each row. The children can make up designs and patterns with colored rubber bands. An alternate method for making geoboards is to push golf tees into squares of Styrofoam™.

Beanbags.   Although Sharifa was a whiz with tools, she was unable to keep the chair because she couldn't sew. Agnes MacGruder was able to salvage the chair and sew a new cushion from an old discarded coat. The children can sew beanbags just as Agnes sewed a new cushion. Cut an old shirt or pair of pants into squares. Use a glue gun or fabric glue to make a bag. Fill the bag with dried beans and glue the fourth side together. Give children large needles and yarn to sew around the beanbags.

Beanbag Games.   The children can use their beanbags to play a variety of games.

- Have them place the beanbags on different body parts, following auditory directions and visual cues.
- Have them place the beanbags on their head and walk around the room, not letting the beanbag fall.
- Make a beanbag toss using numbers, letters, shapes, or colors. Use only numbers or only colors at one time. Direct the children to toss the bag on the color red, the number two, and any other selections.
- Have the children create their own games using boxes and beanbags.

Buttons.   Remove buttons from old clothes or ask parents to send old, unmatched buttons to school. Children can sort the buttons according to different attributes including size, color, and shape. Children can count the buttons and make them into sets for their friends to count.

How Many?   Before rereading the story to the children, have them estimate how many things the chair might be. Ask the children to try and keep track of how many different things the chair was during the course of the story. They can use the information to check their estimations.

Seasons. While reading the story, ask the children to estimate how much time passed from when Martha Jenkins threw away the chair until she found it again. Help them attend to the seasons through the text and the illustrations. Illustrate to the children through simple pictures that summer, autumn, winter, and spring always occur in the same order and that the passing of the seasons marks the passing of time. A simple way to illustrate this is to divide a paper plate into four sections. On each section draw a picture illustrating each season (swimming, orange leaf, snowman, umbrella). Attach a pointer with a brad fastener to the center of the plate. When the pointer goes all around the plate, a year has passed.

Woodworking Math. Many math skills can be reinforced at the woodworking center. Children can count tools, screws, nails, and other items. They can measure the wood and other objects using screws and nails as units of measurement. They might also enjoy measuring, using a ruler and a yardstick as a unit of measurement. The children can sort nails, screws, and nuts according to size. The teacher can label containers with numerals or pictorial sets, and the children can put the appropriate number of screws, nuts, or nails in the container. Tools can be arranged according to length—shortest to longest or longest to shortest. The weight of tools can be compared on a balance scale—What is heavier/lighter, the hammer or the pliers? The weight of nails, nuts, and screws can also be compared using a balance scale. How many nuts weigh the same as one screw? The math possibilities are endless; children will enjoy experimenting with and manipulating the objects in their own way.

Garage Sale. Discuss with the children that many people conduct garage sales when they no longer need or use clothes and household items. Set up a garage sale in the dramatic play area of the room. Children can categorize the items according to function—clothes, kitchen items, tools, and so on. Help them make price tags for the items and supply them with play money and bags. The children can take turns being the shoppers and the vendors. Use a play cash register for sorting and keeping track of the money.

Garage Sale Memory Game. Put three to five "garage sale" items in a shopping bag. The number of items will depend on the age and developmental level of the children. Take the items out of the bag and show them to the children. While the children cover their eyes, put all but one item back in the bag. Place the item out of sight. When the children open their eyes, empty the bag and have them try to guess what's missing. Have the children take turns filling the bag and removing an item.

Role Play. The children may wish to act out the story. The roles are quite simple to play. The children can take turns role playing the different characters. Consider using these props—a rocking chair, a garbage can, a dog and a leash, a broken radio, a cat and milk bowl, scooter boards, a rake, an old coat, and a foot stool. Classroom objects can "stand in" for the props.

If the classroom doesn't have a rocking chair, try to borrow one while this book is being used. The children will enjoy rocking in it and sitting around it while the teacher reads.

Scooter Boards. The Weller twins carried the red rocking chair home on their skateboards. Point out to the children the similarities and differences between skateboards and scooter boards. Divide the children into pairs, each child sits on a separate scooter board. Challenge them to sit on the scooter board and hold onto an item together (hula hoop, yardstick, stuffed animal, etc.) while moving their scooter boards toward a goal. Expand the activity by setting up an obstacle course for the pairs of children to move around while carrying the "rocking chair" home.

Teeter-Totter. Let the children play on a teeter-totter if your school has access to one. The children will enjoy experimenting with their weight and the way in which the teeter-totter moves. Pair children differently so they can see how the activity changes depending on the size and weight of the partners. The children can make up simple rhymes while teeter-tottering. One example is: "Teeter-totter, I don't care, this teeter totter used to be a rocking chair." An old favorite is "Teeter-totter, bread and water."

Suggested Home Activities. Send home a synopsis of *The Old Red Rocking Chair*, and inform parents of some of the activities in which the children are involved. Parents and children can do the following activities together:

- *Box Inventions.* Parents and children can put their heads together and use their imaginations. Ask the parents to help their child find an old box (any size will do). They can turn the box into anything they want to. This activity doesn't have to be elaborate, they can simply pretend the box is something else. Ask the parents to have their child dictate a sentence or two telling about the box. Boxes can be shared at school.

- *Something Old, Something New.* Ask the parents to help their child look around the house to find something that is old or unused. Together think up a new use for the item. Have the children dictate a sentence or two about the item and its new use. The items can be shared at school.

- *Discarded Treasures.* If it happens to be garage sale season, encourage the parents to visit a garage sale with their child. Children will see that just because items are no longer of use to one person or family, they can still be treasures for someone else. The children will enjoy purchasing an item with their own money.

Related Literature (Other Cumulative Tales)

Butler, Dorothy. *My Brown Bear Barney.*
Galdone, Paul. *Cat Goes Fiddle-di-fee.*
Parkinson, Kathy. *The Enormous Turnip.*
Van Laan, Nancy. *Possum Come A'Knockin.*
Willard, Nancy. *Simple Pictures Are Best.*
Wood, Audrey. *The Napping House.*

Story Sequencing Activity

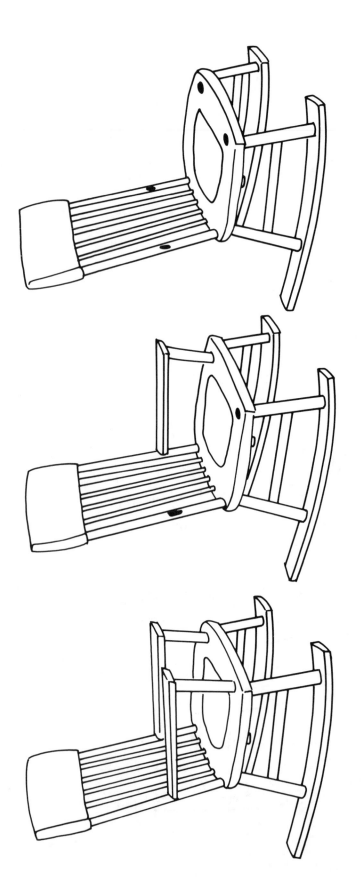

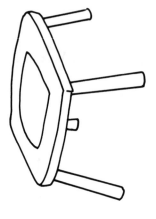

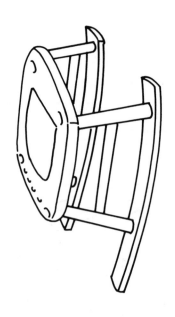

MONKEY SOUP
by
Louis Sachar

Developmental Activities Chart	Language & Cognitive Development	Fine Motor Art	Gross Motor	Perception	Social Skills	Math	Dramatic Play	Cooking Snack	Science	Music, Fingerplays, Poems
1 Sick in Bed										X
2 Eating Right	X	X						X		
3 Monkey Soup	X	X			X					
4 Blow Your Nose										X
5 Staying Healthy	X	X			X				X	
6 Bad Germs	X								X	
7 Dramatic Play	X				X		X		X	
8 Wash and Scrub		X					X			
9 Exercise to Grow			X							
10 Healthy Faces		X		X						
11 New Ways to Paint		X								
12 Bubble Prints		X								
13 Bubble Recipe		X						X		
14 Band-Aid™ Math			X			X				
15 Band-Aid™ Patterns			X			X				
16 Healthy Snack								X		
17 Orange Juice Smoothie		X						X		
18 Say "Aaah" Math					X	X				
19 Get Well		X			X					
20 Smell and Tell	X			. X					X	
21 Aaaaachoo Picture		X								
22 Feeling Better	X									
23 Balloon Fun	X	X	X		X				X	
24 Suggested Home Activities	X							X	X	
25										
26										
27										
28										
29										
30										

MONKEY SOUP
by Louis Sachar
Alfred A. Knopf, 1992

With the help of her toy monkey, a little girl thoughtfully prepares some soup for her daddy who is sick in bed. The soup is full of Band-Aids™, bubbles, buttons, crayons, and other ingredients that are bound to help daddy feel better because all the things included make her feel good!

Sick in Bed (to the tune of "Home on the Range")

Sick, sick in his bed
With red eyes and a cold in his head.
I'll make monkey soup,
So dad won't get the croup.
Soup will make him feel all better soon!

Eating Right.   Chicken soup and monkey soup help someone who is sick feel better. But to stay healthy, it is important to eat the right foods. Talk about the major food groups—milk and cheese group, meat and protein group, fruit and vegetable group, bread and cereal group. Provide grocery ads and magazines. Children cut pictures and make food group collages that can be displayed in the classroom.

Monkey Soup.   Divide children into small groups. Give each group a large piece of kraft paper cut into the shape of a cooking pot. Children brainstorm a list of things that would help someone who is sick feel better and fill their "cooking pot" with ingredients they find in catalogs, magazines, and advertisements. The children can dictate their recipe for monkey soup on the back of their pot. Some groups may want to include reasons for selecting the special "ingredients." The groups can all take turns sharing their recipes. The pictures and recipes can be stapled or sewn together with yarn to make a class book. The book can be sent home to sick family members or classmates throughout the year.

Blow Your Nose (to the tune of "Row, Row, Row Your Boat")

Blow, blow, blow your nose
Gently when it's red.
Throw away, throw away, throw away, throw away
Kleenex™ and bad germs.

Staying Healthy.   Daddy was sick in bed with a cold. Have children share experiences about times they have been sick. Brainstorm a list of things children *should* do to keep themselves healthy. Some examples include:

- Take a nap and get enough sleep at night
- Play to get fresh air and exercise
- Eat good food
- Keep yourself clean: wash hands before eating and after using the bathroom, and brushing your teeth
- Use tissue when you sneeze
- Cover your mouth when you cough

Children can draw pictures to illustrate their ideas. Pictures can be displayed in the classroom or made into a class book to keep in the science center.

Bad Germs. Germs cause people to become sick. Daddy used a tissue when he sneezed so that his germs wouldn't spread. Demonstrate how germs can spread if we don't cover our mouths and noses when we cough and sneeze. Fill a balloon with confetti or the paper circles from a hole punch. Carefully blow up the balloon and tie the end. Hold the balloon and pop it with a pin. Watch the germs spread!

Dramatic Play. Encourage children to share their experiences about seeing the doctor/nurse when they were sick or when they went for a checkup. Talk about what they saw and the equipment the doctor/nurse used. Set up a doctor's office, infirmary, or sick room in the dramatic play area. Students can take turns being doctors, nurses, moms, dads, and others caring for sick patients and dolls. Props to provide could include white or blue shirts for the doctors and nurses to wear, a purse to use as a medical bag, cotton balls, cotton swabs, Band-Aids™, gauze, small empty medicine bottles and containers, eyedroppers, scale, tape measure, tongue depressors, Ace™ bandages, plastic gloves, pencil and pad of paper for writing prescriptions, blanket, pillow, and any other items the children suggest.

Wash and Scrub. Fill the sensory table with warm water. Provide small bars of soap, a container of soft soap, nail brushes, cloths, sponges, and plenty of dry towels. Children can wash the dolls from the play area or practice washing their own hands.

Exercise to Grow. Children need play and exercise to help them develop strong bones and muscles. Teach children some simple warm-up and cool-down body stretches. Encourage them to stretch before and after running, jumping, hopping, skipping, galloping, and other strenuous activities.

- Stand next to a wall for support. Pick up your right foot with your right hand and gently pull your foot up behind you and feel the stretch. Hold; then repeat with the other side.
- Stand up straight, bend over slowly and reach to the floor, without making bouncing movements. Repeat several times.
- Stand up straight balancing on tip toes. Raise arms and hands overhead to reach and stretch to the sky. Repeat several times.

Healthy Faces.   When daddy was sick, his face was pale and needed more color. Provide sheets of manila paper and a supply of brightly colored crayons or paints so that children can draw a picture of people with healthy faces.

New Ways to Paint.   Children paint a mural using tissue and napkins instead of brushes. Put each color of paint in a shallow container (pie plates work well). Show children how to squeeze together and wad up napkins or several pieces of tissue. Children gently dip the paper into the paint and print on the mural paper. Use a new wad for each color used.

Bubble Prints.   Bubbles made the little girl laugh, so she poured them into her soup for dad. Children will enjoy making bubble pictures. Make a solution of liquid dishwashing soap, water, and food coloring in small margarine containers. Prepare several colors, varying the amount of food coloring to get different shades. Have a supply of straws available, and let children practice blowing bubbles in plain water before they begin. Each child blows in the solution until big bubbles form and rise over the top. He or she then carefully places a piece of white paper on top of the bubble container. The colored bubbles form a delicate picture.

Bubble Recipe.   Make this recipe and blow big bubbles like the dad in the story did. Give each child a set of plastic rings from a six-pack of canned soda to use as a wand. Pour bubble solution into a 9" × 13" cake pan or cookie sheet. To avoid foaming, do not stir wands in the suds.

    2   cups Joy™ dishwashing detergent
    6   cups water
    ¾   cup Karo™ light corn syrup

Combine, shake, and let the bubble mixture settle for a few hours. Caution: The bubble solution causes a slippery surface when it's on the ground.

Band-Aid™ Math.   Provide a variety of different sized Band-Aids™, including circles, squares, and rectangles. Children can sort the Band-Aids™ by size and shape. Then graph, count, and compare the various Band-Aids™.

Band-Aid™ Patterns.   Using a variety of different sized and shaped Band-Aids™, children can create interesting patterns, such as large circle, small rectangle, large circle, small rectangle, or large rectangle, small square, small rectangle, large rectangle, small square, small rectangle.

Healthy Snacks.   Children can help prepare some healthy snacks:

- peanut butter on apple slices
- celery stuffed with peanut butter
- fresh fruit kabobs
- frozen grapes and banana slices
- popcorn
- banana chunks rolled in nuts or coconut
- cut-up veggies
- yogurt mixed with raisins
- cheese chunks
- frozen fruit juice on sticks
- cheese and crackers

Orange Juice Smoothie. Chicken soup and orange juice are the all-time remedies for treating a cold. Children can whip up this delicious orange juice drink for snack time, even if they don't have a cold!

    12 ounces frozen orange juice
     2 cups plain or vanilla yogurt
     2 tablespoons sugar

Mix the ingredients together in a gallon container. Dilute with water to get ½ gallon. Stir thoroughly with a spoon or with a hand blender.

Say "Aaah" Math. Use a permanent marker to write a numeral from 1 to 10 on a set of ten tongue depressors. Place the tongue depressors in a doctor's bag or black purse. Children play the game by taking a tongue depressor out of the bag and making a set to correspond to the number they chose. The children can make sets using cotton balls, Band-Aids™, or cotton swabs.

Get Well. Provide paper, markers, crayons, magazine pictures, and various collage materials for children to use to make get-well cards for family members or friends.

Smell and Tell. Daddy had a cold and could "blow his nose louder than anyone in the world." Talk about how we use our nose. Point out that when people have colds, they temporarily lose their ability to smell. Daddy was probably unable to smell mom's chicken soup. Fill baby food jars or film containers with a variety of substances—cloves, onions, cinnamon, perfume, garlic, peanut butter, coffee, vinegar, lemon juice, and mustard. Place the containers on the science table. Children can smell what's inside the containers and try to identify each substance. A yes/no graph can be made to indicate what smells they liked or didn't like.

Aaaaachoo Picture. Give each child a small paper plate. Using crayons, markers, or paper scraps, children make a face on their plate. Strips of paper or yarn can be glued on for hair. Children cut and glue a strip of paper on the back of the plate to represent arms and hands. They fold the arms forward so that the hands are near the mouth and nose. Glue a piece of tissue on the hands. Display the pictures in the classroom to remind children to use good health habits.

Feeling Better. In the story, the little girl tried hard to help daddy feel better by thinking about and doing things that she liked. Have children complete the sentences.

    Things that make me feel better are _____.
    Things that make me happy are _____.
    Things that keep me warm are _____.
    Things that make soup delicious are _____.
    Things that make me laugh are _____.

Balloon Fun. The little girl knew balloons would help daddy feel better.

- Children can sequence the events of the teacher blowing up a balloon—tell what happens first, next, and last.
- Compare the size, shape, and color of different balloons. Bring in a helium-filled balloon and have children compare it with a regular air-filled balloon. Discuss how the balloons are the same and how they are different.
- Small groups of children can gently tap a balloon around their circle to keep it off the floor.
- Children use crayons or markers to color the balloons on the black line master.

Suggested Home Activities. Send home a synopsis of the story *Monkey Soup,* and inform parents of some of the activities children are doing at school. Send home the list of ideas children developed about ways to stay healthy and encourage parents to reinforce the concepts children are learning about. Remind parents to spend time with their child talking about hygiene and demonstrating the correct way to wash, brush teeth, blow their nose, and so forth. Children will enjoy going to the store to shop for a new toothbrush, tube of toothpaste, bar of soap, sponge, and box of tissue. A fun activity would be making homemade toothpaste:

Mix together 1 tablespoon baking soda, ½ teaspoon salt, and ¾ teaspoon water. Add a few drops of strawberry, orange, lemon, or mint-flavored extract.

Encourage parents to schedule regular doctor and dentist visits for their child to ensure good health.

Related Literature

Cherry, Lynne. *Who's Sick Today?*
Gretz, Susanna. *Teddy Bears Cure a Cold.*

Color the balloons to make yourself feel good!

Balloon Fun Activity

LITTLE NINO'S PIZZARIA
by
Karen Barbour

Developmental Activities Chart	Language & Cognitive Development	Fine Motor Art	Gross Motor	Perception	Social Skills	Math	Dramatic Play	Cooking Snack	Science	Music, Fingerplays, Poems
1 Pizza Sequence	X	X								
2 Class Pizzaria	X	X			X		X			
3 Chef Hats		X					X			
4 Play Dough Pizza	X	X			X		X	X	X	
5 Class Collection					X	X				
6 What Size?	X			X	X	X				
7 Name Your Favorite	X					X				
8 Pizza Math						X				
9 Pizza Puzzles		X		X	X	X				
10 Invented Recipes	X	X								
11 Pizza Walk			X							
12 Pizza Collage		X								
13 Pizza Matching		X		X	X					
14 Little and Big	X									
15 Pizza Patterns		X				X				
16 Helpers	X				X					
17 Cashier						X	X			
18 Pizza Song										X
19 Pizza Recipe	X	X			X			X	X	
20 Suggested Home Activities	X	X		X		X		X		
21										
22										
23										
24										
25										
26										
27										
28										
29										
30										

LITTLE NINO'S PIZZARIA
by Karen Barbour
Harcourt Brace Jovanovich, 1987

Tony enjoys helping his father, Nino, at their small family-owned and -operated pizzaria. He helps with cooking, setting tables, waiting on customers, cleaning up, and distributing leftovers to the homeless people. One day Nino decides to close the small pizzaria and open a large fancy restaurant. Although Tony tries to help, he is only in the way. The story ends on a happy note when Nino reopens the small pizzaria and names it "Little Tony's Pizzaria."

Pizza Sequence. After reading the story and looking at the pictures, ask the children to recall the steps in making a pizza. Use the pictures in the book as cues. (1.) Knead the dough. (2.) Stir the sauce. (3.) Roll the dough. (4.) Put on the sauce. (5.) Put on the toppings. (6.) Bake the pizza. Assemble a construction paper pizza following the sequence. Use different colors and layers to represent the layers and ingredients on a real pizza.

Class Pizzaria. Set up a pizzaria in the dramatic play area of the classroom. Start with a class meeting. Children can suggest and vote on a name for the pizzaria. They can make menus by folding colored paper and "writing" on them. Provide a tablecloth, dishes, silverware, a serving tray, small notebooks for writing orders, pencils, aprons, money, and a cash register.

Chef Hats. The children can make chef hats to wear in their pizzaria. Ask a local bakery to donate white, medium-sized bags or trim off half a large grocery bag and paint the bottom of the bag and the remaining sides white. Cut a 2-inch-wide band out of tagboard or heavy paper to go around each child's head, leaving enough extra to staple the head band. Help the children staple the bag onto the band; the bag will be wider than the band so you will need to make some tucks in the bag when stapling.

Play Dough Pizza. Children can make pizza from play dough with this simple no-cook recipe. Divide the flour and salt mixture into different bowls, and add food coloring to the oil and water to make appropriate colors for the crust, sauce, sausage, pepperoni, cheese, and other items to go on the pizza. Provide a dull knife, a pizza cutter, a garlic press, a grater, and a rolling pin for the chefs.

2 cups flour	2 tablespoons oil
½ cup salt	food coloring
½ cup water	

Mix flour and salt in a bowl. Slowly add water, food coloring, and oil. Knead for 10 minutes. Store in the refrigerator in an airtight container.

Class Collection.   One job that Tony enjoyed was sharing left-over pizza with homeless people. Talk with the class about collecting food or clothing to donate to a local charity. Set a class collection goal (perhaps one item per child). The children can keep a record with tally marks.

What Size?   Cut and color a few small, medium, and large cardboard circles to represent different-sized pizzas. The children can sequence the circles from large to small and small to large. They can categorize them by putting all the same-size circles together. They can use the pizzas to fill an order: "I'd like to order two small pizzas or one large and one medium pizza."

Name Your Favorite.   Make a graph on a large sheet of butcher or craft paper. Draw pictures of different kinds of pizza along the top. Include cheese, cheese and sausage, cheese and pepperoni, anchovy, mushroom, and other combinations that the children volunteer. List the children's names or pictorial representations of the children down the left-hand side of the paper. Take a vote on favorite kinds of pizza. Record each child's response under his or her name. Talk about the class favorite and the least favorite, which type of pizza received the most and least votes, which had zero votes, which had an equal number of votes, and so forth.

Pizza Math.   Provide five to ten circles representing plain cheese pizzas, and label each one with a numeral. Put simple cutouts representing pizza toppings in a bowl (simple colored shapes work well). Ask the children to look at the numeral on each pizza and top it with the appropriate number of toppings. The children can sequence the pizzas from 1 to 10.

Pizza Puzzles.   Give the children tagboard pizza shapes to color. Have them cut their pizzas into five to ten pieces, depending on their age and developmental level. They can reassemble the pieces to make a pizza. The children will enjoy challenging their friends by assembling each other's pizza puzzles.

Invented Recipes.   Make a class pizza recipe book. Each child can dictate his or her favorite pizza recipe, including ingredients and preparation directions. Each recipe should be illustrated. Laminate the pages and assemble them into book form.

Pizza Walk.   Prepare a large circle pizza shape from kraft paper. Divide it into sections. On each section write a direction describing a way for children to move around the pizza. Suggestions include walk, hop, jump on two feet, run, crawl, skip, gallop, and roll. Assist each child to write his or her name on a card and place the cards in a hat or small box. Play music as the children move around the circle. When the music stops, draw a name and help the child "read" the direction he or she is standing on, to determine the next way the children will move around the pizza.

Pizza Collage.   Children can make pizza collages with paper plates. Use a crayon or marker to divide a paper plate into triangular sections, as you would a pizza. Provide a variety of collage materials such as cut-up paper, buttons, yarn, foil, and fabric. The children can glue different materials in each section of the pizza.

Pizza Matching. Copy the black line master provided. The children can find the matching pizzas. After identifying the pairs, they can cut them out. They can use the pieces to play "Concentration" by placing them face down and turning them up two at a time. If the pizzas match, the child gets to keep them; if not, they are turned face down and play continues.

Little and Big. Little Nino's was closed down when Big Nino's was opened. Big Nino's was quite different from Little Nino's. Discuss the concept of big and little, and compare Little Nino's with Big Nino's. Find classroom objects that are big and little and categorize them accordingly. Talk about other things that are big and little—houses, cars, mountains, lakes, people, animals, and so forth. Find pictures of big and little items in magazines and catalogs—cut them out, mount them on paper and classify them by size.

Pizza Patterns. Copy the pizza black line master for each child to color. Colors can be alternated to form patterns. The children can cut their pizzas and mount them on a paper plate.

Helpers. Little Tony was a big help to his father at the restaurant. Even though most children don't help in the family business, they do help the family at home. Talk with the children about what they do at home to help their parents. Remind them that listening and following directions help parents, the same as picking up toys, putting clothes in the hamper, and helping to set the table. Make a list of the many ways the children help at home.

Cashier. The cashier is an important job in any restaurant. The children can take turns acting as cashier. Use a play cash register or a box that has been separated into compartments. Place play bills and coins of various denominations in the different sections. The "customer" can pay the cashier, who then places the different denominations of money in the appropriate section.

Pizza Song (to the tune of "The Bear Went Over the Mountain"). Children will enjoy making up verses for this song. Have the children pantomime the actions.

> We'll knead the dough for the pizza.
> We'll knead the dough for the pizza.
> We'll knead the dough for the pizza.
> And it will taste so good.

Additional verses:

> We'll stir the sauce . . .
> We'll spread the sauce . . .
> We'll grate the cheese . . .
> We'll put the cheese on the pizza . . .
> We'll cut the pizza in pieces . . .

And when our pizza's gone.
And when our pizza's gone.
We'll clean up all of our dishes.
We'll clean up all of our dishes.
We'll clean up all of our dishes.
And we will fall asleep.

Pizza Recipe.   With close supervision, allow the children to grate the cheese and cut and chop the toppings in addition to preparing the dough.

Mix 2 cups Bisquick™ and ½ cup cold water until a soft dough forms. Roll or pat the dough into a 12-inch circle on an ungreased cookie sheet. Pinch the edge to form a rim. Spoon on canned pizza sauce and grated mozzarella cheese. Choose among the following toppings—cooked sausage or sliced pepperoni, chopped mushrooms and onions, circles of green pepper, slices of tomato, and other favorites.

Suggested Home Activities.   Send home a synopsis of the story *Little Nino's Pizzaria.* Inform the parents about some of the activities their children are doing at school. Emphasize that cooking with children strengthens skills in fine motor and language development, perception, and math. It helps to build self-esteem, and it provides an opportunity for an enriching parent and child interaction. Make a copy of the picture recipe for English Muffin pizzas for each family to try at home.

Related Literature

Merriam, Eve. *Daddies at Work.*
———. *Mommies at Work.*

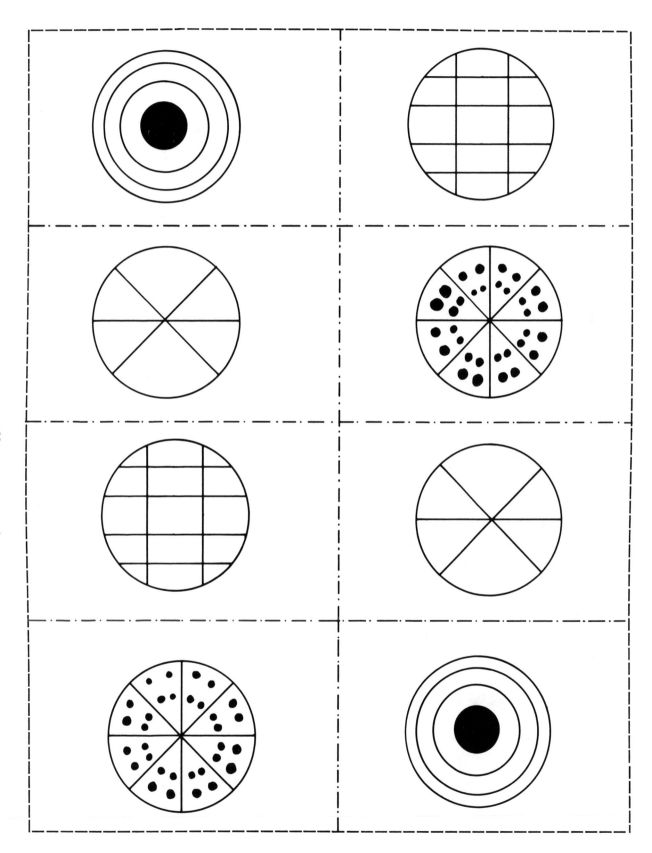

Pizza Matching Activity

Pizza Patterns Activity

English Muffin Pizzas

Ingredients:

½ English muffin

2 tablespoons pizza sauce

3 heaping tablespoons cheese

Spread sauce on English muffin. Top with cheese. Bake until cheese melts. Favorite toppings can be added under the cheese.

Suggested Home Activity

HAPPY BIRTHDAY, SAM
by
Pat Hutchins

Developmental Activities Chart	Language & Cognitive Development	Fine Motor Art	Gross Motor	Perception	Social Skills	Math	Dramatic Play	Cooking Snack	Science	Music, Fingerplays, Poems
1 The Birthday Circle	X				X	X			X	
2 Sam's Party	X				X		X			
3 Calendar	X					X				
4 Paper Chains		X			X	X				
5 Party Bags		X				X				
6 Trail Mix								X		
7 Party Hats		X								
8 Tablecloth		X								
9 Birthday Cake								X		
10 Piñata		X	X		X				X	
11 Guess the Gift	X	X								
12 Pin the Nose on the Clown			X	X						
13 Ball Toss			X			X				
14 Ring the Candle			X							
15 Cake Walk			X			X				
16 Card Search						X				
17 Stilts			X						X	
18 Cake Math		X				X				
19 Growth Charts	X	X				X				
20 Measure Me	X					X				
21 Clap and Tap	X			X	X	X				X
22 Birthday Wishes	X	X								
23 Suggested Home Activities	X					X				
24										
25										
26										
27										
28										
29										
30										

HAPPY BIRTHDAY, SAM
by Pat Hutchins
Greenwillow Books, 1978

It was Sam's birthday and he was a year older. Upon getting out of bed he went to turn on the light but discovered he still couldn't reach the light switch. He also found that he still couldn't reach his clothes or the bathroom faucet. When the postman came to the door with a birthday gift from grandpa, Sam discovered a new source of independence. This delightful birthday story puts familiar feelings into words and pictures. Even though children turn a whole year older, new abilities don't develop overnight.

The Birthday Circle.   It is very difficult for young children to comprehend the meaning of "another year older." One way for children to visualize a year is by paging through a calendar, month by month, discussing the seasons and the special days occurring each month. Another way to help children visualize the passing of a year is to sit in a circle. Pass a ball or globe around the circle. On the first complete trip, show a picture of the birthday child at 1 year old. On the second complete circle, show a picture of the birthday child at age 2, and so on until reaching the child's present age. Explain to the children that the earth revolves around the sun. When it has made a complete circle, a year has passed.

Sam's Party.   It is impractical to have a full-scale birthday party for every child in the class. Since birthdays are fun to celebrate, try having a class birthday party. Choose an otherwise quiet time of the year, perhaps around President's Day. If the party is planned at that time, discuss the meaning of the day. The book *Happy Birthday, Sam* can be used to set the stage. The children can help plan the party decorations, snack, and games.

Calendar.   The first step in planning any party is setting the date.

- Look at the calendar with the children and set a date.
- Say the days of the week and discuss which are school days.
- Count how many days are in the week and month and how many weeks are in a month.
- Count how many more days there are until the party. Mark the party day with a cutout of a birthday cake.
- Each day cover the number with a cutout of a party hat and count how many more hats will be needed before reaching the cake.
- Each day reinforce the concept of yesterday, today, and tomorrow.
- Label each child's birthday with a special cutout shape. Count how many months, weeks, or days until each child's special day.

Paper Chains.   The room can be decorated with paper chains made by the children. Each child can make his or her own chain or one large chain can be made as a cooperative effort by the class. Cut 2" × 8" colored strips of paper. The strips of paper are linked together. Color concepts are reinforced when children identify the colors they are using. Math skills are strengthened when children pattern colors, estimate, and measure classroom objects with chain links and lengths. The concept of long and short can be reinforced as the children make the chains. Simple addition concepts can be reinforced as children add links to the chain.

Party Bags.   The children can decorate party bags and brainstorm ideas for filling the bags. Provide plain or colored lunch bags. The bags can be decorated with crayons, markers, paint, or collage materials. Suggestions for party bag fillers might include healthy snacks (raisins, trail mix, pretzels, bread sticks, crackers), coloring pages, stencils cut from cardboard, pencils, homemade play dough, or a teacher-made blank book for coloring or drawing. As the children fill the bags, they will strengthen skills in one-to-one correspondence, counting, and simple addition.

Trail Mix

4 cups Cheerios™	1 cup peanuts
1 cup M&M™ candies	1 cup raisins

Combine in a large bowl. Store in a zip-close bag. Ingredients can be substituted, added, or deleted.

Party Hats.   Use the black line master as a stencil for party hats. Children can trace and cut the shape, roll it into a cone-shaped party hat, and glue or staple it closed. The steps can be modified for younger children and those with delayed fine motor abilities. Punch holes in front of the ears and attach a string to keep the hats in place. The hats can be decorated with Fruit Loops™, colored cotton balls, colorful buttons, and scraps of yarn.

Tablecloth.   Cover the snack table(s) with plain kraft paper. Provide the children with colored markers, paint and sponges, or crayons for decorating the tablecloth. The children can snip around the edges of the paper to create a fringe.

Birthday Cake.   The children will enjoy making, decorating, and eating their own cakes. Use the following recipe for healthy carrot cake cupcakes with cream cheese frosting or make cupcakes by following the directions on the back of a cake mix box. When the cupcakes are cool, give each child enough homemade or canned frosting to cover his or her cupcake. Squeeze tubes of cake decorator gel can be used along with sprinkles to add the finishing touches.

Carrot Cake Cupcakes

1½ cups vegetable oil	3 cups grated carrots
2 cups sugar	4 eggs
3 cups flour	1 cup chopped nuts (optional)
2 teaspoons baking soda	1 teaspoon vanilla
3 teaspoons cinnamon	

Preheat oven to 325 degrees. Line a cupcake pan with individual liners. Combine oil and sugar. Add eggs and vanilla. Mix dry ingredients together and add to above mixture. Blend in carrots and nuts last. Bake for about 20 to 30 minutes or until a toothpick inserted in the center comes out clean. Frost when cool.

Cream Cheese Frosting

    3   ounces cream cheese
1½ cups powdered sugar
    1   teaspoon vanilla

Cream ingredients together until smooth.

Piñata. Piñatas are a tradition at parties in Mexico. A piñata can be purchased or made out of papier-mâché. Purchased piñatas come in a variety of shapes and colors. A homemade piñata will be less spectacular, but the children will be proud of their efforts. Purchase a large balloon, preferably one made out of heavier rubber.

- Inflate the balloon.
- Tear single sheets of newspaper into thin strips.
- Make a thin paste out of flour and water.
- Cover the balloon with a thin layer of oil.
- Dip newspaper strips into the paste, and place the strips over the balloon. Layer strips of newspaper until the balloon has a thick cover.
- Let dry overnight.
- Once dry, the papier-mâché balloon will need to be cut in half to fill with treats. The balloon rubber can be removed when the papier-mâché is cut.
- Poke two holes in the shell and insert a string or yarn to hang from the ceiling.
- Fill the shell with treats such as candy, balloons, crayons, and markers.
- Put the two halves back together and seal with papier-mâché mixture. Let dry.
- Decorate with paint.
- Hang the piñata from the ceiling. The children sit in a large circle on the floor and take turns hitting it with a stick or dowel rod trying to break it open so the treats fall out.

Guess the Gift. A fun part of receiving a birthday gift is guessing what's inside the box and unwrapping it. Explain to the children that the gifts at this party aren't really new but are favorite games and toys from the classroom. Wrap items in different-sized boxes. Give clues to the children about what is in the box. The child who guesses the item gets to unwrap it. Wrap enough gifts so that everyone in the class gets a turn. Clues can be given using color, size, and function as descriptors. The difficulty of the clues will depend on the age and developmental level of the children in the class.

No party is complete without a variety of party games to enjoy. Here is a sampling of some of the favorites.

Pin the Nose on the Clown.   Cut a large circle out of colored kraft paper. Cut hair out of red paper or yarn and place it on the head. Draw eyes and a mouth on the clown. Inflate a small balloon for each child. Blindfold the children one at a time, and hand them the balloon with masking tape on the end. Each child places the balloon where he or she thinks the nose belongs. The game can be played with individual clowns that the children can take home. Use a paper plate for the clown's face.

Ball Toss.   Label three baskets or cartons with the numerals 1, 2, and 3. Line up the baskets in a row. Children stand behind a chalk line and toss a ball into the baskets in numerical order.

Ring the Candle.   Use a soda bottle or a thick dowel rod for a candle. Provide the children with rings or hula hoops to toss around the "candle."

Cake Walk.   Make cutouts of birthday cakes using the black line master. Place enough cakes in a circle on the floor so there is one cake for each child. Play music while the children walk around the circle of cakes. While they are walking, remove one cake. When the music stops, each child must find a cake to stand on. The child or children who are not standing on a cake when the music stops stand in the middle of the circle and pretend to be the candles. Count the candles before starting the music each time.

The following activities are general ideas for a birthday unit; they are not necessarily meant to be associated with the class party:

Card Search.   Provide a deck of cards. The children can look through the deck to find the four cards with the numeral representing their age. Younger children and children with lower-level math skills may need to match numerals by looking at a model. The children can count the symbols on the cards as a self-checking technique.

Stilts.   Sam woke up in the morning expecting to be bigger. When he couldn't reach things on his own, he used the chair given to him by his grandpa. The children can experiment with what it feels like to be taller by making stilts out of cans. Twenty-eight-ounce tomato cans work well, but if they are unavailable, collect 16-ounce cans. Empty the cans from the bottom so that the top has a flat surface intact. Punch a hole on two sides toward the top of the empty cans. Attach heavy string or yarn that will reach up to the children's hands. The children place their feet on the top of the can while holding onto the strings. They will probably require help when first walking on the stilts.

Cake Math.   Make pretend birthday cakes out of play dough or flat pieces of Styrofoam™. Label each cake with a numeral from 1 to 5 or 10. Provide the children with golf tees. They place the corresponding number of golf tees into the birthday cakes. The activity can be extended by asking the children to arrange the birthday cakes in numerical order.

Growth Charts. Children can make and decorate their own growth charts. Measure the children during the course of the year and record growth on the chart. The growth charts can be taken home and parents can record their continued growth at regular intervals. The charts can be made from 4-foot lengths of kraft paper. The children can decorate the charts with crayons and markers. The teacher can use a yardstick to mark inches and feet along the side of the chart. Laminate the charts or cover them with clear Con-Tact® paper to preserve them. When comparing height from one interval to the next, use the terms taller, shorter, larger, smaller, and so forth.

Measure Me. The children will enjoy measuring themselves in different units and recording the results on a graph. Determine what units of measure will be used (blocks, unifix™ cubes, chain links, markers, etc.). Draw pictures of the units of measurement across the top of a sheet of paper. List the children's names along the left-hand side of the paper. Record how many of each unit was used in measuring each child. Children can compare their heights according to units of measurement.

Clap and Tap. The children can clap and tap their age. Classmates will need to listen very carefully to determine the age of their friend. Vary the activity by asking children to clap their brother's or sister's age or the age of their pet.

Birthday Wishes. Children are familiar with the tradition of making a wish and blowing out the candles. Provide the children with paper cut into candle shapes. They can draw a picture of what their wish would be. Some children might enjoy looking through magazines or catalogs to find a picture of their wish to cut out and mount on the candle. Ask the children to dictate a sentence or two describing their wish. Mount the candle wishes on a large sheet of kraft paper cut to resemble a birthday cake.

Suggested Home Activities. Send home a synopsis of *Happy Birthday, Sam*. Inform parents about the kinds of activities their child is doing at school. Parents can reinforce the concept of age at home by looking through picture albums with their child and talking about how old the child was in each picture. Parents can describe what the child was able to do at each age. Encourage parents to label the home calendar with family birthdays and other special days. As the special days approach, children will enjoy counting how many days until the special day.

Related Literature

Asch, Frank. *Happy Birthday, Moon.*
Keats, Ezra Jack. *A Letter to Amy.*

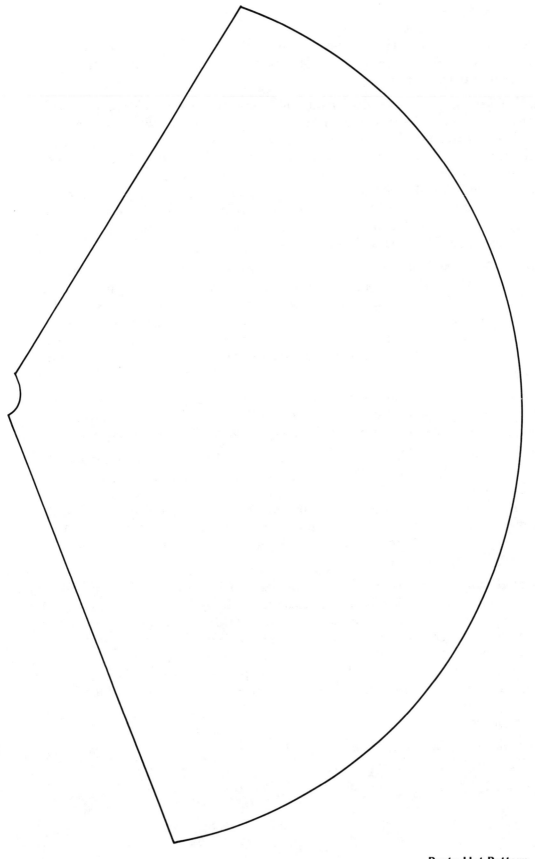

Party Hat Pattern

Cake Walk Activity

APPENDIX

Readiness Books

ALPHABET BOOKS

Anno, Mitsumasa. *Anno's Alphabet.* Thomas Y. Crowell, 1975. This alphabet book uses capital letters that give the look of having been carved from an oak. The borders detail many objects beginning with the same letter sound.

Aylesworth, Jim. *Old Black Fly.* Henry Holt, 1992. This ABC rhyme describes 26 things Old Black Fly did on a very busy bad day.

Barton, Byron. *Applebet Story.* Viking Press, 1973. Children can guess the word that goes with each letter, telling an alphabet story in sequence.

Bayer, Jane. *A, My Name Is Alice.* Dial Books, 1984. Animals sell their wares in this wonderfully illustrated version of a bouncing ball chant. Children can make up verses based on their own name.

Boynton, Sandra. *A Is for Angry: An Animal and Adjective Alphabet.* Workman Press, 1987. Each alphabet letter interacts with a corresponding animal. Children can guess and pantomime the adjective.

Ehlert, Lois. *Eating the Alphabet: Fruits and Vegetables from A to Z.* Harcourt Brace Jovanovich, 1987. This colorfully illustrated alphabet book shows fruits and vegetables from apples to zucchini.

Eichenberg, Fritz. *Ape in a Cape: An Alphabet of Odd Animals.* Harcourt Brace Jovanovich, 1952. Large and colorful animals are involved in silly and unusual rhyming activities, such as a carp with a harp.

Gardner, Beau. *Have You Ever Seen? An ABC Book.* Dodd, Mead, 1986. Dynamic graphics combine each alphabet letter with something that it typically does not go with.

Lobel, Arnold. *On Market Street.* Greenwillow Books, 1981. Clever ABC of people made out of apples, books, clocks, and other items.

Lyon, George Ella. *A B Cedar: An Alphabet of Trees.* Orchard Books, 1989. This unusual alphabet book shows a leaf and fruit sample for each tree, one per alphabet letter, and a silhouette drawing of each tree below.

MacDonald, Suse. *Alphabatics.* Bradbury Press, 1986. A clever acrobatic book where letters change into different objects.

Merriam, Eve. *Where Is Everybody? An Animal Alphabet.* Simon & Schuster, 1989. An alliterative alphabet book that shows an animal in a place corresponding with each letter.

MATH CONCEPTS

Anno, Mitsumasa. *Anno's Counting Book.* Harper & Row, 1975. This book shows country scenes and events in nature and in the lives of people that lend themselves to counting.

Aylesworth, Jim. *One Crow: A Counting Rhyme.* J. B. Lippincott, 1988. Rhyming couplets of one to ten farm animals shown first in summer and then repeated in winter. Children can count the animals, compare summer and winter, and repeat each rhyme.

Carle, Eric. *1, 2, 3 to the Zoo.* Philomel Books, 1968. Children can follow and count the animals in the train cars leading to the zoo.

———. *Rooster's Off to See the World.* Picture Book Studio, 1972. Rooster takes his friends on a trip. Children can count forward and backward on this delightful journey.

Christelow, Eileen. *Five Little Monkeys Jumping on the Bed.* Clarion Books, 1989. The familiar chantable rhyme that children can recite "one fell off and bumped his head."

de Regniers, Beatrice Schenk. *So Many Cats!* Houghton Mifflin, 1988. This counting story in verse shows how easily one sad and lonely cat can turn into 12.

Ehlert, Lois. *Fish Eyes: A Book You Can Count On* (pre-1). Harcourt Brace Jovanovich, 1990. The book has simple rhymed text and cutout holes for children's little fingers on each page.

Eichenberg, Fritz. *Dancing in the Moon: Counting Rhymes.* Harcourt Brace Jovanovich, 1975. Numbers 1 through 20 are shown by a variety of animals moving with a rhyming word.

Fleming, Denise. *Count.* Henry Holt, 1992. A boldly illustrated animal counting book from 1 to 10 and then in tens to 50.

Galdone, Paul. *Over in the Meadow: An Old Nursery Counting Rhyme.* Prentice Hall, 1986. An old familiar counting rhyme that children can recite.

Hoban, Tana. *Count and See.* Macmillan, 1972. The book moves from 1 to 15, then in tens to 50, then to 100. Clear, easy-to-recognize photographs.

Hutchins, Pat. *1 Hunter.* William A. Morrow, 1982. A hunter walks through the jungle and children can count various animals 1 to 10.

Leedy, Loreen. *A Number of Dragons.* Holiday House, 1985. A call and response rhyming 10 to 1 and back again dragon counting book.

Lionni, Leo. *Inch by Inch.* Astor-Honor, 1962. An inchworm measures all the birds.

Miller, Jane. *Farm Counting Book.* Simon & Schuster, 1986. Color photographs of favorite farm animals help introduce children to simple number concepts.

Schwartz, David M. *How Much Is a Million.* Scholastic, 1985. A million, billion, and trillion are explained so that children can visualize the vastness of numbers.

Sendak, Maurice. *One Was Johnny: A Counting Book.* Harper & Row, 1962. A counting rhyme to act out in sequence, about Johnny and all the intruders who destroy his peace and quiet until he issues an ultimatum.

Serfozo, Mary. *Who Wants One?* Macmillan, 1989. A big sister offers her stubborn little brother an array of rhyming animals and objects, from 1 to 10.

GENERAL CONCEPTS

Brenner, Barbara. *Mr. Tall and Mr. Small.* Young Scott, 1966. A giraffe and his mouse friend can't decide if tall or small is better until a forest fire brings out their best qualities.

Hoban, Tana. *Big Ones, Little Ones.* Greenwillow Books, 1976. Black-and-white photographs show young and adult animals.

——. *Circles, Triangles, and Squares.* Macmillan, 1974. Shapes are everywhere, if you look for them in everyday objects. The shapes are shown in black-and-white photographs.

——. *I Read Signs.* Greenwillow Books, 1983. Photographs of familiar signs are shown in the book.

——. *I Walk and Read.* Greenwillow Books, 1984. Photographs of objects children see and read as they walk in familiar places are shown.

——. *Is It Red? Is It Yellow? Is It Blue?* Greenwillow Books, 1978. Photographs of city life show objects of different colors, shapes, and sizes.

——. *Is It Rough? Is It Smooth? Is It Shiny?* Greenwillow Books, 1984. Children can look at photographs of objects and answer the questions the title asks.

————. *Over, Under & Through, and Other Spatial Concepts.* Atheneum, 1973. Photographs demonstrate spatial concepts expressed in 12 words.

————. *Push-Pull, Empty-Full.* Macmillan, 1972. Children can figure out opposite word pairs by looking at the full-page black-and-white photographs.

————. *Round and Round and Round.* Greenwillow Books, 1983. Photographs show a variety of objects that are round.

Kalan, Robert. *Blue Sea.* Greenwillow Books, 1979. Fish of different sizes illustrate the concepts of size and space relationships.

Noll, Sally. *Jiggle Wiggle Prance.* Greenwillow Books, 1987. This rhyme helps teach action words.

Serfozo, Mary. *Who Said Red?* Macmillan, 1988. Colors are described by a farm girl and her brother.

Walsh, Ellen Stoll. *Mouse Paint.* Harcourt Brace Jovanovich, 1989. Three white mice discover three pots of paint—red, yellow, and blue—and dive in.

Predictable Books

Bang, Molly. *Ten, Nine, Eight.* Penguin Books, 1985. A predictable, rhythmical story depicting the bedtime rituals a little girl shares with her father.

Burningham, John. *Hey! Get Off Our Train.* Crown, 1989. A young boy takes a trip around the world. Along the way, endangered animals board the train and ask for sanctuary. The special journey has a surprise ending.

————. *Mr. Gumpy's Outing.* Henry Holt, 1971. Although Mr. Gumpy warns his boat passengers to behave, the children squabble, the rabbit hops, the cat chases the rabbit, and the rest of the animals misbehave until the boat capsizes.

Carle, Eric. *The Grouchy Ladybug.* Harper & Row, 1977. Unwilling to share food with a friendly ladybug, the grouchy one looks from morning to night for someone bigger. All day she challenges everyone to fight. In the end the grouchy ladybug ends up where she began, chaste and hungry.

————. *The Mixed-Up Chameleon.* Harper & Row, 1984. As the chameleon's wishes come true, he becomes the combination of the ten creatures that he envies the most.

Hutchins, Pat. *Good-Night, Owl.* Macmillan, 1972. Owl can't sleep because of the noise made by the insects, birds, and animals of the forest.

Kraus, Robert. *Oh, A-Hunting We Will Go.* Atheneum, 1974. A classic folk song that encourages children to make up their own verses.

————. *Where Are You Going, Little Mouse?* Mulberry Books, 1986. A little mouse runs away from home to find a nicer family, but when darkness comes, he misses them and realizes how much he loves them.

————. *Whose Mouse Are You?* Macmillan, 1970. A young mouse saves his mother from a cat, frees his father from a trap, brings his sister home, and welcomes his new baby brother.

Lobel, Arnold. *A Treeful of Pigs.* Greenwillow Books, 1979. A farmer's wife tries everything to pry her lazy husband out of bed. She has the help of some cooperative piglets.

Martin, Bill, Jr. *Brown Bear, Brown Bear, What Do You See?* Henry Holt, 1983. A call and response story in which children can learn about colors and animals.

McGovern, Ann. *Too Much Noise.* Scholastic, 1967. A folktale about a man who couldn't sleep until he acquired and then let go a houseful of animals.

Numeroff, Laura Joffe. *If You Give a Moose a Muffin.* HarperCollins, 1991. A sequel to *If You Give a Mouse a Cookie.* Children enjoy guessing what the moose could possibly want next.

————. *If You Give a Mouse a Cookie.* Harper & Row, 1985. A cause-and-effect story about what a small mouse might request after giving him a cookie.

Rounds, Glen. *I Know an Old Lady Who Swallowed a Fly.* Holiday House, 1990. A version of an old song about an old lady who dies from overeating a strange variety of animals.

Shaw, Charles. *It Looked Like Spilt Milk.* Harper & Row, 1947. A white cloudlike shape is silhouetted on a blue background for every page.

Tafuri, Nancy. *Have You Seen My Duckling?* William A. Morrow, 1984. A story of mother duck and her ducklings swimming around a pond trying to find a lost duckling.

Williams, Sue. *I Went Walking.* Harcourt Brace Jovanovich, 1990. During the course of a walk, a young boy identifies animals of different colors.

Wood, Audrey. *The Napping House.* Harcourt Brace Jovanovich, 1984. On a rainy day, a granny, boy, dog, cat, and mouse nap together on a cozy bed until a wakeful fly bites the mouse, starting a chain reaction that gets everyone up.

Wylie, Joanne and David. *A Funny Fish Story.* Regensteiner, 1984. The narrator describes the fish he caught in words that keep increasing its size.

Multicultural Books

Albert, Burton. *Where Does the Trail Lead?* Simon & Schuster, 1991. The short story traces the steps of an African-American boy on Summer Island as he follows a trail along the beach until he reaches his family at a seaside picnic.

Aliki. *Corn Is Maize, The Gift of the Indians.* Harper & Row Junior Books, 1976. A learn-and-find-out science book tells the story of corn from planting to final products.

Anno, Mitsumasa. *Anno's Flea Market.* Philomel Books, 1984. A flea market takes place in a town. The market combines objects and people from many times and cultures.

Baker, Keith. *The Magic Fan.* Harcourt Brace Jovanovich, 1989. A Japanese boy averts tragedy with his visionary building projects.

Bang, Molly. *Yellow Ball.* Greenwillow Books, 1991. A book with large ideas and few words. Three beachgoers interrupt a game of catch to build a sand castle on a busy sandy stretch. Unbeknown to the children, the big yellow ball is carried away on the tide and begins a long journey out to sea.

Barbot, Daniel. *A Bicycle for Rosaura.* Kane/Miller, 1991. A picture book from Venezuela details the predicament of Señora Amelia when her handsome hen Rosaura asks for a bicycle for her birthday.

Bogart, Jo Ellen. *Daniel's Dog.* Scholastic, 1990. A young African-American boy is shown adjusting to two big changes in his family life: the birth of a baby sister and the death of his grandfather. Daniel copes by inventing an imaginary dog which he is eventually able to share with his Asian playmate Norman.

Breckler, Rosemary. *Hoang Breaks the Lucky Teapot.* Houghton Mifflin, 1992. A young Vietnamese boy breaks a teapot that houses good spirits. He tries to repair the damage to keep away evil spirits and bad fortune.

Brown, Tricia. *Hello, Amigos.* Holt, 1986. Frankie Valdez is a Mexican-American boy who lives in San Francisco's Mission District. This is a special day in his life—his birthday!

Cohen, Caron Lee. *The Mud Pony.* Scholastic, 1988. A folktale about a Native American boy who wakes up one morning and the mud pony of his dreams has come to life.

Crews, Donald. *Shortcut.* Greenwillow Books, 1992. Although the children were told to stay off the tracks, they decide to take a shortcut home. They hear the train coming!

Cummings, Pat. *Clean Your Room, Harvey Moon.* Bradbury Press, 1991. Like most kids, Harvey Moon has to be told to clean his room. A humorous rhyming text lists the extraordinary items poor Harvey has to find a place for.

dePaola, Tomie. *The Legend of the Indian Paint Brush*. Scholastic, 1988. A young Native American boy learns to paint the sunset. This story captures the spirit and beauty of the Native American legend of the paintbrush.

Everett, Gwen. *Li'l Sis and Uncle Willie*. Rizzoli International, 1992. Based on true memories, Li'l Sis delights in hearing the stories her uncle shares of distant places he has seen. Uncle Willie is the great African-American painter, William H. Johns.

Everett, Louise. *Amigo Means Friend*. Troll, 1987. Jose and George speak different languages, but it doesn't stop them from being friends.

Flournoy, Valerie. *Patchwork Quilt*. Dial Books, 1985. As she quilts, Grandmother tells Tanya family stories. When she becomes ill, Tanya keeps working on the heirloom quilt.

Gobel, Paul. *The Gift of the Sacred Dog*. Aladdin Books, 1980. A legend about a Plains Native American boy who asked the Great Spirit for help for his hungry people. In response, horses were sent to help the people hunt buffalo.

————. *The Race of the Birds and Animals*. Bradbury Press, 1985. A Native American legend regarding a race called by the creator to determine whether people should eat buffalo or buffalo should eat people. Magpie, the slowest of the birds, helped the two-legged (people) win the race. To this day, people honor the birds by wearing their beautiful feathers.

Greenfield, Eloise. *Grampa's Face*. Philomel Books, 1988. When Tamika sees her grandfather's usually loving, kind face turn cold and mean while he's practicing for a play, she becomes frightened that he might look at her like that some day.

————. *Me and Neesie*. Thomas Y. Crowell, 1975. Janell's high-spirited imaginary best friend leaves for good on the first day of school.

Grifalconi, Ann. *Osa's Pride*. Little, Brown, 1989. Osa is too proud for her own good until her grandmother helps her learn an important lesson. Set in an African village.

Grossman, Virginia and Sylvia Long. *Ten Little Rabbits*. Chronicle Books, 1991. A counting rhyme with illustrations of rabbits in Native American costumes, depicting traditional costumes such as rain dances, hunts, and smoke signals.

Havill, Juanita. *Jamaica's Find*. Houghton Mifflin, 1986. Jamaica has mixed feelings about keeping a toy dog she finds in the park.

————. *Jamaica Tag-Along*. Houghton Mifflin, 1989. Jamaica remembers how she felt when her older brother excluded her, and she decides to play with a younger child.

Heide, Florence Parry and Judith Heide Gilliland. *The Day of Ahmed's Secret*. Lothrop, Lee & Shepard, 1991. A young boy in Cairo is bursting to share the news that he can write his name.

Hort, Lenny. *How Many Stars in the Sky?* Tambourine, 1991. An African-American boy is kept awake at night by a question that nags at him: Just how many stars are there up in the sky? Illustrations depict a nighttime suburban neighborhood as well as city and rural scenes.

Howard, Elizabeth Fitzgerald. *Aunt Flossie's Hats (and Crab Cakes Later)*. Clarion Books, 1991. Two sisters visit their great aunt and play with her collection of hats, each of which tells a story.

Hudson, Cheryl Willis and Bernette G. Ford. *Bright Eyes, Brown Skin*. Just Us Books, 1990. An upbeat rhyming text describes four distinctly individual African-American children engaged in typical preschool or day care activities.

Isadora, Rachel. *At the Crossroads*. William A. Morrow, 1991. Children in a South African village excitedly await their father's return from a long stint in the mines.

————. *Over the Green Hills*. Greenwillow Books, 1992. Zolani, who lives in a rural black homeland in South Africa, goes with his mother to visit his grandma, Zindzi.

Jeffers, Susan. *Brother Eagle, Sister Sky.* Dial Books, 1991. A message from Chief Seattle encourages children to care for and preserve our environment.

Johnson, Angela. *Do Like Kyla?* Orchard Books, 1990. A typical day in the life of a young African-American girl and her old sister, Kyla, who she lovingly imitates.

———. *One of Three.* Orchard Books, 1991. It's hard being the youngest of three sisters, until Mama and Daddy find things for her to do at home, making her feel not left out.

———. *When I Am Old with You.* Orchard Books, 1990. The story of an African-American grandfather and his grandson's ideas about things they'll do together when the child is as old as the grandfather.

Kalman, Maira. *Sayonara, Mrs. Kackleman.* Viking Kestre, 1989. While watching *The Mikado,* Alexander asked his big sister Lulu to take him to Japan. Off they fly to Tokyo, taking in all the local sights and customs. This imaginary adventure introduces young readers to the traditional Japanese culture.

La Capa, Michael. *The Flute Player.* Northland, 1990. An Apache folktale about a young boy and girl who were attracted to each other. They communicated from a distance through his flute playing. The girl responded by sending a leaf downstream. The girl becomes ill when the boy goes on a hunt and she no longer hears his flute.

Levine, Ellen. *I Hate English.* Scholastic, 1989. Having moved from Hong Kong to New York with her family, Mei Mei resists speaking English until a new teacher helps her.

Lewis, Richard. *All of You Was Singing.* Atheneum, 1991. A retelling of an Aztec legend that recounts how music came to Earth.

Lexau, Joan. *Benjie.* Dial Books, 1964. A shy boy finds his grandmother's lost earring and gains confidence in the process.

Lobel, Arnold. *MingLo Moves the Mountain.* Scholastic, 1982. MingLo and his wife lived at the bottom of a large mountain. His wife decided that the Mountain should be moved.

Martin, Bill Jr., and John Archambault. *Knots on a Counting Rope.* Henry Holt, 1987. A young blind Native American boy and his grandfather tell the story of the boy's birth and his first horse race. The strong love between grandfather and his grandson is interwoven into the tale.

Marzollo, Jean. *Pretend You're a Cat.* Dial Books, 1990. Preschoolers from diverse racial backgrounds engage in imaginative play next to inset drawings of the animals they're pretending to be.

McKissack, Patricia C. *Nettie Jo's Friends.* Alfred A. Knopf, 1989. Determined to find a sewing needle to make a new dress for her doll, Nettie Jo asks for help from her friends, all of whom seem to be too busy to help her.

Medearis, Angela. *Dancing with the Indians.* Scholastic, 1991. A young girl and her family join the Seminoles for a pow-wow. Ancestors of this Indian nation rescued her grandfather from slavery and accepted him as part of their own.

Mennen, Ingrid and Niki Daly. *Somewhere in Africa.* Dutton Children's Books, 1990. A beautifully illustrated book about home in an African city far from where the animals roam.

Mosel, Arlene. *Tikki Tikki Tembo.* Scholastic, 1968. A folktale from China. A story about two brothers and the Chinese custom of giving the first born son a long name, creating a problem for Tikki Tikki Tembo.

Osofsky, Audrey. *Dream Catcher.* Orchard Books, 1992. In the land of the Ojibwa, a baby sleeps, protected from bad dreams, as Ojibwan life goes on around.

Oughton, Jerrie. *How the Stars Fell into the Sky.* Houghton Mifflin, 1992. A Navajo folktale that answers the age-old question.

Robbins, Ruth. *How the First Rainbow Was Made.* Houghton Mifflin, 1980. One winter long ago, it rained so much on Mt. Shasta that the Indians could not gather seeds for food. All creatures had to work together.

Roe, Eileen. *Con Mi Hermano/With My Brother.* Bradbury Press, 1991. A preschool-aged Latino boy describes all the things he admires about his teenaged brother and looks forward to the time he'll be big.

Rogers, Jean. *Runaway Mittens.* Greenwillow Books, 1988. In an Eskimo village, an Inuit boy loves the mittens his grandmother knit him, even though he constantly misplaces them.

Root, Phyllis and Carol Marron. *Gretchen's Grandma.* Raintree, 1983. Gretchen's grandmother came to visit from Germany, where people do not speak the same language with words. Understanding came from the heart in doing things together.

Serfozo, Mary. *Rain.* McElderry Books, 1990. The story shares the small wonders that a young African-American girl notices during a gentle rain.

Springstubb, Tricia. *The Magic Guinea Pig.* William A. Morrow, 1982. Upset when he can't do anything right in his family's eyes, Mark helps out a bumbling witch who gives him an unexpected pet.

Ward, Leila. *I Am Eyes • Ni Macho.* Greenwillow Books, 1978. A small girl in Kenya awakens and joyfully observes the world around her.

Science/Stories About the Earth

ANIMALS

Goodspeed, Peter. *A Rhinocerous Wakes Me Up in the Morning.* Bradbury Press, 1982. A boy describes all of the 200 animals who help him through his day.

Martin, Bill, Jr. and John Archambault. *Barn Dance.* Holt, 1986. The story of a boy who sneaks into a barn one night to see the animals dance.

Paxton, Tom. *Jennifer's Rabbit.* Morrow, 1988. A lullaby of a little girl's nighttime trip to sea with her animal friends.

Raffi. *Baby Beluga.* Crown, 1990. A song story about a baby Beluga whale, told by the cold water playmates of the whale.

Reeves, Mona Rabun. *I Had a Cat.* Bradbury Press, 1989. A girl gives her assortment of animals away, leaving only her pet cat.

DAYS AND NIGHTS

Asch, Frank. *Happy Birthday, Moon.* Simon & Schuster, 1988. Convinced the moon is talking to him when all he really hears is his own echo, Bear buys the moon a birthday hat.

————. *Moongame.* Prentice Hall, 1984. Bear plays hide-and-seek with the moon.

Berger, Barbara. *Grandfather Twilight.* Philomel Books, 1984. When the day is done and the shadows begin to deepen, Grandfather Twilight closes his book, puts on his jacket, and goes for a walk in the forest.

————. *When the Sun Rose.* Philomel Books, 1986. The sun visits a little girl in her playhouse and takes on many beautiful shapes. The little girl and the sun play all day long, making rainbows until her friend has to say goodbye at sunset.

Branley, Franklyn. *What Makes Day and Night.* Harper & Row, 1986. This science book for young children explains the revolutions of the earth.

Carle, Eric. *Papa, Please Get the Moon for Me.* Picture Book Studio, 1986. When Monica asks for the moon, her father takes along a ladder and fetches it. Large folded pages open up and out to extend the moon's range as it goes through its phases.

Darling, Kathy. *Little Bat's Secret*. Garrard, 1974. A little brown bat experiences her first night flight. She is separated from her mother soon after their departure, becomes disoriented, and gets lost. The little bat befriends a lightning bug, who helps lead her through the darkness.

Frasier, Debra. *On the Day You Were Born*. Harcourt Brace Jovanovich, 1991. The earth and its creatures celebrate the birth of a child.

Ginsburg, Mirra. *The Sun's Asleep Behind the Hill*. Greenwillow Books, 1982. The sun, the breeze, the leaves, the bird, the squirrel, and the child all grow tired after a long day and fall asleep as night falls.

Himler, Ronald. *Wake Up, Jeremiah*. Harper & Row, 1979. A little boy greets the sun and a new day.

Hines, Anna Grossnicle. *Sky All Around*. Clarion Books, 1989. A father and daughter share a special time when they go out on a clear night to watch the stars. They settle down in their spot on the hill to look for pictures in the sky.

Jonas, Ann. *Reflections*. Greenwillow Books, 1987. The book describes a child's perfect day from sunrise to sunset. Read the book and then turn it upside down and continue reading. Each picture reflects another.

Lindbergh, Reeve. *The Midnight Farm*. Dial Books, 1989. A mother takes her child for a walk outside at night, giving him a chance to meet his familiar animal friends in the darkness of the summer night.

Motyka, Sally Mitchell. *An Ordinary Day*. Simon & Schuster, 1989. The delights of a little boy's ordinary day, filled with things to touch, taste, see, and enjoy.

Palazzo, Janet. *Our Friend the Sun*. Troll, 1982. This book explains why the sun is our friend.

Strand, Mark. *The Night Book*. Clarkson N. Potter, 1985. A rising moon sees a little girl who is afraid of the night and sends down a magic moonbeam to show her the many things to see during the darkness.

Zolotow, Charlotte. *Sleepy Book*. Harper & Row, 1988. Animals, birds, insects, and children sleep in their own special places, in their own special ways.

THE SEASONS

Alexander, Martha. *There's More . . . Much More*. Harcourt Brace Jovanovich, 1987. A talking squirrel guides young Sherri through a tour of spring, from leaves and flowers to smells and feelings.

Asch, Frank. *Mooncake*. Simon & Schuster, 1983. Little bear makes a rocket to take him to the moon. He awakens one day and thinks that he's on the moon, unaware that he has simply awakened in winter.

Bauer, Caroline F. *Midnight Snowman*. Atheneum, 1987. In a town where it hardly ever snows, one neighborhood's children and parents take advantage of a late-night snow by building a gigantic snowman before the snow turns to rain and melts away.

Bennett, David. *Seasons*. Bantam Little Rooster Book, 1989. The Bear Facts bear helps children discover about the seasons. One of a series.

Briggs, Raymond. *The Snowman*. Random House, 1978. Hazy, magical pictures show a small boy who builds a snowman on a wintry day and the snowman comes alive in this wordless book.

Bruna, Dick. *Another Story to Tell*. Metheum, 1978. The wordless story of what a little boy does on a snowy, winter day.

Burton, Virginia Lee. *Katy and the Big Snow*. Houghton Mifflin, 1973. A tractor plows out a town after a snowstorm.

Falconer, Elizabeth and Sara Coleridge. *January Brings the Snow: A Seasonal Hide and Seek*. Franklin Watts, 1989. Two stories are woven into one. In the first, a little boy and girl discover the joys of each month. Then, when the flaps are lifted, there appears a second picture story of a field mouse family enjoying the seasons in their own way.

Fowler, Susi Gregg. *When Summer Ends*. Greenwillow Books, 1989. Convinced that everything good happens in summer, a little girl is reminded by her mother of the wonders of the other three seasons.

Gibbons, Gail. *The Seasons of Arnold's Apple Tree*. Harcourt Brace Jovanovich, 1984. Arnold's apple tree is in his own secret place, and this bright and cheerfully illustrated book allows the reader to share the changes and joys of the four seasons.

Hirschi, Ron. *Winter* and *Spring*. Cobblehill Books, 1990. These books are designed to share nature's wonders.

————. *Summer*. Cobblehill Books, 1991. Easy-to-read text and striking photographs explore how baby animals learn lessons from their parents during the summer.

Ichikawa, Satomi. *A Child's Book of Seasons*. Parents Magazine Press, 1975. Children are engaged in the activities of every season, from one winter to the next.

Miller, Jane. *Seasons on the Farm*. Prentice Hall, 1986. This book displays activities on the farm and the farm animals throughout the four seasons.

Minarik, Else Holmelund. *It's Spring!* Greenwillow Books, 1989. Two cats are delighted with the arrival of a new season, and declare they could jump over a tulip, bush, tree, house, island, mountain, moon, sun, and each other.

Nietzel, Shirley. *The Jacket I Wear in the Snow*. Greenwillow Books, 1989. A rhyming, cumulative story of a little girl whose scarf is stuck in the zipper of her winter jacket.

Robbins, Ken. *Beach Days*. Viking Press, 1987. The book shows what people do at the beach on a typical day.

Rockwell, Anne and Harlow. *The First Snowfall*. Macmillan, 1989. The picture book shows the sights and activities that go with the first snowfall of the year.

Ryder, Joanne. *Chipmunk Song*. E. P. Dutton, 1987. A chipmunk prepares for winter hibernation.

Sasaki, Isao. *Snow*. Viking Press, 1982. The story shows a snowfall from morning to night over a tiny rural train station.

Weber, Robert. *The Winter Picnic*. Pantheon Books, 1970. A little boy singlehandedly prepares a picnic in the snow for his busy mother.

Ziefert, Harriet. *Snow Magic*. Viking Press, 1988. When the year's first snow falls on the first day of winter, the snow people gather for a snow party.

Zolotow, Charlotte. *Something Is Going to Happen*. Harper & Row, 1988. A family awakens one cold November Monday morning with a feeling of anticipation; opening the front door, they find it's snowing.

TIME TO GARDEN

Brown, Marc. *Your First Garden Book*. Little, Brown, 1981. A variety of garden-related projects for beginners are included.

Carle, Eric. *The Tiny Seed*. Picture Book Studio, 1987. The text tells the story of the life cycle of a flower in terms of the adventures of a tiny seed. The journey is dangerous.

Caseley, Judith. *Grandpa's Garden Lunch*. Greenwillow Books, 1990. A little girl and her grandparents prepare a lunch with their home-grown vegetables.

dePaola, Tomie. *Too Many Hopkins*. G. P. Putnam, 1989. The Hopkins family of rabbits win the prize for the biggest and finest garden.

Ehlert, Lois. *Planting a Rainbow*. Harcourt Brace Jovanovich, 1988. A mother and child plant flowers in the family garden. Bulbs, seeds, and plants sprout and grow into a rainbow of colorful blooms.

Kraus, Ruth. *The Carrot Seed*. Harper & Row, 1945. In this classic, a little boy has faith that the carrot seed he planted will come up, in spite of his doubting parents and brother.

Kroll, Steven. *The Biggest Pumpkin Ever*. Holiday House, 1984. Once two mice fell in love with the same pumpkin. One watered and tended the plant during the day; the other repeated the care during the night, unknown to each other.

Kuchalla, Susan. *Now I Know All About Seeds*. Troll, 1982. This book presents several kinds of seeds and shows how they grow into plants.

Le Tord, Bijou. *Rabbit Seeds*. Four Winds Press, 1984. This book sequences the toils and satisfactions of a gardener's year.

Lobel, Arnold. *A Rose in My Garden*. Scholastic, 1984. Beginning with one rose in the garden, the verses in the book build in the "House that Jack Built" style to include the flowers in the garden, a mouse, and a cat.

Maris, Ron. *In My Garden*. Greenwillow Books, 1987. Stepping into a child's garden, the path leads to frogs in the pool, flowers, and a big surprise at the end.

McMillan, Bruce. *Growing Colors*. Lothrop, Lee & Shepard, 1988. Color photos of fruits and vegetables on the vine, plant, or tree are shown.

McNulty, Faith. *The Lady and the Spider*. Harper & Row, 1986. The story of a tiny spider who makes her home in a head of lettuce and the lady who finds her.

Oda, Mayumi. *Happy Veggies*. Parallax Press, 1986. The book takes children on a stroll through Mother Nature's vegetable garden all year long.

Petie, Haris. *The Seed the Squirrel Dropped*. Prentice Hall, 1976. From the seed of a cherry comes a new tree that is cared for by a little boy until he is finally able to pick cherries to make pie.

Rockwell, Harlow. *The Compost Heap*. Doubleday, 1974. This picture book explains how a compost pile is made and how it turns into soil.

Von Olfewrs, Sibylle. *The Story of the Root Children*. Floris Books, 1990. Based on the 1906 German tale of the awakening of the root children. The book and illustrations show children's activities until Mother Earth calls them back under the ground to hide until next spring.

TREES

Ayers, Pam. *When Dad Cuts Down the Chestnut Tree*. Alfred A. Knopf, 1988. A child thinks of all the good reasons to cut down a tree and then thinks of the reasons not to. Finally, a decision is reached.

Baker, Jeannie. *Where the Forest Meets the Sea*. Greenwillow Books, 1987. An extraordinary visual journey through a tropical rainforest, where animals can be discovered hiding within the lush vegetation.

Curran, Eileen. *Look at a Tree*. Troll, 1985. Children learn about the different animals that can be seen in or around various types of trees.

Killion, Bette. *The Apartment House Tree*. Harper & Row, 1989. Children are introduced to the inhabitants of one special tree.

Lavies, Bianca. *Tree Trunk Traffic*. E. P. Dutton, 1989. The book shares one full day in the life of a tree and the animals who live there.

Pike, Norman. *The Peach Tree*. Stemmer House, 1983. The Pomeroy family plants a peach tree on the hill near their home. This is a lesson in ecology.

WATER IS WONDERFUL

Arnold, Carolyn. *A Walk by the Seashore.* First Facts Series, Silver Burdett, 1990. One book in a series that explores this habitat in a simple nature walk.

Bennett, David. *Rain.* Bear Facts Series, Bantam Little Rooster Book, 1989. Young children discover this wonder of nature in a simple way.

————. *Water.* Bear Facts Series, Bantam Little Rooster Book, 1989. Children discover the wonders of water in this picture book.

Carlstrom, Nancy White. *Better Not Get Wet, Jesse Bear.* Macmillan, 1988. Getting wet is okay—for everyone but Jesse Bear. But finally, it is Jesse Bear's turn to splash in his wading pool on a hot day.

Clements, Andrew. *Big Al.* Picture Book Studio, 1988. A very scary-looking and lonely fish teaches other frightened fish that looks alone don't "make the fish," when Big Al comes to the rescue of other fish.

Cooney, Nancy Evans. *The Umbrella Day.* Philomel Books, 1989. With a big, old, dusty umbrella at her side, Missy finds excitement when she wishes it into a toadstool, a wild animal tent, and a boat.

Craig, Janet. *What's Under the Ocean?* Troll, 1982. A colorful introduction to some of the plants and animals that live in the ocean.

Florian, Douglas. *A Beach Day.* William A. Morrow, 1990. Highlights of a day at the beach told in simple rhyming text, with simple crayon and watercolor illustrations.

Ginsburg, Mirra. *Mushroom in the Rain.* Macmillan, 1974. Many animals hide under an ever-expanding mushroom that shields them from weather and a hungry fox.

Goodall, John. *Paddy Under Water.* Atheneum, 1984. Paddy goes underwater to enjoy its pleasures and then comes to the rescue of a small creature with exciting results.

Jones, Rebecca C. *Down at the Bottom of the Dark Deep Sea.* Bradbury Press, 1991. Andrew is frightened by water, especially the water at the beach. While building sand castles, he realizes he can get wet and still be safe.

Oppenheim, Joanne. *Follow That Fish.* Bantam, 1990. A young boy meets a variety of sea animals when the fish on his line pulls him underwater.

Paraskevas, Betty. *On the Edge of the Sea.* Dial Books, 1992. A boy dreams of a long day at the beach. The story is told in rhyme, with simple descriptive illustrations.

Parramon, J. M. *The Four Elements: Water.* Barron, 1985. The book gives very young children all the reasons we should be grateful for water. Other books in the series include *Earth, Fire,* and *Air.*

Rius, Maria and J. M. Parramon. *Life in the Sea.* Barron, 1987. One book in a series, showing plants and animals that grow and live in the sea.

Samton, Sheila White. *Beside the Bay.* Philomel Books, 1987. Seashore colors and creatures are introduced in a rhyming walk along a stone wall.

Schmid, Eleonore. *The Water's Journey.* North-South Books, 1989. The story shows the journey of water that begins high in the mountains in the form of snowflakes and continues on.

Spier, Peter. *Peter Spier's Rain.* Doubleday, 1981. It is a clear, fair summer day as a young girl and her brother go out to play in the yard. A storm comes and the children and their dog explore in the garden, splash out to the park, and study their neighborhood.

ABOUT OUR WORLD

Arnold, Carolyn. *A Walk in the Woods.* First Fact Series, Silver Burdett, 1990. The book explores the wonders of the woods that can be discovered in a simple nature walk.

Other titles include *A Walk in the Desert, A Walk Up a Mountain,* and *A Walk by the Seashore.*

Aruego, Jose. *We Hide, You Seek.* William A. Morrow, 1988. When Rhino is invited to play hide and seek, he tries to find animals camouflaged in their native habitat.

Asch, Frank. *Skyfire.* Simon & Schuster, 1984. Bear discovers a rainbow and fears the sky is on fire.

Baines, Chris. *The Old Boot.* Crocodile Books, 1989. Homes for all kinds of creatures can be found in the most unlikely places and can easily be disturbed if we are not careful.

Burlson, Joe. *Space Colony.* G. P. Putnam, 1978. A story about space with an unusual format children will enjoy.

dePaola, Tomie. *Michael Bird-Boy.* Prentice Hall Books for Young Readers, Simon and Schuster, 1975. This story is a gentle lesson about air pollution.

Ets, Marie Hall. *Gilberto and the Wind.* Penguin Books, 1963. The story of a little Mexican boy who discovers the wind.

Howard, Jane R. *When I'm Sleepy.* E. P. Dutton, 1985. A little girl wonders what it would be like to sleep with the animals wherever they sleep.

Hutchins, Pat. *The Wind Blew.* Penguin Books, 1986. This story shows people frantically trying to retrieve possessions that the wind has blown away.

Peters, Lisa Westberg. *The Sun, the Wind, and the Rain.* Henry Holt, 1988. Two side-by-side stories in one, the first showing how a mountain is created and then worn down and changed; the second, on facing pages, parallels the first, as Elizabeth builds a sand mountain at the beach, only to have it changed by the wind and rain.

Rius, Maria and J. M. Parramon. *Life Underground.* Barron, 1987. Papa Bunny explains to his little bunny rabbit how their underground home was built by digging through various layers of earth. Other titles include *Life in the Air, Life on the Land,* and *Life in the Sea.*

Ryder, Joanne. *Where Butterflies Grow.* Lodestar Books, 1989. The story of a butterfly as it goes through its changes.

Selsam, Millicent and Joyce Hunt. *Keep Looking!* Macmillan, 1989. Although the snow-covered house and yard seem empty, a careful look reveals animals such as chickadee, chipmunk, skunk, and woodchuck going through their routines.

Tompkins, Jasper. *The Sky Jumps.* Green Tiger Press, 1986. The book shows small children all the things the sky can do.

Personal Experience

ADOPTION

Charlton, Michael. *I Am Adopted.* Bodley Head, 1983. Charles and his sister, Sophie, are adopted. Charles describes his life with his special friend and family.

Stein, Sara B. *The Adopted One: An Open Family Book for Parents and Children Together.* Walker, 1979. Joshua feels excluded at a family gathering. After feeling unsure about his place in the family, his parents' response gives Joshua the reassurance he needs.

Turner, Ann Warren. *Through Moon and Stars and Night Sky.* Harper & Row, 1990. The family of this adopted Asian child retell the story of his arrival on a huge plane that came through the night sky.

DISABILITIES

Burns, Kay. *Our Mom.* Franklin Watts, 1989. Four children in a busy family describe some of the daily routines of their wheelchair-mobile mom.

Ominsky, Elaine. *Jon O: A Special Boy.* Prentice Hall, 1977. Jon has Down's syndrome; his difficulties and joys are shared.

Prall, Jo. *My Sister's Special.* Children's Press, 1985. A young boy describes his brain-damaged sister. She can't walk, talk, or use her arms or legs, but she can laugh.

Rabe, Berniece. *The Balancing Girl.* E. P. Dutton, 1981. Wheelchair- and crutches-bound Margaret proves her balancing talents and causes a sensation at the school carnival.

DIVORCE, REMARRIAGE, BLENDED FAMILIES

Baum, Louis. *One More Time.* William A. Morrow, 1986. Simon and his noncustodial dad share Sunday in the city. They say good-bye easily because they know they'll see each other again soon.

Drescher, Joan. *My Mother's Getting Married.* Dial Books, 1986. Katy thinks the idea of her mother getting married "stinks." After being defiant at the wedding, mom reassures Katy of her continued love.

Stinson, Kathy. *Mom and Dad Don't Live Together Any More.* Annick Press, 1985. A preschool girl describes her life since her parents' divorce, wishing they were together. Gradually, she accepts that she has love of both, even though they are not together.

Vigna, Judith. *Daddy's New Baby.* Albert Whitman, 1982. While visiting her father and his new wife, a young girl's space and time are invaded by her baby half-sister.

———. *She's Not My Real Mother.* Albert Whitman, 1980. While visiting his father and his father's new wife, Miles becomes concerned that his acceptance of her would be disloyal to his mother.

FEARS AND FEELINGS

Bourgeois, Paulette. *Franklin in the Dark.* Scholastic, 1986. Franklin, the turtle, is afraid of the dark, making it impossible for him to stay in his shell. He learns to cope with his fear of small, dark places when he realizes that he is not the only one who has fears.

Christelow, Eileen. *Henry and the Dragon.* Clarion Books, 1984. Afraid of a dragonlike shadow on his wall, rabbit Henry wants his parents to check out his surroundings before bed.

Corey, Dorothy. *You Go Away.* Albert Whitman, 1976. Through a variety of separation experiences, preschool children are reassured that their parents will return.

Crowe, Robert L. *Clyde Monster.* E. P. Dutton, 1976. Young monster boy, afraid to go to bed in his dark cave, confides his fear of people to his parents who reassure him that we're quite harmless.

De Groat, Diane. *Alligator's Toothache.* Crown, 1977. Alligator suffers a painful toothache and he's afraid of the dentist. His friends trick him into treating himself.

dePaola, Tomie. *Oliver Button Is a Sissy.* Harcourt Brace Jovanovich, 1979. Oliver doesn't like doing the things other boys enjoy doing. Oliver is teased by the boys while the girls stick up for him. The story has a surprise ending.

Grossnickle, Anna. *Grandma Gets Grumpy.* Houghton Mifflin, 1990. Grandma runs out of patience when the children spend the night.

Hazen, Barbara Shook. *Fang.* Atheneum, 1987. A boy with many fears has a huge dog who looks fierce but is scared of everything.

Holabird, Katherine. *Alexander and the Dragon*. Crown, 1988. Afraid of the dragon under his bed, a young boy armed with helmet, shield, and sword is prepared to bash it until he realizes it's friendly.

Hughes, Shirley. *Dogger*. Lothrop, Lee & Shephard, 1988. David is heartsick when he loses his favorite stuffed animal.

Kachenmeister, Cherryl. *On Monday When It Rains*. Houghton Mifflin, 1989. A young boy describes in text and photographs of his facial expressions, the different emotions he feels each day.

Mayer, Mercer. *There's an Alligator Under My Bed*. E. P. Dutton, 1987. A boy must lure out an alligator he knows is there.

————. *There's Something in My Attic*. Dial Books, 1988. When the city girl moves out to a farm, she's afraid every night of the nightmare lurking in her attic.

Polacco, Patricia. *Thunder Cake*. Philomel Books, 1990. The narrator relates how, when she was a child, her Russian grandmother Babushka helped her overcome her fear of thunderstorms by baking a cake before the storm came.

Russo, Marisabina. *Why Do Grown-Ups Have All the Fun?* Greenwillow Books, 1987. When Hannah is in bed unable to sleep, she imagines all the fun the grown-ups are having—doing all the things she herself likes to do.

Viorst, Judith. *Alexander & the Terrible, Horrible, No Good, Very Bad Day*. Macmillan, 1972. Alexander has a terrible day from beginning to end. He decides to move to Australia, but finally comes to the conclusion that some days are like that.

Wells, Rosemary. *Shy Charles*. Dial Books, 1988. Charles is so shy he trembles at the thought of meeting other children.

Whitney, Alma Marshak. *Just Awful*. Harper & Row, 1985. When he cuts his finger, James is afraid to go to the school nurse for fear of what she might do.

GROWING UP

Cooney, Nancy Evans. *The Blanket That Had to Go*. G. P. Putnam, 1981. Susie dreads leaving her blanket when kindergarten starts.

————. *Donald Says Thumbs Down*. G. P. Putnam, 1987. A preschool boy kicks his thumb-sucking habit when he's finally ready.

Keller, Holly. *Geraldine's Blanket*. Greenwillow Books, 1984. A young pig, not willing to give up her old security blanket, makes it into a dress for her new baby pig doll.

Robison, Deborah. *Bye-Bye, Old Buddy*. Clarion Books, 1983. Jenny doesn't know how to give up her worn-out, fuzzy baby blanket until she decides to mail it to a stranger picked from a phone book.

ILLNESS AND DEATH

Bunting, Eve. *The Wall*. Clarion Books, 1990. A boy and his father search the wall of the Vietnam Memorial to find the name of the boy's grandfather who was killed in the war.

Clifton, Lucille. *Everett Anderson's Goodbye*. Holt, Rinehart and Winston, 1985. His father has died, and a young boy goes through the five stages of grief. Each stage is simple and depicted on a single page.

Cohn, Janice. *I Had a Friend Named Peter: Talking to Children About the Death of a Friend*. William A. Morrow, 1987. Betsy's parents and teachers help her deal with her best friend's death in a car accident.

dePaola, Tomie. *Nana Upstairs & Nana Downstairs*. G. P. Putnam, 1973. As a grown-up, Tommy remembers the rituals of his visits to the house of his active grandmother shared with his bedridden 94-year-old great-grandmother.

Gaes, Tim and Adam. *My Book for Kids with Cansur*. Melius and Peterson, 1987. Jason's true story about his cancer surgery, chemotherapy, and the bone marrow tests he endured until his remission.

Hickman, Martha W. *Last Week My Brother Anthony Died*. Abingdon Press, 1984. Julie and her parents are trying to cope with the death of her 4-week-old brother.

Hogan, Bernice. *My Grandmother Died, but I Won't Forget Her*. Abingdon Press, 1983. A story about a young boy whose grandmother has just died and the loneliness he feels.

Jewell, Nancy. *Time for Uncle Joe*. Harper, 1981. The changing seasons bring back fond memories of Uncle Joe for a young girl.

Viorst, Judith. *The Tenth Good Thing About Barney*. Atheneum, 1971. To help him deal with his grief over his cat's death, a boy's mother suggests he think of ten good things to tell about the cat at its funeral.

Zolotow, Charlotte. *My Grandson Lew*. Harper & Row, 1974. Lew's grandfather died when he was quite small, but it turns out that Lew remembers him in vivid fragments while he and his mother talk about remembering.

MOVING

Aliki. *We Are Best Friends*. Greenwillow Books, 1982. The boy left behind when his friend moves finds a new boy.

Brandenberg, Franz. *Nice New Neighbors*. Scholastic, 1980. The six field mice children are rebuffed when they try to make friends in their new neighborhood.

Hickman, Martha W. *My Best Friend Moved Away*. Raintree/Steck-Vaughn, 1980. William and Jimmy are best friends, but William moves away, leaving Jimmy with all the familiar things except his best friend.

Keats, Ezra Jack. *The Trip*. Greenwillow Books, 1978. A move to a new neighborhood leaves Louie with no friends.

Komaiko, Leah. *Annie Bananie*. Harper & Row, 1987. The story of two friends who promised to be friends to the end, then one must move away.

Malone, Nola Langner. *A Home*. Bradbury Press, 1988. Moving into a new home is difficult for Molly.

O'Donnell, Elizabeth Lee. *Maggie Doesn't Want to Move*. Four Winds Press, 1987. Upset about moving away from his house, playground, and teacher, Simon claims his toddler sister is the one who's unhappy about the change.

Tsutsui, Yoriko. *Anna's Secret Friend*. Viking Press, 1987. When Anna, a little Japanese girl, moves to a new house, she receives flowers, a paper doll, and a letter from a mysterious person who wants to be friends.

NEW BABY—JEALOUSY

Alexander, Martha. *Nobody Asked Me If I Wanted a Baby Sister*. Dial Books, 1971. This story subtly teaches about brotherly love.

Caseley, Judith. *Silly Baby*. Greenwillow Books, 1988. Even though only child Lindsay tells mama "No, thank you," her mother has the new baby anyway.

Clifton, Lucille. *Everett Anderson's Nine Monthes Long*. Henry Holt, 1988. A small boy and his family await the birth of a new baby.

Ferguson, Alane. *That New Pet!* Lothrop, Lee & Shepard, 1986. Siam, the cat, is jealous of the new baby in the household.

Hoban, Russell. *A Baby Sister for Frances.* Harper & Row, 1964. Feeling unloved with the new baby in the house, the badger girl runs away under the dining room table.

Lindgren, Astrid. *I Want a Brother or Sister.* Farrar, Straus, & Giroux, 1988. Peter is jealous of his new baby sister until he starts to help care for her.

RUNNING AWAY—GETTING LOST

Carlson, Natalie Savage. *Runaway Marie Louise.* Scribners, 1977. Mongoose, who feels unloved after her mama gives her a spanking, takes her peanut butter and jellyfish sandwich and sets out to look for a new mama.

Cole, Brock. *No More Baths.* Farrar, Straus & Giroux, 1989. A dirty little girl runs away in disgust when her mother wants to give her a bath in the middle of the day.

Galbraith, Richard. *Reuben Runs Away.* Orchard Books, 1989. Fed up with Anna's careless treatment and lack of respect, her teddy bear Reuben runs away to the big city where he ends up in a secondhand shop, only to be bought and brought back home by Anna's grandfather.

Kent, Jack. *Joey Runs Away.* Prentice Hall, 1985. Kangaroo boy figures it's easier to leave home than clean his room.

Kraus, Robert. *Where Are You Going, Little Mouse?* William A. Morrow, 1986. When it starts to get dark, Little Mouse has second thoughts about running away from home.

Tafuri, Nancy. *Have You Seen My Duckling?* Penguin Books, 1986. A mother duck leads her ducklings around the pond in search of the missing duckling.

SCHOOL

Alexander, Martha. *Move Over, Twerp.* Dial Books, 1989. Now that Jeffrey is old enough to take the school bus, he has to figure out a way to keep the big kids from taking his seat every day.

Butler, Dorothy. *My Brown Bear Barney.* Greenwillow Books, 1988. A little girl takes her brown bear everywhere, and she expects to take it to school also.

Chapman, Carol. *Herbie's Troubles.* E. P. Dutton, 1981. Jimmy John, a class bully, only gets worse when Herbie tries being assertive, shoving, and punching back, as advised by three friends.

Howe, James. *The Day the Teacher Went Bananas.* E. P. Dutton, 1984. The class's new teacher is a gorilla!

————. *When You Go to Kindergarten.* Alfred A. Knopf, 1986. This story is a positive exposure to this childhood milestone, including riding a bus, behavior, fire drills, and other growing-up activities.

Kantrovitz, Mildred. *Willy Bear.* Parents Magazine Press, 1976. A little boy transfers his anxieties about starting school to his stuffed animal.

Oxenbury, Helen. *First Day of School.* Dial Books, 1983. A little girl clings to her mother as they arrive at preschool.

Rogers, Fred. *Going to Day Care.* G. P. Putnam, 1985. A nonfiction book depicting the experiences children will encounter in day care.

Stanek, Muriel. *Starting School.* Albert Whitman, 1981. A young boy prepares to enter school, including learning new skills and visiting the doctor and dentist. After the first day, he leaves with a new sense of independence.

Tyler, Linda Wagner. *Waiting for Mom.* Viking Press, 1987. After the 3:00 bell rings, a young hippo child keeps busy at school when mom is unexpectedly an hour late.

Weiss, Leathie. *My Teacher Sleeps in School.* Frederick Waine, 1984. Because Mrs. Marsh is always in her classroom before the students arrive and always stays after they leave, Mollie becomes convinced that her teacher has no home other than school.

Wolde, Gunilla. *Betsy's First Day at Nursery School.* Random House, 1976. Attending nursery school doesn't seem like a good idea to Betsy, but she goes to visit.

WORKING FAMILIES

Delton, Judy. *My Mother Lost Her Job Today.* Albert Whitman, 1980. Mother arrives home and announces to 6-year-old Barbara Anne that she has lost her job.

Parker, Nancy W. *My Mom Travels a Lot.* Warne, 1981. A picture book about a child who is cared for by her father while her mother travels.

Stecher, Miriam B. *Daddy and Ben Together.* Lothrop, Lee & Shepard, 1981. Ben and Daddy take care of each other when Mommy goes on a business trip. Things don't all go well.

Winning Picture Books

CALDECOTT AWARD BOOKS

Aardema, Verna. *Why Mosquitoes Buzz in People's Ears.* Dial Books, 1975. A cumulative African tale of the chain of events that begin when a mosquito tells a lie to an iguana.

Ackerman, Karen. *Song and Dance Man.* Alfred A. Knopf, 1988. The grandchildren describe how Grampa, once on the vaudeville stage, puts on his wonderful singing, dancing, and music- and magic-filled act for them in the attic when they visit.

de Regniers, Beatrice Schenk. *May I Bring a Friend?* Atheneum, 1964. Set in rhyme, a boy arrives with different zoo animals when invited to tea by the king and queen.

Emberley, Barbara. *Drummer Hoff.* Prentice Hall, 1967. A sequence story in rhyme depicting how the General, Major, Captain, Corporal, Private, and Drummer Hoff loaded and fired a cannon.

Hader, Berta. *The Big Snow.* Macmillan, 1949. When winter snows make it difficult for the woodland animals to find food, people in the stone house help the animals.

Hogrogian, Nonny. *One Fine Day.* Macmillan, 1971. A folktale of the fox who barters for milk to give to the old woman before she will sew his tail back on.

Keats, Jack Ezra. *The Snowy Day.* Viking Press, 1962. The story of a small boy enjoying a day in the snow, making tracks, and watching snow melt.

Udry, Janice May. *A Tree Is Nice.* Harper, 1956. A beautiful story about why a tree is a wonder of nature.

McCloskey, Robert. *Make Way for Ducklings.* Viking Press, 1941. The adventure of two mallard ducks looking for a place to raise their family of ducklings.

Mosel, Arlene. *The Funny Little Woman.* E. P. Dutton, 1972. The story of a little woman in old Japan who liked to make dumplings out of rice and laughed a lot.

Ness, Evaline. *Sam, Bangs and Moonshine.* Holt, 1966. When Samantha tells gullible Thomas a lie that endangers both his life and her cat's, she finally learns the hard way the differences between real and moonshine.

Sendak, Maurice. *Where the Wild Things Are.* Harper, 1963. Max is sent to bed without supper. He imagines a world of bulging-eyed, scary monsters where he is the king.

Tresselt, Alvin. *White Snow, Bright Snow.* Lothrop, Lee & Shepard, 1947. When it begins to look, feel, and smell like snow, everyone prepares for winter.

Van Allsburg, Chris. *The Polar Express*. Houghton Mifflin, 1985. On Christmas Eve a little boy takes a magical ride to the North Pole to receive a special gift from Santa.

Yolen, Jane. *Owl Moon*. Philomel Books, 1987. A small girl tells about a snowy winter night when she went owling in the woods with her father.

FANFARE

Barton, Byron. *I Want to Be an Astronaut*. Thomas Y. Crowell, 1988. A great space book for small children. There are only five short sentences.

de Regniers, Beatrice Schenk, ed. *Sing a Song of Popcorn: Every Child's Book of Poems*. Scholastic, 1988. Over 100 poems illustrated by nine Caldecott artists.

Ehlert, Lois. *Color Zoo*. Harper & Row, 1989. There are exotic animals hiding in the shapes and cutouts that pile up and rearrange on each succeeding page, so for example, a tiger becomes a mouse.

Henkes, Kevin. *Jessica*. Greenwillow Books, 1989. A shy preschooler insists that her friend Jessica is not imaginary and, in the end, she's absolutely correct.

Hoban, Tana. *Exactly the Opposite*. Greenwillow Books, 1990. A concept book that looks at opposites.

Lyon, George Ella. *Come a Tide*. Orchard Books, 1990. This story gives a little girl's account of her family coping with a deluge and digging out.

Martin, Bill, Jr., and John Archambault. *Chicka Chicka Boom Boom*. Simon & Schuster, 1989. A rhythmical alphabet book where letters climb to the top of a coconut tree, overload it, and all fall down.

Rosen, Michael and Margaret K. *We're Going on a Bear Hunt*. McElderry Books, 1989. A retelling of the favorite tale about a family of bear hunters who go through many obstacles before encountering the bear.

Schwartz, David. *If You Made a Million*. Lothrop, Lee & Shepard, 1989. A sequel to *How Much Is a Million*.

Van Laan, Nancy. *Possum Come A'Knockin*. Dragonfly Books, Alfred A. Knopf, 1990. Predictable text told in mountain dialect about a young boy who is tricked by a possum.

BEST BOOKS—SCHOOL LIBRARY JOURNAL

Aardema, Verna. *Borreguita and the Coyote*. Alfred A. Knopf, 1991. Hungry Coyote thinks that Borreguita, the little lamb, would make a tasty meal, but every time he meets her, she manages to outsmart him, leaving him not only hungry but humiliated as well.

Bunting, Eve. *The Wednesday Surprise*. Clarion Books, 1989. A loving story about a proud granddaughter and her successful efforts to teach her grandmother to read.

Hoffman, Mary. *Amazing Grace*. Dial Books, 1991. Hurt and angry when a classmate tells her she can't be Peter Pan in the class play because she's black and a girl, Grace becomes determined to prove herself.

Johnson, Angela. *Tell Me a Story*. Orchard Books, 1991. A black preschooler becomes the storyteller in repeating the family legends her mother told her.

Marshall, James. *The Three Little Pigs*. Dial Books, 1989. While sticking closely to the story, Marshall adds hilarious touches into the dialogue and illustrations.

Polacco, Patricia. *Just Plain Fancy*. Bantam, 1991. While tending their chickens, two Amish girls happen upon an unusual egg and secretly hatch and raise a remarkable peacock chick.

Shaw, Nancy. *Sheep in a Shop.* Houghton Mifflin, 1991. This story in rhyme records the adventures and misadventures of five sheep. Young readers enjoy the tales of their familiar friends.

Tafuri, Nancy. *Follow Me!* Greenwillow Books, 1991. A baby seal leaves his mother's side and follows the lead of a scampering red crab that catches his eye.

Weiss, Nicki. *Where Does the Brown Bear Go?* Greenwillow Books, 1989. Sleepy animals are headed to the quilted safety of a child's bed.

Whipple, Laura. *Animals, Animals.* Philomel Books, 1989. A compendium of poems illustrated by Eric Carle take young children on a colorful swing through the animal kingdom.

EDITOR'S CHOICE

Aardema, Verna. *Traveling to Tondo.* Alfred A. Knopf, 1991. A funny Central African folktale in which a cat gathers his companions, one by one, to join him on his journey to Tondo, where his bride awaits.

Cole, Joanna. *My Puppy Is Born.* Morrow, 1991. Color photographs illustrate the birth and early life of a Norfolk Terrier puppy.

Ehlert, Lois. *Eating the Alphabet.* Harcourt Brace Jovanovich, 1989. A colorful book of fruits and vegetables from A to Z.

Fleming, Denise. *In the Tall, Tall Grass.* Henry Holt, 1991. Rhymed text describes the sights and sounds of a fuzzy caterpillar on a lunchtime excursion through the grass from lunchtime until nightfall.

Garland, Michael. *My Cousin Katie.* Harper/Crowell, 1989. The story tells what it's like on the farm where Katie works and plays.

Hennessy, B. G. *The Missing Tarts.* Viking Press, 1989. The Queen of Hearts is joined by other nursery rhyme characters in the search for her stolen strawberry tarts.

Lear, Edward. *The Owl and the Pussycat.* G. P. Putnam, 1991. This favorite poem is set in lush Caribbean landscape. A beautiful mix of realism and fantasy.

Levine, Evan. *Not the Piano, Mrs. Medley!* Schindler, 1991. Max is frustrated because his grandmother, Mrs. Medley won't go to the beach unless she has her chair, umbrella, bongo drums, and other inappropriate items.

Lindbergh, Reeve. *The Day the Goose Got Loose.* Dial Books, 1990. In this rollicking rhyme, the goose opens his barnyard pen and all the different farm animals and the farm family react in their own individual style.

Pomerantz, Charlotte. *The Chalk Doll.* Harper/Lippincott, 1989. A mother's stories of her Jamaican childhood entertain her daughter at bedtime.

Ringgold, Faith. *Tar Beach.* Crown, 1991. A young girl dreams of flying away from her home, over the Brooklyn Bridge, to a place of equality.

Folk and Fairy Tales

Aesop, adapted by Janet Stevens. *The Tortoise and the Hare: An Aesop Fable.* Holiday House, 1984. A classic story, modernized with running shorts and sneakers in the pictures, although the outcome remains the same.

Aardema, Verna. *Bringing the Rain to Kapiti Plain.* Dial Books, 1981. Cumulative rhyming African folktale about how young Kipat brings rain to the dry Kapiti plain by shooting an arrow into the clouds.

Benchley, Nathaniel. *Red Fox and His Canoe.* Harper & Row, 1984. A tale about an Indian boy who takes too many animals on his canoe and ends with a surprise.

Bennett, Jill. *Teeny Tiny*. G. P. Putnam, 1986. "Give me my bone!" the ghostly voice makes demands of the teeny tiny woman in her teeny tiny bed, in her teeny tiny house, in her teeny tiny village.

Berson, Harold. *Kassim's Shoes*. Crown, 1977. Kassim's old shoes cause trouble when he tries to throw them away and wear his new ones. This is a humorous adaptation of a Moroccan folktale.

Bowden, Joan Chase. *The Bean Boy*. Macmillan, 1979. A greedy fox increases his fortune from bee to boy.

Brett, Jan. *Goldilocks and the Three Bears*. G. P. Putnam, 1987. Classic story richly detailed in a new and creative way with bear-filled borders.

———. *The Mitten*. G. P. Putnam, 1989. A version of a Ukranian folktale about a boy's lost mitten and the animals that find it.

Brown, Marcia. *Stone Soup*. Atheneum, 1986. A classic story about three soldiers on their way home from wars who manage to get a good meal from some very careful French peasants.

Cauley, Lorinda Bryan. *Goldilocks and the Three Bears*. G. P. Putnam, 1981. The traditional story with marvelous illustrations.

Cook, Scott. *The Gingerbread Boy*. Alfred A. Knopf, 1987. The original dough boy runs away from the little old woman who made him and a group of other chasers, until Fox comes along.

dePaola, Tomie. *The Comic Adventures of Old Mother Hubbard and Her Dog*. Harcourt Brace Jovanovich, 1981. A rendition of the nursery rhyme.

de Regniers, Beatrice Schenk. *Red Riding Hood*. Aladdin Books, 1977. This is a very funny version of a favorite story retold in verse.

Galdone, Joanna. *The Little Girl and the Big Bear*. Houghton Mifflin, 1980. After losing her way in the forest and being captured as a bear's servant, a little girl devises a plan for her escape back to her grandparents.

Galdone, Paul. *The Gingerbread Boy*. Clarion Books, 1979. The talking cookie escapes only to meet his end in the jaws of a fox.

———. *Henny Penny*. Clarion Books, 1979. The story of the simple hen who thinks the sky is falling in when struck on the head by an acorn.

———. *The Magic Porridge Pot*. Clarion Books, 1979. The porridge overflows through the whole village and won't stop.

———. *The Three Bears*. Clarion Books, 1979. Goldilocks strikes again in this favorite tale.

———. *The Three Billy Goats Gruff*. Clarion Books, 1979. The story of the three goats and the troll.

———. *The Three Little Pigs*. Clarion Books, 1979. The tale of huffing and puffing leading to the cooking pot.

Grimm, Jakob. *The Bremen Town Musicians,* retold by Anthea Bell. Picture Book Studios, 1988. To save themselves, four old animals band together and head through the woods for Bremen, when they come upon a house inhabited by robbers.

———. *Little Red Cap,* trans. by Elizabeth D. Crawford. William A. Morrow, 1983. A delicately illustrated version of the tale of Red Riding Hood.

———. *Little Red Riding Hood,* retold by Trina Schart Hyman. Holiday House, 1983. A traditional version of the wolf in Granny's clothing.

Heyer, Marilee. *The Weaving of a Dream*. Penguin Books, 1989. This is a retelling of a traditional Chinese tale. When the beautiful tapestry woven by a poor woman is stolen by fairies, her three sons set out on a magical journey to get it back.

McGovern, Ann. *Stone Soup*. Scholastic, 1986. An easy-to-read version about the little old lady and the hungry young man.

Parkinson, Kathy. *The Enormous Turnip*. Albert Whitman, 1986. A turnip grew so big, grandfather needs help pulling it from the garden. For each tug, another helper is added to the lineup, including the whole family, a dog, a cat, and a mouse.

Romanova, Natalia. *Once There Was a Tree*. Dial Books, 1989. A Russian tale about a tree stump and all the animals that lived in and near it.

Stevens, Janet. *Goldilocks and the Three Bears*. Holiday House, 1986. An excellent version of the familiar story.

Tolstoi, Alexei. *The Great Big Enormous Turnip*. Heinemann, 1968. A tale of Russian folklore in which everyone on the farm must work together to pull up the turnip.

Zemach, Margot. *The Three Little Pigs: An Old Story*. Farrar, Straus & Giroux, 1988. An affectionately illustrated version of the familiar story.

Books About Holidays and Special Occasions

BIRTHDAYS

Awdry, The Rev. W. *Happy Birthday, Thomas*. Random House, 1990. Thomas is worried that all his friends have forgotten him on his birthday.

Carle, Eric. *The Secret Birthday Message*. Thomas Y. Crowell, 1972. Tim receives a secret message with rebus shape clues that lead him on a treasure hunt to find his birthday present—a puppy.

Flack, Marjorie. *Ask Mr. Bear*. Macmillan, 1932. Animals advise a young boy on his mother's birthday present.

Hiller, Catherine. *Abracatabby*. Coward, 1981. To stop his friends' teasing, Adam wishes his magical cat to show its tricks at Adam's birthday party.

Keats, Ezra Jack. *A Letter to Amy*. Harper & Row, 1968. Peter worries that his friend Amy won't come to his birthday party.

Moskin, Marietta. *Rosie's Birthday Present*. Atheneum, 1981. Starting with a golden button she finds outside, Rosie trades treasures to acquire the perfect present for her mother.

Russo, Marisabina. *Only Six More Days*. Greenwillow Books, 1986. Ben starts the daily countdown to his birthday and is teased by his sister until she realizes there are only 47 days left to hers.

Willard, Nancy. *Papa's Panda*. Harcourt Brace Jovanovich, 1979. On James' birthday, his father spins a yarn about what would happen if a live panda came to visit, culminating in a present of a stuffed panda.

CHINESE NEW YEAR

Wallace, Ian. *Chin Chiang and the Dragon Dance*. Atheneum, 1984. Afraid his clumsy dancing will anger the Great Dragon, shame his grandfather, and bring bad fortune to his community, Chin Chiang runs off before the Chinese New Year's parade begins.

CHRISTMAS

Balian, Lorna. *Bah! Humbug!* Abingdon Press, 1977. A faithful little girl and her skeptical brother aim to find out if Santa is real when they set a trap in the living room.

Brown, Margaret Wise. *The Steamroller*. Walker, 1974. Daisy's unique Christmas present runs amok and squashes everything and everybody flat.

Collington, Peter. *On Christmas Eve*. Alfred A. Knopf, 1990. How does Santa deal with houses without chimneys? Tiny fairies appear and light the way for Santa. The sleeping girl almost wakes up.

Day, Alexandra. *Carl's Christmas*. Farrar, Straus & Giroux, 1990. The beautifully illustrated wordless story about Carl, a dog, and the baby he watches.

Haywood, Carolyn. *A Christmas Fantasy*. William A. Knopf, 1972. The story uncovers how Santa as a boy tumbled down chimneys and got into the present business.

Hoban, Lillian. *Arthur's Christmas Cookies*. Harper & Row, 1972. Chimp botches up the recipe when he mistakes salt for sugar.

Johnston, Johanna and Tony. *Mole and Troll Trim the Tree*. G. P. Putnam, 1989. Two best friends get into a fight over the right way to decorate a Christmas tree.

Keller, Holly. *A Bear for Christmas*. Greenwillow Books, 1986. When his mother hides Joey's present, he finds it, sneaks a peek, and accidently damages it.

McCully, Emily Arnold. *The Christmas Gift*. Harper & Row, 1988. A wordless celebration of a close-knit mouse family's holiday, from baking cookies and trimming the tree to the trauma of breaking a favorite present.

Merriam, Eve. *The Christmas Box*. William A. Morrow, 1985. On Christmas morning, a large family of six children and five adults find only a very long, thin box, inside of which is, connected together, one present per person.

Prelutsky, Jack. *It's Christmas*. Greenwillow Books, 1981. Twelve holiday poems from a child's point of view.

Thayer, Jane. *The Puppy Who Wanted a Boy*. William A. Morrow, 1986. Out on the street to find a boy for Christmas, shaggy mutt Petey comes upon the Home for Boys where everyone needs him.

Wells, Rosemary. *Max's Christmas*. Dial Books, 1986. Rabbit Max peeks when Santa comes, in spite of his sister Ruby's warning not to.

Ziefert, Harriet. *A New Coat for Anna*. Alfred A. Knopf, 1986. With the war just ended, Anna's mother has no money to buy her a promised coat, but instead barters her treasures in return for services to a sheep farmer, spinner, weaver, and tailor, all of whom help provide a beautiful red wool coat for Christmas. Based on a true story.

EASTER

Friedrich, Priscilla and Otto Friedrich. *The Easter Bunny That Overslept*. Macmillan, 1987. Attempting late deliveries on various holidays, the rabbit finds no one wants eggs until he meets up with Santa.

Wells, Rosemary. *Max's Chocolate Chicken*. Dial Books, 1989. Max spots a chocolate chicken, and the battle for the feast is on between him and his bossy sister, Ruby.

FOURTH OF JULY

Zion, Gene. *The Summer Snowman*. Harper, 1955. The story of a little boy and the winter snowman he takes from the freezer months later.

GROUNDHOG DAY

Johnson, Crockett. *Will Spring Be Early? or Will Spring Be Late?* Thomas Y. Crowell, 1959. A stray plastic flower causes Groundhog to predict spring's arrival in February.

Kroll, Steven. *It's Groundhog Day*. Holiday House, 1987. Roland Raccoon kidnaps Godfrey Groundhog so that spring won't be early.

HALLOWEEN

Adams, Adrienne. *A Woggle of Witches.* Scribner's, 1971. A spooky Halloween story children will enjoy.

Ahlberg, Janet and Allen Ahlberg. *Funnybones.* Greenwillow Books, 1980. One dark night, a big and little skeleton take their dog skeleton for a walk through town and look for someone to frighten.

Asch, Frank. *Popcorn.* Parents Magazine Press, 1979. Bear gets a houseful when he pops too much at his Halloween party.

Bunting, Eve. *Scary, Scary Halloween.* Clarion Books, 1986. A story in rhyme showing trick-or-treaters in costume, witnessed by a cat and her kittens.

Kroll, Steven. *The Candy Witch.* Holiday House, 1979. When young Maggie the Witch's good deeds go unnoticed by her family, she turns to Halloween mischief to make everyone notice her.

Miller, Edna. *Mousekin's Golden Home.* Prentice Hall, 1964. A mouse selects a discarded Halloween pumpkin for winter refuge.

Prelutsky, Jack. *It's Halloween.* Greenwillow Books, 1977. These poems encompass typical trick-or-treat experiences.

Titherington, Jeanne. *Pumpkin, Pumpkin.* Greenwillow Books, 1986. The simple story of the seed Jamie planted.

HANUKKAH

Adler, David. *Malke's Secret Recipe.* Kar-ben Copies, 1989. In the foolish town of Chelm, Berel the shoemaker attempts to duplicate the secret recipe of making potato pancakes, but his wife's interference makes his plan go awry.

Kimmel, Eric. *Hershel and the Hanukkah Goblins.* Holiday House, 1989. Hershel looks forward to celebrating Hanukkah in the local village. When he arrives he finds no candles and no latkes. The villagers are frightened of the local goblins that haunt the old synagogue. Hershel brings Hanukkah back to the village by outwitting the goblins.

Manushkin, Fran. *Latkes and Applesauce: A Hanukkah Story.* Scholastic, 1990. A blizzard has made it impossible to dig potatoes and gather apples for the traditional Hanukkah dinner. Supplies are running low; nevertheless, the poor family takes in a stray cat and dog. On the eighth night, a miracle occurs.

Zalben, Jane Breskin. *Beni's First Chanukah.* Henry Holt, 1988. The symbols of the holiday are mentioned without information overload. A young bear helps his mother prepare latkes, plays "Spin the Dreidel," and recites a prayer with his father.

MOTHER'S DAY

Bunting, Eve. *The Mother's Day Mice.* Clarion Books, 1986. Three young mice brave the dangers of the field to bring a strawberry, a fluff ball, and a song home to their mother for her Mother's Day gifts.

NEW YEAR'S DAY

Modell, Frank. *Goodbye Old Year, Hello New Year.* Greenwillow Books, 1984. On New Year's Eve, pals Marvin and Milton set their alarm clocks for midnight but oversleep till 5:30 A.M. when they go outside with pots and pans to welcome in the dawn.

PASSOVER

Zalben, Jane Breskin. *Happy Passover, Rosie*. Henry Holt, 1990. This Passover, Rosie's the youngest, so she has the most important job of all. She has lots to do before the celebration.

ST. PATRICK'S DAY

Schertle, Alice. *Jeremy Bean's St. Patrick's Day*. Lothrop, Lee & Shepard, 1987. All his classmates tease him when Jeremy Bean forgets to wear green on March 17, until his principal helps out.

Shute, Linda. *Clever Tom and the Leprechaun*. Lothrop, Lee & Shepard, 1988. Tom ties a red garter around the boliarin bush to mark the place where a leprechaun claims his gold is buried, runs off for a spade, and returns to find a garter on every bush in sight.

THANKSGIVING

Johnston, Johanna. *Speak Up, Edie*. G. P. Putnam, 1974. Edie is confident about her big part in the class Thanksgiving play until she faces the audience.

Prelutsky, Jack. *It's Thanksgiving*. Greenwillow Books, 1982. This is a light-hearted book of poems.

Schatell, Brian. *Farmer Goff and His Turkey Sam*. Harper & Row, 1982. A pie-loving prize turkey "pigs out" at the County Fair.

Sharmat, Marjorie Weinman. *One Terrific Thanksgiving*. Holiday House, 1985. Irving Morris Bear learns that Thanksgiving means more than eating good food.

Ziefert, Harriet. *What Is Thanksgiving?* Harper Children's Books, 1992. Little mouse learns about Thanksgiving from his mother. The book explains the first Thanksgiving in simple terms. Little mouse also learns how his family celebrates the holiday.

VALENTINE'S DAY

Bunting, Eve. *The Valentine Bears*. Clarion Books, 1984. Mrs. Bear sets her alarm clock for February 14 so she and Mr. Bear can share their first Valentine's Day ever.

Carlson, Nancy. *The Mysterious Valentine*. Puffin Books, 1987. When she receives a valentine from a secret admirer, Louanne Pig tries to find out who sent it.

Hoban, Lillian. *Arthur's Great Big Valentine*. Harper & Row, 1989. Until he figures out how to make up with his ex-best friend Norman, Chimp Arthur is friendless, reduced to having snowball fights with himself on Valentine's Day.

Modell, Frank. *One Zillion Valentines*. Greenwillow Books, 1981. Marvin and Milton make Valentines for everyone in the neighborhood and more to spare.

Prelutsky, Jack. *It's Valentine's Day*. Greenwillow Books, 1983. Fourteen poems for all aspects of the day.

All-Time Favorite Books

Bemelmans, Ludwig. *Madeline*. Viking Press, 1939. This is the story about the 12 little girls, including the heroine, Madeline, who attend school in Paris. Madeline gets appendicitis and needs an operation.

Bridwell, Norman. *Clifford, The Big Red Dog*. Scholastic, 1985. The adventures of a little girl and the gentle giant dog named Clifford.

Brown, Margaret Wise. *Goodnight, Moon*. Harper & Row, 1947. Little rabbit says goodnight to all the familiar things in his room and outside his window before going to sleep.

────. *The Runaway Bunny.* Harper & Row, 1977. A comforting story of a bunny's imaginary game of hide and seek and the loving mother who finds him every time.

Burton, Virginia Lee. *Mike Mulligan and His Steam Shovel.* Houghton Mifflin, 1939. Together Mike and his mighty machine dig a new Town Hall cellar in only one day.

Ets, Marie Hall. *In the Forest.* Viking Penquin, 1944. A little boy leads a grand parade of talking animals through the forest before the spell of his daydream brings him safely to his father.

Flack, Marjorie. *Ask Mr. Bear.* Aladdin Books, 1986. Danny searches for the perfect present for his mother and learns the best gift of all.

────. *The Story About Ping.* Viking Press, 1933. The classic about a Yangtze River duckling who hides to avoid a spank from the master of his boat.

Freeman, Don. *A Pocket for Corduroy.* Viking Press, 1978. Lisa and Corduroy accompany Lisa's mother to the laundromat, when Corduroy has an adventure leading him to the realization that he needs a pocket.

Hutchins, Pat. *Rosie's Walk.* Macmillan, 1971. Rosie the hen goes for a walk around the barnyard and unknowingly outwits the fox. She innocently leads him to one disaster after another.

Johnson, Crockett. *Harold and the Purple Crayon.* Harper & Row, 1955. Harold goes for a walk in the moonlight and draws adventures along the way with his purple crayon.

Keats, Ezra Jack. *Goggles.* Macmillan, 1987. Peter and his friend, Archie, find motorcycle goggles. Big boys try to take them away.

────. *Jennie's Hat.* Harper & Row, 1985. Jennie's new hat is disappointingly plain, until her bird friends help transform it into a hat she could only wish for.

────. *Pet Show.* Macmillan, 1972. When Archie can't find the neighborhood stray cat in time, he brings a jar for his entry in the pet contest.

────. *Whistle for Willie.* Viking Press, 1964. Peter yearns to be able to whistle so that he can call his dachshund Willie.

Krauss, Ruth. *A Hole Is to Dig.* Harper & Row, 1952. This book is a first book of childlike "definitions."

McCloskey, Robert. *Blueberries for Sal.* Viking Press, 1948. Sal and her mother, out blueberry picking, get all mixed up with Bear and his mother on Blueberry Hill.

Piper, Watty. *The Little Engine That Could.* Platt & Munk, 1961. The Little Blue Engine uses positive thinking to pull a load up a mountain.

Potter, Beatrix. *The Tale of Peter Rabbit.* Warne, 1902, 1987. A naughty rabbit is trapped in Mr. McGregor's garden.

Rey, H. A. *Curious George.* Houghton Mifflin, 1941. This is an introduction to George, the trouble-making monkey. George gets into trouble with the fire department and a balloon man, in this first of the series.

Sawyer, Ruth. *Journey Cake, Ho!* Penguin Books, 1978. This version of a mountain folktale tells how Johnny chased the Journey Cake home and brought all the lost animals with him.

Seuss, Dr. *The Cat in the Hat.* Random House, 1966. When the cat visits two children on a rainy day, trouble follows.

Udry, Janice May. *What Mary Jo Shared.* Albert Whitman, 1966. A shy little girl thinks of the perfect thing to share for show-and-tell—her father.

Waber, Bernard. *Ira Sleeps Over.* Houghton Mifflin, 1972. When Ira is invited to spend the night with best friend Reggie, he debates whether or not to take his teddy bear along.

Williams, Margery. *The Velveteen Rabbit*. Doubleday, 1926, 1958. The story of the rabbit who stuck by a boy even through illness. A magic fairy turns the Velveteen Rabbit real and gives him a home with other rabbits.

Zion, Gene. *Harry, the Dirty Dog*. Harper & Row, 1976. Harry hated baths so much he buried the scrubbing brush and ran away from home.

Zolotow, Charlotte. *William's Doll*. Harper & Row, 1972. A boy wants his own baby doll, much to his father's chagrin. William's wise grandma comes to his rescue.

More Picture Books to Enjoy

Asch, Frank. *Bear's Bargain*. Simon & Schuster, 1985. Bear teaches Bird how to be big in return for Bird teaching Bear how to fly. The two friends cooperate creatively.

Bauman, A. F. *Guess Where You're Going, Guess What You'll Do*. Houghton Mifflin, 1989. A variety of situations are described, and children can guess the resulting destination and activities on the following page.

Burke, Rose. *Amelia's Fantastic Flight*. Henry Holt, 1992. A young girl builds her own airplane and flies around the world.

Cazet, Denys. *I'm Not Sleepy*. Orchard Books, 1992. Dad tells a bedtime story to Alex with humorous results.

Crews, Donald. *Freight Train*. Greenwillow Books, 1978. A freight train hurtles across the pages day and night with speed and color.

Fox, Mem. *Night Noises*. Gulliver/Harcourt, 1989. Old Lily Laceby dozes by the fire with her faithful dog Butch Aggie at her feet as strange night noises provide a surprise awakening.

Gauch, Patricia Lee. *Dance, Tanya*. Philomel Books, 1989. Tanya loves to dance, but she's too little for lessons. Instead, she practices a wonderful sad swan at home.

Ginsburg, Mirra. *Asleep, Asleep*. Greenwillow Books, 1992. Everything is asleep except for the wind and one wakeful child.

Hurd, Edith Thacher. *I Dance in My Red Pajamas*. Harper & Row, 1982. A little girl remembers all the reasons why she loves visiting her grandparents.

Long, Earlene. *Gone Fishing*. Houghton Mifflin, 1983. A boy and his dad get up before dawn, see all sorts of creatures on their expedition, catch two fish, and have a good time.

Morris, Ann. *Bread, Bread, Bread*. Lothrop, Lee & Shepard, 1989. The story celebrates the many different kinds of bread and how it may be enjoyed.

———. *Hats, Hats, Hats*. Lothrop, Lee & Shepard, 1989. This book introduces a variety of hats.

Nightingale, S. *A Giraffe on the Moon*. Harcourt Brace Jovanovich, 1991. A sleeping child is surrounded with books and toys that have been transformed in a dream world of amusing surprises.

Pizer, Abigail. *It's a Perfect Day*. J. B. Lippincott, 1992. A colorful rebus story in simple, repetitive text. Barnyard friends enjoy a perfect day moving and making their sounds.

Quinlan, Patricia. *Anna's Red Sled*. Annick Press, 1989. A little girl and her mother enjoy an old, small red sled.

Rylant, Cynthia. *The Relatives Came*. Bradbury Press, 1985. One summer, a whole group of relatives gets up before dawn to come for a visit, creating chaos, commotion and confusion.

Sis, Peter. *Going Up!* Greenwillow Books, 1989. As the elevator moves up from the first floor to the twelfth, various people dressed in different colored costumes get in, all bound for a birthday surprise on the twelfth floor.

Stanovich, Betty Jo. *Big Boy, Little Boy*. Lothrop, Lee & Shepard, 1984. A boy and his grandmother share an afternoon together.

Ward, Cindy. *Cookie's Week*. Putnam & Grosset, 1988. Cookie, a mischievous cat, creates a household disaster each day of the week, leaving children to imagine what Cookie will do on Sunday.

Williams, Barbara. *Kevin's Grandma*. E. P. Dutton, 1975. Kevin tells how his grandma is different: she practices yoga and judo and brings Kevin peanut butter soup on her Honda, and she even sky dives.

Williams, Vera. *Three Days on a River in a Red Canoe*. Greenwillow Books, 1981. Mom, Aunt Rosie and two children make a three-day camping trip by canoe.

Wolkstein, Diane. *Little Mouse's Painting*. William A. Morrow, 1992. Little Mouse has painted a picture, but no one knows what she has painted.

Additional Books for Young Children

WORDLESS BOOKS

Anno, Mitsumasa. *Anno's Journey*. Philomel Books, 1978. One man in a small boat arrives at an unknown shore. The shore gives way to meadows, forest, farmlands, and a European city.

———. *Topsy-Turvies: Pictures to Stretch the Imagination*. John Weatherhill, 1970. A story of humor, imagination, and optical illusions.

Aruego, Jose. *Look What I Can Do*. Scribner's, 1971. The story of two caribous who get carried away trying to outdo each other and almost come to a sad end.

Bang, Molly. *The Gray Lady and the Strawberry Snatcher*. Four Winds Press, 1980. This eerie, imaginative adventure involves a basket of strawberries, a skateboard, and more.

Barton, Byron. *Where's Al?* Seabury Press, 1972. Al, a puppy, chases after a stick and gets lost in a big city. His young owner worries about Al and vows to find him.

Carle, Eric. *Do You Want to Be My Friend?* Harper, 1971. A little mouse wants someone to play with. He follows a lot of tails before finding the right friend.

———. *I See a Song*. Thomas Y. Crowell, 1973. Children can create their own music or stories to go with the colorful pictures.

Collington, Peter. *The Angel and the Soldier Boy*. Alfred A. Knopf, 1987. After a pirate story, a little girl falls asleep with some little toys on her pillow. The soldier boy comes alive and tries to defend the child's piggy bank from the pirate. The angel rescues him.

Crews, Donald. *Truck*. Greenwillow Books, 1980. A bright red tractor trailer truck pushes its way across the United States to deliver a cargo of tricycles.

Day, Alexandra. *Good Dog, Carl*. Simon & Schuster, 1985. Carl, a dog, is responsible for looking after the baby, and together they share many adventures. Other titles include *Carl Goes Shopping*, and *Carl's Afternoon in the Park*.

dePaola, Tomie. *Flicks*. Harcourt Brace Jovanovich, 1979. Five silent movie situations and dilemmas are presented, each with a surprise ending.

———. *Pancakes for Breakfast*. Harcourt Brace Jovanovich, 1978. A little old lady attempts to have pancakes for breakfast but her pets interfere.

Goodall, John. *Paddy's New Hat*. Atheneum, 1980. Paddy, a lovable, and accident-prone pig, is led into a series of adventures when he purchases a straw hat that is blown off by the wind.

————. *The Surprise Picnic.* Atheneum, 1977. Cat and her kittens explore a small island and are surprised when their picnic lunch disappears. One surprise leads to another.

Hutchins, Pat. *Changes, Changes.* Macmillan, 1971. The story shows the transformation of two figures, a man and a woman, and brightly colored blocks that turn into a boat, a wagon, eventually even into a house.

Krahn, Fernando. *The Creepy Thing.* Houghton Mifflin, 1982. A little boy catches something strange on a fishing trip. When it escapes, the boy begins a search to find it.

————. *Here Comes Alex Pumpernickel!* Little, Brown, 1981. Little Alex causes a flood while trying to stop a leak, faces a fly that refuses to be swatted, and deals with other sticky situations.

————. *The Secret in the Dungeon.* Houghton Mifflin, 1983. A little girl on a sightseeing tour wanders off and discovers a surprising secret in the dungeon.

Mayer, Mercer. *Frog Goes to Dinner.* Dial Books, 1974. Frog can't resist the temptation to stow away in an empty pocket when the family goes to a fancy restaurant for dinner.

————. *Frog Where Are You?* Dial Books, 1980. A boy and a dog search for their missing frog friend.

McCully, Emily Arnold. *Picnic.* Harper & Row, 1984. It's a perfect summer day, so the mouse family sets off in a red pickup truck to have a picnic by the lake.

Ormerod, Jan. *Moonlight.* Lothrop, Lee & Shepard, 1982. The story shows a family retiring on a typical day.

Turk, Hanne. *Max Packs.* Alphabet Press, 1984. Max, a mouse, has a lot to pack in his pink suitcase. What he eventually brings on his trip is quite different.

————. *Snapshot Max.* Alphabet Press, 1984. Max, a mouse, readies himself to take some vacation snapshots.

————. *A Surprise for Max.* Alphabet Press, 1982. Max, a mouse, opens a surprise gift that he loves!

Turkle, Brinton. *Deep in the Forest.* E. P. Dutton, 1976. Three bears visit a forest cabin after a human mama, papa, and young girl leave the house.

Ueno, Noriko. *Elephant Buttons.* Harper & Row, 1973. Out from under the buttons on the elephant's belly springs a buttoned horse who produces a lion, then a seal, monkey, duck, and mouse.

Winter, Paula. *The Bear and the Fly.* Crown, 1976. A bear tries to catch a fly with silly and disastrous results.

POETRY—ANTHOLOGIES

Cole, Joanna. *A New Treasury of Children's Poetry: Old Favorites and New Discoveries.* Doubleday, 1984. Over 200 poems, one per page, sorted into nine general areas.

dePaola, Tomie. *Tomie dePaola's Book of Poems.* G. P. Putnam, 1988. A compilation dealing with weather, hiding places, games, Halloween, siblings, old age, animals, and seasons.

Hopkins, Lee Bennett. *More Surprises.* Harper & Row, 1987. Short, snappy poems about various topics are included in the book.

————. *Side by Side: Poems to Read Together.* Simon & Schuster, 1988. Old and new poems are included in this book.

Prelutsky, Jack. *Read-Aloud Rhymes for the Very Young.* Alfred A. Knopf, 1986. An assortment of more than 200 short poems, with an oversized format.

Whipple, Laura. *Eric Carle's Animals, Animals.* Philomel Books, 1989. A poetry and picture book of animals that swim, creep, fly, and leap.

POETRY—SINGLE AUTHOR

Carlstrom, Nancy White. *It's About Time, Jesse Bear.* Macmillan, 1990. More antics of Jesse Bear are written in short verse.

Greenfield, Eloise. *Honey, I Love and Other Love Poems.* Crowell/HarperCollins, 1978. A collection of short poems about emotions and ordinary childhood experiences. The illustrations are appealing.

Lobel, Arnold. *Whiskers & Rhymes.* Greenwillow Books, 1985. Bouncy original nursery rhymes are included in this book of poems.

Merriam, Eve. *You Be Good & I'll Be Night: Jump-on-the-Bed Poems.* William A. Morrow, 1988. More than 24 simple, nonsense-filled rhymes are included.

Prelutsky, Jack. *Ride a Purple Pelican.* Greenwillow Books, 1986. Poems filled with people and animals from all over the United States and Canada are included.

Rossetti, Christina. *Color.* HarperCollins, 1992. An introduction to colors and poetry for very young children.

Silverstein, Shel. *Where the Sidewalk Ends.* Harper & Row, 1974. Children will enjoy the nonsense verses and humorous poetry.

Smith, William Jay. *Laughing Time: Nonsense Poems.* Delacorte, 1980. More than 100 entertaining and silly poems will delight and entertain children.

MOTHER GOOSE

The Glorious Mother Goose, compiled by Cooper Edens. Atheneum, 1988. Over 40 of the best-known nursery rhymes are included.

Mother Goose: A Collection of Classic Nursery Rhymes, compiled by Michael Hague. Holt, 1984. This book is in picture book format with one large painting per rhyme.

The Mother Goose Treasury, compiled by Raymond Briggs. Dell, 1986. This version is a huge classic collection of over 400 rhymes taken from Iona and Peter Opie's compilations.

The Real Mother Goose. Rand, 1916. This oversized collection of more than 200 nursery rhymes has the original illustrations.

Richard Scarry's Best Mother Goose Ever, compiled by Richard Scarry. Western, 1970. This version includes large double-page picture spreads for each of 50 rhymes.

Tail Feathers from Mother Goose: The Opie Rhyme Book, compiled by Iona and Peter Opie. Little, Brown, 1988. These rhymes include a selective compilation of over 60 mostly lesser-known rhymes and songs.

Tomie dePaola's Mother Goose, compiled by Tomie dePaola. G. P. Putnam, 1985. Almost 200 rhymes with large, cheerful paintings are included.

HISTORICAL BOOKS

Adler, David. *A Picture Book of Christopher Columbus.* Holiday House, 1991. A historical account of Christopher Columbus, beginning with his childhood in Italy. The story tells about his early days as a sailor as well as his four voyages to America.

Other historical books by David Adler include:

A Picture Book of Abraham Lincoln.

A Picture Book of Benjamin Franklin.

A Picture Book of Eleanor Roosevelt.

A Picture Book of George Washington.

A Picture Book of Helen Keller.

A Picture Book of Martin Luther King, Jr.

A Picture Book of Thomas Jefferson.

Aliki. *The Story of Johnny Appleseed.* Trumpet Club, 1963. The story of Johnny Appleseed and his relationship with the environment, settlers, and Native Americans.

Lyon, George Ella. *Who Came Down That Road.* Orchard Books, 1992. A mom and child think about the past and discuss who might have traveled down the old, old road. They think back to pioneer days and to days of prehistoric animals.

Marzollo, Jean. *Happy Birthday, Martin Luther King.* Scholastic, 1993. The story of Martin Luther King and how he worked for freedom.

————. *In 1492.* Scholastic, 1991. The story of Columbus' voyage and subsequent discovery of the Bahamas. The story is told in rhyme.

Sanders, Russel Scott. *Aurora Means Dawn.* Bradbury Press, 1989. Watercolor pictures and simple text give a historical view of settlers in the 1800s.

Stories in Rhyme

Ahlberg, Janet and Allen. *Each Peach Pear Plum.* Viking Press, 1979. An "I Spy" rhyme book in which nursery rhyme characters are hidden in the drawings.

Carlstrom, Nancy White. *Jesse Bear What Will You Wear?* Macmillan, 1986. Jesse Bear enjoys his day, morning until night, wearing his favorite clothes, such as pants that dance.

Cauley, Lorinda Bryan. *The Three Little Kittens.* G. P. Putnam, 1982. The old rhyme of lost mittens and naughty kittens.

Causley, Charles. *"Quack!" Said the Billy Goat.* J. B. Lippincott, 1986. Because Farmer Brown has laid an egg, all the barnyard animals make the wrong noises.

Cherry, Lynne. *Who's Sick Today?* E. P. Dutton, 1988. Animals suffer from a variety of ailments, from beavers with fevers to cranes with pains.

Cole, William. *Frances Face-Maker: A Going to Bed Book.* World, 1963. Every night, Frances plays a face-making game with her dad.

Degen, Bruce. *Jamberry.* Harper & Row, 1983. A bear that speaks in nonsense verse guides a young boy through lush berries.

Dobbs, Dayle-Ann. *Wheel Away!* Harper & Row, 1989. This story in rhyme traces the path of a boy's bicycle wheels.

Gag, Wanda. *Millions of Cats.* Coward, 1928. The classic story of a peasant goes in search of a cat to keep himself and his wife company.

Grossman, Bill. *Tommy at the Grocery Store.* Harper & Row, 1989. Left behind at the grocery store, little Tom, a pig, is mistaken for a variety of things until his mother finds him.

Guarino, Deborah. *Is Your Mama a Llama?* Scholastic, 1989. A young llama asks all its animal friends that question, but then figures out the answers from their rhyming descriptions.

Hayes, Sarah. *This Is the Bear.* J. B. Lippincott, 1986. The tale of a teddy bear dumped in the garbage and the boy who searches for him.

Hennessy, B. G. *The Missing Tarts.* Viking Press, 1989. The Queen of Hearts is joined by other nursery rhyme characters in the search for her stolen strawberry tarts.

Hoberman, Mary Ann. *A House Is a House for Me.* Viking Press, 1978. The story that answers what lives where, from animals to objects.

Hutchins, Pat. *Don't Forget the Bacon.* Greenwillow Books, 1976. A young boy on a shopping errand confuses the order and forgets the bacon.

Komaiko, Leah. *I Like the Music.* Harper & Row, 1987. A little girl who loves the music of the street learns that the symphony is also good music when she attends a concert with her grandmother.

Kudrna, C. Imbior. *To Bathe a Boa.* Carolrhoda, 1986. The silly story of the boy trying to get an unwilling snake into the tub.

Lindbergh, Reeve. *The Day the Goose Got Loose.* Dial Books, 1990. The day the goose got loose on the farm, all the different farm animals and the farm family reacted in their own individual style.

McMillan, Bruce. *One Sun: A Book of Terse Verse.* Holiday House, 1990. Simple, striking photographs show a pair of things that rhyme at the beach.

Sendak, Maurice. *Chicken Soup with Rice.* Harper & Row, 1962. This favorite soup is applauded each month of the year in rhymes and pictures.

Seuss, Dr. *The Cat in the Hat.* Random House, 1966. When the cat visits two children on a rainy day, trouble follows.

Shaw, Nancy. *Sheep in a Jeep.* Houghton Mifflin, 1986. *Sheep in a Ship.* Houghton Mifflin, 1989. *Sheep in a Shop.* Houghton Mifflin, 1991. These stories in rhyme record the adventures and misadventures of five sheep. Young readers enjoy the tales of their familiar friends.

Siebert, Diane. *Truck Song.* Thomas Y. Crowell, 1984. This book tells the realistic story of a trucker's run, on the road with the rest of the rigs.

Winthrop, Elizabeth. *Shoes.* Harper & Row, 1986. A rhyme about the uses of shoes for kids.

Yektai, Niki. *Bears in Pairs.* Bradbury Press, 1987. The story of bears in a hurry to get to a tea party.

RECIPE INDEX